THE ARKWRIGHTS

R. S. FITTON

The ARKWRIGHTS
Spinners of fortune

MANCHESTER UNIVERSITY PRESS
MANCHESTER AND NEW YORK
DISTRIBUTED EXCLUSIVELY IN THE USA
AND CANADA
BY ST MARTIN'S PRESS

Published by Manchester University Press
Oxford Road, Manchester M13 9NR, UK
and Room 400, 175 Fifth Avenue,
New York, NY 10010, USA
Distributed exclusively in the USA
by St. Martin's Press, Inc.,
175 Fifth Avenue, New York, NY 10010, USA

British Library cataloguing in publication data
Fitton, R.S.
    The Arkwrights:spinners of fortune.
    1. England. Cotton manufacturing industries.
    Arkwright, Sir Richard – Biographies
    I. Title
338.7′67721′0924
Library of Congress cataloging in publication data
Fitton, R.S.
    The Arkwrights:spinners of fortune/R.S. Fitton.
    p. cm. Bibliography: p. 301.
    Includes index. ISBN 0-7190-2646-6:$35.00 (U.S.: est.)
    1. Arkwright, Richard, Sir, 1732–1792. 2. Cotton
    manufacture-Great Britain – Biography. I. Title.
TS1440.A75F57 1988   338.7′67′7210924-dc19   [B]

ISBN 0-7190-2783-7 paperback

Reprinted in paperback in 1996

Designed by MaxNettleton
Typeset in Poliphilus and
printed in Great Britain
at the Alden Press, Oxford

CONTENTS

ILLUSTRATIONS

ABBREVIATIONS

A.F. MSS	Arkwright family papers
B.M.	British Museum
B. & W. MSS	Boulton & Watt collection
B.J.R.L.	*Bulletin of the John Rylands Library*
B.R.L.	Birmingham Reference Library
C.I.S.	Co-operative Insurance Society
C.J.	*House of Commons Journal*
D.A.J.	*Derbyshire Archaeological Society Journal*
D.C.R.O.	Derbyshire County Record Office
D.N.B.	*Dictionary of National Biography*
D.P.L.	Derby Public Library
Fitton and Wadsworth	R. S. Fitton and A. P. Wadsworth, *The Strutts and the Arkwrights*
G.M.	*Gentleman's Magazine*
L.C.R.O.	Lancashire County Record Office
L.G.	*London Gazette*
M.C.R.L.	Manchester Central Reference Library
N.S.A.	New Statistical Account
O.S.A.	Old Statistical Account
P.B.R.	Preston Borough Records
P.P.	Parliamentary Papers
P.R.O.	Public Record Office
S.F.	*The Trial of a Cause by Write of Scire Facias to repeal a Patent granted to Richard Arkwright*
T.L.C.A.S.	*Transactions of the Lancashire and Cheshire Antiquarian Society*
Wadsworth and Mann	A. P. Wadsworth and J. de Lacy Mann, *The Cotton Trade and Industrial Lancashire, 1600–1780*

ACKNOWLEDGEMENTS

THE BOOK is in the form that Bob intended it to be. He would have wanted me to thank the late Colonel and Mrs Peter Arkwright for their interest and the use of the material belonging to the family; his many friends and colleagues at Manchester Polytechnic for their help through the years; and the librarians and archivists in many parts of the country but especially Mr H. Horton of the Reference Department of the Manchester Central Library.   J.M.F.

FOREWORD

CONTRIBUTING THIS PREFACE to the first major modern biography of
Arkwright was to have been an occasion of gladness and celebration. Alas, with Bob
Fitton's death on 1 March 1987 it has become an obituary — introducing what is his
most substantial scholarly work but now also his principal academic memorial. It
represents virtually his lifetime's commitment, long delayed through illness and
personal constraints, virtually complete well before his death.

We had met first in T. S. Ashton's seminar in London. Latterly we were more
closely in touch when I became external examiner, at his suggestion, for a new business
history course and M.A. in the economic and social history of the Manchester region
at the Polytechnic. My telephone would ring, unexpectedly, every few months, and
there would be Bob — worried, tentative, apprehensive about imposing or becoming
a nuisance, shocked by the latest derelictions from scholarly standards which he had
just experienced, so aware of all the obstacles standing in his way, but eager to discuss
progress with *Arkwright*.

He suffered grievously from rheumatoid arthritis, which almost incapacitated him
at times. He worked agonisingly slowly, a perfectionist according to his own standards,
taking few into his confidence, fearful that others might exploit the documents he had
discovered and therefore worried lest premature publication (particularly in the form
of articles to blaze the trail for a longer study) would allow others to overtake him. With
his difficulties of health and awareness of all the failings of the world he was doubtless
at times a difficult colleague. But always the academic flame burned steadily and was
never extinguished as long as life remained. He never gave up, tenacious to the last,
imposing the highest standards upon himself, returning to the text whenever time,
physical ability and confidence of mind allowed. This book is therefore a memorial to
an individual of great courage and humanity as well as to a scholar.

R. S. Fitton was born in 1925, in Blackpool, and educated at Blackpool Grammar
School. He served in the Royal Air Force during the second world war as a navigator
in Lancaster bombers. Following demobilisation, he took his B.Sc. (Econ.) at the
London School of Economics, continuing there for the Ph.D. degree. In T. S.
Ashton, then professor and head of the department of economic history at LSE, Bob
Fitton found his mentor — fellow Lancastrian, recently arrived from the University of
Manchester. Ashton had brought lustre to economic history in general and to the
industrial history of Lancashire in particular. Under his supervision Bob prepared a
doctoral thesis on the English Sewing Cotton Company, whose records were placed
at his disposal by Professor Arthur Redford, professor of economic history at Manches-

ter (and T. S. Ashton's brother-in-law). From LSE Bob returned, predictably, to Lancashire – the only place where he really felt at home and with which he could identify – first to Burnley Technical College and then, in 1955, to the College of Commerce in Manchester, later to become Manchester Polytechnic, where he worked until 1984 as Principal Lecturer.

Bob Fitton's research in economic and business history lay squarely within what might be called the 'Manchester tradition'. T. S. Ashton gave it eminence in the monographs he wrote at Manchester, on the coal industry, iron and steel in the eighteenth century, and Peter Stubs, the Warrington file maker; but it embraced a wider genealogy, including George Unwin, Joseph Sykes, G. W. Daniels, Arthur Redford and A. P. Wadsworth. Manchester University Press established its reputation in this field of scholarship by bringing their work into the public domain, and it is eminently right that *The Arkwrights* should also appear under its imprint.

The hallmark of the 'Manchester tradition' lay in empirical studies, based on primary sources (wherever possible the archives of the businesses and the individuals concerned). Industrial history was thus set upon the firm foundation of business records; built up from the microcosms of individuals, firms and families who were the operational agents of the activities concerned. The studies sought to provide specific answers: to say what actually happened, how businessmen actually ran their affairs, what profits they made, how they disposed of them, what the working hours of their labour force were, how they were recruited, what were the problems of developing new technology, how were such endeavours financed? The answers to questions like these were sought from the critical analysis of primary sources, in a historiographical tradition long established in political and diplomatic history.

This first generation of industrial and business history in England, as we can now identify it, which set quite new professional norms, grew to maturity in years of much grand theorising about the historical process, invoking the cosmic destinies of capital-ism and socialism according to various, and self-contradictory, methodological ab-solutes. In longer perspective we can see monographs in the Manchester tradition establishing a corpus of knowledge of individual cases, doubtless unrepresentative in any statistical sense, but intrinsically irrefutable within their own horizons, and establishing islands of reality in an ocean of limitless and quite unoperational theoretical speculation. Predictably they have survived to contribute still relevant data and conclusions where the great theories remain as intellectual curiosities in the history of economic and political thought.

Into such a tradition of research and scholarship Bob Fitton was inducted as a graduate student of T. S. Ashton. It characterised his own work, from the thesis down to this present book. His first main publication came with *The Strutts and the Arkwrights: a Study of the early Factory System* (1958), Part I written in collaboration with A. P. Wadsworth (who had previously collaborated with Julia de Lacy Mann in an important earlier study, *The Cotton Trade and Industrial Lancashire, 1600–1780* (1931)). His next work, involving great labour, and undertaken at the persuasion of T. S. Ashton, was to rescue another major source of contemporary data in the social context of industrialisation by editing the late Frances Collier's study *The Family Economy of the Working Classes in the Cotton Industry, 1784–1833* (1964). In fact his primary interest still lay with Arkwright, and the foundations of the present book were laid partly in the research undertaken in the 1950s for *The Strutts and the Arkwrights* and partly from new sets of documents which came to his notice in the 1960s. The papers of E. G. Holiday, a descendant of John Smalley, Arkwright's first partner, had been deposited with the Department of the History of Science and Technology in 1967. On the basis of these papers Bob wrote a short article for *Advance* (a journal published by UMIST) which came to the notice of Colonel Peter Arkwright, a direct descendant of the first Richard Arkwright. He revealed to Bob that there were more family papers, as yet unseen by historians, in his possession. Those papers, in turn, provided the main new documentary base for the present book.

There is no need, in such a foreword as this, for a substantive introduction to the book itself. The text speaks for itself, and Bob was an experienced historian requiring no interpreter for his own words. The remarkable thing, in retrospect, is that the first Richard Arkwright, acknowledged by all as the archetypal pioneer of the factory system in the textile industry, has not attracted a major biography long before this. Doubtless the elusiveness of contemporary primary sources has remained the principal explanation. Of Arkwright's primacy there is no doubt. Contemporary travellers (including Samuel Johnson) looked to his mills, conscious that they were witnessing a phenomenon which would transform the future. Such diverse early nineteenth-century writers as Carlyle, Babbage, Ure, Marx and Engels recognised the same transcendent significance in Arkwright, although refracted through the different lenses of interpretation with which each regarded the dynamics of industrialisation. Arkwright was not the great inventor, nor the technical genius, but he *was* the first man to make the new technology of massive machinery and power source work as a system – technical, organisational, commercial – and, as proof, created the first great personal fortune and received the accolade of a knighthood in the textile industry as an industrialist, rather than as a merchant or a 'putter out' in the 'proto-industrial' phase of industrial development.

The present biography enables us to evaluate all this in context. Moreover the study is firmly set in the dynastic context of the Arkwright family, which gives it an important additional dimension. Family continuity and succession, family motivations; even family financial logistics, set much of the dynamics of the firm, where ownership was identical with management. A family biography which spans two generations in depth reveals such continuities with great clarity. The creation of Hampton Court, the Arkwright estate in Herefordshire, bought by Richard Arkwright II, was the subject of an important article by Professor E. L. Jones in 1967.[1] The present work offers us the longer perspective through which this can be seen in relation to the industrial fortune and the business of Richard Arkwright I.

It is tragic that Bob Fitton did not live to see the appearance of this, his most important publication, and to appreciate the interest it will arouse. For those who knew him well

[1] E. L. Jones, 'Industrial capital and landed investment: the Arkwrights in Herefordshire, 1809–43', in E. L. Jones and G. E. Mingay (eds.), *Land, Labour and Population in the Industrial Revolution*, London, 1967, pp. 48–71.

– family, friends and colleagues – no further testament is required to confirm his standing as an economic historian. But the book will establish his reputation, alas belatedly and retrospectively, among economic and business historians as a whole.

PETER MATHIAS
Master's Lodge
Downing College, Cambridge

CHAPTER I

Arkwright in Lancashire

RICHARD ARKWRIGHT, whose spinning machines revolutionised the manufacture of cotton, was, perhaps even more importantly, a business genius of the first order. The founder of the modern factory system, he was the creator of a new industrial society that transformed England from a nearly self-sufficient country, her economy based on agriculture and domestic manufactures, into the workshop of the world. Admired yet feared in his own lifetime, the nineteenth century recognised him as one of the cornerstones of its prosperity, an 'Historical Phenomenon', as Carlyle put it, who had given England the 'power of cotton' which had enabled her to finance the successive coalitions against Napoleon and without which 'imperial Kaisers were impotent'.[1]

The first Sir Robert Peel (whose father Arkwright had accused of infringing his patents and who, himself, had been a leading opponent of Arkwright's exclusive patent rights[2]) compared his achievements to those of Nelson and Wellington.[3] Arkwright, he testified before a Select Committee of the House of Commons in 1816, was 'a man who has done more honour to the country than any man I know, not excepting our great military characters'.[4] And four years later the Prime Minister, Lord Liverpool, told Parliament that 'England was indebted for her commercial power and greatness' to men like Arkwright who had been 'as useful to their country, in their generation, as any of the legislators of old were in theirs'.[5]

By early Victorian times he had become a hero of classical political economy. The creation of the factory system, wrote Andrew Ure, 'required . . . a man of a Napoleon nerve and ambition . . . . Such was Arkwright, who, suffering to stay or turn aside his progress, arrived gloriously at the goal, and has for ever affixed his name to a great era in the annals of mankind.'[6] To Samuel Smiles he was the epitome of the self-made man — and more: 'Arkwright was a man of great force of character, indomitable courage, much worldly shrewdness, with a business faculty amounting to genius.'[7]

But for all the bold assertions there was — apart from Arkwright's undoubted success — surprisingly little to go on. Seven years after his death his son, Richard (his own sons at Eton and on his way to becoming the richest commoner in England), made some enquiries as to his father's early life but unearthed practically nothing. Arkwright was to remain, indeed, one of the biographical enigmas of the eighteenth century.

When questioned in later life as to his ancestry Sir Richard Arkwright is reputed to have replied, 'I can plainly prove, on the best of all authorities, that Noah was the founder of our family, for he was undoubtedly the first Arkwright in the world.'[8] Certainly the name Arkwright is derived from the Old English *arc*, 'ark', and *wyrhta*, 'a maker of arks, chests, etc.[9]' but when in 1787 Sir Richard applied for a grant of arms he guarded the names of his forebears as zealously as he had his patents, depositing no pedigree at the College of Arms. And when a little over half a century later the family appeared in the early editions of Burke's *Landed Gentry* they supplied a pedigree stretching back only as far as Sir Richard.

From the Middle Ages Arkwrights had lived in or on the edge of the Fylde, a gently undulating, well watered country forming the western part of the Lancashire hundred of Amounderness. The earliest of whom we have record is untypical. He is Gilbert de Arkewright of Ellel in the parish of Cockerham, who at Henry III's assize at Lancaster in 1246 was held to be a villein of Grimbald de Elhale, to whom he was ordered to be given up.[10] The John Arkwright who in the fifteenth century held a close of land at Broughton, four miles north of Preston, had clearly advanced in status. By the seventeenth century the greatest number of Arkwrights were to be found at Broughton but there were others near by at Cottam, Kirkham, Claughton, Lytham, Newsham, Whittingham, Alston and Preston, all place names of Old English origin and all north of the river Ribble.[12]

Our first glimpse of the Arkwrights in Preston is to be found in the Rolls of the Guild Merchant of 1562 when William, a 'taylyer', and his son Thomas were admitted as stallengers, a privilege which, while not conferring the status of burgess, allowed them to live in the town and to set up stalls at its market. At the next Guild, in 1582, William Arthwright (there are a dozen variants of the spelling, all, with the possible exception of Atrick, readily recognisable) again appears, together with his three sons, Thomas, William and George. All are recorded as foreign burgesses, as is Thomas Arkwrighte, whose name is listed in 1602 and again in 1622.

Midway between the Guilds of 1622 and 1642 Preston was ravaged by bubonic plague probably originating in an outbreak of typhus fever similar to the one that preceded the London epidemic of 1625. Lancashire, reported the Lord President of the North in September 1631, was 'miserably distressed with the pestilence' and the greatest urban sufferer at this time was Preston, where between 8 November 1630 and 4 November 1631 some 1,100 burials, most of them victims of the plague, were registered. According to a contemporaty account corn rotted in the surrounding countryside for lack of reapers. 'Heare begineth the Visitation of Almighty God, the plague,' record the parish registers at the beginning of what may well have been the worst calamity Preston ever witnessed. It is, indeed, probable that it suffered proportionately as severely as any English town in the history of the bubonic plague, yet there is no reason to suppose that it was depopulated, as the disease was incapable of bringing this about. Undoubtedly many of its inhabitants temporarily deserted the town, but it is certain that more than half the population survived.[13]

The Arkwrights could well have been among those families that moved out, for none is listed in the Guild Rolls of 1642, and whether or not Thomas Arkewright, Sir Richard's great-grandfather, whose name appears with his sons William, Henry and George in the rolls of 1662, was descended from the Arkwrights of earlier Guilds it is unfortunately not possible to determine.

Certainly Thomas was living in Preston, although not as a 'free Burgess', when his eldest son, William, was born in November 1647. This is clear from the first Court Leet, held on 21 October 1653. 'Wee find,' it is recorded, 'there are great numbers of fforrayners crept into this Towne . . . [who] have continued soe long untill they could not conveniently be removed . . . and take to themselves the priviledges and p'fitts wch onlye belonge to free Burgesses.' Listed among the fourteen 'fforrayners' brought before the court that day was 'Thomas Arthwrite [who] keepeth alehouse', the continuance of which offence was punishable by a fine of 20s a month.[14]

Shortly afterwards Thomas enrolled as a 'free Burgess', which, like regular admission during the Guild proceedings, involved the payment of a fee or fine. In September 1655 he was living in Friargate at the birth of his second son, John, who died the following month in an epidemic which trebled the number of deaths usual in September and October. Two years later when his third child, Jennet, was born his occupation was given as 'yeoman', a description repeated in the 1667 will of Richard Turner, shoemaker, of Preston, under which he received 20s and a pair of gloves. Thomas had two other sons, Henry, who went to Dublin, where he died in 1729,[15] and George born in September 1662. In 1660 Thomas had become an Overseer of the Poor[16] 'in the Church-gate and ffishergate' and two years later a churchwarden[17] at the parish church of St John. The following year he was paying tax on three hearths.[18] Until his death on 18 November 1691 Thomas continued to live in Preston and to make his appearances before the Court Leet usually, though by no means exclusively, as a juryman.

William Arkwright, who like his father became a churchwarden at St John's, lived successively in the Back Weind, in Friargate Barrs and in Friargate, where he followed the occupation of husbandman and saddler. Of his children three sons and one daughter reached maturity. The eldest, Mary born in 1686, married at twenty-eight Thomas Anderton, shoemaker, of Preston, and raised three children.[19]

On 6 January 1703, when almost fourteen, William's eldest son, Richard, was apprenticed 'By the Town' and 'at the Towns charge' to Thomas Kilshaw of Preston, saddler, 'for the term of seven years'.[20] He had probably benefited from a practice formalised three years later when the council 'Ordered that the Overseers of the poor of this Town do make an exact list of all such poor Boys and Girls as are fit to be put out Apprentices'.[21] In 1721 Richard, then living in the Back Weind, was described as an innkeeper,[22] an occupation no doubt carried on alongside his trade of saddler, but whatever his employment he had become a minor man of property before his death in 1727 at the age of thirty-eight.[23] To his wife, the former Ellen Beesley, whom he had married in 1715, he left various properties, including two of his four houses in Friargate, one a 'new built brick Messuage or Dwelling house' he had bought from William Taylor of Liverpool in 1724 and another rented to Dr John Escolme at £9 a year. In addition Richard was the owner of a row of houses and a new stable in the Barkside, land and buildings close to the river Ribble and eleven acres of meadow in North Meadow Lane and Back Weind.[24]

John Atrick (like his brother Richard, he spelt his name that way) became a shoemaker, and the Register of Apprentices gives the names of several boys put out to serve their time under him at the usual fee of £5. In 1721 he became a churchwarden[25] 'For the Lower End of the Parish' and in 1746 an Overseer of the Poor.[26] John's house in Friargate was assessed at £10 a year for Poor Tax purposes. He also owned two houses, both of which he let out, and a shippon. John, who in 1719 had married Jennet Jolly, had no family and according to Arkwright tradition[27] left to his widow a handsome fortune which upon her death went to his numerous nephews and nieces. Unhappily the story is unfounded, for John left only 'above £40'. He had worshipped at St George's Chapel (where his grave is still to be seen) and bequeathed his seat there to his niece, Ellen Plant.

Thomas Arkwright, William's second son and the father of Sir Richard, served his apprenticeship as a tailor.[28] He married by licence at St Peter's Church, Liverpool, on 29 August 1717, twenty-four-year-old Ellen Hodgekinson. The register records both as being 'of Preston'. Thomas and Ellen returned to Preston, and by 1732 (how much earlier is not known) were renting at £3 2s 6d a year a house owned by Margaret Hankinson and Lawrence Wall, Mayor of Preston in 1722-23, in Chapel Yard, a short, narrow street running between Friargate and the recently built St George's Chapel.[29]

Ellen was to survive her husband by almost a quarter of a century. Some time after his death in 1753 she went to live with her daughter Mary, the wife of James Charlton, 'surgeon', of Manchester.[30] It was a move that may well have been dictated by financial consideration, since from 1767 to 1773 she received 2s 6d each year from the funds of a charity founded by Henry and Eleanor Rishton, the income from which was distributed among the poor of Preston at

Christmas.[31]

A short reminiscence of Thomas and Ellen has come down from the Charltons' daughter Mary, the wife of Joseph Fletcher:

> I never knew my Grandfather Arkwright; I think he died before I was born. My Grandmother died in Manchester, at my Mother's house, aged 93 years; had all her faculties perfect to the last, except hearing; she was very deaf; she could see to thread a smallish needle without spectacles, but she did use them. When I think of her now I admire her as a wonder at her age; she was particularly fair, little, but very good looking; her maiden name was Hodgkinson, I think a native of Preston: I have no recollection of her ever saying anything of her relatives.[32]

Ellen's age corresponded to that given in the burial registers of St John's Church, Manchester: 'Apl 22 [1778] Ellen Arkwright Widow 93 y[ears] Decline'. She was in fact several years younger, having been born at Preston on 22 January 1693.

The Poor Tax return for 1732[33] records Preston as having 851 houses, which would give it a population somewhere in the region of 5,000 to 6,000. A description of the town about the time Thomas and Ellen were bringing up their family of seven — two sons and five daughters[34] — is given by Daniel DeFoe, who passed through in 1727:

> Preston is a fine town, and tolerably full of people, but not like Liverpoole or Manchester; besides, we come now beyond the trading part of the county. Here's no manufacture; the town is full of attorneys, proctors, and notaries, the process of law here being of a different nature than they are in other places, it being a dutchy and county palatine, and having particular privileges of its own. The people are very gay here, though not perhaps the richer for that, but it has by that obtained the name of Proud Preston. Here is a great deal of good company, but not so much, they say, as was before the late bloody action with the northern rebels; not that the battle hurt many of the immediate inhabitants, but so many families there and thereabout, have been touched by the consequen- ces of it, that it will not be recovered in a few years, and they seem to have a kind of remembrance of things upon them still.[35]

'Proud Preston', strategically situated on the north bank of the Ribble at its lowest bridging point, and where the west-coast road to Scotland is joined by the route down the Ribble valley, had had its moments of history. Granted the earliest of its charters by Henry II in 1179, Edward I, moving to subdue the rebellious Scots, issued two proclamations from it in 1306. Robert the Bruce burnt the town, the point of his farthest advance in his expedition of 1322. During the Civil Wars it became the Royalist headquarters in Lancashire and saw amongst other hard fighting Oliver Cromwell's decisive victory over the Duke of Hamilton and General Marmaduke Langdale in 1648. In 1715 'Priest's-town' — always a Catholic stronghold — proclaimed the Old Pretender at the cross in its market place, as it did the Young Pretender thirty years later.

According to family tradition Thomas and Ellen's eldest son William, born in 1725, had joined Prince Charles Edward on his march south. If so (he has probably been confused with the William Arkwright executed at Gallows Hill[36] for his part in the 1715 rebellion) the story was given a doubly romantic ring when on 4 October 1746 he married sixteen-year-old Martha Charlton at Manchester's collegiate church. William, whose name appeared from 10 June 1734 to 15 February 1735 in the register of the Boys' Charity School, a 'free Catechistical School . . . for the Christian Education of Poor Boys in the town of Preston',[37] followed his father's trade and set up his tailor's shop at 50 Sugar Lane, Manchester,[38] a business in which his two sons were to follow. He died of asthma (a complaint that also afflicted his more distinguished brother) when just short of fifty and was buried at St John's Church. His wife died in 1796 of 'Old Age' and was buried with him.

Three of William's sisters married Manchester men. Mary's husband as we have seen, was William's brother-in-law, James Charlton, while the eldest, Ellen, married at the collegiate church on 2 September 1736 John Hulme, a peruke maker. (John died in 1763, aged forty-nine, and three years later Ellen married Ralph Barber, a bricklayer.) The third sister, Jennet, born in 1727, married Matthew Green, a reed maker, of Hanging Ditch and later of Spring Gardens.[39] Two of her children, Richard and Thomas, were pupils at the Manchester Grammar School.[40]

Thomas and Ellen's two other daughters remained in Preston. Ann, born in 1720, married when in her early twenties Richard Bramwell, a tailor, while the youngest daughter, Elizabeth, followed her brother, William, to the Bluecoat charity school and in March 1742, together with other pupils, received a Bible valued at 2s 8d. 'The Trustees for Mr. Maddock's Legacy, of Twenty Pounds, to the Girls School only,' reads a note in the accounts, 'agree, that the Interest shall be laid out in Bibles, & other Religious Books, to be dispos'd of to such Children, as are capable of Reading, & in some degree, of understanding what they read, when they leave the School; in order to keep & improve that little knowledge they have already attain'd.'[41] The school's declared aims were thus modest enough, and Elizabeth, like her sister Ann, never learned to write. Elizabeth married at Preston in June 1755 Richard Melling, and their son William, clerk to attorney Nicholas Grimshaw, seven times Mayor of Preston and twice Guild Mayor, was to accompany his uncle to Cromford, where he remained until Sir Richard's death.[42]

Richard, Thomas and Ellen's youngest surviving child, was born at Preston on 23 December 1732 and baptised there on New Year's Eve. His formal education did not stretch as far as the Bluecoat School and Whittle, the historian of Preston, tells us that he attended an evening school during the winter months and that his uncle Richard taught him to read.[43] But Uncle Richard had died in 1727, and if there is anything at all in the story he is more likely to have been helped by his cousin, Richard's daughter Ellen, who is said to have recounted 'many anecdotes of Sir Richard's ingenuity when quite a youth, he was very partial to her, as she took more notice of him than any of his other relatives, and she frequently encouraged him in studying, and inventing any little sort of machinery, &c.'[44]

Richard was apprenticed to a barber at Kirkham,[45] west of Preston, and in 1750 moved on to Bolton, then known as Bolton le Moors, a town of perhaps 3,000 inhabitants, 'a Staple for fustians of divers Sorts' which were brought in 'from all Parts of the Country' for sale at its weekly market and at its one-day fairs, held in June, July and August.[46] A short account of Arkwright's eighteen-year residence in Bolton was given by Thomas Ridgway in 1799 in response to an enquiry from Arkwright's son, then seeking information about his father's early life. Thomas, the son of James Ridgway, a Bolton fustian dyer, had with his brother John founded a large bleaching concern in Bolton and, in 1775, at Wallsuches, near Horwich, which became the largest in Lancashire.[47] Ridgway's letter reads:

My first knowledge of your father, was about the year 1750 when he came to reside in Bolton and was I think then about the Age of 18. He entred into the employment of one Edward Pollit[48] A peruke maker there, on whose death he remained with his widow for Sometime — He then married your Mother, and began business for himself; which he pursued with most indefatigable industry and with some success. He might now be considered in a comfortable situation; he had a decent House, a cleaner one coud not be and his friends and acquaintance always found in it a cordial reception from him. These were Persons of no mean consideration in the town, but such as were in Superior Stations to himself. To these he recommended himself by his character for neatness, sobriety, industry and good Sense. The Latter part of his time at Bolton was not so pleasant as it had been. He became necessitous in consequence of taking a public house, which did not answer his purpose and upon which he expended much money on alterations. He was obliged to leave the house and had a many interruptions caused by an inveterate asthma, which brought him very low in every sense of the word. Notwithstanding this, I believe there was only one Person to whom he owed Money, when he left the town and his credit [was] otherwise good.[49] His customers that had employed him in his business were generally of the better sort, he might probably have done better coud he have Stooped to the vulgar, but his spirit was much superior to it, And always seemed to have something better in view. His genius for Mechanics was observed it was perceived in his common conversation which often turned on subjects of that kind.[50] I well remember we had often great fun with a Clock he put up in his shop, which had all the appearance of being worked by the smoke of the chimney and we have caused a many to believe it was so; I have often seen Him cut pasteboard into different shapes such as forming squares from oblongs without adding or diminishing, and a Hundred curious knackey things that one cannot find words to explain. He was always thought clever in his peruke making business and very capital in Bleeding & toothdrawing and allowed by all his acquaintance to be very ingenious man.[51]

Ridgway's account may be filled in a little. After leaving Pollit's widow, Arkwright set up for himself in a barber's shop in Deansgate, at the end of a

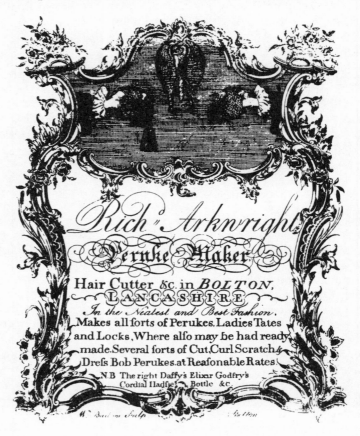

Arkwright's business plate when he was a barber in Bolton

passage leading to the White Bear public house.[52] Here, tradition had it, he 'shaved chins in subterranean apartments at a penny-a-piece'.[53] It was about this time that he married. His wife was Patience, daughter of Robert Holt of Bolton, a friend of the Ridgways and a property-owing schoolmaster of some means.[54]

Their marriage was by licence on 31 March 1755 at Bolton parish church, Arkwright being described in the register as 'Peruke maker'. The entry follows another of the same date recording the marriage of Patience's sister, Ellen, and

Thomas Wood, a Bolton fustian weaver, who in 1776 was to take out a patent for a machine 'for carding and roving silk, cotton, and sheep's wool'.[55] And it was about this time that Wood joined with William Cockshott (until recently in business with Thomas Plumbe and Peter Drinkwater as fustian manufacturers in Bolton)[56] and with Robert Pilkington in a series of partner-ships at Tottington,[57] near Bury, at Macclesfield[58] and, more surprisingly, at Taplow[59] in Buckinghamshire on the river Thames. Wood and Pilkington were to give evidence for Arkwright in the great patent trials of 1785.[60]

A son, Richard, was born to the Arkwrights on 19 December 1755 and baptised a month later at the Bank Street Presbyterian chapel, the Holts' place of worship. Patience died on 6 October 1756 and was buried in the same grave as her mother at the parish church. Holt was soon to lose two of his sons, both of whom had seen service in the Seven Years' War: twenty-one-year-old Robert died in 1761 and Thomas four years later at the age of thirty-five. They were described as 'Mariner' on the family gravestones and after Thomas's name his father had inscribed, 'he served his King and Country with Honout 16 Years.'[61]

Although at first Arkwright seems to have got on well with his father-in-law (sufficiently so for Holt to lend him £60, which was repaid in 1762)[62] the relationship did not last. A hint of discord is perhaps to be seen in the wording, 'Patience Third Daughter of Robert and Jennet Holt', on the gravestone. Arkwright is not mentioned. Nor is he, except indirectly, in Holt's will, drawn up and initialled only with difficulty on the last day of his life. 9 October 1783. In it he denied Arkwright even the proverbial shilling, bequeathing instead to the 'son of my Son-in-Law, Richard Arkwright the sum of One Shilling'.[63]

On 24 March 1761, almost four and a half years after Patience's death, Arkwright married at Leigh parish church Margaret Biggens, of Pennington. A daughter, Susanna, was born at Bolton on 20 December 1761 and, like her half-brother, was baptised at the Bank Street chapel.[64]

In April 1762 Arkwright applied for a licence 'to carry on the Business of an Innkeeper' and having satisfied 'the Minister & Churchwardens . . . and other inhabitants of Bolton . . . as a man of sober life and conversation And well qualified to keep a Publick House'[65] became for the next two years landlord of the Black Boy.[66] It was probably about this time that he moved into a barber's shop opposite the Man and Scythe in Churchgate and took on a skilled wig maker, John Dean of Leigh, as his assistant.[67] This enabled him to spend part of his time travelling the country to buy women's hair to make into wigs.[68] He is said to have had a valuable method of dyeing hair which wig makers held to be superior to any in Lancashire.[69]

It was now that Arkwright's career took a decisive turn. In addition to carrying on his businesses of barber, peruke maker and publican he began to devote an ever-increasing amount of his time to the development of a machine to spin cotton by rollers. For a quarter of a century since 1740 the Lancashire cotton manufacturs had experienced a period of greatly increasing trade, and the expansion of the demand for twist and weft (as also in the Midlands and in London) may well have begun to place a strain on the supply even before the 1760s, when the fly shuttle, a simple but important improvement to the loom, patented in 1733 by John Kay, a reed maker of Bury, in Lancashire, came into general use.[70] Weaving could now be done more quickly and only one person (instead of two) was needed to produce a wide cloth. Small wonder, then, that the improvement of spinning was much in the air, and many men up and down Lancashire were working at it.[71] The chief use of cotton yarns at this time was in the weft of materials of which the warp was linen, worsted or silk;[72] it was Arkwright's success in taking up and perfecting the idea of roller spinning that transformed the method of producing yarn and virtually created an industry based solely on cotton, and conducted in factories.[73]

The first use of cotton in Lancashire in a textile material appears to have been at the beginning of the seventeenth century in the manufacture of fustian, a fabric with a cotton weft and a linen warp. These fustians, it seems probable, were one of the 'new draperies' that had been introduced into East Anglia by Walloon and Dutch immigrants, although how extensively the Norwich immigrants carried on the manufacture of the cheaper fustians which Lancashire adopted remains uncertain. The earliest reference discovered to the manufacture is of 1601, when the name of George Arnould, fustian weaver, of Bolton,[74] appears in the records of Quarter Sessions. And in a petition of 1621 the London fustian dealers recounted to Parliament how:

> about twenty yeeres past diverse people in this Kingdome, but chiefly in the Countie of Lancaster, have found out the trade of making of other Fustians, made of a kind of Bombast or Downe, being a fruit of the earth growing upon little shrubs or bushes, brought into this Kingdome by the Turkie Merchants, from Smyrna, Cyprus, Acra and Sydon, but commonly called Cotton Wooll.[75]

Early seventeenth-century Lancashire was a relatively remote and backward part of England, its textile industries being given over to the manufacture of the coarsest woollens and linens. Woollens were made in the upland valleys of the Pennines, linens in the remainder of the country from flax imported mainly from Ireland.

Fustians first took hold in the hilly country between Bolton and Blackburn, and by the 1630s they had also become firmly established in the neighbourhood of Middleton, Chadderton and Hollinwood. By this time cotton was pushing its way slowly against wool and linen, alongside which it grew and which it was first to overshadow and then to replace. Throughout the seventeenth century the drift of enterprise was away from the corporate towns to the freer atmosphere of the countryside, and it was in places like Manchester, Bolton and Rochdale, where society was more fluid, that progress was most rapid. The Manchester fustian dealers distributed raw materials to smaller capitalists who were the country spinners and weavers; and, as time went on, the putting-out system increased at the expense of the independent producer. Such was the develop-ment that before Arkwright established the first successful cotton-spinning factories the population of Lancashire south of the Ribble had been gradually transformed from a community of independent landowners with whom spinning and weaving were subordinate to agriculture to one of cottagers almost entirely dependent on the making of textiles. Yet is spite of the strides made by capitalist organisation in the seventeenth and eighteenth centuries, the agrarian background remained largely unchanged until long after the factory system had emerged.[76]

Although Lancashire manufacturers were neither conservative by nature nor inclined to neglect technical improvements,[77] almost the entire expansion of the textile industry before Arkwright patented the water frame had been obtained without the assistance of power-driven machinery. Nevertheless, there had been no shortage of attempts to mechanise both spinning and weaving operations. As early as 1678 Richard Dereham of the City of London and Richard Haines[78] of Sussex had patented a machine to shorten the slow process of making yarn by hand spinning, and eight more attempts were made before Lewis Paul, over half a century later, began his experiments to produce yarn by a revolutionarty methods, that of roller spinning.

It was in 1738 that Lewis Paul, the brilliant but wayward son of the French refugee who became physician to Anthony, third Earl of Shaftesbury, patented a machine the idea behind which was to do for spinning what Kay's fly shuttle was ultimately to do for weaving.[79] In this activity Paul was assisted by John Wyatt, a former master carpenter with whom he had first become acquainted in Birmingham in 1732.[80] It was probably soon after the start of their association that Paul had broached to Wyatt the idea of a machine for spinning by rollers, and on 24 June 1738 (almost two years after the original application) he was granted a patent for his invention. According to the specifcation, wool or cotton, already carded and made into rovings, would be

> Put betwixt a pair of rowlers, cillinders, or cones, [and then through] a succession of other rowlers, cillinders, or cones, moving proportionably faster than the first, [so as to] draw the rope, thread, or sliver, into any degree of fineness which may be required.[81]

But even now Paul was far from having a marketable invention. Ten months after the grant only the original model of the machine was in existence and Paul therefore sold licences to operate his spindle to several adventurers. Three of these were intimate acquaintances of his friend and correspondent Dr Samuel Johnson: they were Edward Cave, founder of the *Gentlemen's Magazine*, Johnson's first employer and the publisher of his first important poem; Thomas

Warren, a Birmingham bookseller who published Johnson's *Lobo*; and Dr Robert James, an old schoolfellow and the inventor of a famous fever powder, whom Johnson helped with his *Medical Dictionary*. That Johnson had brought these backers to Paul is to be seen in his letter to him of 31 January 1741, in which he refers to 'my assiduity in expediting the agreement between you'. In it Johnson urged Paul to settle differences which had arisen between the parties, and exactly two months later he is again writing to Paul of his hope of a 'more pleasing employment than that of reconciling variances' and of 'interposing in controversises which grow every [day] more distant from accomodation'.[82]

The first of the Paul–Wyatt mills was set up during the summer of 1741 in a warehouse in the Upper Priory in Birmingham, its motive power being supplied by 'two asses walking round an axis'. Within two years, however, the mill (apparently managed by Paul himself) was almost derelict. Meanwhile Cave, who may have had an interest at Birmingham, took a warehouse probably on the Turnmill brook, a little to the north of Fleet Bridge, at the back of Field Lane, Holborn, where he installed machines worked by hand. But in spite of Paul's personal superintendence the mill proved unprofitable and was abandoned.[83]

After making enquiries throughout the country for a suitable water mill Cave found one by 1742 at Northampton, where on the river Nene he established a rudimentary spinning factory the machines in which were turned by water power. Little is known of the venture after 1743, although a period of control by Samuel Touchet, the great Lancashire and London merchant, whose many-sided and meteoric career made him a government contractor and a man of significance in war, politics, finance and industry, seems to have lasted until 1755. A fourth Paul–Wyatt mill was set up by Daniel Bourn at Leominster, Herefordshire, possibly in 1744, although the earliest mention of it is in 1748. Bourn may well have been a native of Lancashire, as was his only known partner, Henry Morris, a yarn dealer who in 1743 had bought a grant of spindles from Paul. The mill, which was probably the only one outside the control of Paul and his backers, was destroyed by fire in 1754 and was not rebuilt, although Bourn and his partners had considerable hopes of it.

Paul's enterprises did not fail owing to shortage of capital or to lack of markets for his yarn. His backers included men of substance, while Samuel Touchet and James Johnson of Spitalfields, the first to experiment commercially with his roller-spinning machine, were both intimately concerned with the manufacture of checks for the African market.[84] To them the promise of cheap yarn of a quality comparable with that from India opened up exciting prospects.

Matthew Boulton, who saw the Birmingham mill when a boy of thirteen, told James Watt forty years later, in 1781, that it was 'a good Cotton spinning Mill . . . that would have got money had it been in good hands'.[85] And certainly there were management problems, not least with labour: 'I have not half my people come to work to-day,' Cave confided to Paul on one occasion, 'and I have no great fascination in the prospect I have to put myself in the power of such people.'[86]

Equally important, the machinery had mechanical defects which the partners, for all their ingenuity, failed to solve satisfactorily, and the resulting mechanism had a large number of small, fragile parts which proved extremely expensive to maintain in good working order. But the main reason for Paul and Wyatt's lack of success is that their machine was based on the wrong principle for spinning cotton.[87] They failed to separate the drawing or drafting stage (during which the carded cotton is stretched so as to form a yarn of the correct thickness) from the twisting or spinning stage (in which the fibres are locked firmly together). This separation, which the skill of the hand spinner was able to achieve, is essential in a machine with continuous spinning and winding. Paul may well have realised that it was a problem, for in 1758 he took out another patent in which he seems to have abandoned the idea of roller spinning. The following year he died, having, according to Robert Dossie, the first historian of the Society of Arts, 'carried this application of mechanics to the greatest extent it is perhaps capable of . . .'.[89]

In 1748 Paul had secured a patent[90] for carding, and after the breaking up of the Northampton mill the machine was bought by a hat manufacturer of Leominster and used for the carding of wool for hats. According to John Kennedy, one of the greatest of the Manchester spinners and an early historian of the cotton industry, 'about 1760 it was introduced into Lancashire, and re-applied to the carding of cotton, by a gentleman of the name of Morris [probably Bourn's partner at Leominster], in the neighbourhood of Wigan'.[91]

The remainder of Paul's machinery disappeared, but knowledge of his roller-spinning machine (if not the machines themselves) spread to Lancashire, brought there initially, perhaps, by those associated with the Northampton and Leominster concerns. Arkwright himself heard of roller-spinning; he was certainly applying himself to the idea by 1767, already well aware of the problem ('several gentlemen have almost broke themselves by it') that had confronted Paul and his associates almost thirty years earlier.[92]

Many romantic legends grew up to explain how Arkwright came upon a solution to the spinning problem. Some believed his roller-spinning machine was developed as a by-product of a search for perpetual motion, or that he had studied the silk-throwing machines at the Lombes' famous Derby Silk Mill.[93] A partner's son maintained that the method had been suggested to him by the working of a cylindrical wire-drawing machine, others that 'he gradually rose in the acquisition of . . . vast wealth by the accidental purchase of a single piece of mechanism, called the spinning jenny, the invention of an [unnamed] ingenious carpenter, who . . . offered it for sale from mere necessity'.[94] There were tales that in his barber's shop he had overheard a sailor describe a wonderful Chinese machine[95] and that 'during his chin-scraping operations, he weekly pulled the nose of the real inventor — a poor illiterate cabinet-maker of the name of Brown, a fellow of infinite genius and most excellent fancy, and perhaps equal as a machinist to anyone in the country'.[96]

Putting aside all these unlikely stories, there remains the key question of Arkwright's much disputed association with Thomas Highs (Hayes) and John Kay. From 1761, the year of his marriage to Margaret Biggens, Arkwright was a frequent visitor to Leigh, where he took up a half-worked-out invention of the reed maker Thomas Highs and developed it. About 1763 or 1764 Highs, then of the Walk, Leigh, had as his neighbour John Kay, a former Warrington clock maker, whom he employed as an assistant in his machine-making experiments. According to Richard Guest, Highs's biographer and apologist, the pair were at this time engaged in making a spinning jenny (which Guest claimed preceded that invented by James Hargreaves) but, after several months of toil, 'All their trouble and pains were . . . abortive, and one Sunday morning, in a fit of despondency, they threw the machine through the garret window, into the yard.'[97] Ridiculed by neighbours who made repeated enquires for weft, Kay gave up. Highs, less easily discouraged, collected together the broken wheels and, taking them back to his garret, eventually succeeded in making a jenny capable at first of spinning six threads. It must have been about 1764 or 1765 — the time Highs[98] was later to claim he had first become acquainted with Arkwright — that, again assisted by Kay, he began work on a machine for spinning cotton by rollers. In this he was not wholly successful, for although the drawings and description of his machine (reported by Guest but with what accuracy is not known) seem to show that he was working on the right principles, and make apparent his machine's similarity with that later patented by Arkwright, they also reveal vital differences which show that despite his great mechanical abilities he was unable to develop the finer points of roller spinning.

The precise nature of Arkwright's association, direct or otherwise, with Highs remains an unsolved mystery. Of that with Kay we know more. Having made his acquaintance by March 1767,[99] Arkwright met him again six months later in Warrington, to which place Kay had returned from Leigh, and there persuaded him to make one or more models of the roller-spinning machine he had built under Highs's supervision. Kay and Arkwright now asked Peter Atherton (probably then of Warrington but afterwards of Liverpool) to build a machine, only to have their request refused because of the poverty of Ark-wright's appearance. Later the same day, however, Atherton is said to have agreed to lend Kay a smith and a watch-tool maker to build the heavier part of the machine. Kay himself undertook to make to clockmaker's part of it and to instruct the workman.[100]

Towards the end of 1767 Arkwright took the machine to Manchester,[101] staying perhaps with one of his sisters, before going on to Preston, a town soon to be convulsed by the violence of the famous Burgoyne election of March 1768.[102] During the three-month campaign the claims of the rival Tory (or Corporation) and Whig candidates (supported by the Earl of Derby) were pressed by hired bands of ruffians brought in from the surrounding country-side.[103] Their depredations, said the anonymous writer of a letter printed in the *Gentleman's Magazine*, 'exceed belief; murdering, maiming, pulling down of houses, destroying places of public worship, and breaking the furniture and burning the effects of each other, are among the acts of the enflamed mob'.[104]

Arkwright's activities at this time may be traced in the records of the inquiry subsequently held to determine the right of persons to vote in the bitterly contested election. The first entry against his name reads, 'Arkwright Richd Barber has been in Town pretty constantly since 5th January 1768 followed Clockwork.' Arkwright's votes, cast on 25 March in favour of the Tory candidates Sir Peter Leicester, Bart, and Sir Frank Standish, Bart[106] (but only, it is said, after he had persuaded his friends to 'procure him a suit of clothes', his own being 'in such a ragged state, that he could not for shame go up to the poll'),[107] were rejected, as were those of many others, on the grounds of non-residence. Sent to Westminster as the town's representatives were the Whigs Sir Henry Hoghton, Bart, and Colonel John Burgoyne, now remembered for his surrender of the British forces after the battle of Saratoga, turning point in the War of American Independence.

Kay, who had accompanied Arkwright to Preston, told the same inquiry that he had 'known him 12 Mo^s is a serv^t assisting him in making a machine — his Wife & Children with him — his Wife here 5 Weeks ago, knows not where he came from but by Lr from Manch^r — works ab^t a Machine — known not what its for, but bel^s to find out Longitude'.[108] Kay's story was supported by the Rev. Ellis Henry, headmaster of the Free Grammar School in Stonygate,[109] to which post he had been elected in 1765 in succession to the Rev. Robert Oliver, who had been dismissed sixteen years earlier for 'having been greatly remiss and negligent in the performance of his duties'.[110] The inquiry also recorded of Arkwright that '*Mr Henry* let him some rooms in his house — has resided there since Janry at 7 Gs. P. An: — making a Machine to find out the Longitude. Apprehended he was a freeman when he let him the rooms — does not know why he apprehended so.'[111]

The Rev. Ellis Henry may well have believed the story of the longitude machine. And certainly it was more credible than another circulating at the time to the effect that two aged women, whose thatched cottage was separated from Rev. Henry's house only by a garden filled with gooseberry bushes, maintained that they heard strange noises, of such a humming nature, that the devil was tuning his bag-pipes, and that Arkwright and Kay were dancing a reel:.[112]

It was during the turmoil of the Burgoyne election that Arkwright brought

Legend:

■ Arkwright estates
● Mills which the Arkwrights worked
◆ Other locations referred to in text

Newcastle-upon-Tyne

Scarborough

Skerne ■

◆ Preston
◆ Chorley
Birkacre ● ◆ Bolton
Manchester
Liverpool ● Stockport ● ◆ Mellor and Marple
◆ Warrington
Macclesfield ◆ Buxton ■ Sutton Hall
Holywell ◆ Chatsworth House
Willersley Castle ■ Darley Hall
CROMFORD ● ■ Crich
◆ Ashbourne
Rocester ● Derby ◆ ● Nottingham
◆ Burton-upon-Trent
■ Dunstall Hall
Lichfield ◆
◆ Tamworth
■ Normanton Turville
◆ Birmingham

■ Hampton Court
◆ Cambridge

■ Mark Hall

London
Taplow ◆ ◆ Eton

Rye ◆

Arkwright interests in England and Wales

his machine near to completion. The method of spinning which he was to perfect was based on the continuous spinning principle of the Saxony (or flax) wheel, the flyer of which inserts twist into the fibres and (revolving round the spindle) simultaneously winds the resulting yarn on to a bobbin. Linen yarn had long been produced by this method in the country to the south of Preston, and Arkwright may well have realised that the Saxony wheel had the obvious action to attempt to mechanise, provided a way could be found of imitating the part played by the spinner's fingers in drafting or stretching the fibres being fed into the yarn on the spindle.[113]

In order to draw out the cotton for spinning Arkwright at first used four (later three) pairs of rollers with suitable gearing to make each set rotate successively faster. The top rollers were covered with leather and the bottom ones were made from wood, with a metal core, and fluted. The back pair, where the thick cotton roving entered, rotated the slowest, and each succeeding pair turned faster, thus drawing out the roving.

But however much Arkwright may have used the ideas of others two essential features are to be found in his spinning machine (subsequently known as the water frame) which did not appear on earlier ones.

First, he recognised the importance of placing the pairs of rollers which draw out the cotton at the correct distance apart for the staple length of the fibres being drawn. If too close rollers would grip both ends of the same cotton fibre and snap it, or it too far apart would not grip it properly and so produce uneven, lumpy yarn.[114]

Secondly, he weighted the top rollers so that they pressed firmly against their lower counterparts. Without the weights the twist would have run between the rollers and locked the fibres together in the drafting zone, causing uneven drafting and uneven yarn. (with the Saxony wheel the spun yarn was held by the spinner so as to prevent the twist running back to the drawing thread, which was held in the other hand.) Paul and Wyatt did not weight their rollers, nor do they appear to have realised the vital importance of the staple length.

Yet despite these differences the roller-spinning machines of Paul and Arkwright had much in common, and it is perhaps hardly surprising that, on allowing Samuel Johnson to inspect his machine, Arkwright — a newspaper reported — declared him to be 'the only person who, on a first view, understood both the principle and powers of his most complicated piece of machinery'.[115]

NOTES

1 T. Carlyle, *Chartism*, London, 1840, p. 85.
2 J. Wheeler, *Manchester, its Political, Social and Commercial History, Ancient and Modern*, Manchester, 1836, p. 521.
3 E. Baines Junior, *History of the Cotton Manufacture in Great Britain*, London, 1835, p. 503.
4 P.P. 1816 (397) III, *Select Committee on the State of the Children employed in the Manufactories of the United Kingdom*, p. 134.

5 *Hansard*, 1820, I. p. 621 (16 May 1820).

6 A. Ure, *The Philosophy of Manufactures,* London, 1835, p. 16.

7 S. Smiles, *Self Help,* London, 1859, p. 66.

8 *Stockport Advertiser,* 2 December 1830.

9 P. H. Reaney, *A Dictionary of British Surnames,* London, 1958, p. 11.

10 Colonel J. Parker, 'A Calendar of the Lancashire Assize Rolls preserved at the Public Record Office', printed for the *Record Society of Lancashire and Cheshire,* XLVII, 1904, p. 40. P.B.R., Assize Roll of Guild Merchants.

11 H. Fishwick, *The History of the Parish of Preston in Amounderness in the County of Lancaster,* Rochdale, 1920, pp. 251, 263.

12 E. Ekwall, *The Place Names of Lancashire,* Manchester, 1922, p. 239. (Kirkham, thought by Ekwall to be Old English, may of course be Scandinavian).

13 J. F. D. Shrewsbury, *A History of the Bubonic Plague in the British Isles,* Cambridge, 1970, pp. 362–3; E. B. Leach, 'The parish registers of Lancashire', *T.L.C.A.S.,* LVII, 1946, pp. 150–1, 155; W. A. Abram, *Memorials of the Preston Guilds,* Preston, 1882, p. 42; R. Sharpe France, 'A history of the plague in Lancashire', *Historical Society of Lancashire and Cheshire,* XC, 1939, p. 60.

14 P.B.R., Court Leet Records; and see A. Hewitson, *Preston Court Leet Records, Extracts and Notes,* Preston, 1905, pp. 10–11, 12.

15 For Henry see Oifig Iris Puibli, Dublin, and the reference to his will dated 4 October 1729 in *Betham's Genealogical Abstracts.* This will did not survive the destruction of the office in 1922.

16 L.C.R.O., PR 1480, p. 31.

17 *Ibid.,* p. 34.

18 H. Fishwick, *Preston in Amounderness,* p. 434.

19 L.C.R.O., PR 1480, p. 53, describes William Arkwright as Churchwarden. Court Leet Records: Backweind Court Leet, 1698, p. 60; Friargate Barrs Court Leet, 1703, p. 34; Friargate Court Leet, 1709, p. 113, No. 17, and 1712, p. 150. P.B.R., Preston Guild Records, 1722, a Saddler.

20 P.B.R., Register of Apprentices.

21 P.B.R., Preston Council Minute Book, 1703–65, p. 251. On 18 November 1735 'It is ordered that the sons of freemen have preference' (P. 252).

22 L.C.R.O., D 199, Abstract to Mrs Ellen Plant's title to certain premises in Preston.

23 P. A. Whittle, *Bolton-le-Moors, and the Townships in the Parish,* Bolton, 1855, p. 383 n., which states, 'buried at St. John's Churchyard, Preston ⸍ a flat stone on south yard 'Richard Arkwright died 9 August 1727 aged 38"'.

24 P.B.R., Regulation Poor Tax of the Burrough of Preston 1732; L.C.R.O., Will, Richard Arkwright, 1727.

25 L.C.R.O., PR 1480, p. 128.

26 *Ibid.,* p. 158.

27 D.P.L., Hurt MSS (uncatalogued).

28 Preston Guild Records, 1742.

29 Regulations Poor Tax, 1732.

30 M.C.R.L., St John's Church, Manchester, Register of Burials, 3 May 1793.

31 P.B.R., Mr and Mrs Rishton of Bath's Charity.

32 Hurt MSS, written about 1819.

33 Regulation Poor Tax, 1732.

34 A third son, John, lived less than a month. John was born 23 December 1736 and buried 20 January 1737. The oft repeated story that Arkwright was the youngest of thirteen children seems to have appeared first in Dugald Bannatyne's account in the *Supplement* of the *Encyclopaedia Britannica* (1816 or a little earlier), III, 1824 edition, p. 393.

35 D. Defoe, *A Tour through England and Wales*, Everyman's edition, II, London, 1928, p. 268.

36 C. Hardwick, *History of the Borough of Preston*, Preston and London, 1857, p. 235; E. Baines, *History of the County Palatine and Duchy of Lancaster*, IV, London, 1836, p 326; Hewitson, *Preston Court Leet*, p. 198, n. 1, for mention of Arkwright and the position of Gallows Hill.

37 See L.C.R.O., PR 1490, *A Book for the use of the free Catechistical School erected by Mr. Roger Sudell & other Charitable Persons for the Christian Education of the Poor Boys in the Town of Preston*. A note in front of the book reads, 'Wheras it is evident to common observation that the growth of vice debauchery & Irreligion is greatly growing owing to the gross ignorance of the Principles of Christianity, especially among the Poorer Sort of People; because Christian virtue can proceed from no other Root than Christian Principle' (1703).

38 See Mrs Elizabeth Raffald's *Manchester Directory*, 1772 and 1773 editions.

39 Raffald's 1772, 1773 and 1781 editions and Lewis's *Manchester Directory*, 1788

40 Rev. J. Finch Smith, *The Admission Register of the Manchester School*, I, 1730–75, 1866, pp. 157, 162.

41 L.C.R.O., PR 1491, Account of the two Charity Schools in Preston: p. 97 for 20 March 1732/1733; 9 June 1786, 'Placed in the School Gallery in Church 50 Prayer Books, one for each Boy & Girl the practice of more than one using the same book having tempted them to whisper to each other. The above with Carriage from London £13 13s 0d'; 16 August 1786, 'placed in the Girls School Taylor's antidote ag' Popery £0 6s 2d'.

42 William Melling, born 19 September 1764, who went to Cromford and was left an annuity of £30 by Sir Richard, was at one time clerk to Nicholas Grimshaw of Preston (A.F. M.S.S, letter of E. Evans, a granddaughter of Ellen Plant, of 40 Orange Street, Swansea, wife of a Dissenting minister to Richard Arkwright II, 4 December 1833). Nicholas Grimshaw, born 14 October 1757, died 7 January 1838, was a pupil of Manchester Grammar School and the son of Thomas Grimshaw, died 1787, attorney of Preston (L.C.R.O., Will, Thomas Grimshaw, 1788).

43 Whittle, *Bolton-le-Moors*, II, p. 213.

44 E. Evans to Richard Arkwright II, 4 December 1833.

45 *Fitton and Wadsworth*, pp. 60–1, for letter from Thomas Walshman to Richard Arkwright II, 1 March 1799.

46 T. Read, *The English Traveller*, III, London, 1746, p. 12.

47 Sir A. J. Sykes, *Concerning the Bleaching Industry*, Manchester, 1925, p. 81.

48 Edward Pollit is possibly a mistake for Edmund Pollit, of Great Bolton, who died 22 November 1752. In 1756 Edmund's widow Mary, became the landlord of the Angel public house, Bolton, and on 4 November 1757 married, at Bolton, James Markland, a weaver. The Pollit family had for several generations been established as barbers and peruke makers in Bolton and Manchester. See the Manchester directories for 1772, 1773, 1781 and 1788.

49 The *Quarterly Review*, CVII, 1869, p. 59, states, 'One gentleman near Bolton, has informed us that his grandfather having ordered a wig of Arkwright, was required to pay a guinea for it in advance. Before the wig could be made, Arkwright had left town in pursuit of his spinning-machine project on which the whole energies of mind had become bent.'

50 Sir R. Phillips, *A Personal Tour through the United Kingdom; describing living objects and contemporaneous interests*, II, London, 1828, p. 118, states, 'A spirit of detraction would make it appear that Arkwright stole the invention of another but Mr. William Strutt, who knew him well, and is a competent judge on such subjects, assured me that Arkwright was a man of very superior talents as a mechanic, and quite equal to such an invention. I saw two portraits of him in the Strutt's house, and no higher proof could be given of

his personal respect for Arkwright, while he never failed to speak of him with enthusiasm, as a man of original talents.'

51 Letter of 25 March 1799 in Strutt MSS, Fitzwilliam Museum, Cambridge.

52 G. J. French, *Life and Times of Samuel Crompton*, London, 1859, p. 40, n. 45, writes that his first shop was 'in the passage leading to the old *Millstone* Inn, Deansgate'.

53 *Mechanic's Magazine*, I, No. 13, 22 November 1823, p. 107.

54 L.C.R.O., Great Bolton Land Tax, 1783, shown Holt having twelve houses assessed at £20 9s 6d for Land Tax purposes.

55 Patent No. 1130.

56 *L.G.*, 21–25 November 1775, 9–13 July 1776.

57 A. G. Rose, 'Early cotton riots in Lancashire, 1769–1779', *T.L.C.A.S.*, 73 and 74 1963–64, p. 62.

58 *L.G.*, 10–12 September 1781, 6–9 October 1781, 10–13 January 1784.

59 *L.G.*, 10–13 March 1781, 5–8 January 1782, 10–13 January 1784, 1790 pp. 85, 515, 579, 1802 p. 376 (Taplow now a corn mill).

60 *S.F.*, pp. 52, 56, 59, 150, 152.

61 M.C.R.L., Owen MSS, vol. 35.

62 Bolton Public Library, deed dated 5 November 1762. The sum was repaid from an £80 legacy that Arkwright's second wife, Margaret, had received under the will of John Harrison of Blackrod (L.C.R.O., 1747).

63 L.C.R.O., Will, Robert Holt, 1783.

64 There were two other children of the marriage, Ellen born 26 February 1764 and baptised 18 March 1764, and Anne. Both died young (Hurt MSS).

65 Harris Museum and Art Gallery, Preston, QS/B3.

66 Property pulled down 1927 or 1929.

67 R. Guest, *A Compendious History of the Cotton Manufacture: with a Disproval of the Claim of Sir Richard Arkwright to the Invention of its ingenious Machinery*, Manchester, 1823, pp. 14–5.

68 J. Aikin and W. Enfield, *General Biography*, I, London, 1799, p. 391; *S.F.*, p. 63.

69 Guest, *Compendious History*, p. 21.

70 Wadsworth and Mann, p. 472.

71 A. P. Wadsworth, *Manchester Guardian*, 5 May 1934.

72 T. S. Ashton, *Economic Fluctuations in England*, Oxford, 1959, p. 78.

73 T. S. Ashton, *The Industrial Revolution, 1760–1830*, Oxford, 1948, p. 34

74 Wadsworth and Mann, pp. 15, 19–20.

75 Guildhall Library, London, Beta, *Petitions and Parliamentary Matters, 1620–1621*, no. 16.

76 Wadsworth and Mann, pp. 11, 16, 25.

77 *Ibid.*, p. 475.

78 Patent No. 202; see Wadsworth and Mann, p. 413.

79 Ashton, *Industrial Revolution*, p. 33.

80 For Paul and Wyatt see Wadsworth and Mann, pp. 419–31.

81 Patent No. 562.

82 R. W. Chapman (ed.), *The Letters of Samuel Johnson*, I, Oxford, 1952, pp. 17, 19.

83 Wadsworth and Mann, p. 433, n. 3; F. Espinasse, *Lancashire Worthies*, London and Manchester, 1874, I, p. 350; S. Smiles, *The Huguenots: their Settlements, Churches, and Industries*, London, 1867, p. 422.

84 J. H. Thornton, 'The Northampton cotton industry — an eighteenth century episode', *Northamptonshire Natural History Society and Field Club*, XXXIII, June 1959, pp. 250–1.

85 B.R.L., B. & W. MSS, Boulton to Watt, August 1781.

86 Wadsworth and Mann, p. 433, undated letter, Cave to Paul, printed in *Birmingham Weekly Post*, 22 August 1891.

87 R. L. Hills, *Power in the Industrial Revolution*, Manchester, 1970, p. 50

88 Patent No. 724.

89 *Transactions, Society of Arts*, I, 1786, p. 197.
90 Patent No. 636.
91 J. Kennedy, 'A brief memoir of Samuel Crompton', *Memoirs of the Manchester Literary and Philosophical Society*, second series, V, 1831, p. 326 n.
92 *S.F.*, p. 63, evidence of John Kay.
93 *G.M.*, 1772, p. 863.
94 J. M. Britton and E. W. Brayley, *The Beauties of England and Wales*, III, London, 1802, p. 519.
95 See D. J. Jeremy (ed.), *Henry Wansey and his American Journal*, Philadelphia, 1970, p. 6.
96 *Mechanic's Magazine*, II, No. 44, 26 June 1824, pp. 255-6.
97 Guest, *Compendious History*, p. 13.
98 *S.F.*, p. 59.
99 L.C.R.O., DDPd/11/51, 'A State of the Poll at the Election at Preston the 21ˢᵗ of March 1768'.
100 Aikin and Enfield, *General Biography*, I, pp. 391-2.
101 L.C.R.O., DDPd/11/51; *S.F.*, p. 63.
102 L.C.R.O., DDPr 138/7, Miscellaneous Papers.
103 W. Dobson, *History of the Parliamentary Representation of Preston*, Preston, second edition, 1868, p. 35.
104 7 March 1768.
105 L.C.R.O., DDPr 138/7.
106 L.C.R.O., DDPd/11/51.
107 Whittle, *Bolton-le-Moors*, II, p. 216.
108 L.C.R.O., DDPd/11/51.
109 Whittle, *Bolton-le-Moors*, I, p. 84.
110 P.B.R., Council Minute Book: 3 February 1747–48; 10 June 1765.
111 L.C.R.O., DDPd/11/51.
112 Whittle, *Bolton-le-Moors*, II, pp. 215–16.
113 R. L. Hills, 'Hargreaves, Arkwright and Crompton: why three inventors?', *Textile History*, 10, 1979, pp. 116, 121.
114 Hills, *Power in the Industrial Revolution*, pp. 62–3; 'Hargreaves, Arkwright and Crompton', pp. 121–3.
115 Sir J. Hawkins, *The Works of Samuel Johnson, together with his Life, and Notes on his Lives of the Poets*, XI, 1787, p. 215. The statement appears earlier in the *European Magazine*, January 1785, pp. 51, 54–5, quoting an unnamed newspaper.

CHAPTER II

Partners and patents

IN THE SPRING OF 1768 Arkwright, accompanied by Kay, left Preston with his plans for a roller-spinning machine and, like James Hargreaves with his spinning jenny about the same time, sought his fortune in Nottingham, the centre of the cotton hosiery industry. A town of some 15,000 inhabitants, said by the young German traveller Karl Philipp Moritz to be one of the finest and certainly the cleanest outside London, it was surrounded on three sides by fields subject to common rights. This prevented the natural outward expansion of the town, but despite this many of the houses had stretches of garden and, sometimes, orchards attached to them.[1]

Nottingham had been growing in social significance since 1674, when the Duke of Newcastle had begun the building of his Palladian mansion, with its sixty-four-acre deer park on the site of the old castle. His example was followed, among others, by the Plumptres, the Willoughbys and, not least, by George Smith, the banker. The aristocracy and gentry of the region not only gravitated to the town on important social occasions; some of them actually lived there.

From the last decade of the seventeenth century the stocking manufacturing industry, based on the Elizabethan invention of William Lee, the Nottingham parson, had been moving away from London to the Midlands, where control by the Framework Knitters' Company was ineffectual and where labour and other costs were lower. In 1730 a Nottingham workman, using Indian spun cotton yarn on the stocking frame, produced the first pair of cotton hose ever made by mechanical means. Twenty years later the Nottingham hosiers are said to have provided employment for 1,200 frames working in wool and cotton as well as for a considerable number of workpeople in the ancilliary industries. In 1759 Jedediah Strutt obtained a patent for his Derby rib machine, a highly ingenious mechanism which, when placed in front of the stocking frame, enabled the fashionable ribbed stockings to be made by machine instead of by hand. Strutt's invention was followed by a succession of innovations which enabled the framework knitter to produce almost every kind of mesh by mechanical means: in 1764 it was adapted to the making of eyelet holes, the first step towards the manufacture of machine-made lace; in 1767 velvet was made on the stocking frame and two years later brocade.

Nottingham thus offered many advantages to the prospective machine spinner. It provided a ready market for cotton yarn, in which the Midland manufacturers were largely dependent for their supplies on Lancashire, where they had to compete with other users, or from India, yarn from which was expensive. To hand in Nottingham were mechanics long skilled at working upon the stocking frame, a complex machine for the time, and who since the days of Lewis Paul had given much thought to the problems of machine spinning. And it is possible too that the attitude towards inventors aiming at exclusive patent rights was less hostile than in Lancashire.

Arkwright was soon joined in Nottingham by three of his distant relatives — John Smalley of Preston, through whom he had rented rooms at the Free Grammar School, and two Liverpool men, David Thornley and his brother-in-law, Henry Brown, watchmaker, of Ranelagh Street.[2]

Forty-year-old Smalley, landlord of the Bull inn (later the Bull and Royal), was described as a 'Grocer and Painter' in the Guild Rolls of 1762. The following year he became a Bailiff of Preston and in 1765 a Corporation Steward. The second son of John Smalley, chapman, of Blackburn, he had married at Preston in 1751, Elizabeth Baxter, whose mother Ellen, the widow of Arkwright's uncle Richard, had married Christopher Baxter, husbandman, on the last day of 1730, just over three years after the death of her first husband.[3]

Thornley's mother, Sarah, daughter of Richard and Ellen Arkwright, had married by licence at Penwortham, near Preston, on 21 June 1738, David Thornley, carrier, and David, their only son, was born three years later, On 4 November 1766 this David married Mary, daughter of Joseph Brown, roper, at St Peter's, Liverpool, the church at which Thomas Arkwright and Ellen Hodgkinson had married almost half a century before. In *Gore's Directory* for 1767 David is described as 'merchant' and his wife as 'milliner' of Castle Street, Liverpool. The following year — perhaps earlier — Thornley began his active association with Arkwright when he joined him in Preston, an event recorded in the inquiry into the qualifications of those who had voted in the Burgoyne election: 'Thornley David from Liverpoole his wife is a Milliner she never was at Preston but one Night in her road from Manchester, no children 1st. Febry never stay'd above a Night or two.'[4]

On 14 May 1768 Arkwright, Smalley and Thornley became partners at Nottingham. Richard Arkwright, the agreement recited, had 'lately Invented and constructed an Instrument or Peice of Machinery for the more Expeditious and better Spinning of Cotton, Worstead and Flax into Yarn' and had agreed that John Smalley and David Thornley became 'Joint Adventurers and Partners' for a term of fourteen years or, if a patent could be obtained, for a longer period. Each partner was to have three one-ninth shares and was to advance such money as might be necessary to apply for a patent 'and for Improving Enlarging Using and Working the Machine already Invented and

The specification in the petition for royal letters patent reads: 'NOW KNOW YE, that I, the said Richard Arkwright, in compliance with the said proviso, do hereby describe and ascertain the nature of my said Invention, and declare that the Plan thereof drawn in the margin of these Presents is composed of the following particulars (that is to say):- *A*, the cogg wheel and shaft, which receive their motion from a horse; *B*, the drum or wheel which turns *C*, a belt of leather, and gives motion to the whole machine; *D*, a lead weight which keeps *F*, the small drum, steady to *E*, the forcing wheel; *G*, the shaft of wood which gives motion to the wheel *H*, and continues it to *I*, four pair of rollers (the form of which are drawn in the margin), which act by tooth and pinion, made of brass and steel nutts, fixt in two iron plates *K*. That part of the roller which the cotton runs through is covered with wood, the top roller with leather, and the bottom one fluted, which lets the cotton, &c. through it, and by one pair of rollers moving quicker than the other, draws it finer for twisting, which is performed by the spindles *T*. *K*, the two iron plates described above; *L*, four large bobbins with cotton rovings on, conducted between rollers at the back; *M*, the four threads carried to the bobbins and spindles, by four small wires fixt across the frame in the slip of wood *V*; *N*, iron leavers with small lead weights, hanging to the rollers by pulleys, which keep the rollers close to each other; *O*, a cross piece of wood to which the leavers are fixed; *P*, the bobbins and spindles; *Q*, flyes made of wood, with small wires on the side which lead the thread to the bobbins; *R*, small worsted bands, put about the whirl of the bobbins, the screwing of which tight or easy causes the bobbins to wind up the thread faster or slower; *S*, the four whirls of the spindles; *T*, the four spindles which run in iron plates *V*, explained in letter *M*; *W*, a wooden frame of the whole machine.'

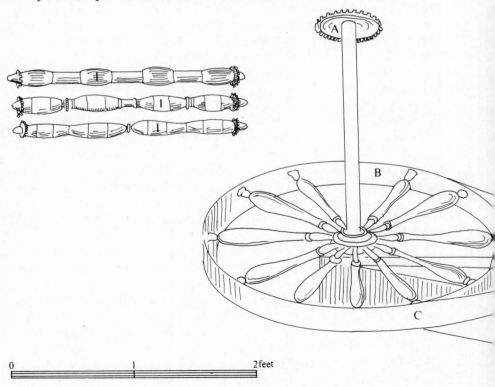

0   1   2 feet

others thereafter to be Constructed for the same or like purposes'. Profits were to be equally divided 'as often as they might think convenient' but in the event of each partner's share exceeding £500 a year Richard Arkwright 'should be Allowed Ten Per Cent: of the Surplus . . . more than either of the other partners'.[5] After two years no partner was to 'carry on or follow any other Business Trade or Employ without their Mutual Consent' and if any partner died before the end of the agreement his heirs were to receive his share of the profits after making 'a reasonable allowance to those surviving for Extra trouble in running affairs'.[6]

The partners had agreed 'that they some or one of them should as soon as might be Apply for a Patent' and on 8 June 1768 Richard Arkwright, 'Clockmaker of Nottingham', submitted his petition, which was granted thirteen months later. John Smalley and Bigoe Henzell ('Clerk to Henry Rooke Esq.') signed as witnesses. The long interval between the petition for the patent and the final grant (there was to be no such delay with Arkwright's carding patent of 1775) suggests that the partners had difficulty in raising the £55 that had to be paid at various stages.

Certainly this was the case with David Thornley (an eventuality already anticipated under the terms of the partnership agreement), and on 19 June 1769, finding it 'not Convenient . . . to advance . . . a full equal Share of Money'. he assigned to Smalley, 'with the Consent and Approbation of . . . Richard Arkwright', a one-ninth share in the partnership in return for the capital. Thornley was still to take 'the full and just sum of Five Hundred Pounds' a year but, beyond that, Smalley was to have an additional one-ninth share of the profits.

It is tempting if idle to speculate as to why in these circumstances Thornley was able to take up a three-ninths share in a patent and in a partnership so obviously dominated from the start by Arkwright — and an Arkwright short of money. One can only suspect that, perhaps together with his brother-in-law, Henry Brown, he had played some vital but unknown part in the development of the water frame.

The patent secured, the partners began the search for premises in which to build and set up their machines and on 29 September 1769 agreed with John Miller of Nottingham upon a ninety-one-year lease at £105 plus a yearly rent of £50 of 'All that Messuage Burgage and Tenement with the Outhouses Buildings Maltrooms Barn Stable Yard Garden Close or Paddock thereunto Adjoining . . . in Nottingham . . . in or near two certain Streets or Places there called Goosegate and Hockley and being the Corner house and Premises next and adjoining to a certain other Street or place called Coalpit Lane late in the Tenure or Occupation of the said John Miller'. Close by James Hargreaves had already established his mill and in the spring of 1769 had advertised in the *Nottingham Journal* for machine makers.[7]

Tradition has it that, with Smalley's resources by this time stretched to their limit, Arkwright sought assistance from Ichabod and John Wright, the Nottingham bankers, who agreed to support him provided that 'if his plan should succeed, they were to share in its profits'.[8] Dugald Bannatyne's account in the *Supplement* of the *Encyclopaedia Britannica* (1816 or a little earlier) is the first to mention the Wrights and that they, 'finding the amount of their advances swell to a larger sum than they had expected, while there seemed to them little prospect of the discovery being brought into a practical state', turned Arkwright over to Samuel Need, a wealthy Nottingham hosier, and partner since 1762 with Jedediah Strutt, inventor and patentee with his brother-in-law, William Woollat, of the Derby rib machine.[9] The device had made possible a great expansion of the hosiery industry, and Need, having profited so much from this successful patent, was ready to exploit another. As, the story goes, he asked Arkwright 'to carry the model of his machine to Mr Strutt . . . [who] told Mr Need that he might with great safety close with Mr Arkwright; the only thing wanting to his model, being an adaptation of some of those wheels to each other, which, from a want of skill, the inventor, with all his powers of contrivance, had not been able to accomplish'.

And so on 19 January 1770 Need and Strutt, on payment of £500, became co-partners with Arkwright, Smalley and Thornley for the remainder of the patent's fourteen-year term. The new partners, the agreement recited, were to be allowed to continue in their hosiery concerns, but otherwise no partner was to engage in any other business.[10] Arkwright and Thornley were to be responsible for the day-to-day management of the mill and each was to have £25 a year 'for their personal and constant Attendance upon the Managem[en]t & superin-tendence of the Works & Servants'. As in the agreement of 14 May 1768, Arkwright was to have 10 per cent of any additional profits once each partner had received £500. Should any partner die, his share in the concern was to be carried on on behalf of his executors, who were to receive profits due to him, less '£60 a Year for the Wages of a proper person to Officiate in his place'.[11]

With the financial backing of Need and Strutt Arkwright was able to commission Samuel Stretton, a Nottingham builder, to convert the recently leased property into a mill, driven by horses turning a capstan.[12] The mill was, however, still in the experimental stage — it is said not to have been 'brought to work' until Christmas 1772 — when in 1771 the partners, Thornley excepted, took the momentous decision to go to Cromford, near Matlock, and apply water power to machinery still far from perfect. Their experiment was to prove a major turning point in the history of the factory system. The only power mentioned in the patent specification had been that of horses, and while nothing more had been attempted at Nottingham the idea of a factory system based on water power had long been in the air. In 1702 Thomas Cotchett had set up a mill for twisting silk by water power on an island in the river Derwent at

Derby. His enterprise failed but was soon revived and extended by John and Thomas Lombe, whose Derby Silk Mill, built and equipped, it is said, at a cost of £30,000, must have been well known to Strutt, whose hosiery business included the manufacture of silk at Derby.[13] By the 1760s silk mills were working at Stockport, Congleton, Macclesfield, Sheffield and Watford. In cotton the factory Lewis Paul had established at Northamptom by 1743 — and which in so many ways resembled Arkwright's — was driven by water. The use of water power for spinning had also been contemplated in two machines neither of which received a serious trial: those of James Taylor, a clockmaker, of Ashton-under-Lyne, and John Kay, of Bury, whose 'invention for spinning of cotton by water' is referred to in his letter to the Society of Arts in 1767.[14]

The Cromford venture had its visible beginnings on 1 August 1771, when the partners agreed with Robert Nall, hosier, of Chesterfield, and a trustee of William and Mary Milnes of Aldercar Park, near Heanor, to lease land upon which to build a water-powered spinning mill.[15] A yearly rent of £14 secured for them a twenty-one-year lease extendable by a further sixty-three years of:

> All that River Stream or Brook called Bonsall Brook Situate and being within the Liberty of Cromford . . . together with the Stream of Water Issuing and running from Cromford Sough in Cromford . . . into the said Bonsall Brook with full Liberty and power . . . to divert Turn and carry the said Brook Stream and Water down the South Side of the High Way in Cromford . . . and under or over the said Highway And also all that piece or parcel of Ground situate . . . between the said Bonsall Brook and the intended new Cutt and extending the length from the Turnpike road leading to Matlock Bath to a Garden in the Possession of James Cooper . . . Together with full and free Liberty Power and Authority . . . to Erect and Build one or more Mill or Mills for Spinning Winding or throwing Silk Worsted Linen Cotton or other Materials and also such and so many Waterwheels Warehouses Shops Smithies and other Buildings Banks and Dams Gails Shuttles and other Conveniences as they should think proper for the effectual Working the said Mills.

Nine years later Arkwright was to tell John Lee, his counsel, why the site had been chosen. Cromford, he said, was 'a place affording a remarkable fine Stream of Water, And [was situated] in a Country very full of inhabitants vast numbers of whom & small Children are constantly Employed in the Works'.[16] The district was not new to water-powered ventures. As early as the thirteenth century Cromford had had its 'ancient corn-mill' on the Bonsall Brook just above its confluence with the Derwent, and the agreement of 1771 specifically stated that Arkwright's activities were in no way 'to prejudice the corn-mill in the possession of Mr. Baxter, by taking away or diminishing the quantity of water . . . used or necessary for working the . . . corn-mill'. Close to Cromford Bridge and but a short distance from the corn mill stood the smelting mills at which, observed a visitor in 1749, 'they melt down the Lead Ore, and run it into a Mold, whence it become *Pigs*, as they call them. The Bellows are kept in continual Motion by running Water.'[17]

Shortly before the partners' arrival at Cromford other adventurers had started to make use of the neighbourhood's water power. In 1768 George White had taken a ninety-nine-year lease of land in the manor of Matlock 'to build Mills and Erect Water-Wheels upon a parcel of Land adjoining to the River Derwent called Masson' and in July the following year John Barber and George Goodwin obtained a twenty-one-year lease enabling them 'to Erect Water-Wheels & other machines on the East side of River Derwent adjoining a piece of Land called the High Tors Wood & also near Matlock Bridge for the purpose of Unwatering Mines'. In 1771 Robert Shore and George White built a paper mill near New Bath at Matlock, adding additional buildings in 1772 and signing an agreement with the lords of the manor to convey water to the paper mill for a period of twenty-one years.[18]

The Arkwright partners can hardly have been unaware of these develop-ments and could well have had some additional incentive to move to Cromford in the tradition that the waters of Cromford sough, draining from the Wirks-worth lead mines and joining Bonsall brook just above the proposed mill site, had never been known to freeze.[19] Otherwise, apart from the potential labour supply of lead miners and their families, Cromford had little to offer. The turnpike from the north of England to Derby and London (the main source of raw cotton) ran through Brassington, some miles to the west, Derby was fourteen miles away, Nottingham twenty-six and Manchester forty-five. The direct route to Derby ran over the moorlands; the valley road, now the A6, was not built until 1820.[20]

The country around Cromford afforded stark contrasts. Arthur Young on his tour in 1771 was:

> agreeably surprized to find the country from *Derby* to *Matlock* in general enclosed and cultivated. *Derbyshire* being generally reputed as waste a county as any in *England*; I was led to expect large tracts of uncultivated country in every quarter of it; but all the southern parts of it are rich: in this track are some un-inclosed commons, but they bear no proportion to the cultivated land.[21]

Yet the following summer Thomas De Quincey's father noted that on ap-proaching Matlock Vale from the direction of Chesterfield:

> there are four miles of road over a very extensive moor, covered in some places with fern, but every where with large stones sticking out of the earth, and exhibiting a black, desolate, and melancholy appearance; the hills are not comparable in height to the mountains of several northern counties, or even to some in the more western parts of this; however they are steep enough to oblige any but a daring traveller to alight and walk down, and a the foot of most a brook or rather a small torrent pours impetuously along. Nature seems also to have

[29]

debarred improvement in this dreary waste, having placed an insurmountable object in the way of cultivation, by fixing upon it those prominent rocks.[22]

Such was the country in which the partners chose to expand their activities. Steephill Grange, a house built by Robert Greensmith in 1714, was bought and its stone used to build a mill which is still to be seen from the road connecting the A6 and Cromford Bridge.[23] Like the Derby Silk Mill, upon which it is said to have been modelled, it had a design of great functional simplicity. Its five storeys consisted of rectangular masonry boxes, with timber beams and posts supporting each floor. Combined in a single design, the long, narrow proportions, height, ranges of windows (so well caught in the paintings of Joseph Wright of Derby) and large areas of relatively unbroken interior space had no counterpart in English architectural history and became the basic design in industrial architecture for the remainder of the eighteenth and throughout the nineteenth centuries.[24]

The mill's bell, cast by Pack & Chapman of Whitechapel, bears the date 1771 and in December that year the partners are seen advertising in the *Derby Mercury* for clockmakers, a smith and other machine makers. Also required were weavers and women and children. The labour force was being got together. The notice reads:

Cotton Mill, Cromford,   10th Dec. 1771

WANTED immediately, two Journeymen Clock-Makers, or others that understands Tooth and Pinion well: Also a Smith that can forge and file. — Likewise two Wood Turners that have been accustomed to Wheel-making, Spole-turning, &c. Weavers residing in this Neighbourhood, by applying at the Mill, may have good Work. There is Employment at the above Place, for Women, Children, &c. and good Wages.

N.B. A quantity of Box Wood is wanted: Any Persons whom the above may suit, will be treated with by Messrs. Arkwright and Co. at the Mill, or Mr. Strutt, in Derby.[25]

Some few indentures from these early days have survived. The oldest is that of George Hodges, a Nottingham labourer who on 30 May 1772 was bound for £10,000. (Arkwright was hardly the man to allow any of his workmen to get away with selling his mechanical or other secrets.) Hodges agreed to work thirteen hours a day, six days a week. His wages, to be paid 'Weekly and every Week', were to be 10s during the first year, 11s for the second and 12s from the third until the end of his contract in 1783. He agreed to work 'within the Town of Nottingham or elsewhere' and was to receive in addition to wages:

any Reasonable Charges in Removeing his Family and Goods and . . . is to be at Liberty not to work for them [the partners] and Longer than the Space of Six Months from and after he shall give Notice of his Intention so to do and the said

Copartners or any of them are to be at Liberty to give the said George Hodges Six Months Notice of their Intention for him to Quit their Service whenever they shall think Proper so to Do. And the said George Hodges shall and do from time to time during the Continuance of the said Patent and so long as the said shall be in force keep secret and not on any occasion whatever directly or Indirectly disclose or make known to any Person or Persons whatsoever the form Construction use or Manner of Working any Machine or Machines belonging to the said Richard Arkwright and Company.[26]

A lengthy, vigorous and ill spelt letter of March 1772 from Arkwright to Strutt gives something of the spirit of this early period. Some few legends have come down about it, the most credible being that of Strutt using a piece of chalk to stop the 'licking' — the catching of the yarn — on the front rollers of the spinning frame. Above all, Arkwright's letter reveals his unbounded confidence in himself and (as Thomas Ridgway noted of his Bolton years) an extremely practical turn of mind. He is getting on with the making of more frames. (Machine production was dependent on the production of machines, and the earliest factory masters had to make their own.) His head is full of ideas about the uses his yarn could be put to, not only in hosiery but also in the whole range of cotton fabrics — from calicoes to fustians, and he looked forward to worsted. Need, then aged fifty-three, is shown as the cautious partner, content to make a success of the Nottingham mill and more set in his ways than the ambitious Arkwright, still not quite forty. And Need had the money. It was a situation shrewdly summed up in the memoirs of Elizabeth Grant of Rothiemurchus, a visitor to Need's daughters in the early 1820s: 'Arkwright was the head, Strutt the hands, and Need the sinews, for *he* had the purse.'[27] Arkwright's letter reads:

Cromford Mar,[h] 2.[d] 72

Sir,

Yours yesterday came to hand together with a bill from M.[r] Need Value £60. I have sent a little cotton spun on the one spindle & find no Difficanty in Geting it from the Bobbin & Dubel.[d] & Twist.[d] in the maner you see it at one opration one hand I think will do 40 or 50lb of it in one day from the bobins it is spun upon that is in the new whay I am sertain of it ansuaring & one person will spin a Thousand Hanks a Day so that wee shall not want 1/5 of the hands I First Expect.[d] not withstanding the Roaving takeing so few I see Greate Improve, ments Every day, When I rote to you last had not thorowly prov.[d] the spining several things apening I could not a count for sinse then has proved it — I have made trial to twist it for Velverets & find what the[y] do with five operations [I] Can do with one that is duble & twist it Redey for wharping at one time, first they reel second wind third Duble fourth twist 5 wind redey to wharp & all these done one thred at a time Except Twisting shold Like you try a little of this hard in a rib.[d] fraim i think it shold not be whet but beate Plais to send the solft to M.[r] Need one has a slacker throw then the other naither of [them] perfect but

shold like to see a stockin or part of one pray Bring a Little with you. Mr Need
of wanting Thos Bell & a turner but Cant see what they whant Thos for I spok
to Coniah & dar say he will come if he was properly aploy.^{d} to or they might
get a man from Hibisons but there is no person at the mill that will put
themselves out of their whay to be of aney Servis Except teas Mr Needs hart out
with a continual want & uneasiness as to sending aney hand from hear I can.^{t}
think of doing for where they get a Shiling Cleair there shall in a few months
40 I am posative if Mr Need thinks best Can go one or two days p. wheek to
Nottingham & Shall Shortly Suply them with Roavings from hear if wee can.^{t}
spin 2000 Hanks a Day which I an Sertain I can in four months at the outside
and now as solfter can be spun faster than hard stocking yarn will ansuar best
& will be Dubled with very Little Expence — at the mill the[y] whant Cards
puting on andrew might do that as it Requires no greate Judgement but I sopose
he is a deal taken up in those Looms & the profits of wich will Scairsly pay
whare house room if he can be got to wheave by the Pees or yard & out of the
mill shold sune set that plase in Better order but while he is in it is scairsly posable
Except he has his own whay no good will be don with justis or him & what
I sade to George is what I shold say again it whas unraisenable in a few weeks
shall move for wee can do without them all it is onley seting an other pair of cards
&c hear wee have begun of them shold Like to know if aney acount is come
from Hallifax^{29} lately he has sent som other Cards but not the quantety I Rote
for and no Letter or bill with them shold Rote to Mr N. but has not time &
wold when I do send to send some twe threds solft and as Even as silk I am
sertain I can [make] the first fraim I have hands to make three fraims in a fortnet
it shall be don you may depend upon it but I whant sombody to look after the
spining &c I have rote to Kay yesterday if he will not come can you think of
sombody a yonge man was hear this Wheek sade he had spoke to you this is his
Riteing I send Inclosed what do you think of him he seems a Likely person but
has all to Lern I am afraide no one man will know all that I shold Expect the[y]
might. Rich^d has hit upon a method to spin woostid with Roulers it is quite
sertain & only altering the shape that is Round on one side and flat on the other
so that the twist gets under or betwixt them at sertain time it will ansuar I am
sertain, Querey will not Cotton make whip coard as good as silk properly
Twisted it may be don all at onst from the bobins pray Rite to Mr N. what he
thinks best I Cant think of stoping this Con[c]ern hear as that at notting.^{m} his
[not] or Ever will be aney thing in comparison to this, there is hands to be got
there & if he wold have mee com over I shall but not take aney from hear I ask.^{d}
Mr Whard to get som Let pipes to bring the water into the mill they are
continially fetching it might be Brought in the Rooms wold it not be best to fix
a Crank to one of the lying shafts to work a pump or Ingon in case of fire bring
the belts with you Desire ward to send those other Locks and allso Some sorts
of Hangins for the sashes he & you may think best and some good Latches &
Catches for the out doors and a few for the inner ons allso and a Large Knoker
or a Bell to First door I am Determin.^{d} for the feuter to Let no persons in to Look
at the wor[k]s except spining the man Mr Whard Bo.^{t} the ash Board from Call.^{d}

the other shorlty I am tired with riteing so Long a Letter & think you can scairsly Reed it Excuse haist

and am yours &c.

R. Arkwright

John Kay, the former Warrington clock maker, and three of Arkwright's early workmen may be identified in the letter. They are Thomas Bell, a joiner who in 1785 stated that he had worked for Arkwright five years '17 years ago',[30] Richard Briddon, who joined Arkwright in 1771 and later became a partner with his son at a cotton-spinning mill at Rocester, Staffordshire,[31] and Coniah Wood, a Nottingham turner who took out a patent in 1772 for a machine for spinning wool or jersey and who, according to Gravenor Henson, a gatherer of much tradition, rescued Arkwright from Needs's scorn when, early on, the performance of his machines failed to match his promises.[32]

The next we hear of the partners' activities concerns their position under the law. Early in the century, jealous of the finished fabrics — calicoes and chintzes — brought in by the East India Company, the woollen and silk manufacturers had secured from Parliament the imposition of a double excise duty and, for printed calicoes, an almost complete prohibition of sale and manufacture. In 1736 the Lancashire cotton industry had obtained by the so-called Manchester Act a relaxation for printed goods made of flax warp and cotton weft, and this, it seems, had come to cover the bulk of the industry's production, including the growing part of it that consisted of printed goods made entirely of cotton. Technically, however, from 1736, only half-cotton material was free to be made (subject to the 3d a yard excise).

The machine-spun twist from the Arkwright patent machines was now entering the calico-printing trade and was being treated inconsistently by the excisemen. In Lancashire the new printed calicoes were allowed through at 3d a yard duty (as for cotton-linen prints) while in London they were charged at double that rate. Under the Act of 1721 they should have been confiscated, but so completely had the situation changed that no action was in fact taken and the question of prohibition remained in doubt. The earliest hint we have of this is in an anonymous letter, doubtless inspired by the Arkwright partners, in *Prescott's Manchester Journal* of 18 December 1773 suggesting that steps should be taken to alter the law if, indeed, it did forbid the manufacture:

To the Printer of the *Manchester Journal*.

Sir

I shall be much obliged to any of your Ingenious Readers who wil favour me with answers to the following QueriesA.B.1. What is the duty on Printing all cotton good being manufactured in this kingdom?

2. Is there any law that prohibits the wear of such cotton goods, provided they are of English manufactory?

3. If there be such a law, would it not be prudent to look for redress?

4. Provided we have no such law, how must we distinguish our English printed cottons, from those printed Callicoes commonly called muslins, so much wore at this time among us?

5. Are the printed Callicoes or printed muslins prohibited? If so, what is the penalty?

6. Is it not consistent with reason, when we can manufacture goods equal to foreigners, to give employment to our own people, rather than to inrich other nations?

The partners in all likelihood had already considered seeking redress by legislation, for on 25 February 1774 their petition — from 'Richard Arkwright and Company, of Nottingham, Spinners of Cotton, and Manufacturers of British Cotton Stuffs' — was presented to the Commons. It recited how, under the 1769 patent, cotton yarn for warps had been spun by machine, and how 'with such warps, there are wholly made in Great Britain, from raw Materials, Velverets, and a Variety of other Goods, particularly a new Manufacture of White Cotton Stuffs, adapted for Printing'. A few pieces printed in Lancashire had been charged with two duties of $1\frac{1}{2}d$ a yard, $3d$ in all; others sold to calico printers 'in and about London' had been charged as calicoes with two duties of $3d$, $6d$ in all. Orders had been countermanded 'to the great Prejudice of a new and promising British Manufacture'. The petition contended that they should be charged at $3d$ and that a $6d$ duty would act as a prohibition, adding that doubt had arisen whether such 'White Cotton Stuffs' were not, when printed, prohibited from being used and worn in Great Britain. It went on, with some prescience:

the Petitioners assure themselves, the said Manufacture, if not crushed by so heavy an Duty as Six Pence a Yard, will rapidly increase, and find new and effectual Employment for many Thousand British Poor, and increase the Revenue of this Kingdom; and that it is probable such Warp, made of Cotton which is manufactured in this Kingdom, will be introduced in the Room of the Warps before used, made of Linen Yarn (great Part of which Linen Yarn is imported ready-spun from Foreign Parts) in making Lancashire Cottons, in regard Cotton Goods so made wholly of Cotton will be greatly superior in Quality to the present Species of Cotton Goods made with Linen Yarn Warps, and will bleach, print, wash, and wear better, and, by Means thereof, find further Employment for the Poor.

They prayed that the Commons give leave to bring in a Bill legalising the white cotton stuffs, settling the duty when printed at $3d$, and extending to them the export drawback allowed to British and Irish coarse linens.[33]

Clearly the partners had not managed their parliamentary affairs skilfully, for their petition was allowed to lie on the table for more than two months, its supporters not being ready to follow it up. Strutt, who early in February had

The Headmaster's House in Preston,
where Arkwright developed the water frame

overleaf The water frame

A shows a full size water frame originally worked by the Arkwrights at Cromford Mill (now at The Museum of the Lancashire Textile Industry, Helmshore). The double-sided frames were worked in pairs driven by the central wheel itself attached to gearing and powered by the mill's water wheel. Note the timber-framed construction, only the precise parts, sometimes referred to as 'clockwork', would be made of metal. The picture illustrates the cotton rovings in the upper part of the frame being drawn through rollers (in these more advanced frames containing 3 rather than 4 pairs of rollers) and on to the spindles. Note the weights which were used to apply pressure to the rollers.

B shows details of a full size water frame (now at the North West Museum of Science and Industry), in particular the rollers and the gearing.

The quality of the final cotton yarn was itself dependent upon the quality of the rovings that fed the frame, to improve this quality a range of preparatory machinery – the lapping machine, the carding engine, the lantern frame, the jack-in-a-box and the drawing frame – were devised (these can be seen at The Museum of the Lancashire Textile Industry, Helmshore).

C illustrates a carding engine originally worked at Cromford Mill.

D illustrates one of the lesser-known machines, the lantern frame, so named because the conical container was opened at the side like a lantern.

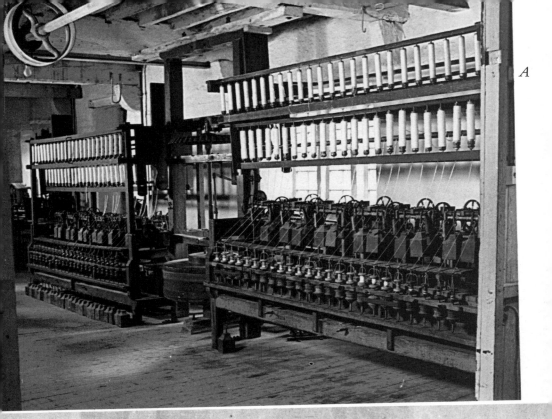

C

D

Stanley Bell Mill

Masson Mill

come up to London to take charge of the parliamentary proceedings (he lodged with his brother Joseph in Newgate Street), settled down to wait, his wife coming up to join him the following month and finding his 'business goes so slowly'.[34] On 2 May the petition was read again and referred to a committee of the House. The named members were Lord Howe, the admiral, who although since 1757 member for Dartmouth had close political connections with Nottingham,[35] and John Plumptre,[36] since 1761 one of the Nottingham members. Lord Howe reported from the committee on 6 May. Jedediah Strutt had 'produced a Piece of plain white, and a Piece of printed, Cotton Stuffs (the Warp being Cotton, and spun by the said [1769 patent] Machine) manufactured from raw Materials, near *Blackburn*, in *Lancashire*, which he said was better adapted for Printing than any Thing of the Kind heretofore used for that Purpose', and Stephen Williams, a linen draper of Poultry, who described his difficulties with the London excisemen and his unsuccessful appeal to the Commissioners of Excise when after having had printed 'about 300 Pieces . . . of the said Cotton Stuffs . . . the Officers of Excise demanded a Duty of Six Pence *per* Yard as Callicoes, being the same Duty that is paid upon Callicoes imported from the *East Indies*'. Strutt, recalled, said that:

> the Petitioners had expended upwards of £13,000 in the said Manufacture; that if charged with the said Duty of Sixpence *per* Yard, it would totally hinder the Growth, and obstruct the Sale, of this promising Manufacture, which, in all Probability, will become a flourishing Trade, if encouraged, and be the Means of employing many Thousands of Poor People, there being already upwards of 600 Persons of all Ages employed in this Branch of Business; that Children of Seven Years old, and upwards, are employed, and they prefer Children from Ten to Twelve Years old, for the preparing and spinning Cotton by the said machine.[37]

Leave was given to Lord Howe, Frederick Montagu (member for Higham Ferrers and a Nottinghamshire landowner) and Plumptre to bring in a Bill. This had its second reading on 17 May, its third on 1 June, was passed by the Lords without amendment, and received the royal assent on 14 June.[38]

In the interval between the two petitions the partners had submitted to the Lords of the Treasury the 'Heads of an intended Act of Parliament pursuant to the Petition of Richard Arkwright and Company'. Among its proposals was a scheme by which the 'New Manufacture' (which 'if properly encouraged, will rapidly increase and find effectual Employment for many Thousand British Poor, and encrease the Revenue of this Kingdom') could be distinguished from imported calicoes.[39] Arkwright's suggestion was that each piece of cloth made with cotton warp should be marked with three blue threads at both ends of the piece ('Proviso that the East India Company or any other Person or Persons' importing 'Callicoes Muslins or other Goods from the East Indies' so marked should forfeit the manufactures and in addition suffer 'the Penalty of £100 Sterling for each Piece').[40] These proposals were referred to the Board of Excise on 8 April and thirteen days later the Commissioners, all nine being present, proposed to the Treasury an alternative which would 'be more effectual to prevent Frauds'. This was that the blue threads should be in the selvage, 'going through the whole length of each piece'; a stamp at each end of the piece should have 'instead of the Word Callicoe which stands for Foreign Callicoes', the works 'British Manufactory'. This was embodied in the Bill; the British all-cotton stuffs were to be distinguished from the foreign by having three blue threads in the selvage (the first, third and fifth) and by the stamp.[41]

Arkwright did not figure in the Commons proceedings, nor was he associated with Need and Strutt's gift, thirteen months later, of a piece of the new manufacture to Lord Howe for his wife. Strutt's draft letter (written on the back of one from his daughter of 2 July 1775) ran:

> Mr N & Mr S Compl[iment]s to Ld Howe begs his Lordships acceptance of this peice of British Calico for Lady Howe as a small acknowledgment for the great trouble we gave your Ldship last summer in obtaining the Act for the printing & wearing of them in England. We wish the choice of the print may be a recommendation. The piece itself is not exquisite, has nothing extraordinary in it, but that it is British Manufacture. We have since this time 12 months made about 5000 pieces & have pleasure to inform your Lordship that when we have made the necessary allowance for the difficulties & prejudices attending all new manufactures of concern we are then so far successful. I am, my Lord, for Mr N & self yr L[ordship]s most obt most obligd & most Hmble Sert J S[42]

Eight years after the passing of the Calico Act Arkwright, then putting forward his case for the statutory extension of his patent rights, recounted a version of the episode which had some dubious points:

> By the united Effects of these important Inventions [his patents], and the Perseverance and Spirit with which the Undertaking was pursued, the most excellent Yarn or Twist was produced; notwithstanding which, the Proprietors found great Difficulty to introduce it into Public Use. A very heavy and valuable Stock, in Consequence of these Difficulties, lay upon their Hand; Inconveniencies and Disadvantages of no small Consideration followed. Whatever were the Motives which induced the Rejection of it, they were thereby necessarily driven to attempt, by their own Strength and Ability, the Manufacture of the Yarn: Their first Trial was, in weaving it into Stockings, which succeeded; they then endeavoured to prevail on the Manufacturers in *Lancashire* to weave it into Callicoes, but they absolutely refused. The Proprietors, therefore, themselves made the Attempt, and succeeded; and soon established the Manufacture of Callicoes, which promises to be one of the first Manufactures in this Kingdom. Another still more formidable Difficulty arose; the Orders for Goods which they had received, being considerable, were unexpectedly countermanded, the

Officers of Excise refusing to let them pass at the usual Duty of 3*d*. *per* Yard, insisting on the additional Duty of 3*d*. *per* Yard, as being Callicoes, though manufactured in *England*: Besides, these Callicoes, when printed, were pro, hibited. By this unforeseen Obstruction, a very considerable and very valuable Stock of Callicoes accumulated. An Application to the Commissioners of Excise was attended with no Success: The Proprietors, therefore, had no Resource but to ask Relief of the Legislature; which, after much Money expended, and against a strong Opposition of the Manufacturers in *Lancashire*, they obtained.[43]

It was a coloured narrative. Arkwright was then at the beginning of his bitter struggle with the Lancashire manufacturers, who, he claimed, had conspired to deprive him of his hard-earned patent rights. There is no reason to suppose that the partners turned to using their yarn in the manufacture of stockings and of calicoes only when they had large unsaleable stocks on their hands. Ark-wright's letter to Strutt of 2 March 1772 does not support that, nor does the letter of 14 February 1774 from Mrs Strutt to her husband in London just before the partners' petition to the Commons:

one Waddington of Nottingm, a long with the man at yr Nottingm Cotton Mill went to Cromford & has took what Layloc Stripd was left there, then came to Derby in hopes to find ours not disposd off but there was but 2 pieces left, he said if there had been a hundred of those small patterns you took in your box he wou'd have took em all & thought him self obligd to you to let him have them, he has took a great number of white pieces from Cromford and sent to print, from what I hrd by the by betwixt your man and Waddington Arkwright has sold the white pieces so that he wish'd you & Mr Need wou'd print no more, he told me that you might Sell them in the White as fast as Cou'd make em, we have heard nothing more either from Cromford . . .[44]

There is no direct evidence to support Arkwright's contention that the Lan-cashire manufacturers refused to take his yarn or that they opposed his appli-cation to Parliament. No Lancashire members are referred to in connection with his Bill, nor are any divisions on it recorded. A declaratory amendment, probably of Lancashire inspiration, that 'nothing in this Act . . . shall extend to Cotton Velvets, Velverets, or other Fustians, manufactured in *Great Britain*' was accepted, leaving the position of these stuffs under the Manchester Act unimpaired.[45] The Lancashire members were at this time more concerned with pushing through a panic measure to prevent the export of textile machinery. Arkwright failed to get an export bounty such as was already allowed on British and Irish coarse linens, although this is hardly surprising, since four years earlier the Lancashire manufacturers had been refused one for their checks and cottons for printing.

The revenue returns for the first nine years of the new duty under the Calico

Act show the enormous increase in the trade and its effect on imported calicoes. Duties levied on British calicoes amounted to £710 in 1775, £1,289 in 1776 and £2,515 a year later. By 1780 the figure had risen to £14,288; it more than doubled to £28,987 in 1781 and reached £44,732 in 1783. In terms of yardage the statistics for British calicoes reveal a similar trend. Production in 1775 amounted to 56,814 yards, almost doubled the following year and did so again a year later; in 1780 1,143,043 yards were produced, in 1781 2,318,972 yards and in 1783 3,578,590 yards. Statistics of imported foreign calicoes, on the other hand, show an almost continuous decline from 2,111,439 yards in 1775 to 1,194,495 yards in 1781 and to 770,922 yards in 1783.[46] It is against this background that the great expansion of the partners' activities must be judged.

The successful establishment of the Cromford enterprise coincided with changes in the partnership. The death of thirty-one-year-old David Thornley on 27 January 1772, almost two months after that of thirty-four-year-old Henry Brown (both were buried at St Mary's Church, Nottingham),[47] had given Arkwright the opportunity of buying out Thornley's widow, Mary, who returned to her millinery business in Liverpool. Smalley was by this time back in Preston, where on 28 February 1771, the Council Minutes reveal, he 'was chosen a Councilman in the room of Mr Thomas Jackson deceased'. His name countinues to appear in the minutes until his last recorded attendance, on 19 May 1772.[48]

It was perhaps then, but more likely in October 1773, when he sold the Bull Inn (by this time known as the White Bull) to Lord Stanley,[49] that, accompanied by his family, he returned to Cromford as mill manager. Certainly the Smalleys were living in Cromford by August 1774 and created a favourable impression on Jedediah Strutt's eldest daughter, Elizabeth, who on 5 September wrote to her father, who had stayed on in London after the death there of his wife four months earlier, 'I was at Cromford last Wednesday but one along with my Uncle, & we return'd on Thursday. Mr Smalleys family is there. They seem to be very agreeable people & I could spend a week with them with great pleasure.'[50]

But whatever the precise date of Smalley's return to Cromford he soon found himself at loggerheads with Arkwright. So much so that on 14 September 1774 Jedediah's eldest son, William, then aged eighteen, felt constrained to write to his father:

> You begin to be much wanted at Home, & may also be at Cromford; I was there last Sunday but one, & heard very unfavourable accounts of Mr A's behaviour. I suppose he is going to leave you. Mrs Smalley does not seem at all happy in her new situation, & they had a bad misfortune last week for one of the Children broke a Leg.[51]

This was not the only hint of trouble. A draft letter by Strutt on the back of one of 28 September 1773 from his wife must have been to Smalley. The draft (words in italic are crossed out) reads:

> Recd yours & am sorry to find matters betwixt you & Mr Arkwright are come to such extremities (*It is directly contrary to my disposition*) & wonder he shoud persist in giving you fresh provocations. I said what I coud to persuade him to oblige you in any thing that was reasonable & to endeavour to live on good terms at least & my wife has said a great deal to him. (*and what can I do more I cannot stop his mouth nor is it in my power to convince him*) nor when I come to consider the matter seriously and the circumstances I am at a loss to think about what we can do it, you must be sensible when some sort of people set themselves to be perverse it is very difficult to prevent them being so. We cannot (*stop his mouth or prevent his doing wrong*) prevent him saying Ill-natured things nor can we regulate his actions, neither do I see that it is in our power to remove him otherwise than by his own consent for he is in possession & as much right there as we. Nay further suppose we was to discharge the Man that has been the occasion of all this he may say he shall not be discharged & if they two agree what could we do to pretend to do that by compulsion that we [breaks off][52]

Arkwright was by this time rapidly rising in the world, the poor adventurer of the Preston and early Nottingham years being left far behind. A glimpse of his new prosperity was given by Elizabeth Strutt in a letter of 2 July 1775 to her father in London:

> Mr Arkwright came here [Derby] on wednesday night & brought his daughter a very pretter letter from her Brother & — would you think it — a very elegant little watch whitch he bought for her at Manchester — on thursday morning they sett off from here to Birmingham my sister & Miss Arkwright in genteel riding dresses & provided with pen & ink & Memorandum Books that they may see which writes the best journal. They seem'd very happy & I hope they will have a deal of pleasure. They talk'd of going to France & the whole Town believes they are gone there but every body thinks they will not like it. I suppose you will see them before you receive this.[53]

A promise of even greater affluence lay in Arkwright's proposals, now nearing completion, to take out a patent for an all-embracing carding machine covering every stage of the spinning process. Parts were, indeed, already in use at Cromford, but so valuable did Arkwright believe his machine to be that he determined to deny its use to his partners and at the same time to sever his connections with them, and with Smalley in particular. Accordingly early in 1775 Arkwright sought the opinion of forty-three-year-old Lloyd Kenyon, who, already making more than £4,000 a year, was to enter Parliament as MP for Hindon in 1780, succeed Lord Mansfield as Chief Justice in 1788, and die worth an estimated £300,000 in 1802.[54]

After reciting the agreements of 1768 and 1770 Arkwright went on to give

Kenyon details of another:

By Memdum of Agreem.^t signed & made the 12th Novr 1774 Betw. s.^d Arkwright Need & Strutt — said Arkwright agreed wth s.^d Need & Strutt for them to take all his share or shares in a business than carried on betw.ⁿ them jointly under his Ma[jes]tys letters patent for spinning of Cotton &c And in consn of the above Need & Strutt agreed to pay s.^d Arkwright 1000.^t p Ann. if so much sho.^d be cleared for his share or shares, If it did not amount to so much *all that* his share or shares may amount to less than that sum for so long as the Patent may continue and to be paid every three Months.

There followed six questions with a space after each for Kenyon's reply:

Qre 1st Are not the first Articles of Partnership between R.^d Arkwright John Smalley and David Thornley entirely at an End by their Entring into the subsequent ones in conjunction with Need and Strutt notwithstanding they were never cancelled & the Term not expired.

[Answer] Arkwright, Smalley & Thornley by the Deed of 12 June 1770 have recd Need & Strutt as partners in the discovery & patent upon the Terms of that Deed. But I do not see why any of the stipulations of the 1.st Deed, which are consistent with the 2.^d Deed, are rescinded by the 2^d Deed.

2^d Can R. Arkwright follow any Business on his own Acct. (as all the o.^r Partners do) not interfering with the Lres Patent It being agreed that an Allowance of 25.^t a Year apiece be made to him and Thornley for their personal and constant Attendance upon the Managem^t & Superintendence of the Works & Serv^{ts} used & employed in the said Trade.

[Answer] By the 1st Deed, none of the parties thereto were to follow any other business &c in Case the Trade &c with.^t their mutual Consent. By the 2.^d Deed Arkwright & Thornley were to receive the stipulated Sallary for their constant Attendance. Both these Agreem^{ts}, as it appears to me, continue in force, & unless Mr Arkwright can follow *any business on his own Acct.,* with^t infring^g the words of these Articles, I conceive he cannot follow it at all, altho' it may not interfere with the Letters Patent.

3^d R. Arkwright has invented sev.^l other Machines besides that for which the Patent was obtained & having put the same in use for the Companys benefit withut having obtained any Patent or Patents for them. Can he now take out a Patent for the same on his own Acc.^t & thereby prevent the Company the use of them; If you are of Opinion it will not prevent the company the use of those already made will not such Patent if obtained Prevent their making any new Ones of the same construction.

[Answer] If Mr Arkwright is the real Inventor of the new Machines to wch this Question applies, & has not admitted the Company to a partnership in these new machines, & his new Invention, I conceive he may obtain a patent or patents for his new Invention; & as the Articles do not extend to them, there is no Colour to say that the partners can have any right to an Interest in the patent or patents to be obtained. The Machines already made *& bro.^t into the partnership* must belong to the partnership Concern.

[40]

4th Arkwright Need & Strutt having executed the Agreem.^t of the 12.th of Novr 1774 whereby Arkwright sells his share to them for the consn therein ment.^d yet notwithstanding the parties finding It co.^d not conveniently be carried into Execution verbally agreed that there sho.^d be an End of it & the Partnership has gone on ever since as before but the same has not been cancelled.

Is the same binding on s.^d Arkwright if it is does it comprehend any other Inventions besides that for which the Patent was obtained And wou'd it not be advisable for Mr Arkwright as the Business now goes on as usual to get the same cancelled.

[Answer] I am of opinion that a parol Agreem^t, if fully proved, will put an End to the Agreem.^t referred to But to obviate future disputes on the subject, it certainly will be prudent to cancel that Agreem.^t I see no foundation for supposing that the Agreem.^t extends to future Inventions.

5th If a Person obtains a Patent for a Machine for one Use, can he or any other Person take out a Patent for the same Machine for another Purpose.

[Answer] I think no other patent can be taken out for the same Machine. It is the Machine, & not the application of it, that is the object of the patent.

6th Some of the new invented Machines ment.^d in the 3.^d Qre *have been got at by five or six Persons in the Neighbourhood* who have *made use* of them for three Qrs of a Year.

Will such new Inventions being in five or six different Hands for that time comprehend publick use so as to prevent Mr Arkwright the Person who can most clearly prove himself the Inventor from applying for a Patent And if such Patent is obtained will it prevent those five or six persons from using those Machines or only all others who shall not have used them at the time the Patent is obtained.

[Answer] I think the publication men^d in the Qre will not prevent Mr A: from apply^g for a patent. If any psons have got at the new Invention by Mr Arkwright's permission I think he cannot prevent them from using Machines so got, but after a patent is obtained he may sue those who make or use *new Machines* of the same Construction with his Invention.

A copy of Kenyon's reply of 22 February 1775[55] was sent on to Arkwright the following day by Thomas Wilson (son of the Rev. Benjamin Wilson of Wakefield who as Dr Primrose was the hero of Goldsmith's novel).[56] An accompanying letter reads:

S^r

On the other Side is a Copy of the Ques as to your Case with Mr Kenyons Answers thereto.

Possibly you may not fully comprehend his Answer to the 3^d Quers where he says if *you have not admitted the Company to a Partnership in those new Machines.* I therefore askt him whe^r your having suffered them to be workt for the partnership Trade & the profits equally divided was Admitting them into the partnership he is very Clear it is not.

With respect to the 6th Quere I take it that the Machines were Got by those persons without *permission* if so your Patent will prevent their using them.

[41]

If any further Explanation now is wanted write me a Letter & I shall be Answering you forthwith. I hope this will find you well after your Journey & am &c Yr mt hbe Svt,

Tho: Wilson
M: Temple
23 Feb 1775

By the end of 1775 Arkwright was ready to apply for a patent for 'those new Machines' and on 16 December the carding patent was sealed. Four months were allowed for the lodging of the specification, which was not witnessed and presumably not fully disclosed until 10 April 1776.[57] The witnesses were John Hacket, one of Arkwright's workmen, and W. D. Crofts ('Clerk to M.ʳ Evans in Nottingham'), both of whom were to figure in the great patent trials of 1785. There is no mention of Strutt in the various stages of the patent, and it is perhaps not without significance that in spring 1776 he was contemplating ending his hosiery partnership with Need.[58] There was to be no break, but was Strutt, already aware of Arkwright's intentions, planning to raise capital in preparation for branching out on his own in cotton spinning?

The patent secured, Arkwright, undeterred by Kenyon's unpromising opinion as to the indestructability of the partnership except by mutual consent, determined that the time had come to rid himself of Smalley. By January 1777 all was ready for his offensive. But Smalley showed spirit. He rejected Arkwright's ultimatum with its almost derisory offer for his share in the business and called in John Aspinall of Standen, Serjeant at Law, and Recorder of Preston.[59]

There had, as in 1773, been trouble with the men, and one might almost be tempted to suppose that 'Michael . . . a Vile wretch' had been put up to it. Aspinall advised that it was in Need's and Strutt's interest to support Smalley: after all, he was not the first partner to come under attack, Mrs Thornley having been 'frightened out' of the partnership at her husband's death. And when Arkwright talked of his own son working in the mills Smalley reminded him that he himself had been 'at the origin of these works [and] found the first money'.[60]

Arkwright now threatened to 'set off to London & there take such measures, one way or another, as shall procure a separation'. Both Need and Strutt did their best to calm things down. Strutt advised that Arkwright had now consented to arbitration as to the terms upon which Smalley could quit. Smalley agreed, and his compensation was settled at William Lovatt's New Bath at Matlock.[61]

The successive stages in this brief but revealing encounter may be seen from the surviving letters (words in italics are crossed out):

John Smalley to Samuel Need   Chorley 21ˢᵗ Janʸ 1777

Sir

I have rec'd yours dated the 10ᵗʰ Insᵗ — since which time I have been to
consult Mʳ Aspinall Serj.ᵗ at Law a Genᵗ of great repute as most in the Kingdom
both for his great abilities & Honest Character I shewed him all the Partnership
deeds & some Letters & gave him as many Particulars of the Transactions from
the first as lay in my Power & nothing but the Truth — he says that the deeds
are so strong & binding to each other that they cannot be broke into but (*to the
great detriment of those who puts in Practice such designs*) by the consent of the Whole
as to that paper signed by the Men I told him you & Mʳ Strutt was able to
contradict it indeed theres some of the Men I dont know by their Names but as
to Michael he's a Vile wretch & I wou'd not be answerable for his Wickedness
in this affair on any Accᵗ whatsoever the rest of the Men That I know (*nothing
to them but*) I hope are very good but I never Injured them either by word or deed
— false Pretensions & Assertions will but cutt a poor figure when they come
to be proved so in a court of Justice it will not Answer either to Credit or Profitt
the Serjᵗ says he wou'd not have me sell out & that he both can & will Protect
me from injustice let the works be carried on where they may if its in the Kings
dominions he says that you & Mʳ Strutt shou'd Join me for if you'll look
backwards into the usuage that I have been treated with from the beging of this
affair with the Present designs now wickedly contriving against me I suppose it
cannot be paralleld — for truths must come out if I am injured & time will
discover — he says as to me taking 1000£ p an & got me 1280£ last year its
the greatest absurdity imaginable & as the works may be increased to get almost
as much money as you please he says he shou'd take me to be a Mad Man
— & as to talking of his Son working them he says if he can anybody may for
its a Joint concern to the Partners only equally Moiety according to the
Proportions of Shares as the deeds directs — now I shou'd be glad to know what
I have done that I shoud go out can anything be proved against me no I say
otherwise & that I was at the orrigin of these works found the first money & have
endeavoured ever since to be of any service possible cou'd lie in my power which
was vilely wrested out of my hands has instance Manchester for one time.

Now I might as well say that I shou'd go and erect a Building & begin of
working it in the same manner & point out one of you & say with Pretensions
for my interest that you shall have nothing to do with it only so much a year of
a stipend as I shall allow wou'd you think I was acting like an honest Man nay,
even if I had it my power what wou'd you think of me — I am well Assured
that my share may amount to a great many thousands a year & in a very little
time — (*I must have one pray what must become of the rest I shou'd be glad to be informed
but I will never be frightened out of it as poor Mʳˢ Thornley was, notwithstanding if you'll
give me anything like adequate to the Value of it so that I may live independent I will still
sell out but I must & will stand by my family*) now I shoud put my self out of the
way to serve either you or Mʳ Strutt but this matter is of so great importance that

I am in duty bound to use my Best & honest endeavours for my Family's interest my Wife joins me in our best respects to Mrs Need you & all your good family

—

Sir your most obligd Hbl^e Servt

John Smalley

Jedediah Strutt to John Smalley   Derby Feb: 9: 1777

Sir

I am to acquaint you, that Mr Need rec'd your Letter & has wrote the purport of it to Mr Arkwright, both which I have seen & the affair is still in the same unsettled state it was in before — Mr Arkwright has been here today to acquaint me, & is now gone to Nott^m to acquaint Mr Need of his absolute determination of a separation betwixt him & you, & if something is not done preparatory thereto betwixt this & next Thursday morning, he will then set off to London & there take such measures, one way or other, as shall procure a seperation, & mentions various ways by which it may be brot about. He was very desirous of your being acquainted with his resolution time enough to prevent his going, is the reason of sending this special messenger. The sum you mentioned in your last Letter but one was tho't too much, & the sum Mr Need mention'd to you, you seem to think too little, but if you woud agree to seperate from Mr Arkwright, he has proposd to leave the conditions to such indifferent persons as he & you shall make choice of. Now as this is become a Matter of serious consequence to all of us & as this seems to be the most equitable as well as the most probable method of accommodation that will be attended with any satisfaction, it seems to require some attention to be paid to it. I think we are all considerable sufferers already by this unhappy difference, & shall certainly be more so very soon if there is not some end put to it. What I wish you Just now to consider is, whether you think that by haveing the case properly stated to proper persons they woud not allow you a compensation adequate to the profits you woud be likely to receive by continuing in the partnership (I shoud think they woud) and whether this compensation before a break has taken place will not be more than you or any of us shall receive when there is an open rupture & a Law Suit commenc'd, & a business carried on in opposition to this; all which I believe will be the case if not prevented. I wish you seriously to consider these circumstances in that point of view that immediately affects your own interest without mentioning how much I & Mr Need shall be injured who shoud have no concern in this quarrel. Nor woud I lead you by any thing I have said to think I have any interested views of my own. On the contrary I will not knowingly advise, or say or do, anything that will influence, or mislead you from your own best interest & advantage. Mr Arkwright had mentiond something of this in a Letter to Mr Need & I had desir'd he woud write to inform you of it, but I dont know at present if he has. You must pray give some answer to this by return of the bearer, for him to leave at Cromford in his way back, as I promisd Mr Arkwright he shoud for his satisfaction, & if anything can be done that will be satisfactory this way or any other that you can think of, it woud be best if you coud come over; & if you give us a line to that purpose Mr Need & I will meet you at Matlock the time you appoint. If Mr Arkwright & you shoud agree to leave this dispute to some indifferent persons who will be the most impartial & the best Judges abt it there may then be a reasonable time allowd to chuse who shall be the Judges & to deliberate on all the other circumstances. I beg my best respects to Mrs Smally & all your family & am your

Sincere friend & Hum^{le} Servt

J Strutt

John Smalley to Jedediah Strutt   Chorley 12th Feby 1777

Sir

When your Messenger came here yesterday, I was at Preston, otherwise he might have return'd back sooner. I have perus'd your Letters, & I am willing to conform to your proposalls that it may be refer'd to two honnest Men, you or Mr Arkwright, or Mr Need may mention one & I will bring a Gent.^{n} along with me & meet you at Matlock Bath on Monday the 24 Ins^t, if that time be agreeable please to let me know in a Post or two, as to M.^{r}Arkwright saying of disolving the Partnership by force it's impossible but my Motive is in consenting to your request that you may be made easy, both for your benefit & Satisfaction I am with Due respects to your Family

Sir your mo: Hum: Sev.^{t}

John Smalley

Jedediah Strutt to John Smalley   Derby Feb: 17: 1777

Sir

I recd yours on Fryday night & on Saturday a Letter from Mr Arkwright desiring I woud send him a copy of the Letter I sent to you which I did which he approves & has declind his Journey to London in hopes something will be done to the satisfaction of all parties. I intend to go over on Wednesday as I have not been there since before Christmass. I have wrote to Mr Need & sent him your Letter but have not heard from him since but you may expect us to meet you at Lovats the 24th Inst which I think is the time you mention. I have been thinking woud it not be best to enter into Arbitration Bond, the first thing that is done. It woud prevent disputes afterwards & I think might be best for you; but as I have not seen either of the other parties I can say nothing what is their opinion. We shall know more when we meet till then I an S^r

Yr obt Hum^{le} Servt

J Strutt

I beg my Compts to M^{rs}
Smally & all your family

The 'two honnest Men' meeting at the New Bath on 24 February 1777 reached agreement over the valuation of Smalley's one-fifth share in the patent and in the Nottingham and Cromford mills, and the following day Smalley transferred his rights to Arkwright, Need and Strutt for £3202 16s 5½d plus interest at 5 per cent until payment had been completed. This figure was based upon the value of the mills (including the 'new erected Spinning Mill' at Cromford) at the partners' 'Annual Settlement' of the previous November. In addition Smalley was to receive £100 each month until the expiry of the patent in 1783. In all he received exactly £10,751.

Although Smalley had agreed not to 'set up Work and carry on any Machine Engine or other Device to infringe upon the Right Granted by the . . . Patent' the spring of 1777 found him at Holywell, Flintshire, where on a stream already used for industrial ventures, and reputed like that at Cromford never to freeze,[62] he set up a spinning mill thirty-three yards long, eight yards wide and three storeys high, powered by a large waterwheel.

Here, no longer 'unhappily within the baneful influence of a tyrant rival', the traveller and naturalist Thomas Pennant records, Smalley prospered. He died at Holywell aged fifty-three on 28 January 1782, eight months before Arkwright had completed his plans to take legal action against him as well as other infringers of the 1769 patent.[63]

Smalley's departure made no apparent difference to the relationship between Arkwright and Strutt. Both families continued to remain in close and friendly association, although it is worth noting that in 1776 Strutt financed alone the building of the first of his mills at Belper,[64] a village on the Derwent seven miles by road south of Cromford and midway between there and Derby. The mill began working in 1778, a year after Strutt, again on his own, bought two iron forges, a slitting and 'Rowling' mill and other properties on both banks of the Derwent at Milford, two mile below Belper.[65] Here, in addition to cotton spinning, he established his bleachfields and machine-making shops.[66]

On 14 April 1781 Samuel Need died at his lodgings in Bread Street, Cheapside, 'advanced in Years and after a very long Illness'. He is 'said to have died immensely rich'.[67] Need's wife Elizabeth, daughter of John Gibson, laceman, of Lawrence Lane, Cheapside, and partner in Gibson Johnson & Co., discount bankers, had died, aged forty-three, less than three months earlier.[68] Although their eldest son, John, for a time managed a cotton mill at Penny Foot Garden,[69] Nottingham, Need's executors sold out to Arkwright and Strutt on 20 September 1782[70] for a sum in the region of £20,000. Among the executors were John Wright the banker and Need's brother-in-law Thomas Gibson, partner in Gibson Johnson & Co., soon to be brought down by the collapse of the ill fated Livesey Hargreaves & Co. The failure hit Need's old partners hard, for in the bankruptcy proceedings Arkwright proved a debt against Gibson Johnson & Co. of £32,534, his son one of £9,163 and the Strutts one of £5,817.[71]

NOTES

1 Unless stated otherwise references to early Nottingham are from C. P. Moritz, *Travels of Carl Philipp Moritz in England in 1782*, London, 1924; J. D. Chambers, Population change in a provincial town: Nottingham 1700-1800', in L. S. Pressnell (ed.), *Studies in the Industrial Revolution*, London, 1960; C. W. Chalklin, *The Provincial Towns of Georgian England: a Study of the Building Process, 1740-1820*, London, 1974.

2 Was Henry Brown related to the Henry Brown of J. M. Wagner & Co. a Liverpool concern having connections with Fuhrer & Wagner, in which the Venetian, Benedict Paul Wagner, husband of Margaret Arkwright's cousin Elizabeth, was a partner? See Nottingham Public Library, Stretton MSS, p. 35, for Brown's administration.

3 Elizabeth Smalley (John's widow, died 1796) in her will of 23 November 1790 (National Library of Wales) bequeathed to her son Christopher her pew in St George's Chapel, Preston. Elizabeth had a one-seventh share in the Holywell Cotton Twist Company. With William Douglas, Daniel Whittaker and William Harrison, the other partners, she had lately bequeathed to Christopher Smalley a one-third part of her one-seventh share.

4 L.C.R.O., DDPr 138/7.

5 Unless stated otherwise references to the Arkwright partnership in this section come from the E. G. Holiday documents at U.M.I.S.T.

6 Case, from Lloyd Kenyon, 22 February 1775, p. 2, para. 2

7 *Nottingham Journal*, 1 April 1769 (the advertisement is dated 29 March). James Hargreaves obtained his patent (No. 962) on 12 June 1770.

8 Ichabod Wright (1700-77), a trader in timber, iron and hemp with the Baltic, had founded the bank in 1759 or 1769 (J. D. Chambers, *Nottingham Journal*, 29 June 1949). There is probably some truth in this legend: John Wright (1723-89), Ichabod's son, was named as an executor and trustee in Need's will (Somerset House, 1781) by which he received £100. For information about the Wrights see S. Glover, *The History and Gazetteer of the County of Derby*, II, Derby, 1833, p. 201; *Nottingham Journal*, 6 September 1777; *G.M.*, 1789, p. 1212; *Derby Mercury*, 23 December 1789, 22 July 1790.

9 For a full account of the activities of the new partners see Fitton and Wadsworth. Also M. L. Walker, *A History of the Family of Need of Arnold, Nottinghamshire*, London, 1963.

10 Need and Strutt, Strutts and Woollat.

11 Case, from Lloyd Kenyon, 22 February 1775

12 Stretton MSS, p. 179, 'built by Samuel Stretton at the bottom of Goosegate, Nottingham 1769'.

13 W. Hutton, *History of Derby from the remote Ages of Antiquity to the year 1791*, London and Derby, 1791, pp. 195-8.

14 Wadsworth and Mann, p. 463.

15 A.F. MSS.

16 A.F. MSS.

17 Read, *The English Traveller*, I, 1746, p. 244. The position of the mills, which were to remain a prominent feature of Cromford until the 1790s (B.M., Add. MS 6666, p. 357, black ink), is clearly shown on William Brailsford's map of Edwin Lascelle's Willersly farm estate.

18 B.M. Add. MS, 6669/6670

19 D. P. Davies, *A New Historical and Descriptive View of Derbyshire*, Belper, 1811, p. 91; J. Farey, *General View of the Agriculture and Minerals of Derbyshire*, I, London, 1811, p. 487. Cromford sough had been in existence at least as early as 1704.

20 See Burdett's map of Derbyshire, 1762-67.

21 A. Young, *The Farmer's Tour through the East of England*, I, London, 1771, pp. 194-5.

22 *A short Tour in the Midland Counties of England performed in the Summer of 1772: together with a similar Excursion undertaken September 1774*, London, 1775 (note inside book: 'Presumed to be the work of Thomas Quincey of Manchester, father of Thomas De Quincey'). See

W. A. Axon's *Lancashire Gleanings*, Manchester, 1883, p. 285. For the scene in 1792 see J. P. Malcolm in *G.M.*, 1793, pp. 505⁄6.

23 Rev. J. C. Cox, 'The Wolley manuscripts', *D.A.J.*, XXXIII, 1911, p. 185, citing B.M., Add.M.S, 6670 232.

24 W. H. Pierson junior, 'Notes on early industrial architecture in England', *Journal of the Society of Architectural Historians*, 8, 1949, pp. 5⁄6.

25 *Derby Mercury*, 13 and 20 December 1771.

26 The indenture was witnessed by John Hacket and John Middleton, both of whom were to become mill managers after leaving Arkwright's service, the former in Penicuik, Scotland, and the latter in Derbyshire.

27 Lady J. M. Strachey (ed.), *Memoirs of a Highland Lady: the Autobiography of Elizabeth Grant of Rothiemurchus afterwards Mrs. Smith of Baltiboys, 1797⁄1830*, London, 1898, p. 381.

28 See A. Seymour⁄Jones, 'The invention of roller drawing in cotton spinning', *Transaction of the Newcomen Society*, I, 1920⁄21, and the Boulton & Watt papers for a facsimile of the original.

29 Halifax was then, as later, in the card⁄making area. W. B. Crump (ed.), *The Leeds Woollen Industry, 1780⁄1820*, Leeds, 1931, p. 8.

30 *S.F.*, p. 160.

31 Richard Briddon had been clerk to Richard Arkwright II at Bakewell.

32 G. Henson, *The Civil, Political and Mechanical History of the Framework⁄Knitters in Europe and America*, I, Nottingham, 1831, pp. 369⁄70. The legend is hardly credible in so far as Henson writes, 'The sanguine spirit of Arkwright bore against all these difficulties (yarn of wretched quality) for five years; his partner Need, had expended £1,200 and had realised no profit when he at length became impatient, and had resolved to abandon the concern as hopeless!'

33 *C.J.*, XXXIV, pp. 496⁄7.

34 Letter from Elizabeth Strutt to her children, April 1774 (Fitton and Wadsworth, p. 119).

35 Sir L. B. Namier, *The Structure of Politics at the Accession of George III*, I, London, 1929, pp. 115, 117–18.

36 *C.J.*, XXXIV, p. 695.

37 *C.J.*, XXXIV, p. 709.

38 *C.J.*, XXXIV. The Act was 14 George III, c. 72, Duties on Cotton Stuffs, etc.

39 P.R.O., Correspondence of Board of Excise with Treasury.

40 Baines, *Cotton Manufacture*, p. 170, 'Under the Act liable to lose goods, and to forfeit £10 for each piece. The penalty of death was attached to the counterfeiting of the stamp, or the selling of the goods knowing them to have the counterfeited stamps.'

41 P.R.O., Correspondence of Board of Excise with Treasury.

42 D.P.L., Strutt MSS.

43 *The Case of Richard Arkwright and Company*, London, 1782, p. 2.

44 Strutt MSS.

45 *C.J.*, XXXIV, p. 795.

46 Excise Revenue, 1662–1827. Quantities, Rates and Amounts of Excise Duties 1684⁄1798. All by permission of HM Commissioners of Customs and Excise.

47 Stretton MSS, p. 135.

48 In Hodges's indenture of 30 May 1772 Smalley is listed as 'Merchant', of Preston, in the list of partners.

49 L.C.R.O., Derby Muniments, II, pp. 531⁄2, Bundle 797 1 and 2.

50 Strutt MSS.

51 *Ibid.*

52 *Ibid.*

53 *Ibid.*

54 *G.M.*, 1802, pp. 337⁄9.

55 The copy of the Kenyon letter sent to Arkwright had its date altered to 23 February. Was

he anxious of suggesting a day's delay with Arkwright? (Franked 23 February.)

56 H. A. C. Sturgess (complier), *Register of Admissions to the Honourable Society of the Middle Temple*, I, London, 1849, for 12 November 1740, 'Thomas Wilson, son and heir of the Reverend Benjamin Wilson of Wakefield, Yorks., clerk'. See also *G.M.*, 1764, p. 450, and 1780, p. 495; also J. W. Walker, *The History of the old Parish Church of All Saints, Wakefield*, Wakefield, 1888, p. 193.

57 A.F. MSS.

58 Fitton and Wadsworth, pp. 50⁄2.

59 For John Aspinall see W. Abram, *Parish of Blackburn, County of Lancaster: History of Blackburn, Town and Parish*, Blackburn, 1877, p. 409, and H. O. Aspinall, *The Aspinwall and Aspinall Families of Lancashire*, Exeter, 1923, p. 63⁄5. John Aspinall married in 1764 Maria, daughter of Mail Yates, brother⁄in⁄law of Thomas Ridgway.

60 Was Smalley at Chorley possibly preparing for Birkacre?

61 *Derby Mercury*, 26 June 1772.

62 *Manchester Mercury*, 6 November 1792, cited by E. J. Foulkes, 'The cotton⁄spinning factories of Flintshire, 1776⁄1886', *Journal of the Flintshire Historical Society*, XXI, 1964; see also P. S. Richards, 'The Holywell textile mills, Flintshire', *Industrial Archaeology*, VI, 1969.

63 T. Pennant, *The History of the Parishes of Whiteford and Holywell*, London, 1796, p. 214. Pennant had on 20 March 1790 sold to the Holywell partners land and water rights at Holywell. And see n. 3 above.

64 Guildhall Library, MS 7253, Royal Exchange Registers, 4/76867 (November 1779); Fitton and Wadsworth, p. 78.

65 *Anis's Birmingham Gazette*, 14 April 1777; *Manchester Mercury*, 12 April 1781.

66 Fitton and Wadsworth, p. 295.

67 *Derby Mercury*, 20 April 1781; *Nottingham Journal*, 21 April 1781.

68 Walker, *Family of Need*, p. 14.

69 *Derby Mercury*, 3 and 17 January 1793.

70 Date from the preamble to the James trial.

71 Fitton and Wadsworth, p. 96; Walker, *Family of Need*, pp. 14⁄15, 22, 28.

CHAPTER III

The Arkwright empire

GREAT AMBITIONS — nothing less than the creation of a cotton-spinning empire — lay behind the all-embracing carding patent of 1775, and the following decade saw a remarkable expansion of Arkwright's activities not only in Derbyshire but also in Lancashire, in Staffordshire and in Scotland.

The great burst of activity began at Cromford, where during the summer of 1776 over 200 workmen erected another large cotton mill 120 ft long and seven storeys high.[1] The mill, completed in September, must eventually have made possible a doubling of Cromford's output. Power was supplied by two overshot wheels erected in a pit some 20 ft deep from which water was channelled to the river Derwent through a massive stone-arched culvert more than a quarter of a mile in length.

Cromford Mill

Arkwright, already rich and famous, returned to Lancashire in 1777 and agreed with John Chadwick, of Burgh, to build a spinning mill on the site of a forge on the river Yarrow at Birkacre, near Chorley. The mill, the higher and lower forges, a corn mill, three weirs, a house and cottages were then leased to Arkwright on 29 November 1777 for eighty-four years at £150 a year, together with a further thirteen and a half acres of land at a yearly rent of £31. He was joined in this venture by Jedediah Strutt and Samuel Need, and by two new partners, Thomas Walshman,[2] a Preston woollen draper and one of his oldest acquaintances, and John Cross, a Preston attorney.[3]

Under the direction of Walshman 'shops or Departments for Turners and some other Artists employed about the Works' were set up, a counting house was built, and plans were made for carrying on the 'whole Process of Picking Carding Roving Spinning and Reeling of Cotton'.[4] By the autumn of 1779 'part of the numbers of Spindles agreed for were at Work . . . making Yarn or Thread of a superior Quality to any other now spun from Cotton'.[5]

Altogether, according to the partners' estimates, upwards of £4,400 had been spent, some of it on 'another large new Building', when on Monday 4 October 1779 a mob 'to the number of 4 or 5,000 with considerable Quantity of Fire Arms and other Offensive Weapons and meeting with little or no resist-ence . . . broke into the Mill and destroyed all the Machinery then Attacked the Building with Pickaxes Hatchets &c to demolish it but at last as a shorter Method . . . set fire to it & burnt it to the Ground'.[6]

Birkacre had first come under attack on 2 October, receiving the special attentions of the hand workers of west Lancashire, who, in a time of bad trade, revolted against not only the Arkwright 'Patent Machines'[7] but against all those which had passed beyond the stage of hand work. Josiah Wedgwood, on his way to Bolton to visit his ten-year-old son at a school run by the Rev. Philip Holland, minister of the Bank Street chapel, was a witness to the disturbances and on 3 October wrote to Thomas Bentley from there:

In our way to this place, a little on this side of Chowbent, we met several hundred people in the road. I believe there might be about five hundred; and upon inquiring of one of them the occasion of their being together in so great a number, he told me they had been destroying some engines, and meant to serve them all so through the country. Accordingly they have advice here to-day that they must expect a visit to-morrow; the workmen in the neighbourhood having muster'd up a considerable number of arms, and are casting bullets and providing ammunition to-day for the assault to-morrow morning. Sir Richard Clayton brought this account here to-day, and, I believe, is in the town now, advising the inhabitants upon the best means for their safety; and I believe they have concluded to send immediately to Liverpool for a part of the troops quarter'd there. Many of the workmen having been turn'd off lately, owing to a want of demand for their goods at foreign markets, has furnish'd them with an excuse for these violent measures. The manufacturers say the measures which the Irish have adopted in their non-importation agreements have affected their trade very much. These are melancholy facts, upon which I forbear to comment. They do not stand in need of much illustration, but we must pray for better times.

With the events leading to the War of American Independence trade with the colonies had declined, a movement which steepened when in 1778, upon Franklin's signing of treaties of commerce and alliance with Vergennes, Britain promptly declared war on France, thus making the conflict world-wide. In June the following year Spain joined in the hostilities against Britain, besieging Gibraltar and closing the Mediterranean to British shipping. The Irish non-importation agreement cut off another important outlet for trade. Small wonder that an anonymous writer felt the need to explain:

> Do not you think the war a more probable cause of the badness of trade, than the number of spinning-mills and jennies; that the loss of three millions of customers; the war with France and Spain and America at the same time; and the Irish non-importation agreements, are sufficient to interrupt your trade, and produce all the distresses you feel of fear?[9]

In marked contrast to the heady days of 1759, misfortune had indeed succeeded misfortune. Early in August 1779 news had reached Lancashire that the island of St Vincent had submitted to the French: 'The Distress of the West-India Merchants, on receiving this disagreeable Intelligence is inconceivable.'[10] Then on 28 September confirmation arrived of the capture by the French of the important cotton-producing island of Grenada,[11] whereupon 'a *report* that a proprietor of one of the large machines (when cotton was advanced upon the news of the loss of the Island of Grenada) offered to spin cotton at a lower price than what was generally given' was the immediate cause of the rioting.[12]

In a further letter to Bentley on 9 October Wedgwood continued his account of the disturbances:

> I wrote to my dear friend last from Bolton, and I mention'd the mob which had assembled in that neighbourhood; but they had not then done much mischief; they only destroyed a small engine or two near Chowbent. We met them on Saturday morning, but I apprehend what we saw were not the main body; for on the same day, in the afternoon, a capital engine or mill, in the manner of Acrites, and in which he is a partner near Chorley, was attacked; but from its peculiar situation they could approach to it by one passage only; and this circumstance enabled the owner, with the assistance of a few neighbours, to repulse the enemy and preserve the mill for that time. Two of the mob were shot dead upon the spot, one drowned, and several wounded. The mob had no fire-arms, and did not expect so warm a reception. They were greatly exasperated, and vowed revenge; accordingly they spent all Sunday and Monday morning in collecting fire-arms and ammunition and melting their pewter dishes into bullets.

They were now join'd by the Duke of Bridgewater's collier and others, to the number, we are told, of eight thousand, and march'd by beat of drum and with colours flying to the mill, where they met with a repulse on Saturday. They found Sir Richard Clayton guarding the place with fifty Invalids armed, but this handful were by no means a match for enraged thousands; they (the Invalids) therefore contended themselves with looking on, whilst the mob completely destroyed a set of mills valued at 10,000l.[13]

This was Monday's employment. On Tuesday morning we heard their drum at about two miles' distance from Bolton, a little before we left the place, and their professed design was to take Bolton, Manchester, and Stockport in their way to Crumford, and to destroy all the engines, not only in these places, but throughout all England.

Arkwright was alerted by express of the mob's intentions. Nothing short of 'regular military fforce', wrote Walshman and Cross, would thwart:

these butchers [who] have put everything they threaten into execution . . . . They are much more formidable than anyone can conceive, but those who have The misfortune to see them . . . . These Devils Incarnate wou'd hear nothing the Justices said to them but declared that one and all, let the consequences be what it would, were determined to destroy the whole works. It was thought by the Gentlemen as this resolution cou'd not be removed, that the Invalids were not a sufficient force, therefore agreed for the men to be drawn off, that the mob might go into the works and destroy them, but save the buildings. They then went in about 2 o'clock and before 4 destry'd all the machinery, the Great Wheel, and set fire to the broken frames in the yard, rear'd some of them agt. the wall which communicated to ye building and ended it . . . . My poor Boy is in greatr distress than I can describe, his fondness of the employ, added to what we suffer takes away all his spirits. I have sent him with a good stout companion to Birkacre to give directions for collecting everything worth saveing and putting them into some place of safety.[14]

Arkwright passed on his partners' letter to the Mayor of Derby, who, urgently appealing to the Secretary at War for military assistance, added that the rioters, now twenty miles closer and growing in number, were as determined as ever to raze the five Derbyshire mills, worth in all some £50,000. No troops could be spared but the almost simultaneous arrival of the Horse Guards Blues, Elliot's Light Horse and the 19th Light Dragoons, all on the march towards Manchester, helped ease public anxiety.

Arkwright meanwhile was busy preparing for all eventualities. A letter of 9 October from Cromford to 'a Gentleman in Manchester' spoke of feverish activity:

In your last you expressed some fear of the Mob coming to destroy the Works at Cromford, but they are well prepared to receive them should they come there. All the Gentlemen in this Neighbourhood being determined to support Mr.

Arkwright, in the Defence of his Works, which have been of such Utility to this Country. Fifteen hundred Stand of small Arms are already collected from Derby and the neighbouring Towns, and a Battery of Cannon raised of 9 and 12 Pounders, with great Plenty of Powder and Grape Shot, besides which, upwards of 500 Spears are fixt in Poles of between 2 and 3 Yards long. The Spears and Battery are always to be kept in Repair for the Defence of the Works and Protection of the Village, and 5 or 6000 Men, Miners &c. can at any Time be assembled in less than an Hour, by Signals agreed upon, who are determined to defend to the very last Extremity, the Works, by which many hundreds of their Wives and Children get a decent and comfortable Livelihood.[15]

But the rioters never got within fifty miles of Cromford, and it was never threatened again.

Those prosecuted at the assizes were a representative group of the industrial population — weavers, spinners, colliers, nail makers, labourers, joiners and even a 'cotton tradesman' wealthy enough to pay £20 damages. They were accused of attacking ten mills, including that at Birkacre, the largest, for which a women, Mary Leicester, was convicted at Preston with having destroyed twenty of each of the following machines: spinning frames, spinning engines, carding engines, roving engines, twisting engines, twisting mills, cotton wheels and cotton reels. For this she was sent to prison at Lancashire Castle for twelve months. The heaviest sentence — two years in gaol — was given to Giles Fletcher, an Aspull miner who had led the Birkacre riot.

In February 1780 Arkwright sought the opinion of John Lee as to whether an action could be brought against the Hundred to recover damages sustained at Birkacre under the Acts 1 George I, C. 5, or 9 George I, c. 22, and if so whether these would be confined to the value of the buildings only or whether the damage done to machinery could be included. And further, 'whether the Offence of which the Rioters have been Guilty is Felony within either the above Acts or that of the 9th of the present King respecting the Destruction of Mills or upon any other Statute and in what way would you recommend them to be Indicated and presented. The Proclamation in the Riot Act was not made.' Lee advised that although no action was possible under the first two Acts 'it seems to me that the last Statute of 9th G 3d may without straining be extended to a case like this'.[16]

All this was a prelude to a petition presented by Walshman to the House of Commons on 27 June 1780 'that a Satisfaction be made to your petitioner and other Proprietors for the great Injury they have suffered by this lawless Proceeding in such Way as to the Wisdom of Parliament shall seem expedient'.[17]

Four days earlier Cross had sent to Sir Thomas Egerton, Tory MP for Lancashire, 'the . . . Petition, without any other Recommendation; tho' I assure you it would be supported by All your most respectable ffriends here . . . . Other Members will be applied to, but it is particularly wished that the Business may have the Sanction of being Introduced by you.' The partners had in mind 'The Disposition shown by [the] Government to make Satisfaction to the private Sufferers by the late Riots in London', but the Commons turned a deaf ear.

Birkacre was not rebuilt as a cotton mill. The lease was surrendered on 20 September 1780 on payment of £200, 'Richard Arkwright and his partners thinking it insecure to proceed in their intended Business in that place'.

On 6 November of the same year, 1777, as had seen the beginnings of the ill fated Birkacre venture Arkwright agreed with his near neighbour, Philip Gell of Hopton Hall, for the fifty-year lease of fifty-three acres of land at Great and Little Lumford and at Holme bank in the parishes of Bakewell and Longstone, Derbyshire, at an annual rental of £68.[18] The situation was well suited for water spinning, and although the lease was not to become effective until the following March Arkwright at once set about building[19] on the river Wye at Lumford, just outside the manor of Bakewell, a mill 200 ft long, 30 ft wide and four storeys high.[20] Near by a bridge was built over the Wye, and some time before 1786 an extension 60 ft long and 16 ft wide was added over the mill's tail race at right angles to the original building. The undershot waterwheel was fed from a five-acre reservoir into which water from the Wye was diverted by means of a newly constructed weir below which the river was straightened so as to cut off a meander which had previously crossed land now occupied by the reservoir.

Arkwright's activities did not escape the attention of the Duke of Rutland, lord of the manor of Bakewell, who contended that, as a result, his corn mill now received only an intermittent supply of water, his trout fishing was impaired, and his common damaged owing to the removal of soil and clods.[21] The duke set out the precise nature of his grievances in an almost feudal preamble to terms which the younger Arkwright, owner of the mill since July 1783,[22] was obliged to accept in December 1786 after a long-drawn-out wrangle. The preamble reads:

> Whereas the said Charles Duke of Rutland is Lord of the Manor of Bakewell . . . And whereas the said Charles Duke of Rutland and his Ancestors have for time immemorial been seized and possessed of a certain ancient Corn Mill situate . . . within the said Manor of Bakewell and turned and worked by the said River Wye . . . at which Mill the tenants of the said Duke of Rutland . . . have of ancient right and custom been used to have their Corn Ground paying the customary Toll . . . And the said Richard Arkwright the elder and Richard Arkwright the younger both or one of them have erected upon the said piece of ground called Lumford a Cotton Mill and have likewise without the leave or licence of the said Duke or of John Duke of Rutland his late Grandfather deceased made erected built and set up Divers Wares Sluices

Dams and other Obstructions upon and about the said River Wye within the said Manors of Ashford and Bakewell and have made great Dams Pools or Reservoirs in the Grounds called Great and Little Lumford and have diverted the Waters of the said River Wye from its ancient course thro' the said Ground called Lumford into the said Pools for the purpose of impounding the Water and for the turning the Wheels and Engines of the said Cotton Mill and have thereby prevented and obstructed the Water of the said River from flowing in its ancient and usual course to the aforesaid Corn Mill Of the said Duke of Rutland Whereby the same is obstructed and injured and the ffishery of the said Duke is affected and prejudiced And whereas the said Richard Arkwright hath also cut through the ancient Mill dam of the said Corn Mill and hath taken and carried away the Stone Gravel and Soil from the same as well as digged up and taken away Clods Stone and Soil from the Commons and Waste grounds belonging to the said Duke of Rutland within the said Manor of Bakewell for the making of the said Dams and Mounds.[23]

Under the terms of settlement the younger Arkwright agreed to pay a nominal rent of £10 a year for a forty-two-year lease of the waters of the Wye between Crackendale and Holme Bridge and secured the right to repair existing bridges, dams and sluices provided that no damage was done to the duke's corn mill. He also agreed to restore the Wye to its original course if asked to do so at least two years before the end of the lease.

The elder Arkwright, by no means a stranger to the workings of the law, can hardly have been unaware as to the outcome of his actions. Believing that the duke would refuse to agree to his plans, he had decided to act first and negotiate afterwards. And not without reasons, for the duke's opposition ran deeper than the damage done to his properties. He feared above all that an influx of mill workers and their dependants would be detrimental to the interests of his estates.

His misgivings were not entirely unfounded, for although the elder Arkwright recruited the greater part of his work force locally White Watson, the Bakewell sculptor, antiquary and mineralogist,[24] records that with the building of the mill 'wages were raised immediately and hands came from Manchester, introducing good-natured girls . . . to whom the town was a stranger'. Further, from the outset Arkwright took steps to provide housing for his workpeople within the manor of Bakewell, agreeing on 5 December 1778 to buy from Thomas Marsden a messuage and croft for £300 only to discover later the same month that a part of the property, Lady Croft, had already been leased to John Renshaw, who refused to surrender the title. 'I don't see I have any real Dispute with M.ʳ Renshaw,' Arkwright told Thomas Ince, his attorney, on 23 March 1779. 'The contract he hath made with Marsden at Presant Doth not efect me. I have nothing to say only when M.ʳ Renshaw in Inclianable to take his . . . money I will pay it.' But for whatever reason (is the duke's hand to be seen?) it was not until January 1782 that Arkwright was able to obtain the land upon which he built the substantial cottage houses in New Street, the present-day New (or Arkwright's) Square.

In October 1792 the younger Arkwright sold to his brother-in-law Samuel Simpson a half share in the Bakewell mill for £21,000.[25] Profits for the year ending October 1793 amounted to £6,279 15s, and for the following year to £5,095.[26] By 1814 Arkwright's son Robert, then living at Stoke Hall,[27] was managing the mill, which was formally conveyed to him by his father in 1812, when his brother Peter was named as co-partner.[28] The concern was to remain in Arkwright hands until 1860, when it was sold to the Duke of Devonshire by Robert's third son, the Rev. Godfrey Harry Arkwright, for £14,500.[29]

It was also in 1777 that Arkwright leased further land, together with an ancient walk mill, now being used as a corn mill, from Philip Gell.[30] This was at Millers Green, half a mile outside Wirksworth, on the turnpike road to Derby.[31] Here on the Ecclesbourne, a tributary of the Derwent, he built a small brick-and-stone mill[32] (the present-day Haarlam Mill) which was apparently com-pleted and perhaps working by June 1780, when a young man was killed while attempting to climb on its wheel.[33]

To help supplement the sometimes inadequate supply of water Arkwright installed a reciprocating engine, probably supplied by Francis Thompson of Ashover.[34] It was described over thirty years later, when, with the mill's machinery and other equipment, it was put up for sale, as being 'in excellent Repair' and 'well adapted for a Coal Pit'; it had a 'main Beam . . . 26 feet long, 2 feet square; the Fly Wheel 18 feet diameter the Cylinder 31 inches diameter, and remarkably strong cast'.[35] The engine, of a type frequently employed to pump water from the Derbyshire mines, was the first ever to be used in a cotton mill[36] and attracted the attention of John Southern, assistant to Boulton and Watt, now seeking orders for the rotative engine patented by Watt in March 1782. He reported to Matthew Boulton on 30 July 1782 on his visit to Wirksworth:

Mr Southern was with M.r Arkwright this morning & had conversation with him a considerable time . . . told M.r A —— that J. S[outhern] had seen his fire Engine at Wirksworth and was sorry that he Mr Ark.t had not incouraged the Patent steam Eng.n there and durst ingage that 1/5th of the Coal wou'd raise an equal quanty of water in same time on the patent construction if made use on there. after a good deal more M.r A ——t say'd he wd show me a model of construction which he sd farr execaded M.r Boulton &c or Pickards or any other — so was introduced wth 4 other Gentln from Manch.r to see this wonder — I aplauded the invention for simplicity and (suspend saying further here) ended with saying yt Mr Boulton woud be at Matlock Bath I believed this afternoon & evening and wished M.ʳ A ⸺ wou'd see him so conveniantly for both — he seem'd startled at this & answ.ᵈ he shou'd be glad to see M.ʳ Boulton — I then said Mʳ B ⸺ n intended himself the pleasure of calling on M.ʳ A ⸺ last summer when at Bath but was told M.ʳ A ⸺ was very Ill — Mʳ A ⸺ remembered this but did not say further on seeing Mʳ Boulton — but thank'd M.ʳ Southern very kindly for calling on him.

In the conversation M.ʳ A ⸺t say'd he had been made to understand (rather believe) that M.ʳ B⸺s Engine was so subject to disorder & so complex prevented him from calling in M.ʳ B & W assistance. This I told him was from yᵗ Ignorant being Tompson, he reply'd it was he on this I cou'd not contrain — told him Tompson had given out publickly that M.ʳ A⸺ had thefted from him great part of his mechanism and obtanid a patent of such — here he laughed at yᵉ ignorance of T⸺ and concurred in that he knew nothing.[37]

The mill (for which shortly before Southern's visit Jedediah Strutt obtained a 'capital large Bell'[38] at a cost of £6 10s)[39] was by 1789 said to be providing employment for almost 200 workpeople. Three years later it was sold to Thomas Eley, a Derby mercer and linen draper, after whose death it was carried on by his widow, Mary, and her brother-in-law Robert Sykes, a Nottingham woollen and linen draper,[40] until 1799, when Robert became sole proprietor.

Shortly after Arkwright had agreed with Philip Gell to lease land on which to build his mills at Bakewell and Wirksworth he also negotiated through him with John Barker, agent to the Duke of Rutland, for the lease of a corn mill at Alport on the river Lathkill, four miles south of Bakewell. These nego-tiations, which took place in March 1778, once again reveal clearly the duke's hostility towards industrial development and explain why Arkwright was forced to abandon his plans to bring cotton spinning to Alport.[41]

The first hint of Arkwright's intention is given in a short note of 3 March 1778 from Gell to John Barker at Bakewell:

> M.ʳ Arkwright & I waited upon you today with an intent to have made some proposals relative to a part of the Duke of Rutlands property in this Country, we were disapointed in not finding you at home, & shall be glad to know when we may have a little conversation with you.

Gell's proposals were set out in greater detail in his letter to Barker of 16 March 1778:

> As I cou'd not conveniently wait upon you last week I desired M.ʳ Outram[42] who was going to Bakewell to mention to you that I shou'd be glad to take yᵉ Corn Mill at Alport, & give his Grace a very considerable advance of Rent to what he now receives provided I might have a Lease. By what he tells me I rather imagine the matter has not been rightly understood, as he said you had an objection to Dams being made upon the River, which was never intended by M.ʳ Arkwright only to repair the present Mill Damm or if that shou'd be any

way prejudicial to let it still Lower than it now is, & make a freer course to the Water. I had an intention to desire you to make our proposals to the Duke, but if there are any material objections I shall be glad to know them before we proceed any farther as I shou'd be sorry to give his Grace or you any unnecessary trouble.

Barker, as his reply of 19 March shows, was hardly convinced. Further, there was the all-important queation of the 'new manufactures':

The Corn Mill at Alport is the only Mill I know of upon the Lathkill that is not greatly prejudicial to his Grace's Mines, nor is there I think any other place upon y^r River where fresh Damms cou'd be made without being of great prejudice to the Mines. Whether his Grace wou'd be willing to destroy the Corn Mill at Alport, or how far his Grace may have altered his Mind relative to the Objections he has so long since & so often made against establishing any new Manufactures upon his Estates I cannot say, but if you choose to make any application to his Grace, it may be as well to do it soon as Mr Smedley[43] & myself shall shortly be over at Belvoir when his Grace may receive such information from us as to facts as his Grace may choose to ask for.

Also on 19 March Gell wrote reassuringly as to the benefits of Arkwright's proposed manufacture, stressing the advantages the duke might obtain:

I never meant to apply to his Grace for any other place than the Corn Mill at Alport for which I wou'd give a very considerable advance of Rent, & lay out a large Sum of Money in Building. the present Mill you know is greatly out of Repair & must cost money to support it, so that there will be a loss instead of gain to his Grace. no Manufacture will be introduced (except what will employ the Children hired by the Day) nor will one person be added to the list of Paupers, so that no disadvantage can possibly attend the Building a Mill at Alport, & I shall be obliged to you if you will lay this before the Duke. Upon a former application from Mr Arkwright to him he said as it was a settled Estate he must consult his Heir, now being certain that Ld Granby wishes to encourage it I venture to make this second application which I an sure if you state the affair rightly will succeed.

In his letter of 23 March Barker saw no hope and feared that he would be blamed for the duke's stand against the introduction of manufactures:

I rec'd your favor of y^c 19.th & shou'd not have wished to give you y^c trouble of an Answer till I had laid you application before his Grace which I wou'd have done as impartialy & clearly as I cou'd but an expression in y^c close of your Letter makes me trouble you with this.

You say you are sure if I state the case rightly it will succeed. I am sorry so far to differ from you in opinion as to be equaly sure that I cannot state y^c Case so as it will succeed. therefore as on y^c one hand I have no expectation of succeeding, & on y^c other I find I must bear y^c blame from you if it does not succeed I shou'd be very glad y^t you wou'd apply to his Grace either by yourself or any other Person.

My Reason for saying I shall not succeed is that some Years ago application was made to me for erecting a Silk Mill at Bakewell. I looked upon this as a very advantageous proposal for his Grace & as such applyed to his Grace to consent to its going forwards. His Grace said he wou'd take some time to consider of it, & some time after told me that he had considered of it & had advised with some Friends about it, & y^t he was well persuaded y^t it was not for the Interest of his Estates to encourage manufactures upon them. I believe his Grace has ever since been of the same opinion & most likely thinks so still.

Mr Arkwright may possibly think that his Application did not succeed because I *did not State ye Case rightly* & as you declare you shall think so, I only beg leave to add y^t I known of no other reason why Mr Arkwright did not succeed than what had been given Years before about ye intended Silk Mill, & I apprehend ye same reasons will prevent your application or any other of ye same kind from succeeding unless his Grace has much altered his way of thinking.

PS As to Ld Granby's[44] opinion upon this Business if you know y^t it is in your favor you may fairly urge it, but as I am an entire stranger to his Lordships sentiments on this head I can not say any thing about it.

Four days later Gell's reply signalled the end of Arkwright's attempt to lease the Alport corn mill. But by this time his mill on Gell's land outside the duke's manor of Bakewell was already under construction:

I am very sorry there shou'd be any thing exceptionable in my Letter, I beg leave to assure you it was not in the least my intention, & I am happy that by your pointing out the expression in your Letter I have an opportunity of explaining what was my meaning in saying 'if the Case was fairly stated we shou'd succeed' I was told last Year and you have since informed me that his Grace has an objection to establishing Manufactorys upon his Estates, which objection cou'd arise from no other motive than burthening his tenants with Poor, now as I endeavoured to demonstrate to you, y^t ye erecting a Mill of the Kind Mr Arkwright wants wou'd not either increase the Inhabitants, im-poverish ye people or introduce any manufacture more than a Corn Mill, (except producing Money to the Poor for purchasing the Product of the latter) I think I might without impeachment say if these things were fairly or clearly stated we shou'd succeed, for no man can be so cruel as to prevent the Poor earning their Bread by their own Labour, more especialy when instead of loosing he may be a gainer by it. but it is needless for me to say more upon this subject to you who I dare say have seen the advantages of the introduction even of the Spinning Jennys both at Bakewell & Youlgreave, however I shou'd be extreemly averse to desiring you to do any thing disagreeable to yourself which the mentioning this to the Duke seems to be therefore wish you to give yourself no further trouble about it.

It was most likely the following year, 1779 that Arkwright (whether father or son is uncertain) leased from John Baker, hosier, of Litton, Derbyshire, a part of Litton Frith,[45] land that had been awarded to him at the enclosure of the manor of Litton sixteen years earlier.[46] Here on the Cressbrook, immediately above its confluence with the river Wye, Arkwright erected a small spinning mill, probably in 1783.[47]

Certainly by October the following year his builder, William Newton, until recently employed by the Duke of Devonshire as a head carpenter in the building of the Crescent at Buxton,[48] could confide to Anna Seward, 'Except not from me, my affectionate friend, either elegant prose or verses, who am confined fourteen hours each day to Mechanical drudgery in a ——— Cotton Mill; and for months together enjoy not the conversation of one man of Letters or Taste.'[49] Newton, Anna Seward's 'Minstrel of the Peak', was, according to her, at this time 'articled for seven years, upon a salary of L.50 per annum, as machinery-carpenter in a cotton-mill, in beauteous Monsaldale.'[50] But on 15 November 1785 a fire 'occasioned by a lighted candle falling amongst some waste Cotton' swept through the mill.[51] It was only 'with difficulty', Anna Seward was to recall, that Newton 'escaped from its sudden and midnight conflagaration. His tools, purchased gradually, and which cost him L.30, were consumed.' 'He was,' she maintained, 'refused any compensation for them'[52] (an act which, if true, seems more readily attributable to the elder Arkwright than to his son).

There was to be some delay in rebuilding. John Baker had died in 1783 and neither of his elder sons, Joseph and Edmund, was willing or able to raise the £3,000 for which under the terms of his will they could have acquired the property.[53] In 1787, however, the younger Arkwright bought the Litton estate for this sum,[54] and it was probably then that the mill was rebuilt. Ninety-seven feet long, thirty feet wide and three storeys high, the second Cressbrook mill was erected on Newton's foundations, the lower inner walls of which still bore traces of the fire upwards of a century later.

Cressbrook remained in the younger Arkwright's possession until 1793,[55] when he sold to Samuel Simpson for £3,100 the freehold of Litton Frith together with 'all that Edifice or Building . . . lately erected for the purpose of Spinning Cotton Wool with the several Outbuildings adjoining or standing near the same'.

On 10 October 1781 the elder Arkwright turned to Staffordshire when he bought from William Horsley of Eaton, Derbyshire, 'All that Water Corn Mill and one Fulling or Walk Mill commonly called Rocester Mills', together with various properties and water rights on the river Dove. The agreed price was £820. He at once set about converting the mills for cotton spinning, but in January 1783 sold out for £3,000 to his son, who, three years later, took into partnership 'in the Trade Art and Mystery of Spinning Cotton' Richard Briddon, his clerk at Bakewell, conveying to him a one-third part of the business

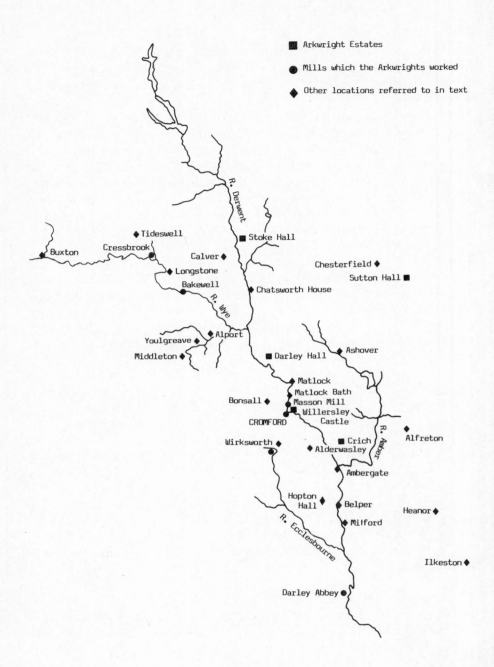

The Arkwrights in Derbyshire

for £3228 14s. This sum included £1,500 'to be paid as a premium for taking the said Richard Briddon into such Copartnership'. Briddon was to receive £25 a year for superintending the mill.

The partnership, originally for fourteen years, was extended until 12 July 1803, by which time its effects were valued at £34,773 19s 10d. Arkwright's share of this came to £5489 12s 11d, and 'he having at various times', with Briddon's consent, 'received several sums of money from and out of the said Trade or Business' sold out to him for than amount.[56]

Despite the destruction of his Birkacre mill Arkwright made a further attempt to spin in Lancashire when late in 1780 or early the following year he leased from Sir John Parker Mosley, Bart, lord of the manor of Manchester, land on the north side of Miller's Lane, stretching back towards Angel Street, on the then outskirts of the town. The site had been advertised in the *Manchester Mercury* at various times from August to October 1780 as 'all that Close of Field, situate at the Top of the *Shude-hill*, in Manchester . . . late in the Occupation of *John Pickford*, deceased, containing upwards of two Acres, and used as a Brick Yard, in which there is now a fine Breast of Clay upwards of two Yards high, and Plenty of Water'.[57]

On this land, opposite the lower group of almshouses in Miller's Lane, Arkwright erected a 'brick built & slated' mill 171 ft long, 30 ft wide and five storeys high.[58] The building, 'intended for a Cotton Manufactory', was insured for £3,000 with the Royal Exchange Assurance in October 1782; £1,000 was added the following year for 'Utensils and Stock in Trade',[59] sums which corresponded to the 'upwards of 4,000l' which Arkwright in 1782 claimed to have spent on the 'very large and extensive Building in *Manchester*'.[60]

By 1786 another 'Mill for Spinning Cotton', 218 ft long, 30 ft wide and five storeys high, a 'Blacksmiths shop Cotton-room Store-Room and other buildings', had been erected, and a reservoir extending almost to two-thirds of an acre dug.[61] The mill's chimney, the highest in Manchester, occupied a base of forty square yards,[62] dominating the landscape to the awe of the crowds who flocked to see it in process of construction.[63]

Arkwright's partners in this venture were two well-to-do Manchester cotton merchants, William Brocklehurst and John Whittenbury, of Market Street Lane and of Piccadilly respectively, Both, until 1784, were also partners with Samuel Swann as 'Manchester Warehousemen' of 50 Friday Street in the City of London,[64] from which premises Whittenbury, who also owned property at 87 Watling Street, carried on business on his own account. In Manchester Brocklehurst and Whittenbury were, until 1794, in partnership with Robert Spear as cotton merchants of 1 Pall Mall.[65]

For whatever reason Brocklehurst and Whittenbury did not long remain in partnership with Arkwright, who in April 1782 was advertising in the

Manchester Mercury the sale 'by Private Contract' of 'That large BUILDING, on the side of *Miller's Lane*, in *Manchester*, lately erected by Mr. *Richard Arkwright*'. His price was apparently too high, for on 1 January 1784 he sold out to his son, who while continuing to live at Bakewell, brought in Samuel Simpson and his brother John as partners and managers. Almost three years later (October 1786) when the younger Arkwright withdrew from the partnership the books showed £20,640 15s 4d owing to him by the Simpsons, who in settlement agreed to pay him, in addition to interest, £7,640 15s 4d in October 1787, £3,000 in October 1788 and a further £2,000 a year for the five years beginning on 10 October 1789.[66] A clause in the agreement held the Simpsons responsible for the recovery of 'all or any part' of the unspecified 'several Ballances . . . then owing from David Dale of Glasgow Merchant John, Walter, and George Buchanan of the same place Merchants and Samuel Oldknow of Stockport Cotton Manufacturer'. Had Dale's New Lanark, the Buchanan brothers' concern and Oldknow's new spinning venture obtained a part of their machinery or equipment from the younger Arkwright?[67]

The Miller's Lane mill attracted the attention of James Ogden, the early historian of Manchester,[68] who noted in July 1783:

> a firm built and capital engine-house, in which the floor beams are all made to spring against their own length and the incumbent weight, by first sawing strong deal balks through the middle, and letting in oak spars to spurn at obtuse angles upward, the divided balks being then screwed together with iron pins, so as to resist the pressure above. Here it is that Mr. *Arkwright's* machines are setting to work by a steam engine, for carding and spinning of cotton.

Ogden had witnessed Arkwright's attempt to obtain rotary power from a single-stroke atmospheric engine of the Newcomen type.[69] He had, in fact, bought two such simple atmospheric engines from Thomas Hunt of London, who in 1783 was advertising that 'any Gentleman who chuses may be accommodated with a neat model, for two guineas'. Hunt claimed that he had also erected engines 'for turning of mills in various branches of manufactory' in and about London, Birmingham, Southampton, Bristol and Liverpool.

As early as 1781 Arkwright's experiments had come to the notice of Matthew Boulton. 'I have heard of no Engine improvements at Manchester except what Arkwright has pretended to,' he wrote to Watt on 7 August, a month after Arkwright's loss of his carding patent in the Court of King's Bench. ' . . . The Manchester folks will now erect Cotton Mills enough but want engines to work them.'[70]

Arkwright's efforts were unsuccessful. As Ogden was describing the 'capital engine-house' James Bateman, a Manchester ironfounder and engine maker, noted that 'Mr. Arkwright's works to go by fire engine are all to pieces,'[71] and by October 1783 Arkwright had abandoned his attempts to use rotary power and instead was employing his engine to replenish his reservoir by pumping back into it water that had already passed over the waterwheel.[72]

According to Watt all this had been readily foreseeable. 'We told Mr Arkwright,' he wrote to Joseph Wilkes, cotton spinner, of Measham, on 20 October 1783, 'that the machine which he propose to erect at Manchester could not answer; but he was obstinate, & the event verified our prediction.'[73] To Boulton Arkwright's failure gave promise of regained opportunity. 'I think Fire Mills will in the end rival Water Mills in such cases as employ numbers of People in Manufactories which require uniformity,' he told Watt on 28 October. 'I think if we were to receive an order for a Mill Engine at Manchester it would do us no harm, as it would show that there are other men in the world almost as ingenious in the Engine way as Mr. Arkwright, and might be a useful example. However I shall not go far out of my way in quest of orders.'[74]

But the first Manchester order for a Boulton & Watt engine did not materialise until 1789, when Peter Drinkwater ordered one of 8 h.p. for his newly built Piccadilly Factory.[75] And it is from a letter of Drinkwater about this time that we learn that the Manchester mill was not yet fully working. 'The factory at Shude Hill which your Mr. Southern has seen has been more than 7 years in filling with machinery,' he reported to Boulton and Watt on 3 June 1789, adding, 'I am doubtful whether with convenience it could have been filled much sooner.'[76] An order for a 6 h.p. Boulton & Watt engine followed a letter of 20 October 1791 from Peter Ewart, the recently appointed Soho partners' agent in Manchester, who had received his training under John Rennie: 'Mr. Barton (Messrs Simpson's manager) desires me to inform you, that they intend taking down their old Engine and putting one of yours in its place — They have set at present 4000 spindles & preparation in the Mill and they mean to put 1000 or 1500 more in it.'[77] It was the second Boulton & Watt engine to be erected in a Manchester mill.

Meanwhile in 1782, the year the Miller's Lane mill was put up for sale, Arkwright was advertising that 'Writing-Paper, of all Sorts' was to be had at his warehouse at the lower end of Cannon Street.[78] There is no mention of these premises in Elizabeth Raffald's *Manchester & Salford Directory* for 1781, and they could well have been rented in consequence of Arkwright's apparent decision to supply the Lancashire market from his Derbyshire mills.[79]

Certainly in March 1783 he took steps to establish his own warehouse when he bought from Joseph Furnival, a Birmingham joiner, for £315 'two dw[ellin]g houses one workshop and two stables with a yard . . . situate . . . near to a certain place called Cock Pit Hill' bordering on Market Street Lane. In September there followed another and presumably larger purchase when he acquired from Charles Upton of Derby some three and a half acres of land, together with buildings, also at Cock Pit Hill, for £2,117 10s. Arkwright 'soon after' demolished the property and erected 'one or more edifices or buildings fronting into a Court or Street . . . laid out by him . . . and called Cromford Court buildings'. The court, 7 yd 33 in wide 'at the least', was connected to Market Street Lane by a passage four yards wide. It was here, close to the Exchange, that many spinners and cotton merchants had their premises, among them Samuel Oldknow, who on 25 March 1788 leased from Arkwright a warehouse for twenty-one years at £40 a year.[80]

Also in the early 1780s Arkwright's first mill, that at Nottingham, was rebuilt following the disastrous fire reported in the *Derby Mercury* of 15 November, 1781:

> A Letter from Nottingham dated Nov. 9, says, 'Yesterday morning between Four and Five o'Clock, a dreadful Fire broke out in the Cotton-Mill at the Bottom of Hockley, in this Town, the Property of messrs. Arkwright, Need, and Strutt, which raged with such Fury, that in two Hours after the spacious Building was reduced to a mere Shell: All the Machines, Wheels, Spindles, &c. employed for spinning and winding Cotton, were entirely consumed, and not a single Article contained therein, (the Books excepted) could possibly be saved, notwithstanding the Exertions of many Inhabitants, who used their utmost to preserve it and the adjacent House, from the Inveitable Destruction. From what Cause the Fire originated we are not able to tell; various Reports are current, but none seemingly founded on Facts. A Centinal keeps Guard there Night and Day.'

How far the new mill corresponded in size with that of 1769 we have no means of knowing, nor can we be certain as to its exact measurments. What little information we have is to be found in the rough plans drawn up by Boulton & Watt in 1790, the year following Arkwright's tentative but urgent enquiries about one of their engines. According to these plans the new mill would appear to have been some 117 ft long and 27 ft wide. As many as six storeys are suggested in one plan but four are perhaps more likely, while the distance between the upper floors — 12 ft — is probably excessive. In the 1769 mill the horse-wheel, 27 ft in diameter and 9 ft high, was situated in a wheelhouse 30 ft square and 11 ft high 'at one end of the building & under part of the spinning rooms'. A note added to the drawing reads, '6 Strong horses at a time — Mr Arkwright said 9 horses'.

Arkwright's enquiry about a Boulton & Watt engine had come in a letter of 20 June 1789 from Joseph Fletcher at Cromford: 'Sir Richd Arkwright desires you will in form him p return of Post in how short a time you could erect him a fire Engine to work his Cotton Mill which is situate in Nottingham as he will want one at the place very shortly.'[81]

There was at the outset some confusion as to the number of horses required. 'I have directions from Sir Richd Arkwright to inform you he has received your favour of the 23rd Inst in which it appears you imagine it takes 10 Horses to drive his works at Nottingham [but] there is only 8 Horses at work at one time,'

Boulton & Watt were advised on 26 June 1789.[82] Four days later came the explanation:

> We were led to think that a 10 horse engine might be necessary to your works from a conversation you had with our J.W. at Birmingham when you mentioned that you needed 9 horses at a time, wrought them very hard, & changed them often, which makes an essential difference in their power, & we also know you choose to have your work done effectively. We however by no means wish to prescribe to you.

By 23 February 1790 the matter had been resolved. 'Sir Richd Arkwright,' Fletcher told Boulton & Watt, 'desires you will forward the Engine that has been long talked of for his Mill in Nottingham as soon as possible, to have the power of *Twelve Horses* he wishes you to send the drawings either here [Cromford] or to Nottingham that preparations may be making against it is ready your speedy compliance . . . will much oblige.' But even now doubt still lingered, as the following letter of 5 April to Boulton & Watt reveals:

> I am directed by Sir Richd Arkwright to inform you he has received your proposals for erecting a Steam Engine at Nottingham, and agree to pay you the same as other people does but you say *Twelve Horses* he says he never heard of more than Nine at one time and sometimes Eight — you will order such a one as will answer, and send an Instrument for him to make it binding to each party he will do the needfull to it and leave the rest to you.

William Stretton, Arkwright's builder and Thomas Lowe, his millwright, now set about preparing for the installation of the engine, and on 29 May Boulton & Watt were advised, 'We have compliated our reservoy for the steam Engin likewise Mr Lowes works is perfectly ready our Building will be compliated in a very short time beg we may have the Engin here soon as Possible Please to drop a line pr return of Post and say when we may expect it here'.[83]

This had not been the earliest or only prompting. As technical details were passed to and fro a constrained but impatient Arkwright had urged 'that everything may be going forward with all expedition possible and the sooner tis compleat the better',[84] and requested on behalf of 'Mr Lowe our Mill-wright . . . how many stroaks the Engin will make pr minute and when it will be here so that he may be prepar'd against that time. The Perpendicular height from the bottom of the well to the fly wheel shaft is 52 feet, the well will be readey in the course of a day or two, a Line pr return of Post will oblige . . . . Please to say *when the Pump will be here.*'[85]

'We are going on with every thing that is necessary as fast as possible Viz the Framing Building &c suppose we shall be compliately readey in the course of a Month. Please to drop a Line and say when you think the Engin will be here,' Boulton & Watt were told on 16 April, and on 8 July they were advised 'all things has been perfectly readey for this last fortnight past, the Boiler is on the ground and all things are waiting'.[86]

A letter of 16 September from Cromford informed Boulton & Watt that the newly installed engine 'has stoped two or three times, whether it is the fault of the Engine or the people who is Managers of the same (I do not know) but probably it may be in the Managers, they being unaccquainted with the Management of it. If it should stop at different times it will be attended with a very great loss but hope it will not any more.'[87]

And on 30 December Arkwright sought Boulton & Watt's assistance:

> The people who looked after the Mill at Nottingham have been discharged from thence, the Son who had learned to work the Engine said he would not instruct any other and since he left the Engine has worked very indifferently for 3 or 4 Days and People are of Opinion they have done something at it. This is to desire you to send Low's Son or some other to instruct a Man with all the speed possible, a Line signifying your Intention will oblige.

It was not until 8 September 1790, when Arkwright asked Boulton & Watt 'if Mess.rs Peel's of Warrington paid in the same proportion for theirs' that he made any detailed inquiry as to the cost of the engine. But on 29 October, having received the account, he demanded to be told 'by return of Post' the amount of discount allowed and on 23 December when enclosing a draft on Smith Payne & Smith's for £242 18s, 'which Balances the Acc.t the rec.t' by Return', he set out additional queries:

> I desire to know the particulars of Lowe & Sons Time Worked at Nottingham Mill, that is what days they Work in every week from their first coming to their Leaving I have large Charges at Nottingham for what was Incurd through the fire Engine say Upwards to nine hundred pounds. This was more than I was led to believe it woud amount to, am apprehensive this Business has not been attended to as it should have been. I wish you to make some Enquiry of your people who was there perhaps some light may be thrown upon this by them. This large Expence will prevent me having one at Wirksworth.[88]

Whether Arkwright was otherwise satisfied with the engine we do not know. In 1792 the mill was sold to Robert Heptinstall, haberdasher, of Ludgate Hill, London, who worked it until his death in 1796.[89]

The installation of a Boulton & Watt engine at Nottingham drew comment from William Stretton: 'Mr. Arkwright's Cotton Mill, Hockley, first worked by Steam 1790 . . . Other Mills were then, & had for some time been working by Steam, but he could not be brought into a belief that a good thread could be spun by that means till his own Eyes convinced him.'[90] But this view is misleading. In November 1777, less than two years after the beginning of Boulton & Watt's partnership, Arkwright, already a visitor to Soho, had become the first cotton spinner to enquire as to the expense of a reciprocating engine, one capable of 'throwing up 6[0] Ton of water p.r Min. 29 ft. high', for his recently built Cromford mill.[91] He was ahead of his time. 'As to the expense of the Engine,' he was told, 'I cannot speak accurately to that point as we have not yet erected any engines but what have been much larger or much smaller than the one you require.'[92]

Arkwright failed to reply to Bolton & Watt's detailed letter, and it was not until 1780 that he made a further enquiry, this time for an engine to raise ten tons of water a minute 18 ft high. 'Mr Arkwright of Cromford sent for me last night,' Watt told Boulton on 12 October, 'he has built a mill and the miners have lett down his water so that it cannot move.' As in 1777 Arkwright failed to respond to Boulton & Watt's suggestions, a matter about which four years later Watt commented tartly in a letter to his father-in-law:

> Some years ago he applied to us at two different times for our advice which we took the trouble to give him, in one or more long letters, which he never had the manners to answer but followed his own Whims till he threw away several 1000£s and exposed his ignorance to all the world, & then in disgust gave up the scheme . . . . Our rotative engines which we have now rendered very complete, are certainly very Applicable to the driving of cotton mills in every case where the conveniency of plaicing the Mill in a town or ready built Manufactory will compensate for the expense of coals & of our premium. Our premium we have fixt at £5 p^r annum for every horses power the machine is equal to & the Coals are about 10 pounds weight p^r hour for each horse.[93]

But Arkwright's natural caution (rightly so, as it turned out) had made him sceptical of Watt's claims as to the quantity of coal consumed by his engines. It was, indeed, not until 1786, six years after the second of Arkwright's inquiries, that an engine supplied by the Soho partners began work in a cotton mill, that of the Robinsons at Papplewick, Nottinghamshire, who experienced some eighteen months of anxiety in the purchasing and setting up of their comparatively small engine.[94] And by this time Arkwright's Wirksworth and Manchester mills were already making use of steam power.

Although in the mid-80s Arkwright was to extend his enterprise to the banks of the Clyde and the Tay, his machines had, a few years earlier, been introduced into Scotland by adventurers who gambled that mere distance would allow their illicit use of the water frame to go unchallenged.

Scotland's first cotton mill, that at Penicuik in Midlothian, was built 'under the inspection and direction'[95] of John Hacket, Arkwright's former workman and an acquaintance of James Hargreaves. The owners were Peter Brotherston and Bertram Gardner & Co. bankers, of Edinburgh, who, on the formation of the partnership in 1776, had feued some five Scottish acres 'with the use of water for mills and other machinery' from Sir James Clerk of Penicuik. The venture was financed by the bankers, Brotherston 'not [being] possessed of any capital, . . . merely contributed his personal skill and labour in superintending

Arkwright and the early cotton-spinning mills in Scotland

and conducting the work'.[96]

Rothesay, the second mill to be built in Scotland, soon came to rely on Arkwright workmen versed in machine making. In 1778 David Loch, General Inspector of Fisheries in Scotland, noted that three weeks before his visit to Rothesay an English engineer had planned 'the buildings, water courses, dams and machinery for a large spinning manufactory to be erected above the town, where the mills for beating lint formerly stood'.[97]

The site had been leased on 'very liberal terms' from the Earl of Bute by James Kenyon and Francis Wheelhouse, already in partnership as watchmakers, and Jonathan Moore, 'victualler', all of Sheffield.[98] On 7 December 1778 Wheel-house and Moore withdrew from the partnership, whereupon Kenyon had 'the address to buy off from about Mr Arkwright's works some men who were known to understand the construction and making of machinery'.[99] Even so, Rothesay was not without its problems, and when in 1785 the mill, advertised as having 'near 1000 Spindles' and 'about Twenty Spinning Jennies',[100] was put up for auction at the Tontine Coffee House in Glasgow it realised £1,500, somewhat less than a third of what it had cost to build.

The early 1780s saw the beginnings of cotton spinning in Renfrewshire. In 1780 a mill 76 ft long, 28 ft wide and three storeys high was built by Stewart Dunlop & Co. on the site of an old corn mill on the banks of the river Levern at Dovecothall in the parish of Neilston,[101] while another built the same year at Busby began working in June 1781.[102]

In 1782 'the art of cotton spinning according to Sir Richard Arkwright's method' was introduced into the west of Scotland by Robert Burns, a partner in Corse Burns & Co., a concern established that year at Johnstone, new Paisley,[103] where the six-storeyed 'Old End' of the mill is still to be seen.[104] 'When to contract was entered into, Mr Robert Burns was not acquainted with the machinery of a cotton mill; but having a turn for mathematics, he applied himself closely to the study of machinery . . . [and] by close attention and skilful management . . . retrieved the affairs of the Company from the most disastrous to the most flourishing situation.'[105] These 'persevering exertions', it was said, cost him his health and 'finally his life'.[106]

The disruption of trade with the Virginia plantations during the War of American Independence dealt a severe blow to the old tobacco atistocracy of Glasgow. With the coming of peace these and other merchants set about re-establishing their connections with the American planters, activities in which they were assisted by the newly formed Glasgow Chamber of Manufacturers, which held its first meeting on New Year's Day 1783 under the presidency of Patrick Colquhoun, Lord Provost of the city. It was a situation in which Arkwright perhaps sensed the opportunity of mobilising capital to develop the cotton-spinning industry, something that would do much to thwart the ambitions of his Manchester rivals. Certainly during the autumn of 1784 he visited Scotland, where at Paisley on 29 September 'for his good deeds done and to be done for the well and utility of the Burgh . . . [he] was by the magistrates and Town Councill . . . Made and Created a free Burgess'.[107] Early October found him in Glasgow:

> Thursday last [reported the *Glasgow Mercury* of 7 October 1784] George Dempster, Esq; of Dunnichen, member of Parliament for the Boroughs of Dundee, Perth, &c. arrived here on his tour through Scotland, to procure infomation relative to the state of the Manufactures Fisheries, &c. Richard Arkwright, Esq; of Cromford in Derbyshire, the ingenious manufacturer of cotton-yarn, was in town, on a tour to view the Manufactures of Scotland, previous to Mr. Dempster's arrival. On Friday, [1 October] they were entertained by the Lord Provost and magistrates in the Town-hall, and Mr. Arkwright presented with the freedom of the city, Mr. Dempster having received that honour on a former visit. They were invited to dine with the Lord Provost at Kelvin Grove on Saturday. The manufacturers of Anderston, through which they had to pass, in order to testify their gratitude to Mr. Dempster, the patron of manufactures in Scotland, and their esteem for Mr. Arkwrgiht, assembled their workmen to receive them. On their arrival, the populace wanted to unyoke the horses from Mr. Dempster's carriage, in order to draw him to Kelvin Grove. This honour he declined, as it has been his uniform wish and practice to lead his countrymen to freedom, rather than put them under the yoke. Mr. Arkwright however was forced to comply with their offer, and the cavalcade proceeded, in a triumphant manner, to the Lord Provost's country seat. .
>
> The inhabitants of Anderston, to testify their joy still further, lighted up bonfires, and prepared flambeaux to accompany them with in the evening upon their return to this city — The procession entered about half past eight, which consisted of five carriages; in the first the Lord Provost, who was followed by Mr. Dempster in the second; his carriage was preceeded by a large transparent gauze-lanthorn, raised upon the top of a pole, inscribed with these words, on the front and back, *The Patriot of his Country*. On the sides, *The Guardians of our Manufactures*. The other carriages were taken up by the Lord Advocate, member of Parliament for this city, &c. Mr. Arkwright, Colonel Campbell of the 9th regiment, &c. In this manner they proceeded to the Saracen's head, where they alighted, amidst the acclamations of many hundreds of the inhabitants.

Dempster was to recall his own part in these activities in a letter of 21 January 1800 to Sir John Sinclair, who had enquired as to 'the circumstances, of the bringing of the spinning of cotton by mills, according to Sir Richard Arkwright's method, into our part of the kingdom':[108]

> I cannot trace that business to its very source, for cotton was spun by mills at Pennycuik in Mid Lothian, and in the Isle of Bute, before ever I had heard of such an invention. But as I had some concern in engaging Sir Richard to instruct some of our countrymen in the art, and also to take a share in the great cotton-mills of Lanark and Stanley, it may not prove unentertaining to one of

your turn for statistical inquires, to mention a few particulars to you; more especially as mere accident occasioned my having any concern in that matter.

Ever since the tax on post-horses, it had been my custom, to perform my journeys to and from Parliament, with my own carriage and horses, making time, as other mechanicians do, supply my want of pecuniary power. To amuse my wife and myself, and to rest my horses, I generally halted a few days at the different watering places by the way; and in the year, I think, 1796,[109] being particularly captivated with the romantic scenery of Matlock, we staid a week or ten days there. In the course of a forenoon's ride, I discovered, in a romantic valley, a palace of a most enormous size, having, at least, a score of windows of a row, and five or six stories in height.[110] This was Sir Richard Arkwright's (then Mr Arkwright) cotton-mills. One of our mess-mates being known to the owner, obtained his permission to see this stupendous work. After admiring every thing I saw, I rode up to Mr Arkwright's house — knocked at the door. He answered it himself, and told me who he was. I said my curiosity could not be fully gratified, without seeing the head from whence the mill had sprung. Some business brought him soon after to London. He conceived I had been useful to him; and offered to assist me in establishing a cotton-mill in Scotland, by holding a share of one, and instructing the people. Private business carried him the following summer[111] to Scotland, where he visited Perth, Glasgow and Lanark, and, I believe, Stanley, for I was not then in Scotland. Mr Dale and I became partners in mills to be erected at Lanark. A company of five or six Perth gentlemen, he and I, entered into partnership in mills to be built at Stanley in Perthshire. Some misunderstanding happening between him and Mr Dale, which they submitted to me, I met them both at Sir Richard's house at Cromford, in December 1786. Each gentlemen offering to take concern, and to take my share also, I awarded the whole to Mr Dale, as being most convenient for him to manage. Mr Dale thinking, I had made him a valuable gift of my share, offered my L.1000 Sterling, by way of equivalent for it; but I was too glad to be rid of so extensive a concern to accept of any compensation for it. Sir Richard instructed Mr Dale's artists and young children gratis, as he did those sent from Stanley. From this last concern I never was able to extricate myself, although it was my intention so to do, as soon as it should become profitable to the adventurers. Mr Arkwright resigned. The war suprised us just when we were beginning to reap the profit of our labours. The price of cotton rose, the value of cotton-yarn fell, and considerable loss was incurred. In the year 1799 the company was dissolved, and those admirable mills are now on sale.

The story goes that after the Kelvin Grove banquet David Dale took Arkwright by post-chaise to view the Falls of Clyde,[112] upon seeing which Arkwright 'exultingly said, that Lanark would probably in time become the Manchester of Scotland; as no place he had ever seen afforded better situations, or more ample streams of water for cotton machinery'.[113] His reported remark may well have been made when, on 4 October 1784, he was presented with a Lanark burgess ticket.[114] The outcome was the decision to build the New Lanark mills.

[73]

The site chosen was described almost a decade later by a topographer of the parish of New Lanark. Below the Cora Linn:

> The next curiosity, on descend the Clyde, that attracts the stranger, is New Lanark, or the cotton mills. The situation of this village is at the western extremity of the Bonninton ground in a low den, and within view of another beautiful and romantic fall called Dundaff Lin, signifying in gaelic *black castle leap*; and no doubt formerly some fortress has been situated hereabouts, although no traces now remain, excepting in tradition; which still points out a rock called Wallace's Chair, where that patriot is said to have concealed himself from the English. This fall is about 3 or 4 feet high, and trouts have been observed to spring up and gain the top of it with ease. This fall, the village, four lofty cotton mills, and their busy inhabitants, together with the wild and woody scenery around, must attract the notice of every stranger.

The building of the first of the New Lanark mills began in April 1785,[115] water for the wheels being channelled through a rock tunnel almost 100 yards long from above the Dundaff Linn. 'Mechanicks were sent to England' to be 'instructed in the business', and spinning began in March 1786. But in December that year the partnership was ended, following a 'misunderstanding' (as Dempster described it) between Arkwright and Dale. This arose, according to Dale's grandson, Robert Dale Owen, when Arkwright, visiting New Lanark for the first time, had a sudden and heated exchange with Dale about the position in which the wooden cupola housing the factory bell had been built.

New Lanark village, by John Winning, 1818

After viewing the Falls of Clyde Arkwright's journey took him to Donside, where the met Alexander Milne, merchant, of Crimonmogate, Aberdeen, and a partner in Gordon Barron & Co., linen bleachers and printers since 1775 at Woodside, near Aberdeen. Arkwright was not slow in pointing out the advantages of the river Don for cotton spinning and offered to provide training at Cromford for workpeople 'in the erection and management of machinery and the manufacture of cotton'. This assistance was accepted, and in 1785 cotton spinning began at Woodside.[116]

By the early months of that year rumours of Arkwright's activities were considered worthy of attention by English newspapers. 'We hear,' reported the *Nottingham Journal* of 19 February, 'that very large Cotton Works are going to be erected at Glasgow, Perth, and Lanark, under the Patronage of Messrs. Dempster, Arkwright, and some capital Merchants, and manufacturers of that Kingdom, and that every Effort to complete the same will be made this Spring.' And three days later the *Manchester Mercury* published dark hints of 'the very great preparations making in Scotland by Mr. Arkwright, joined by several of the most Conspicuous in the Landed and Commercial Interests of that kingdom'.

Three weeks after having been banqueted in Glasgow Arkwright arrived in Perth, where on 27 October 'a deputation the Magistrates and Senate . . . ⁄ presented him with the freedom of that City'.[117] The honour came doubtless in recognition of his already existing involvement in a plan to establish a cotton⁄ spinning mill at Stanley on the river Tay, seven miles north of Perth.

The venture could well have had its beginnings in the summer of 1784 when John the Fourth Duke of Atholl, wrote to his uncle, General James Murray,[118] of his meeting on 14 July at Perth 'with the most Intelligent People belonging to the Linnen Branch' and of their concern as to 'What Effect . . . [Pitt's][119] proposed New Duty would have on that Manufacture'. The 'Unanimous Opinion', he went on, was that it would require 'all the skill and Industry the manufacturers of Linen in this County possessed to be able to Vie with the People of Ireland who had the Superior Advantage'.[120]

About this time the duke received an unsigned ten⁄page memorandum, 'Considerations on the Cotton Manufacture'.[121] It set out Arkwright's achieve⁄ ments — his whole or part interest in 'eleven different Engines', his sales of 'not less than from £12,000 to £15,000 per month', his profits in some years in excess of £40,000 — and surveyed the state and prospects of the textile industries before concluding:

I know but two reasons by which the Linen Manufacturers can escape being ruined by the rapid progress of the cotton Manufacture, one is the Invention of a means of spinning Linen yard by Machines. M.ʳ Arkwright is said to have discovered the art of doing so, But he is too old and too rich to prosecute an uncertain and labourious discovery. The other is for the linen manufacturers to betake themselves to the Manufacturing of Cotton. . . . The more quietly this is undertaken the better chance it has to succeed Little should be said till we are fully possesed of every Machine whether for weaving or spinning that is known and used anywhere else.

The introduction of cotton spinning thus seemed to offer the prospect of relief from the effects of the threatened decline of the linen industry, and on 28 August 1784 the duke agreed with George Dempster, Richard Arkwright and a number of Perth merchants to feu seventy acres of land at Stanley to build a cotton mill.[122]

During the next six months Arkwright was visited by two of his associates, William Sandeman, the owner of a large bleachfield on the Tay at Luncarty, near Perth, and Robert Graham, the impoverished twelfth laird of Fintry. Sandeman was the first to make the journey south. He wrote to the Glasgow merchant Gilbert Hamilton, James Watt's brother-in-law, from Nottingham on 15 November 1784:

> One great object I had in this Journey was to look into the Cotton manufactures in Lancashire being somewhat inspired with the idea of a great riseing trade from the Spirited beginning I had the pleasure to See in your thriving city of Glasgow. And from the short acquaintance I had got of the great M.[r] Arkwright when lately with you I had some desire to visit him and See his great Cotton Mills I have now had that Satisfaction and much pleas'd I am with my visit . . . . I am Sorry that M.[r] Arkwright does not stand so high in esteem with many in his own Country as his Merit deserves I have had access to See both Sides. And if through his means a part of the great Cotton Manufacture now carrying on to the employment of many thousands not only in Lancashire but in Derby & this County Shall be brought to Scotland We will have reason to hold him in that high point of view wherein M.[r] Dempster introduced him to us and your great & thriving city of Glasgow will not repent the honours paid him there. It is possible that the honours he met with there which spread thro' Britain may have occasion'd some little envy from his owne Country for fear of consequences.[123]

Graham's visit took place early in 1785 on behalf of the Duke of Atholl, who on 20 February wrote of it and of his own plans to General Murray:

> I have an Idea of establishing the Cotton Manufacture in this part of the World, I have received proposals for Erecting Mill's &cr in which the famous M[r] Arkwright is to be materially concerned; I thought it such an Object that Fintry took the trouble of going the length of Derbyshire to be satisfied of the Utility and to induce Arkwright to be concerned in this Country; Arkwright in consequence means to be here sometime in March till then I shall enter into no agreement th° some of the men of most Capital and Spirit in Perth want to begin instantly a great supply of water is necessary and no where in the Kingdom is there such a Command as at Stanley & by perforating the Hill I can bring in

any quantity of the Tay I please.[124]

The upshot of Graham's investigations seems to have been a meeting between the Duke of Atholl and Arkwright at the King's Arms inn, Perth. It was now that Sandeman brought in George Penny, who is said to have been responsible for the introduction of the cotton manufacture to Perth some three years before. The story goes that the duke and Arkwright were so impressed by the muslins displayed by Penny and by his assurance that he could teach others to weave that Arkwright declared that work on the Stanley project should be started immediately.[125]

Certainly by 12 May 1785 the *Derby Mercury* was able to report the arrival of trainee workpeople at Cromford:

> A few days since, between 40 and 50 North Britons, with Bagpipes and other Music playing, arrived at Cromford, near Matlock-Bath from Perth, in Scotland: These industrious Fellows left the Place on account of the Scarcity of Work, were taken into the Service of Richard Arkwright, Esq; in his Cotton Mills and other extensive Works, entered into present Pay, and provided with good Quarters. They appeared highly pleased with the Reception they met with, and had a Dance in the Evening to congratulate each other on the Performance of so long a Journey.

Five days later, under an agreement between the Duke of Atholl and the Stanley Company, Arkwright was appointed 'sole arbiter' upon such matters as the length of the lease, the yearly rent and the expenses of the duke, who was to have the 'sole Expense of Building a house fit for the necessary machinery'. On Arkwright's advice it was agreed that the company would pay a rent of £69 10s a year for the use of the existing corn mill and water rights, and that the duke would grant a twenty-one-year lease of thirty acres of land upon which to build a village. He also agreed to spend £2,000 putting up houses, a sum upon which he was to receive interest at $7\frac{1}{2}$ per cent.[126] Anxious to control the development of the village, James Stobie, the duke's factor, drew up the rectangular gridiron plan upon which the present-day village is based. A square (now Duke's Square) was named after Arkwright. Stobie also planned the mill lade, 776 ft long and at one point 127 ft below the top of a hill, to replace the old tunnel built for the corn mill.[127] The earliest mill (the so-called Brick Mill,[128] now known as the Arkwright Mill), 90 ft long and 33 ft wide, has its two lower storeys of stone and the others of brick.[129]

At Cromford on 2 December 1785, in the presence of William Greatorex, his servant, and David Dale, Arkwright signed a document which was registered on New Year's Day 1787 as a provisional contract of co-partnership 'Betwixt Richard Arkwright Esquire . . . [and others] for the purpose of carrying on the business of preparing and spinning cotton-wool in this Country in the way and manner in which it is carried on by the said Richard Arkwright at Cromford'. Arkwright's partners besides Dempster, Sandeman and Graham were three Perth merchants, Patrick Stewart, William Marshall and Andrew Keay,[130] who after a spell at Cromford became Stanley's first manager.[131] (The contract referred to 'Sundry Indentures with different persons to be sent to the said Richard Arkwright at Cromford . . to be taught the constructing and making of the Machinery used by him in preparing and Spining the said wool itself'.)[132] Each of the partners agreed to advance £1,000 towards the capital stock of the company, a share that could be sold only to another partner or with the consent of the majority of the partners. Arkwright was exempted from this clause in that 'whenever the Spining of Cotton . . . shall so far succeed as to become a profitable concern'[133] he could assign his share to Dempster or, if Dempster declined, dispose of it 'in any manner he shall see fitt'.[134]

Arkwright soon exercised his right of withdrawal, for when the feu contract between the Duke of Atholl and the Stanley Company was drawn up on 13 February 1787 he had been replaced by William Stewart, a Perth merchant.[135] What Arkwright had hoped to gain from his involvement at Stanley, a venture for which (as for New Lanark) he had trained workpeople without charge, is unclear. Possibly by 1787 he felt less bitter towards the Manchester men who almost six years earlier he had threatened to ruin for having filched his patent.[136] Or perhaps, as Dempster was to recall, 'He conceived I had been usefull to him.'[137]

A second Perthshire mill with Arkwright connections was that at Deanston, on the river Teith, near Doune, where in 1785 the five sons of James Buchanan, a farmer, of Carston, Stirlingshire, built what were to become known as the Little and Large Mills.[138]

The Buchanan brothers, three of whom were 'intimate acquaintances' of Arkwright, had been in cotton since 1776, when John, Walter and George had become partners 'for the purpose of carrying on the trade of cotton spinning in Glasgow'. Their business went bankrupt in 1788, 'owing solely', claimed George, 'to the failure of other houses'. But six years later, when George — who, it was said, had within a few years 'dissipated near L.50,000 Sterling' — petitioned from a Scottish prison for a warrant of Liberation his brother John had already been for more than a year in the Fleet, where, maintained the objectors, 'he sleeps in the London Coffee-house, which is within the limits of that prison, and pays *eighteen pence a-night for his lodgings*. Double that sum will not keep him in eating and drink, and shows he has plenty of money.'[139]

This was not the first or only time John's business activities had been called into question. When still 'a very young man, who was totally ignorant of every branch of the cotton-manufactory' he had obtained through his uncle, Robert Corse, a position as a book-keeper with Corse Burns & Co. (a concern to which, on payment of £1,000, he was later admitted to a one-sixteen share) but within a few months had 'then got slack so the Company never had accounts shown to them'. Further, 'in the face of the clause of the contract prohibiting any of the partners from commencing any other cotton-concern without the consent of the Company, [he] had nevertheless entered into another concern, called the Elderslie Cotton Company; and not only so but had also undertaken to be their salesman'.[140]

The three concerns of John Walter & George Buchanan (which went bankrupt in 1788), James & Archibald Buchanan (which failed in 1793) and James & Archibald Buchanan & Co. (whose estates were sequestered the same year) were, as was said at the time, 'much interwoven'. George and John (the latter in partnership with James and Walter) each had a 'wareroom' at Oswald's Close, Stockwell, Glasgow,[141] and were Arkwright's first agents for the sale of his twist in Scotland.[142]

When Arkwright visited Glasgow in October 1784 he was greatly impressed by fifteen-year-old Archibald, the youngest of the Buchanan brothers, then an apprentice wright with Bogle Edmiston & Young.[143] He persuaded Buchanan's recently widowed mother to allow him to come to Cromford and, legend has it, duly arrived driving a herd of cattle before him as an offering to Arkwright to pay for his board and instruction in the trade.[144]

The beginnings of the Deanston mills were described by the Buchanans' nephew James Smith, who, from the age of two months,[145] when his father died, had been brought up by Archibald and who was the mills' manager from 1808 until his retirement in 1841:

> John, being in the habit of attending the great cattle-trysts of Doune, was attracted, by the beautiful and powerful stream of the Teith, and the prospect of a plentiful supply of operatives from the village of Doune, to think of establishing a cotton-factory in the neighbourhood. He soon acquired a feu-right . . . of about a mile in length on the banks of the Teith, and extending to about six acres of land, being part of the small estate of Deanston. A lint dressing-mill had been long established on this spot, and there was a good weir or dam-dyke attached to it. The building of the lint-mill was immediately filled with machinery for carding and roving cotton-wool, which rovings were spun into yarn upon hand-jennies, which were placed in a new building erected at some distance from the lint-mill.[146]

Returning from Cromford in 1787, Archibald Buchanan was made manager and at once set about building a larger mill, which he filled with water frames. About this time Arkwright is said to have visited his former pupil and, expressing great enthusiasm for the chosen site, presented his silver spectacles to Buchanan's mother as a memento of the occasion.[147]

Deanston prospered until the crisis at the outbreak of war with France, when it was sold to Benjamin Flounders,[148] a Yorkshire Quaker who retained possession until 1800, when he leased the mills to his manager. Eighteen months later Deanston failed, was shut down and the greater part of its workforce dispersed. In 1806 the mills were bought by James Finlay & Co., a concern founded by James Finlay of the Moss, upon whose death in 1790 it had passed to his son Kirkman, a cousin of the Buchanans. In 1808 Deanston was reopened and ninteen-year-old James Smith, by this time a student at Glasgow University, was brought in an manager. Under him:

> the works were entirely remodelled and the population re-collected. A consider-able number of the old hands returned, but it was necessary to get a great many fresh families, who were chiefly collected from the surrounding country. At this time power-weaving was introduced, in conjunction with the spinning; and Mr. Smith, having been bred practically to the business under his uncle, Mr. Archibald Buchanan, at the Catrine Works, in Ayrshire, was enabled to follow out the same system of instruction and management which had been introduced by his uncle at the commencement of the works. The system of piece-work was generally introduced, which excited the workers to exertion, and the leading hands in all departments earned very good wages.[149]

Another Buchanan mill on the Arkwright principle, that at Ballindalloch on the river Endrick, founded in 1790 by James and Archibald Buchanan in partnership with the Virginia merchant Robert Dunmore, laird of Ballindal-loch and Ballikinrain, came into the possession of James Finlay & Co. in 1793.[150] In December 1791 James and Archibald had taken their brothers John and George (who were employed as clerks) into the concern, together with Gideon Bickerdike, a Manchester cotton merchant, but by September the following year John & Archibald Buchanan & Co. were deep in debt to the Kendal Bank, and in July 1793 the firm's estates were sequestered.

In 1801 Kirkman Finlay became the owner of a third spinning concern, Catrine, on the river Ayr, near Mauchline.[151] Archibald Buchanan was made manager, a position he held until his death forty years later. Catrine had been established in 1786 by Claud Alexander, recently returned from service with the East India Company to take possession of the Ballochmyle estate, and David Dale. The mill was powered by four waterwheels built by Arkwright's millwright, Thomas Lowe,[152] 'at different parts of the building, with a divided fall of 48 feet.'[153] Although, according to William Fairbairn, called in by Buchanan in 1824 to redesign the power system, Lowe's work was 'heavy and clumsy', the waterwheels being 'ill-constructed, deficient in power, and con-stantly breaking down or getting out of repair'; they had 'in a certain way answered the purpose, and as cotton-mills were then in their infancy he was the only person qualified from experience to undertake the construction of the gearings'.[154]

While Arkwright was rebuilding his mill at Nottingham, expanding his empire at Bakewell, Wirksworth and Cressbrook in Derbyshire, at Manchester, at Rocester in Staffordshire, and looking towards Scotland, he was planning the greatest of his mills, the Masson Mill, on the river Derwent above Cromford at the entrance to Matlock Dale. Building began, the legend has it, after Arkwright had abandoned a scheme to supply additional power to the Cromford mills by diverting to the site water from the Derwent.

On 9 October 1780 Arkwright agreed to buy from George White of Winster and Robert Shore of Snitterton land at North Masson (Masson Close) as well as a paper mill they had erected at Upper Masson Close, 'adjoining the River Derwent', nine years earlier.[155] It was here, below the paper mill, that in 1783 he built the Masson Mill, a traditional timber-framed structure of red brick with a Georgian facade and a striking cupola. A hundred and fifty feet long, thirty feet wide and five storeys high, Masson was powered by a single wheel[156] to which water was channelled from a large down-curved weir, Masson's bell has the following inscription:

GEO. HEDDERLEY OF NOTTINGHAM FOUNDER 1785
INTACTUM SELEO PERCUTE DULCE CANO.

The following year Thomas Marshall (or so he claimed) was appointed superintendent of Masson Mill. He is now (like Samuel Slatter, who served his apprenticeship at Jedediah Strutt's Milford mills and 'had opportunity, and an oversight, of Sir Richard Arkwright's works')[157] remembered for his part in the development of cotton spinning in the United States, where Arkwright's workpeople — and, indeed, all who professed a knowledge of his methods or machinery — were at a premium. And certainly Marshall stressed the Arkwright connection when he wrote to Secretary of the Treasury Alexander Hamilton from New York on 19 July 1791, a week after his arrival there:

> Were I weak enough to be vain of any Occurrence in Life, that of my Immediate Tuition under Sir Rich[d] Arkwright wou'd make me so, a Man whom *all* attempt to Imitate in the Business, but few or none can Equal: I enter'd into this Gentlemans employ in 1786, and thus derived my knowledge of the Manufactory upon his Principles and that this method claims a very decided Seperiority over every other Competitor needs no Comment. I Superintended the very last work Sir Richard Erected, at Marsden, Opposite Matlock Bath, Derbyshire, and so late as November last I was all over his Works, and am Consequently fully Acquainted with every modern Improvement, some of which are of material Consequence.[158]

On 7 December 1791 Hamilton appointed Marshall ('an essential, and, . . . a very deserving man')[159] to superintend the cotton mill of the Society for Establishing Useful Manufactures at the Great Falls on the Passiac River at Paterson, New Jersey.[160] His starting salary was to be £100 sterling a year.[161]

Opinions differed as to the effects of Arkwright's activities on the beauty of Matlock Dale, the impressive limestone gorge of the river Derwent. Masson stirred Erasmus Darwin (a friend of Arkwright's who was familiar with his machines) to lyrical heights in the first and most influential of his poems, *The Botanic Garden*. In it Darwin embraces the whole field of knowledge and its industrial application through the mingling of technical description and classical allegory. He thus describes Masson Mill:

So now, where Derwent guides his dusky floods
Through vaulted mountains, and a night of woods,
The Nymph, Gossypia, treads the velvet sod,
And warms with rosy smiles the watery God;
His ponderous oars to slender spindles turns,
And pours o'er massy wheels his foamy urns;
With playful charms her hoary lover wins,
And wields his trident, — while the Monarch spins.
— First with nice eye emerging Naiads cull
From leathery pods the vegetable wool;
With wiry teeth *revolving cards* release
The tangled knots, and smooth the ravell'd fleece;
Next moves the *iron-hand* with fingers fine,
Combs the wide card, and forms the eternal line;
Slow, with soft lips, the *whirling Can* acquires
The tender skeins, and wraps in rising spires;
With quicken'd pace *successive rollers* move,
And these retain, and those extend the *rove*;
Then fly the spoles, the rapid axles glow; —
And slowly circumvolves the labouring wheel below.[162]

Almost half a century later William Adam, in his popular guide to Derbyshire, *The Gem of the Peak* (first edition 1838), gave a similar although more down-to-earth description of the scene:

The view [on entering Matlock Dale from Cromford] . . . is remarkably bold and mountainous: the noble peak of Masson is seen raising its lofty head over the windings of the Dale, which is here narrow, finely curved, and profusely wooded. The road [here] takes a westerly direction, then suddenly turns to the North, disclosing at once the splendid rocks which burst upon the view through a fine opening up the river, exhibiting a beautiful waterfall, foaming over the weir and rough bed below it, also the Wild Cat Tor, and Masson Mill . . . . The clatter of its thousand spindles and the tinkling of its bells, warning the attendant its hank, or proper quantity of yarn is completed, instantly strike upon the ear . . . . The view here at night[163] is exceedingly imposing. The spacious mill with its hundred lights reflecting on the river and thick foliage, mingling the din of its wheels and the noise of the waterfall.

Others saw Masson as detracting from the beauty of the Derwent gorge. Thus the Rev. James Pilkington, while conceding Arkwright's mill to be a

'handsome building', believed that the erection of 'this work and other improvements of art have considerably injured the natural beauty of the dale. Those,
who are pleased with viewing picturesque scenes, will wish, that they could
have been conveniently placed in any other situation.'[164]

And Sir Uvedale Price in his *Essays on the Picturesque*,[165] an attempt to
formulate with precision theories of the picturesque promulgated by that
indefatigable artist and traveller, the Rev. William Gilpin,[166] added support:

Masson Mill

When I consider the striking natural beauties of such a river as that at
Matlock, and the effect of the seven-story buildings that have been raised there,
and on other beautiful streams, for cotton manufactories, I am inclined to think
that nothing can equal them for the purpose of dis-beautifying an enchanting
piece of scenery; and that œconomy had produced, what the greatest ingenuity,
if a prize were given for ugliness, could not surpass. They are so placed, that they
contaminate the most interesting views; and so tall, that there is no escaping from
them in any part.

But, whatever the contemporary judgement, Masson Mill still stands as a remarkable monument to the water-powered phase of the industrial revolution. Although greatly extended in 1911, Arkwright's original building, with its thick walls, heavy oak beams, long workrooms, with low ceilings and small windows, remains in use, although mainly for storage. Masson has been saved from extinction by its massive construction and its remoteness but not least by the continuity of Sir Richard Arkwright & Co.

NOTES

1 *Derby Mercury*, 19 September 1776.
2 Thomas Walshman, woollen draper (Preston Guild 1762); his father, Henry Walshman, barber (Guild 1742), died before the 1762 Guild.
3 *Manchester Mercury*, 17 September 1799.
4 A.F. MSS, Case for the Opinion of Mr Lee, 1780.
5 Mr Walshman's Petition to the House of Commons (*C.J.*, XXXVII, p. 926); A.F. MSS.
6 Case for the Opinion of Mr Lee, 1780.
7 Fitton and Wadsworth, p. 82.
8 Holland was the minister of Bank Street Presbyterian Chapel until 3 January 1789. See James C. Scholes, *History of Bolton*, Bolton, 1892, pp. 350-1, and B. T. Barton, *Bolton and District Historical Gleanings*, III, Bolton, 1883, pp. 322-3, for reference to Bank Street Chapel. For Wegwood to Bently see E. Meteyard, *A Group of Englishmen (1795-1815), being Records of the younger Wegwoods and their Friends*, London, 1871, p. 13.
9 *Letters on the Utility of Machines*, 1780, pp. 12-3.
10 *Manchester Mercury*, 10 August 1779.
11 *Manchester Mercury*, 28 September 1779; *L.G.*, 21 September 1779.
12 *Letters on the Utility of Machines*, p 11.
13 Meteyard, *Group of Englishmen*, pp. 14-15.
14 Jn° Cross and T. Walshman to Richard Arkwright, 5 October 1779 (P.R.O., WO 1/1003 (239-241)), cited by A. G. Rose, 'Early cotton riots', *T.L C.A.S.*, 73, 74, 1963-64, pp. 80-1, 90.
15 *Manchester Mercury*, 12 October 1779; reported in *Derby Mercury*, 22 October 1779.
16 Case for the Opinion of Mr Lee, 1780.
17 *C.J.*, XXXVII, p. 926.
18 Arkwright MSS at Chatsworth (henceforth Ark.), 44
19 1779 is the date given by White Watson in his '"Observations in Bakewell": beginning in the 31 May 1774', *D.A.J.*, XI 1889, p. 160, and by William Bray in his *Sketch of a Tour into Derbyshire and Yorkshire*, London, preface dated November 1777, p. 74, who noted that a mill is 'begun at Bakewell'.
20 J. Tann, *The Development of the Factory*, London, 1970, p. 112; R. Thornhill, 'The Arkwright cotton mills at Bakewell', *D.A.J.*, 1959, pp. 80-7.
21 Ark. 63.
22 J. Byng, *The Torrington Diaries, 1781-94*, London, 1935, II, pp. 190-1, for a short reference to Bakewell Mill and Richard Arkwright junior's house in 1790.
23 Ark. 39.
24 White Watson, author of *Delineation of the Strata of Derbyshire*, died 8 July 1835 aged seventy-four. Monument and tomb at All Saints' Church, Bakewell.
25 A.F. MSS.
26 A.F. MSS.

27 Ark. 58/9.

28 Ark. 61/2.

29 Ark. 93.

30 The same year, 1777, perhaps on the same deed, Arkwright leased from Gell the 'China House & Buildings', also 'The Porcelain Manufacture Buildings' (see D.C.R.O., Wirksworth Land Tax for 1781 and 1782). Arkwright Society *Local History Trail No. 11, Wirksworth*, 1971, revised 1978, says, 'Here [i.e. near Wirksworth Church] between 1745 and 1773 Wirksworth China was made. In 1777 the premises were taken over by Sir Richard Arkwright and used as a cotton warehouse, and also for picking cotton.' I have not been able to obtain sight of these leases.

31 *Derby Mercury*, 10 March 1814.

32 Guildhall Library, London, MS 11,937, Sun Fire Office Registers, Country Series, 17/664245, for Wirksworth Mill (3 July 1797). And see P.P. 1834 (167) XX, *Supplementary Report concerning the Employment of Children in Factories*, D1, pp. 115/16.

33 *Derby Mercury*, 23 June 1780.

34 Francis Thompson took out patent No. 1884 for steam engines on 25 May 1792. (J. Tann, 'Arkwright's employment of steam power: a note of some new evidence', *Business History*, XXXI, 1979, p. 248, says 'Thompson did not, in fact, patent an engine until 1792, when he patented the design of a double acting one.') On 23 August 1780 James Pickard took out patent No. 1263, 'Machine for boring, turning . . . and other work that a mill be capable of performing by a rotative motion'.

35 *Derby Mercury*, 27 January 1814.

36 I refer the reader to J. Tann's contribution and research of this topic.

37 B. & W. MSS, 'Minutes of Conversation & notes with Mr. Arkwright's view upon the subject of employ^g B & W's Engines'.

38 *Derby Mercury*, 10 March 1814.

39 Fitton and Wadsworth, p. 92.

40 *L.G.*, 1792, p. 361.

41 Sheffield Central Library, Bar D 736/6, Barker Papers, Bundle 60108/6.

42 Possibly Joseph Outram or Benjamin Outram, sectretary to the Cromford Canal Company.

43 Probably Joseph Smedley of Youlgreave, Derbyshire, barmaster. Smedley is mentioned in the Kirby collection of lead-mining records relating to the mineral interests of the Duke of Rutland (D1289B/6167 and D1289B/L 169).

44 Marquess of Granby.

45 D.C.R.O., Cressbrook Papers, Release to Richard Arkwright, 1787.

46 D.C.R.O., Cressbrook Papers, Enclosure Award.

47 See Miss M. H. Mackenzie, 'Cressbrook and Litton Mills', *D.A.J.*, LXXXVIII, 1968, pp. 4/5, for the reasons for 1783.

48 Rev. J. M. J. Fletcher, 'William Newton, "The Minstrel of the Peak"', *D.A.J.*, XXXIV, 1912, p. 162.

49 *Ibid.*, p. 166, for Newton to Seward from Tideswell, 24 October 1784.

50 A. Seward, *Letters of Anna Seward*, IV, Edinburgh, 1811, p. 134, for Seward to Rt Hon. Lady Eleanor Butler from Lichfield, 9 December 1795.

51 *Derby Mercury*.

52 Seward, *Letters*, IV, p. 134.

53 Cressbrook Papers, Will of John Baker; Release to Richard Arkwright, 1787.

54 *Ibid.*, 6 October.

55 Cressbrook Papers, Conveyance by release to Samuel Simpson, 23 March 1793; A.F. MSS; Cressbrook Doubling Company Letter Book. In the same year (1793) Simpson sold the estate, except the mill area, to Francis and John Leigh Philips of Manchester, for £5,100. Edmund Baker had been the leading partner, but after his retirement the firm is

always referred to as 'Barker, Bossley & Co.' (D.C.R.O., Land Tax). There is no evidence about how many partners there were or the amount of their shares, but it is clear that from 1800 to the bankruptcy in 1808 the mill was struggling (Miss Mackenzie, p. 10); Cressbrook Mill was closed from January 1809 to May 1810, after the bankruptcy of Barker Bossley & Co. Samuel Simpson had now moved from Bakewell to Dunstall Lodge. John Leigh Philips and Francis Philips, cotton spinners, of Manchester, took a lease of the Frith for thirty-seven years from 25 March 1810 at a rent of £82 per annum (Cressbrook Papers, 22 February 1810). They were interested in the *site*, which was worth buying as a business proposition and for its shooting and fishing. Four years later the freehold was purchased by Francis Philips for £5,500. Samuel Simpson had made a profit of £2,400, which repaid him for the capital he had sunk in the Frith.

56 Staffordshire C.R.O., D 1529; A.F. MSS; Courtaulds at Coventry, typescript and miscellaneous MSS relating to the history of Tutbury Mill; Staffordshire Advertiser, 23 July 1831, for description of mills to be sold - e.g. 70 h.p. Richard Briddon died 13 April 1814 worth 'Inf. £30,000' (Lichfield Diocesan R.O., Will, 2 April 1814). Among the executors were Richard Arkwright of Willersley and Samuel Simpson late of Bakewell but now of Dunstall.

57 C.I.S. Archives, Abstract of the Title of John and Richard Simpson Esq^{res} to freehold land and buildings situate in and near Miller Street in Manchester in the County of Lancaster, relating to the Freehold of Brick Yard or Brick Field purchased December 1783 subject to an annual rent of £75.

58 Abstract; John Rylands University Library of Manchester, Royal Assurance 'Plan of all the Spinning Factories within the Township of Manchester' (1821). The C.I.S. 1815 plan shows only a 'Passage 4 ft 51 ft from the lower end of the first mill.

59 Royal Exchange Registers 7/84787 (28 October 1782), 8/87827 (4 November 1783), 9/b.p. 19 (10 February 1784, 9/b.p. 237 (26 October 1784), 11/95583 (10 December 1785), 13/b.f. 150 (15 December 1787).

60 *The Case of Richard Arkwright and Company*, London 1782.

61 C.I.S., Abstract.

62 C.I.S. Plan and Royal Assurance Plan.

63 P.P. 1816 (397) III, *Children in the Manufactories*, P. 317; J. Aston, *The Manchester Guide*, Manchester, 1804, pp 277-82. B. Love, *Manchester as it is*, Manchester, 1839, p. 11.

64 L.G., 17-21 February 1784.

65 L.G., 29 July–2 August 1794.

66 In 1789 Arkwright had sold to the Simpsons the Miller's Lane land (the freehold of which had been acquired in 1783) and buildings for £7,000 (see n. 57 above).

67 M.C.R.L., Manchester 1122.

68 *A Description of Manchester*, Manchester, 1783, p. 16.

69 *Encyclopaedia Britannica, Supplement*, 1824, 'Cotton Manufacture'. W. H. Chaloner 'Robert Owen, Peter Drinkwater, and the early factory system in Manchester, 1788-1800', *B.J.R.L.*, 37, 1959, p. 91.

70 B. & W. MSS.

71 B. & W. MSS, J. Bateman to J. Seale, 6 July 1783; Tann, *Development of the Factory*, p. 83.

72 J. Wilkes to Boulton & Watt, 19 October 1783, cited by J. Tann, 'Richard Arkwright and technology', *History*, 58, 1973, p. 38.

73 B. & W. MSS.

74 Wadsworth and Mann, p. 491, citing Boulton to Watt, 28 October 1783.

75 Hills, *Power in the Industrial Revolution*, pp. 162, 165.

76 B. & W. MSS., P. Drinkwater to Boulton & Watt, 3 June 1789; Chaloner, 'Robert Owen, Peter Drinkwater', p. 91; Hills, *Power in the Industrial Revolution*, p. 169.

77 *Ibid.*, pp. 169, 192; A. E. Musson and E. Robinson, *Science and Technology in the Industrial Revolution*, Manchester, 1969, p. 441; *L.G.*, 1793, pp. 335–6.

78 *Manchester Mercury*, 9 April 1782. The warehouse was perhaps rented from John Upton, a Manchester timber merchant, who owned several properties in Cannon Street (L.C.R.O., Will, 1 August 1798).

79 The premises were in what became Hanson's Court. Taken down in 1913. See John Loudon, *Manchester Memoirs*, London, 1916, p. 136.

80 Joseph Furnival had inherited the property from his father, Jeremiah, a Manchester shearman, who in 1744 lived there with William Barlow, a schoolmaster, whose 'Kins' women' Sarah he had married (L.C.R.O., Will, William Barlow, 1744). Charles Upton had entered Manchester Grammar School in 1784 (J. Finch Smith, *Admissions*, II, p. 109). He was the son of James Upton, a Manchester calenderer (died 12 February 1755) and nephew of Thomas Furnival a Manchester fustian shearer (died 30 March 1774) and brother of Jeremiah (L.C.R.O., Will, James Upton, 1774 (made 1755)). As to the subsequent history of the warehouse, in 1792 at Sir Richard's death it was valued at £8,000. Richard Arkwright II considered setting up his own warehouse (G. Unwin *et al.*, *Samuel Oldknow and the Arkwrights*, Manchester, 1924, p. 94, Arkwright II to Oldknow from Bakewell, 6 September 1787,' . . . I have not yet opened my new warehouse in Manchester, nor have I got one to open, but I will do it when I think it the best opportunity'); however, he does not seem to have gone ahead ⁄ there is no listing in the Manchester directory of 1788 and in Scholes's *Manchester and Salford Directory* for 1794 the listing is 'Arkwright, Richard Esq: cotton spinner, 9 Cromford c.'. On 23 March 1807 Arkwright II sold for £60 land at Cock Pit Hill, bounded on its eastern side by the warehouse. On 29 and 30 August 1815 further land was sold for £1,600. Then on 26 March 1868 the trustees of the will of Peter Arkwright sold to Richard Greenhalgh of Manchester, paper manufacturer, a plot of land and a warehouse in Cromford Court for £5,500 and to Malcolm Ross of Manchester, merchant, land and a warehouse in Cromford Court for £9,500.

81 This paragraph relies heavily on the researches of the Boulton & Watt MSS by J. Tann, R. Hills and D. M. Smith (*Industrial Archaeology of the East Midlands*, Dawlish and London, 1965).

82 B. & W. MSS, written by Joseph Fletcher.

83 B. & W. MSS, G. Truman to Boulton & Watt from Nottingham.

84 B. & W. MSS, G. Truman to Boulton & Watt, 12 March 1790.

85 B. & W. MSS, G. Truman to Boulton & Watt, 17 March 1790.

86 B. & W. MSS, G. Truman to Boulton & Watt.

87 B. & W. MSS, William Gibson junior to Boulton & Watt.

88 On 16 September 1790 William Gibson, junior, had told Boulton & Watt that Arkwright 'will be glad to have a state of the expences first opportunity he having some thoughts of erecting one this kind at Wirkworth'.

89 *Nottingham Journal*, 2 July 1796.

90 Stretton MSS, P. 179.

91 B. & W. MSS, Richard Arkwright to Boulton & Watt, 21 November 1787.

92 B. & W. MSS, Boulton to Arkwright, 30 November 1777.

93 National Library of Scotland, Watt to James Macgregor (on envelope in Watt's handwrit⁄ing McGrigor).

94 See J. D. Marshall, 'The cotton mills of the Upper Leen', *Trans. of the Thoroton Society*, LX, 1957, p. 42, with regard to the Robinsons' mills. By 1797 (a second engine had been obtained from Soho in 1791) the Robinsons were complaining that Watt's engines were by no means economical in fuel consumption, as was advertised, and double the coal was used.

95 *Encyclopaedia Britannica*, 1810, 'Cotton'.

96 Signet Library at Edinburgh, 449/23.

97 *Essays on the Trade, Commerce, Manufacturies and Fisheries of Scotland*, II, Edinburgh, 1778, p. 138.

98 *L.G.*, 8⁄12 December 1778; Sheffield directories for 1774 and 1787 (Kenyon described as a manufacturer, 1797).

99 R. Reid, *Glasgow Past and Present*, Glasgow, 1884, p. 103, citing MSS of John Blain.

100 *Glasgow Mercury*, 17⁄24 March, 28 July 1785; *Manchester Mercury*, 1, 8, 15, 22 March 1785; *Derby Mercury*, 18 August 1785. (Does this latter mean not quickly sold?)

101 *O.S.A.*, II, p. 153; J. Montgomery, *The Theory and Practice of Cotton Spinning*, Glasgow, 1836, p. 292; *N.S.A.*, VIII, p. 336.

102 *O.S.A.*, XVIII, p. 308; P.P. 1834 (167) XX, *Employment of Children in Factories*, A1, p. 187; Montgomery, *Cotton Spinning*, pp. 292⁄3.

103 Signet, 264/2.

104 J. Butt, *Industrial Archaeology of Scotland*, Newton Abbot, 1967, p. 66.

105 Signet, 388/19.

106 Signet, 264/2.

107 A.F. MSS.

108 *The Correspondence of the Right Honourable Sir John Sinclair, Bart.*, I, London, 1831, pp. 361⁄2.

109 A mistake for 1783 (see below).

110 Masson Mill?

111 I.e. 1784.

112 R. Dale Owen, *Threading my Way*, London, 1874, pp. 8⁄10. If so, Arkwright soon changed his mind, since at Masson the cupola was placed in the centre of the (roof) building.

113 *O.S.A.*, XV, p. 46.

114 A.F. MSS.

115 *O.S.A.*, XV, p. 34.

116 P. Morgan, *Annals of Woodside and Newhills, Historical and Genealogical*, Aberdeen, 1886, pp. 18⁄23, 30; P.P. 1834 (167) XX, *Employment of Children in Factories*, A1, p. 12.

117 A.F. MSS; *Derby Mercury*, 18 November 1784, errs in saying 'last week'.

118 *G.M.*, April 1794, p. 384: General James Murray died 1794, aged seventy⁄two, uncle to the Duke of Atholl, MP for Perthshire. Buried Westminster Abbey.

119 *Manchester Mercury*, 6 July 1784, Chancellor of Exchequer's Budget proposals of Wednes⁄ day 23 June 1784, laying an additional Duty of about 10% at the Rate of 3d. to 1s. per yard *ad valorem* on Printed and Stained Callicos.

120 Atholl MSS at Blair castle, 65/5/22.

121 Atholl MSS, Box 25, Parcel IX, Stanley (1), item 1. See A. J. Cooke', Richard Arkwright and the Scottish cotton industry', *Textile History*, 10, 1979, and A. J. Cooke (ed.), *Stanley ⁄ its history and Development*, Dundee, 1977, for a further account and subsequent history of the mill.

122 Atholl MSS, Box 25, Parcel IX.

123 Glasgow Chamber of Commerce correspondence, Mitchell Library, Glasgow. I am indebted to Dr John Butt for this source.

124 Atholl MSS Box 65/5/43.

125 George Penny, *Traditions of Perth*, Perth, 1836, pp. 250⁄1.

126 Cooke, 'Arkwright and the Scottish cotton industry', p. 198 n. 19; Scottish Record Office, Sheriff Court of Perthshire, Register of Deeds, SC 49/48/99, fos. 307⁄22, Decreet Arbitral between the Duke of Atholl and the Stanley Company, 17 May 1785.

127 Cooke, 'Arkwright and the Scottish cotton industry' p. 202 n. 20, Copies of Plan at Stanley Mill and Blair Castle.

128 P.P. 1834 (167) XX, *Employment of Children in Factories*, A1, p. 160.

129 Cooke, 'Arkwright and the Scottish cotton industry', pp. 199⁄200 and n. 21, adds, 'the rest of brick with segmentally⁄arched sash windows, and bears a strong family resemblance to the early Derbyshire mills . . . '.

130 Scottish R.O., SC 49/48/104, fos. 1⁄5, Contract for Co⁄partnery, 1 January 1787. Cooke, 'Arkwight and the Scottish cotton industry', p. 202 n. 22, gives this refrence and adds, 'This was the date of registration ⁄ Arkwright had signed the document at Cromford on 2 December 1785 witnessed by David Dale.'

131 About Keay as manager see Cooke, 'Arkwright and the Scottish cotton industry', p. 200.

132 Ibid., p. 200 n. 24; SC 49/48/104, fos 1⁄5.

133 Ibid., back of fol. 3.

134 Ibid.

135 Cooke, 'Arkwright and the Scottish cotton industry', p. 202 n. 25, citing SC 49/48/104, fos. 120⁄9, Feu contract between John, Duke of Atholl and the Stanley Co., 13 February 1787.

136 See chapter 4, Mordaunt trial. B. & W. MSS,. Boulton to Watt, 7 August 1781, ' . . . he will ruin those Manchester Rascals whom he has been the making of'.

137 Scottish R.O., Sinclair of Ulbster MSS, microfilm, Dempster to Sinclair, 21 January 1800.

138 P.P. 1834 (167) XX, Employment of Children in Factories, A1, p. 168; P.P. 1839 (159) XIX, Half⁄yearly Reports by Inspectors of Factories, p. 97. In 1792, when John and George were requird to surrender themselves to the Bankruptcy Commissioner, they were described as 'late of Glasgow . . . and formerly of Manchester but now of Carlisle' (L.G., 15⁄19 May 1792, p. 322). Walter was already dead by this time.

139 Signet, 360/16.

140 Signet, 388/19.

141 Nathaniel Jones's Directory, 1787

142 P.P. 1839 (159) XIX, Factory Inspectors, P. 97.

143 Glasgow, The Burgesses and Guild Brethren of Glasgow, Edinburgh, 1925.

144 P.P. 1839 (159) XIX, Factory Inspectors, p. 97; James Finlay and Co. Ltd, privately printed, 1951, p. 61.

145 Farmers' Magazine, 1846. p. 191.

146 P.P. 1839 (159) XIX, Factory Inspectors, pp. 97⁄8. Inverness Courier, 6 February 1839, 'John's cattle supposed to have strayed into the river Teith at site of where the mill was built'.

147 P.P. 1839 (150) XIX, Factory Inspectors, p. 98. Inverness Courier, 6 February 1839, for the story of the silver spectacles.

148 O.S.A., XX, p. 87; Signet, 500/89.

149 P.P. 1839 (159) XIX, Factory Inspectors, pp. 98⁄9.

150 1793, according to George Stewart, Curiosities of Glasgow Citizenship, Glasgow, 1881, p. 182; 1793 in Glasgow Herald, 17 April 1884; but 1798 in James Finlay, p. 61.

151 P.P. 1834 (167) XX, Employment of Children in Factories, A1 p. 23; P.P. 1839 (159) XIX, Factory Inspectors, pp. 74, 96; J. Paterson, History of the County of Ayr, II, Ayr, 1847, p. 336; James Finlay, chapter X; O.S.A., XX, p. 176.

152 W. Pole, The Life of Sir William Fairbairn, Bart., partly Written by Himself (edited and compelted by William Pole, FRS), London, 1877.

153 W. F. Fairbairn, Mills, and Millwork, II, London, 1863, p. 112.

154 Pole, Life of Fairbairn, p. 121.

155 B.M. Add. MSS, 6670, fol. 239; A.F. MSS.

156 R. Warner, A Tour through the Northern Counties of England and the Borders of Scotland, I, Bath 1802, p. 144, notes this paper mill and says, 'Masson moved by two water⁄wheels'. Originally the mill had five storeys, a sixth and a pitched roof added later.

157 Samuel Slater in New York to Moses Brown of Providence, Rhode Island, 2 December 1789. G. S. White, Memoirs of Samuel Slater, Philadelphia, 1836, p. 72.

158 Marshall's letter in Hamilton Papers, Library of Congress, and reproduced in H. C. Syrett (ed.), *The papers of Alexander Hamilton*. VIII, New York and London, 1965, pp. 556—9.

159 Hamilton to Peter Colt, 10 April 1793, in Syrett, *Papers of Hamilton*, XIV, p. 303.

160 Syrett, *Papers of Hamilton*, X, p. 345.

161 Nicholas Low to Hamilton, 4 March 1793 in Syrett, *Papers of Hamilton*, XIV, p. 189.

162 *The Botanic Garden*, London, 1791 (first combined edition), II, pp. 56-8.

163 The Hon. John Byng was likewise impressed by the 'luminously beautiful' mills at night. This was, however, the only aspect of Arkwright's activities that received his approval.

164 *A View of the present State of Derbyshire*, II, Derby, 1803 edition, p. 312.

165 I, London, 1810, p. 198.

166 F. D. Klingender, *Art and the Industrial Revolution*, London, 1972, pp. 72-5.

CHAPTER IV

The great patent trials:
Arkwright on the offensive

WHEN DURING THE CREATION of Arkwright's cotton-spinning empire knowledge of his water frame and carding machine became widespread his 'fame . . . resounded through the land; and capitalists flocked to him, to buy his patent machines, or permission to use them'.[1] So wrote Edward Baines, the historian of the cotton industry, a little over half a century later. According to Arkwright himself, he had by 1782 sold water frames and carding machines, 'and particularly the last', to adventurers in eight counties who together had invested over £60,000 in mills and equipment. In all, as a result of his inventions, there had by this time been established 'a Business that already employs upwards of Five Thousand Persons, and a Capital, on the whole, of not less than 200,000 *l*. a Business of the utmost Importance and Benefit to this Kindom'.[2]

The first Arkwright licensee was John Gardom, a well-to-do Bakewell hosier and founder of Gardom Pares & Co., who in 1778 leased from Sir Thomas Eyre of Hassop land on the west bank of the river Derwent a little to the north of Calver Bridge. Here, on a site previously occupied by a corn mill, he built a small three-storeyed mill which he filled with Arkwright machinery.[3]

Before reaching an agreement with Gardom Arkwright had sought the opinion of Lloyd Kenyon as to whether the sale of his machines would invalidate the 1769 patent and especially those of its clauses prohibiting the creation of a partnership of more than five persons:

> Mr. Arkwright for valuable Considerations has assigned over two undivided third parts of the said Letters patent & of all Liberties Privileges thereby granted unto Mr. Samuel Need & to Mr. Jedediah Strutt & they three jointly in Partnership have made Machines & used them in the Spinning Business but have never yet sold any, are now desirous not only of continuing to make & use the Machines in their Business, but finding many other persons will be desirous of buying Machines of them for Spinning of Cotton they have aggred to sell ten thousand Spindles or Machines to Mr. Gardom & diff[eren]t Quantitie to other people to any Amount not exceed[in]g 24,000 Including the 1000d. Spindles agreed to be Sold to Mr. Gardom.
>
> The Draft of the Articles of Agreem[en]t sent herewith are intended as the

[91]

Form of the Agreem[en]t to be made with all other persons who shall purchase any of the Machines hereafter, but Doubts arising what Power the Patentee & his Partners have of making such Sales on Account of these Clauses in the Patent Mr. Kenyon is desired to peruse these Clauses & the Draft of the Articles of Agreem[en]t sent herewith & to revise his Opinion a Copy of which is left herewith & to consider about the Propriety of the Plan proposed & whe[the]r the Patentee & his Partners can carry such a Plan into Execution without making Void the Patent as they only intend the meer Sales of the Machines without debarring themselves of the making & using for their own Use as many Machines as they think proper since the Money arising from the Sale of these Machines will never be shared by more persons than the Number of five tho' the benefit arising from the Use of them will on this plan be shared and divided amongst all the Purchasers.[4]

Unfortunately the draft of the proposed Articles of Agreement no longer survives, but Kenyon's reply of 6 March 1778 was far from encouraging. This — the illegible sections are indicated by brackets — reads:[5]

We are of opinion that the patentee and his two partners may sell as many of the machines as they please, and to as many persons as they please, and the purchasers may work and sell the individual machines they buy but cannot multiply them. But we are of opinion that any Ingagm[en]t on the part of the Sellers restraining them from mak[in]g and selling to others will be [   ] with whom they contract if the number in the [   ] five will vacate the patent according to the provisions; therefore we advise them not to enter into the Articles proposed.[6]

How Arkwright overcame these difficulties is not known, since no form of agreement with any licensee has come to light. In the case of Gardom Pares & Co. it indeed seems doubtful whether the partners ever possessed one, for when in 1783 they disputed the amount of royalties then payable they were uncertain as to the terms to which they had agreed.[7]

John Gardom (Thomas Pares wrote to his son, Thomas, at Gray's Inn on 31 May 1783) maintained that they had rejected Arkwright's latest demands because in 1778 'upon being ask'd to warrant the Patents they positively refus'd'. But Thomas's son, John, believed that the patents had indeed being warranted, and on calling upon Gardom at his residence at Bubnell his recollections of the meeting with Arkwright were confirmed. 'To my great very great astonishm[en]t,' his father wrote to his brother Thomas, 'I find what Mr A: asserts is true ... so that I expect they'll not only be oblig'd to pay the money but also with the Discredit of attempting to dispute the performing [of] their own Aggreem[t] which is vexatious beyond measure.'[8]

The next day, Sunday 1 June 1783, John Pares wrote from Calver to his father of his now abandoned plan to visit Alexander Bossley of Bakewell, an Arkwright attorney, in order to refresh his memory of the all-important meeting:

I intended seeing Mr Bosley[9] who was present at the only meeting I ever had with M^r. A. & Mr Strut (the time when the Articles were executed) that I might have known what he coud recollect of the conversation but since the receipt of Your Letter I have declined seeing him nor will he know of my having been here — as you say a Personal Conversation seems necessary & it is needless to trouble You further on this unpleasant subject 'till that takes place.

But, whatever the legal niceties, Arkwright's charges (put by the spinners' apologist of 1780 as 'at the rate of 7000l. for every 1000 spindles'[10] and five years later by Robert Peel, grandfather of the Prime Minister, at £2 a spindle)[11] were an open invitation to spinners to search for means of evasion. Some took out patents of their own for machines not entirely dissimilar to Arkwright's. Others sought their fortune in Scotland and Ireland, where only the water frame was patented,[12] while bolder (or less prudent) men chose outright evasion.

Arkwright at length determined to stem what threatened to become a fast rising tide of unlicensed competitors, and in February 1781 opened his offensive. Three infringers of the carding patent, Henry Marsland of Bullock Smithy, near Stockport, Daniel Lees of Oldham and John Middleton of Tideswell (a former Arkwright workman) backed down, whereupon Arkwright had their submissions printed in the Manchester and Derby newpapers as a warning to others.[13]

Fearful of what was to come, the Lancashire manufacturers organised resistance and decided to support any whom Arkwright attacked. On 5 March the Manchester Committee of Trade met 'to take into Consideration certain Matters of the utmost importance'. A further meeting was arranged at the Bull's Head for a week later.[14] On 20 March the Committee of Cotton Manufacturers met there 'to consider the most effectual Means of obtaining the Free and general Use of all Engines and Inventions for the manufacturing of Cotton, and of opposing any Attempts that may be made by any Person or Persons at obtaining a Monopoly of the Use thereof'.[15] Manchester's clearly spelt out opposition was not, however, sufficient to prevent another Arkwright victory. On 29 June John Chorlton, 'Joiner and Machinemaker', of Bullock Smithy, submitted, John Cross, one of the Birkacre partners, being a witness to his signature.[16]

Arkwright pressed on. For some time he had been preparing to bring proceedings against nine concerns which he alleged to be making or using the carding machine without licence: John Barnes of Congleton,[17] Bentley Brooke of Ashton under Lyne, William Clegg of Oldham, Robert Ellison and Ralph Whitehead of Stalybridge, Thomas Leeming of Salford, Charles Lewis Mordaunt of Halsall, near Ormskirk, John Taylor and Joseph Smith of Altrincham, John Whitehead of the Garret Mill, Manchester, and John Philips of Stockport and later of the Salford Engine Twist Company.[20]

Arkwright engaged as his leading counsel James Wallace,[21] MP for Horsham and Attorney General, and John Dunning (later Lord Ashburton),

MP for Calne, 'one of the most distinguished pleaders that ever adorned the English bar', where, it was said, 'His perspicuity was uncommon; his ingenuity unrivalled; his language various, ready, and elegant; and his wit always at command.'[22] After studying Kenyon's replies to the points raised in the case of February 1775 Wallace and Dunning had doubts about his reply to the sixth question, and the case was returned to him ('July 1781 — Mr. Kenyon to reconsider. 3 Gns. *Dispatch* par[ticu]larly requested as this Matter is to be tried *next Tuesday*') with the following note:

> The last Question in this Case is the principal point to be determined upon the Trial of several Actions which come on the beginning of next Week for the Middlesex Sittings & which are brought for Infringements upon the Patent Rights. Mr Kenyon will please to reconsider that part of the Case & his Opinion, as the Counsel concerned in the Action incline to think the publica' tion & use of the Machine as stated sufficient to defeat the Patentees exclusive Right. It wod be considered as very kind if Mr Kenyon wod give his Answer by to Morrow Evening or Monday Morning of 13 July.
>
> It is to be observed that the Machine were got at *without* Mr Arkwrights permission, but his present Actions were not agt those persons who had them before his Patent, but others who lately put them in use.

Kenyon's reply of 16 July reads:

> I do not know that this point has been judicially decided. But I shd think the clandestine use of Machines invented by him, not published with his consent, and therefore not given by him to the publick, will not effect the validity of his patent.

Wallace and Dunning were provided with material expected to be of use in the cross-examination of witnesses. The document is of especial interest as being the only detailed account we have of Arkwright's side of his controversial association with John Kay. There is mention, too, of Shipley, for whom James Hargreaves had made jennies in 1768,[23] of George Whitaker, who had had close connections with Hargreaves for nine years and who had made three cranks for James Grimshaw. Finally there is Arkwright's version of the means by which Mordaunt pirated his machine:

> Some general Observations for cross examining Defts Witnesses
>
> It is presumed that all the Defts Witnesses who have any property are Subscribers or Contributors to the Comon defence of these Actions & they are in general either makers or users of the Machines which Plt contends are his exclusive property & which certainly goes to the Credibility at least of their Testimony.
>
> One Whitaker is in Town Subpena'd for Defts he was a white Smith in Nottingham & was some time ago arrained & Convicted of Felony in Lancshire.
>
> One Kay is also summoned as a Witness upon the Defence, he was one of

the Plts first Workmen & about April 1768 ent:^{d} into Articles to serve him 21 Years, & was bound in £10,000 to perform such service & not disclose any Plts works the Articles are in Court & can be proved Notwithstanding which he pirated many of Plts Inventions & as soon as he found it wo.^{d} be for his Advantages deserted his service. Plt. suspecting his Villainy had his House searched he found several parts of his Machines which Witness had stolen & which are now in Plts Mill. Some of the Witnesses are able to give an account of the association it may not be improper to Question them as to the Extraordin- ary Caution observed at Most of the Works to conceal their Machines — as many they made every Person who entered the Buildings take an Oath not to disclose what they saw & at almost all Strangers & every body but approved Friends were excluded. And this Accounts for the little proof given ag.^{t} the different Defts for it was with the utmost difficulty & Personal Danger that the Plts servants co.^{d} get to make the observations they did.

One Shipley a Cotton Spinner in the Neighbourhood of Nottingham is to prove for Defts the use of the Crank & Needle Bar & you will please to examine him strictly as to the time & manner of his acquiring & using it & if it is found Material Ellen Bromley will prove that 8 years ago last Easter she went in his Mill at Nottingham. She was employed in Carding, i.e taking off from the Cylinder Cards by the Hand. That *about a year* afterwards they got the Crank & Needle Bar made as she believes by one Whitaker, that it was very often out of order & co.^{d} not be worked & after 3 Months Trial it was laid aside. That some time afterwards they tried it again upon a Card called a Tuming Card but not answering it was given up & never afterwards used whilst witness continued in that Work which was about 5 years. Saith it was understood to be Mr Arkwrights Invention & she has heard some of the Partners express their fears he would bring an Action against them if he knew they used it, for which reason they kept their doors locked and were very Cautious in admitting any body into the Works. Shipley declared as he came up to Town that if Defts did not succeeed in these Actions, they were determined to come over him some other Way.

It is expected one Marsland will be procured & attempt to prove that he had the Machine called the ffeeder & Crank before Plts patent about which he must be closely examined & whether on an Action being brought ag.^{t} him he did not submit and sign an Acknowledgement in the publick papers that he had infinged on Plts patent right, the fact is so & Mr Evans can prove it.

Any of Defts Witnesses who know Lancashire & the Manufacturers made from Plts Machines must acknowledge the very great Advantage derived from the Invention.

Two Fellows of the Name of Woodiwiss Father & Son are in Town supposed to be Witnesses for Defts they were both formerly employed in Plts Works & discharged for Drunkeness & Negligence the old Man stole several things from Plt: some of which were upon Search afterwards found in his House That amongst the rest he stole a small spinning frame, with 4 Spindles which discovered the Plts plan of Spinning & which he sold to Deft Mordaunt for

£100 or Gui.[5]

Dawson of Manchester Q. if not a subscriber. If he is Examined ask him if he cannot Work better Goods Velverets &c from Plts Single Thread or Yarn than from 2 threads of common Jenny or hand spinning.

Grimshaw of Nottingham Plt: finding a few years ago Witness had infringed on his patent right & charging him with so doing Witness offered to give up the Machines he had made if Plt: wo.[d] not prosecute him which was agreed & Witness declined the spinning Business.

M.[r] Bynion formerly of Manchester. Has been taking infinite pains from the first beginning of Plts Works to pirate his Invention by getting into his Mills & attempting to seduce the Workmen & he has begun many works of his own & spent a pretty little ffortune & Plt has frequently told him he would do so if he persisted. He has lately been down in Devonshire & getting some partners of property hath spent them near £10,000 with his spinning Enterprizes, & he became so abnoxious to them they sent the publick Cryer of the Town were the Works are, to prevent his incurring more D.[s] on their Account ask if he has not very frequently been in & about Plts Mills for the above purposes.

Also said to have been available to give evidence on behalf of one or more of the defendants was Thomas Highs, unexpectedly and hastily recalled from Ireland, where since November 1780 he had been superintending the building of cotton-spinning machinery for Baron Hamilton's newly erected mill, 'four Stories High and extending in Front upwards of 100 Feet',[25] at Balbriggan, a little to the north of Dublin. Upon receipt of a draft on Benjamin and Thomas Graves of Golden Lane, Dublin, with which to defray his travelling expenses, 'Such was the hurry, and so great the urgency of the summons,' Guest tells us, 'that he left Balbriggan immediately, and rode down to Dublin on a hunter, with all expedition, where he embarked for England,'[26]

But when on 17 July 1781 the trial came on in the Court of King's Bench in Westminster Hall before Lord Mansfield evidence as to the origin and the alleged infringements of the 1775 patent was not needed. The first case to be heard was that against Charles Lewis Mordaunt, cousin to the Earl of Peter-borough and Monmouth, whose 'little work' at Halsall, near Ormskirk, had 600 spindles and gave employment to some 160 women and children.[27] Mordaunt's defence was as simple and successful as it was unexpected. He did not deny that he had infringed Arkwright's patent but pleaded that the specification was void because it was obscure and incomplete. After a six-hour hearing the jury, without leaving the court, gave him the verdict.[28] Arkwright did not proceed with the other cases.

The transcript of the trial which Arkwright, beginning what was to become his usual practice, had taken down by Joseph Gurney, shorthand writer to the Courts of Law and in Parliament, has not survived but an account of the day's proceedings was given four years later in the Court of King's Bench by

Mordaunt's counsel, Edward Bearcroft, MP for Hindon, and a 'respectable veteran of the Bar':

in 1781, Mr. *Arkwright*, ... was the plaintiff in nine causes that he brought here against several persons for invading this patent of his. The fate of those causes was singular; by an accident, I bore, as my learned friend says, something like a principal part of it, I think I do remember very particularly, and I will state it very faithfully.

The nine causes Mr. *Arkwright* was plaintiff in, against persons invading this patent, and using those machines without his licence. Mr. *Arkwright*, who is a sharp man himself, and well advised by a great many very able counsel, most of them upon the northern circuit I believe, except one or two of them, and men born in that district, which is very apt to produce sharp and penetrating men, who managed and marshalled his causes with infinite address and cunning indeed.

It so happened, one of his actions was brought against a colonel *Mordaunt*, a gentleman of family, but not of much fortune, and who did not mend it by dabbling in this kind of manufacture. Mr. *Mordaunt* was thought, from his temper, and from the lightness of his purse, out of all the nine causes, as the fittest to be put in the front. Mr. *Arkwright* had nine: he chose to put the action which was to be tried against colonel *Mordaunt* first. There was a particularity in colonel *Mordaunt's* temper at that moment; it was no reflection upon him; but, somehow or other, he took it into his head to wish to have different council in his cause, to defend it, from the gentlemen concerned in the other eight causes. The gentlemen that were concerned in the other eight had been upon the northern circuit, very able persons, and Mr. *Mordaunt* the colonel was fool enough to come to me, and depended upon my assistance, and I remember Mr. *Erskine* was of counsel in all the causes, and I believe Mr. *Erskine* was my only assistant; for colonel *Mordaunt* I had a brief which was written upon a sheet of paper; my other friends were concerned in the other causes, and I was to defend colonel *Mordaunt*. I was a little piqued, I must confess, and I did heartily wish I could overset Mr. *Arkwright*, notwithstanding my poor paltry fee, and my brief which hardly conveyed any ideas. By good luck, Mr. *Erskine*, who was of counsel in one of the causes was with me, I stole from him his knowledge, I borrowed a witness, he communicated his knowledge out of his other briefs. By good luck I comprehended the matter, by the help of my learned friend's communication; I am very free to acknowledge I am obliged to him for it — it was this; that if this was a new invention, Mr. *Arkwright* had not fairly communicated it by his specification, but had absolutely contrived to hide it. Upon that simple ground we went, we had no other to proceed upon; we picked it up, not from my brief I vow to God, for not a syllable of it was to be found there. Mr. *Erskine* communicated his ideas from his other instructions, and I had the good fortune to comprehend them while they were turning the machine about. I made my objections, he lent me a witness or two, and to the perfect satisfaction of the judge who tried it in 1781, the jury found the patent was of no validity; *for Mr. Arkwright, instead of disclosing his invention, did all he could to hide and secrete it*; and upon that ground a verdict was given for my client, colonel *Mordaunt*; and I don't know whether Mr. *Arkwright* repented putting him in front — but I dare say he imagined the same thing would be done in the others, that, that objection would be admissible, though the cases were somewhat different in their nature from each other there was an end of his patent from that time, and I contend all the world had a right to take it so.[29]

Manchester was jubilant. Arkwright's defeat, proclaimed the *Manchester Mercury*, 'relieves the Public from a Monopoly, which they have too long submitted to, under plausible and mistaken Apprehensions'. And, it need hardly have reminded its readers, 'As the said Patent is now of no Force, the Public are at Liberty to make Use of any Part of the Machinery thereof.'[30]

For Arkwright the verdict threatened disaster. The trade had been thrown wide open. The carding patent had been invalidated; the spinning patent would last only until July 1783. He took his defeat badly. Matthew Boulton, who had recently visited Manchester, wrote on 7 August 1781 to Watt of his own and of Arkwright's reaction to the judgement:

> I have heard of no Engine improvements at Manchester except what Arkwright has pretended to & though he has already built a great building for Cotton works yet he now swears it shall never be worked & will sooner let it for Barricks for Soldiers, swears he will take y[e] Cotton spinning abroad, & that he will ruin those Manchester Rascals whom he has been the making of. It is agreed by all who know him that he is a Tyrant & more absolute than a Bashaw & tis thought his disapointment will kill him. If he had been a man of sense & reason he w.[d] not have lost his patent.[31]

Arkwright now turned to other means. He had before him Thomas Lombe's application to Parliament in 1731 for an extension of his patent for throwing silk (he was in the end awarded £14,000) as well as the recent successful applications of James Watt (whose patent of 1769 had in 1775 been prolonged for twenty-five years by special Act of Parliament), William Cookworthy, Elizabeth Taylor, John Liardet and David Hartley. And Arkwright considered his own claim inferior to none: 'as a Man of Genius', read his petition to Parliament of 6 February 1782 asking for an Act to consolidate his patents and extend the term of the water frame to 1789, that of the recently annulled carding patent, 'Mr. *Arkwright* is certainly entitled to greater Praise and Encouragement, because he was the original Discoverer and Inventor; whilst Sir *Thomas Lombe's* chief Merit consisted in clandestinely bringing from *Italy* the Invention of other Artists and Mechanics'.[32]

The Commons referred the petition to Lord John Cavendish and the Earl of Surrey. It was strongly opposed by the trade. Blackburn petitioned that Arkwright had not 'given the House a true State of Facts', Liverpool that he had 'realised such a Fortune as every unprejudiced Person must allow to be ample compensation for the most happy Efforts of Genius'. [33] Stockport, Lancaster and Chorley all gathered signatures. Within three days the Manchester Committee of Trade was distributing copies of the petition. 'It is apprehended,' read the accompanying letter:

> Mr. Arkwright, has no just Pretensions to such an Indulgence, having already acquired a large Fortune since his Patent commenced; and that the Detriment to the Public, if the Time of the Patent be prolonged, could be far greater than any advantage they had received from the Invention, as other Nations have already erected Works upon the same Principles as his, which will throw a manifest advantage into the Hands of our Rivals in Trade.[34]

A meeting was summoned in the Great Room at the Bull's Head for 19 February, following which 316 persons signed a petition to Parliament against the 'oppressive Attempt'.[35] The Manchester Committee also decided to raise £200 for a Stockport man who had invented a machine to rove cotton and 'likely to be of considerable Advantage to the Trade'. Any surplus money was to be devoted to opposing the petition.[36]

Arkwright failed to get parliamentary support and on 10 December 1782 the Manchester Committee for the Protection and Encouragement of Trade, a body founded in 1774 and which, bitterly hostile to exclusive patent rights, had met thirty times since June 1781, boasted the frustration of his application as among the greatest of its achievements. (But the committee's costs fell short of the contributions it had received by £73 13s 6d.)[37]

While Arkwright had been preparing his petition he was making enquiries about the patents taken out by John Kay (1704–1780) of Park, near Bury in Lancashire, best known for his invention of the fly shuttle, who had died in comparative poverty and almost total obscurity in the south of France in the winter of 1780–81. The reason for Arkwright's interest becomes clear when we read in a letter from Kay's son (John Kay, known in Bury as 'French' Kay, owing to his long residence in France with his father) that after the introduction of the fly shuttle 'to the great benefit of this Kingdom' the inventor 'was obligd to leave his native Country haveing spent large sums in lawsuits in defending his Patent against a combination of Weavers [possibly at Colchester] who had an intention to murder him, and it was with some difficulty that a workman he imploy'd escap'd with his live by being put in a Pack of Wool'.[38]

This information probably came too late for Arkwright to include in his *Case*, a printed memorandum which he had had drawn up and distributed among Members of Parliament about the time of his petition. In it he spoke of his struggles to perfect his inventions, his heavy outlay and losses and — like 'the ungenerous Treatment of poor *Hargrave*' whose 'Invention was cruelly wrested from him; and he died in Obscurity, and great Distress' — of his own prolonged struggles with the ungrateful Lancashire manufacturers. 'True it is, that a Man may safely trust the Efforts of his Genius, his Fortune, or his Life, to the Justice of Parliament, or a generous Public; but what Individual can stand against the Power of Numbers of Men, actuated by Malice and Treachery?' Arkwright conceded that in the case of the carding patent he had 'omitted to give so full and particular a Description of his Inventions, in his Specification' but claimed that he had done so to prevent machines 'of great national Importance' being 'sought after by Foreigners to introduce into other Countries'.

With the failure of his first petition, and with the patent for the water frame due to expire in July 1783, Arkwright had to act fast if he were to retain his monopoly. Accordingly on 5 February 1783 he again petitioned Parliament, this time to extend the life of the carding patent until 1789.[39] The Commons referred the petition to Lord George Augustus Cavendish and Lord John Cavendish, and the Manchester Committee of Trade again took up its predictable stance.[40] Arkwright's move had, in fact, begun as early as October 1782, when his attorney, John Leaper, had been in touch with Henry Strachey, MP for Bishop's Castle, and on 4 February 1783 Leaper 'Paid [£1 19s] express to London to Lord G. Cavendish and Mr. Strac[h]ey respecting your M[a]tters in Parliament'. The same day he paid 'Agents attendance with the Letters by the Express to Lord G. Cavendish & Mr. Strac[h]ey & to deliver the same at 10 o'clock at night 13s 4d' and 'To my Clerks Journey with the petition to parliament for you to sign and Expenses, 14s 8d'.

But these lengthy preparations and lastminute rush were of no avail. The Commons received counterpetitions from Lancashire manufacturers and from Carlisle,[41] and with foreign affairs absorbing so much of the attention of Ministers it is hardly surprising that Parliament took no action.[42]

Meanwhile in the summer of 1782 Arkwright had begun preparations to bring to trial those spinners whom he alleged to have infringed the waterframe patent, which had still a year to run. Among these were Thomas James, the joiner and machine maker who had been James Hargreaves' partner in Nottingham, C. & B. Morley, also of Nottingham, Peter Drinkwater, now of Northwich, Howarth & Peel of Burton upon Trent, and the Holywell Twist Company, in which John Smalley's widow had an interest.

The substance of Arkwright's charges is set out in the case sent to his counsel, John Wilson, [43] who in November 1786 was to be knighted on being appointed by Thurlow to fill the vacancy in the Court of Common Pleas occasioned by the death of Sir George Nares:

> The Great Advantages arising from the business which Mr. Arkwright had brought forward and established by means of his Invention tempted numbers of persons to Infringe on his Patent who erected Mills made use of his Machines under various pretences but conducted their business with great Secrecy &

Circumspection. His workmen & people who had been instructed by him were inticed from him & a knowledge of his Machinery by that & other secret means obtained. It is now certain that several persons had been in the actual Exercise of the Invention for which the Patent was obtained for upwards of Two years prior to the expiration of the Patent in July last [1783] And there can be no doubt of their having benefited thereby.

The earliest we know of Arkwright's detailed preparations to bring an action against James ('in the Name of Mr. Strutt the Surviving Assignee of the Patent') is his summoning of Strutt and the attorney John Leaper to Cromford on 19 September 1782 to talk matters over with John Cross. But by the time they arrived Arkwright had decided that they should all meet in Manchester, and the sole outcome of the Cromford discussions seems to have been that Leaper should make a copy of the descriptive parts of the 1769 specification in order to explain the drawings more clearly.

Eight days later Strutt and Leaper left Derby by coach, and after breaking their journey at Cromford went on to Manchester, where they met Cross at the Bull's Head 'for the purpose of considering ... the propriety of bringing fresh actions & to fix a plan of proceedings'. 'Out 3 days', Leaper's charges came to £3 3s; coach hire from Manchester to Derby, his own and Strutt's expenses at the Bull's Head added a further £2 19s.

On 27 October Leaper sent his clerk to Nottingham to obtain 'the substance of his evidence' from Charles Wilkinson, master of an academy there and a proficient draughtsman. Six days later he was there himself with Francis Evans, a Nottingham attorney,[44] 'to see Mr. Wilkinson & to hear his opinion & sentiments as to the sufficiency of the specification it being intended that he should be an Evidence in the Cause'. Leaper also sent to Nottingham John Horrocks, a Derby attorney, to find out from those who were to have been witnesses against Arkwright in 1781 what evidence they were to have given.

On 7 November Arkwright called Strutt, Leaper and Robert Pilkington to Cromford and asked Strutt and Leaper to go up to London with Thomas Wood, his brother-in-law, who, until 1781, had been in partnership with Pilkington and William Shepherd in a cotton-spinning concern at Taplow, and with William Cockshott and John and Richard Watson as fustian manufacturers at Macclesfield.[45] Leaper took with him to London a copy of the 1769 patent and a seventeen-sheet 'fair Copy of [the] state of [the] Case ... as laid before Mr. John Balguy with additional observations & further state of Evidence to lay before Counsel' (£1 10s). Copies at 15s each were also made for Balguy and for two counsel, James Mansfield[46] (who was appointed Solicitor General the following year and Chief Justice of the Common Pleas in 1804) and William Baldwin.[47]

In the midst of all this activity Arkwright's life was threatened. Whilst staying with William Brocklehurst, his Manchester partner, he received an 'incendiary' letter which he published offering a hundred guineas for the identification of the writer and fifty guineas to the person who posted it if he would tell who gave it to him. The letter reads:

Man. 28th Nov. 1782.

Sir

I am very sorry to hear that you still do all you can to distress the trade of Manr: after you had lost the Cause in London this town thought you would then have been easy the remainder of your Time in the patent out. but you still keep doing all you can and not only that but you have been heard to say that you was determin'd to ruin every person that enter'd into that Business, the purport of this is to Advise you that if you d'not withdraw all your prosecutions before Dec. is out I am determin'd to lay in wait for you either in this town Nottingham or wherever I most likely to find you. I will ashure shute you as your name is what it is dam you think the town must be ruled by such a Barber as you, take notice if you are in town on Saturday next I will make an end of you meet you wherever I can. I am not yours, but a friend to the town of Manchester.[48]

Arkwright was undeterred. On 21 December he again summoned Leaper to Cromford 'to take Instructions' in accordance with which copies were made both of the 1769 patent and of the agreement of 1774 which were sent to Baldwin for his opinion.

On Boxing Day Leaper rode over to Nottingham to seek information from John Wright,[49] Thomas Bell[50] and an unnamed man, 'they being thought material witnesses from Nottingham'. But finding Bell, 'the most Material person to see', away from home, he returned to Nottingham two days later to take down his statement and afterwards called upon Arkwright 'to talk further on various Matters'. On 8 January 1783 Leaper was again at Cromford discussing with Arkwright the state of the case and 'who could prove the Act of Infringement'. The Hilary vacation saw him in Nottingham 'with Mr. Wilkinson[51] an Ingenious Mechanic there, to shew him Specification attending Patent & to hear to his Opinion & Judgment on the sufficiency thereof'.

At Milford on 30 April Arkwright and Strutt gave Leaper definite 'Instructions to proceed in this Cause'. Two visits to Nottingham having proved fruitless 'on account principally of the Secrecy & Caution with which the business was carried on by [the] Defendent', Leaper again went there on 17 May '& from thence to Papplewick ... inquiring after several persons who had worked with [the] Defendant when one Milligan was discovered who was able to give the necessary information'.

At the end of the Hilary vacation a one-guinea retainer was paid to Henry Howarth,[52] the thirty-six-year-old MP for Abingdon, 'one of the first crown lawyers in practice', and said to be making 7,600 guineas a year. But on 11 May Howarth was drowned within sight of his house at Mortlake when his best overturned in a sudden squall. His place was taken by John Wilson, and Arkwright also retained Alan Chambré[53] (who was to be elected Recorder of Lancaster in 1796 and was to succeed Sir Francis Buller in the Court of Common Pleas), both at the same fee as Howarth.

On 14 June Leaper met James Robinson of the Papplewick mills in Nottingham in the hope of being able to find 'some other person besides Milligan[54] who was employed in or had knowledge of the Defendents works that the Infringement might have been proved by more than one Witness, but no other Person could be discovered'. On 16 June a messenger was sent to Cromford 'to acquaint Mr. Arkwright what had been done' and at Notting⁄ ham five days later Arkwright, accompanied by Leaper and Robinson, 'after much difficulty' persuaded 'Milligan to give Testimony in the Cause' and took him 'to see the Machinery belonging to the Plaintiff Mr. Arkwright'.

Early in the Trinity vacation James Milligan, Thomas Bell, John Wright, Robert Seagrave,[55] attorney and Town Clerk of Nottingham, and Samuel Ufton, 'for many Years Clerk to Mr. James, Cotton Manufacturer', were subpoenaed, and after 'many attendances' on Arkwright Leaper finally drew up a ten⁄page brief, copies of which were prepared for Wilson, Chambré and Baldwin.

In London Leaper busied himself with consulting Baldwin at his chambers, at his house in Essex Street, and 'several times' at Westminster Hall in order 'to know when the Cause was likely to come on'. He also made 'Several Attendances in London' on three 'ingenious Mechanics', Samuel More,[56] Secretary of the Society of Arts for almost thirty years until his death in 1799, Richard March[57] (Marsh or Marshe), the holder of patents for the manufacture of hosiery and for the spinning of wool, who had his business 'making Patent Netted Stockings' near Barnstaple, and Josiah Crane, who in 1769 had taken out a patent for a machine 'for shading and brocading' stockings and with March was to obtain another in 1804 for 'double⁄seaming and uniting the insides of stocking network together'. All were consulted 'about the Sufficiency of the Specification'. Particularly anxious to have 'the Specification of M.ʳ Marshe's invention in order to have [the] same produced at the Tryal', Leaper also attended the Rolls Chapel so as to have the originals of both specifications produced at the trial 'by the proper officer'.

The action came on in the Court of Common Pleas before Lord Lough⁄ borough and a special jury in the sittings after Trinity, 'when after a full Discussion of the Merits of the Invention & the sufficiency of Mr. Arkwrights Specification (which last mentioned Circumstance was made the principal Ground of Defence) a Verdict was Given in favor of the Plt Mr. Strutt'.

Unfortunately no record of the day's proceedings has survived, with the exception of the names of those who gave testimony on Strutt's behalf and the expenses they received. Five witnesses came up from Nottingham: John Wright was paid seven guineas to cover his journey and expenses; Seagrave 'out 6 Days', received £13 10s 4d — almost twice the £7 4s paid to Ufton, who was away double that time. Bell, 'out 13 days', was given thirteen guineas, a sum which included 'travelling Charges in part for himself & Milligan' (who was paid £6 'for loss of time he being out 13 days & Expences down again'). Attorney Rogers Jortin[58] attended with the letters patent (£1 1s) and More, March and Crane as witnesses, perhaps especially to explain 'the Models produced on the Tryal of this Cause'. 'Expences of all the s[d] Witness[s] & of Plt & M[r] Arkwright & his Agent & Attorney for travell[g] Charges Board & Lodging &c' amounted to £66 4s 5d. Leaper's account came to £32. 0s 5d. This was in addition to a 'General Bill' for £254 10s 9d.

At the time of the trial Strutt was 'unprepared to prove any special Damage (as indeed he must be on account of the Great Caution and Secrecy with which the Def[endan]t had carried on his business) he received nominal Damages only'. Additional questions were therefore put to John Wilson, whose replies are given:

Quere 1st What will be the proper mode of proceeding in order to recover Compensation from Mr. James for an Infringement of the Patent & the benefit arising to him therefrom? May he not be called upon by Messrs Arkwright & Strutt by Bill in Equity to set forth & discover the Advantages that have accrued to him from the Exercise of the Invention before the Expiration of the Patent? *Ansr* Mr. Strutt in the action brought by him against James recovered a Satisfaction in Damages for the Injury he had sustained by Mr. James's Violation of his Patent as in that action he complained of the whole Injury it was his business to have been prepared to prove it & therefore it will now be taken that he recovered damages for the whole Injury that he sustained by James's Infringement of his Patent & he will not now be permitted, as Tronceive to recover any further Satisfaction against James either at Law or in Equity.

Quere 2d May not Messrs Arkwright & Strutt also call upon the several persons who have been in the actual enjoyment and exercise of Mr. Arkwrights very lucrative Invention for a Considerable time previous to the expiration of the Patent by Bill in Chancery (altho' no action at Law has been Commenced against them) and will not Messrs Arkwright & Strutt be intitled to a satisfaction for such Infringement and an amount of the Profits. Or how else will it be advisable for them to proceed against such persons? *Ansr* I think the proprietor of the Patent when the Infringement of it happened may call for amounts from the persons who infringed it by Bills in Equity though no actions at Law have been previously commenced against them As it seems the Injuries were Committed very much in Secret there is no other way for Messrs. Arkwright & Strutt to obtain an adequate Satisfaction. I rather think that a separate Bill must be filed against each Invader of the Patent & this will make It necessary for the Patentees to Consider whether any Injury they can have sustained just before the Expiration of their Patent can make it worth while to enter upon so extensive a field of Litigation

J. Wilson

Linc Inn 22 Decr 1783

Arkwright and Strutt do not appear to have taken any further action.

Encouraged by his success against James, Arkwright began preparations in the Michaelmas vacation of 1783 to recover the carding patent that had been lost in the Mordaunt affair two years earlier. His choice of defendant was his nearest neighbour, Peter Nightingale of Lea,[59] a former High Sheriff of Derbyshire, landowner, lead merchant and one of the proprietors of Cromford Sough. The great-uncle of Florence Nightingale, this eccentric sporting squire, known throughout the county as 'Mad Peter Nightingale', had gained notoriety as a dare-devil horseman, a rider in midnight steeplechases and a layer of wagers, given to hard drinking and low company.[60] This was not the only friction with Arkwright; towards the end of 1783, while getting labour together for his newly built mill, Nightingale was accused of 'seducing and employing a Manufac-turer'[61] from Cromford and at Matlock Bath was ordered to pay twenty guineas in damages and costs.

Before this latter case came on Arkwright had invited George Goodwin, attorney, of Winster, to Cromford to discuss Nightingale's alleged infringment, a consulation for which Goodwin's fee was 10s 6d. Preparations continued throughout the whole of 1784. In the Hilary term Baldwin and John Wilson were commissioned and on 16 March, upon being summoned to Cromford, Goodwin was 'Order'd . . . to go to London', where early in April he discussed with 'Mr Moore of the Adelphi, Mr Lawson[62] & others respecting the Cause'. This London visit cost Arkwright eighteen guineas plus a further seven guineas for 'Coach-hire up and down'.

On 15 and 22 April Goodwin was again at Cromford, while visits on 26 and 30 April were followed by his calling on Nightingale 'at the Lea & the Mill'. After further consultations with Arkwright in May little is recorded until 11 November, when Goodwin was instructed to give notice of the trial.

In January 1785 events began to move rapidly. On the 5th Arkwright called in Thomas Ince to advise 'as to many Particulars respecting this Cause . . . & on several other matters'. The next day Goodwin was told he was to be assisted by Ince, who was soon at work examining the briefs and other papers relating to the Mordaunt trial. On the 10th Goodwin visited him at Wirksworth to discuss matters concerning the forthcoming trial.

Notes from Arkwright compelled Ince's attendance at Cromford on 14 and 15 January, and two days later both he and Goodwin spent the greater part of the day there, it then being 'determined to give Notice of the Tryal for the Sittings after the Hilary Term'. Goodwin, it was decided, should retain Mr Serjeant Adair,[63] a supporter of John Wilkes in 1770 and Recorder of London since 1779, while Ince was to draw up 'a full state' of Arkwright's case to form a part of Adair's brief (eleven sheets £3 13s 4d; fair copy, £1 7s 6d). But no sooner had Ince left Cromford than Arkwright sent a messenger asking him to return the following day, when he was 'directed ... to wait on D' Darwin on the Business'.

On 24 January, Arkwright being away in London, the younger Arkwright called upon Ince and with him read over the case before going on to Cromford in order to meet Darwin. Darwin, however, was otherwise engaged but agreed to meet Ince at one o'clock the next day to discuss 'Objections made to the specification and the Answers to such Objections'. It was about this meeting and of his views on the Mordaunt trial that Darwin wrote to Matthew Boulton from Derby on 26 January:

> I was desired lately to look at the specification of M.ʳ Arkwright's patent, about which He had a trial last year [a mistake for 1781]; & it was in my opinion unjustly given against him. He has made many improvements in the machine since, all which I am master of, & could make more improvements myself in respect to diminishing the friction — but the essential parts of the machine are described in the specification in my opinion.
>
> Now if patents are to be so easily overthrown — does your patent or act of parliament stand on firm foundation? — suppose one should say, you have not mentioned your working your piston *in oil*; & if any one should copy your machine, & working their piston with oil, should say, your specification was not similar to your machine; & therefore would infringe it? would this be just?[64]

Four days later Arkwright, now back from London, sent for Ince, who the following day went over the case with both of the Arkwrights and with Goodwin. It was then agreed that Ince and Goodwin should leave for London on 2 February and that in the meantime the younger Arkwright should travel to Yorkshire to consult the Rev. John Michell, FRS a contemporary of Darwin at Cambridge (where in 1762 he had been appointed Woodwardian Professor of Geology) but now rector of Thornhill, near Wakefield.[65] A friend of Joseph Priestley and a close associate of the founders of the Lunar Society, he was well known for his researches in magnetism, optics and astronomy. Arkwright took with him material as to the sufficiency of the specification; his mission, no doubt, was to seek Michell's opinion regarding its adequacy and if possible to persuade him to give evidence at the trial.

Ince and Goodwin (who had taken with them to London a 'Copy of Gurneys short hand Notes of the 1st Trial & a Book') were joined there by the remainder of Arkwright's party, accommodation for whom had been arranged at the Swan Tavern, Feathers Tavern, Crown and Anchor, Clement's Coffee

House and at two private houses at a total cost of £31 14s.

The case was fought out in the Court of Common Pleas before Lord Loughborough on 17 February 1785. Arkwright's case was led by Adair, assisted by Wilson, Chambré, Baldwin and John Anstruther,[66] an active supporter of Charles James Fox and one of the managers of the impeachment of Warren Hastings. Nightingale's counsel were Edward Bearcroft [67] and Thomas Erskine,[68] a future Lord Chancellor.

Like that against Mordaunt, the trial turned entirely on the sufficiency of the patent. The question of the originality of the inventions which Arkwright claimed as his own was yet to come. Witnesses were called by Adair to prove that they had actually made from the specification and its accompanying drawings one or more of the parts that together went to make up the carding patent. Other Arkwright witnesses testified that they believed it possible for any competent and well instructed mechanic to do so. Altogether prosecution and defence called upon twenty-two witnesses.

Adair opened with a eulogy of his client:

> I have no doubt that the name of Mr. Arkwright is well known to every man who hears me; I need say no more of him, than in one word, that he is not only one of the most ingenious mechanics that this or any other country has produced; but, which is more material to this country, he has been one of the most useful mechanics, and inventors, and one of the greatest improvers of the manufacturers of this country, that this country has ever known ... He is the inventor of several of the most ingenious and most useful machines, and in particular, I believe I may venture to say, that he is the most indisputable inventor, (I have never yet heard that point brought into question) of the very ingenious and useful machine, which you will presently see, and have explained to you; and which is the subject of the present action ... It is well known, that all the most useful discoveries that have been made in every branch of arts and manufactures, have not been made by speculative philosophers in their closets; but by ingenious mechanics, conver-sant in the practices in use in their time, and practically acquainted with the subject matter of those discoveries.[69]

At the Mordaunt trial, Adair went on to contend, neither Arkwright's distinguished counsel nor the 'ingenious mechanics' called as witnesses had understood 'the real question to be tried; because the objections came by surprize upon the parties'. The principles of the machines in use before the patent had been taken out had not been explained, and further confusion had arisen with the display in court of a model which did not correspond to the drawings and specification owing to the inclusion of several improvements made since 1775 by Arkwright as well as by those who had infringed his patent. To make these points clear, three models were now to be put on view: the machine in use before the patent, a model made exactly to the specification, and the improved machine, although this was 'only a more finished way of making the same thing, and of producing the same effect'.

Among those who testified that the machine could be made from the specification and drawings alone were such distinguished witnesses as James Watt, Erasmus Darwin and Samuel More (whose evidence in 1781 — 'In the former trial, I considered myself as strictly bound to the *form* of the machine only' — must have done much to bring in a verdict in favour of Mordaunt).

James Watt, an early Arkwright witness to go into the box, was introduced by Baldwin as follows: 'Though the gentlemen of the jury may not know you, sir, I do. I believe you are the gentleman that made some improvements upon the fire-engines'. The key to Watt's evidence, guarded in the extreme, is well illustrated by his reply to Baldwin's final question:

> If you had had the old machine before you, and knew the manner of working it, could you, from that specification and description, have made, or directed to be made, a machine that would have answered the purpose?[70]
>
> I beg [answered Watt] to explain, before I answer that question. It was necessary also I should have known the methods Mr. Arkwright practiced in his spinning, which were then publicly known, as I understood; when I understood the nature of them perfectly, I think I might have made it out; but I deliver this as a matter of opinion, and desire it may be understood so.

And again when cross-examined by Erskine:

Q If you had been the inventor of that particular machine, with the improvements which have been stated, and which are the subject of that specification, could not you, with the greatest ease, have described it so as to have avoided all that puzzle we now have? Could not you have described it so that it would have been easy for any mechanic to make it?

A I could have done it, but I might have failed on some other side. I think I could have described it better.

Q There is no difficulty in describing it better?

A I don't know that; because, in describing any machine of that kind, the things necessary to be described are the parts that are new. People are supposed to know the things that are old, or else they are not masters of their business. I have told you that piece-meal I understood this thing; but I can't say what I should have done if I had been describing it, possibly I might have described only the new parts, and mentioned the old, or I might have described the whole together; but I think I could have described it better.

This sort of evidence was hardly decisive. One wonders if Arkwright begrudged Watt the £42 he received in expenses.

Dr Darwin, whose speech impediment gave the court some trouble, was familiar with both the old and the new machines. He testified that he would 'not have had the least difficulty' in directing the construction of the machine from the specification and the drawing even had he never visited Cromford.

Darwin ('I am so used to machinery'), who was to spend so much time with Arkwright and his advisers over the patent issue, received expenses in this instance of £137 10s.[71]

The reason why Arkwright's attorney was so anxious to consult Richard March about the sufficiency of the specification and to have March's own specification to hand at the James trial became apparent towards the end of Bearcroft's cross-examination of Darwin. The outcome of Darwin's evidence, Bearcroft contended, was that Arkwright had specified 'a new and meritorious invention, the application of which to an old machine, in the letters patent, they have not described in that way at all ... I have known that objections lead to a nonsuit.' But Lord Loughborough would have none of it: 'I have known it over-ruled. In all the oilet hole work that there were patents for the machines are additions to the old stocking frame, and they are not so described ... there was no reference to the old machine.' And, not unexpectedly he was supported in this by Adair: 'I can speak of that with certain recollection; and the same was the case in Marsh's patent two years ago.'[72]

Samuel More, who claimed, 'no man in this kingdom, I believe, is so often consulted upon matters of patent as I am, who gets nothing by it', recalled that in 1781 he had been told by Erskine that he was to compare the improved machine then displayed in court, and which he had first seen the previous day, with the drawing and specification. He had said then as he did now that he could not do it. But, he went on, had he then been acquainted with the machine in use before Arkwright's patent he could with the aid of the drawing and description have instructed an 'ingenious working mechanic' to make a machine inside a week: 'It might not perhaps have accorded exactly in form with the machine that we were intending to imitate and make; but I do really believe that, with due application, such a machine might have been made.' It was, in short, a matter of 'whether patents are granted for *principle* or for *form*'.

Another witness who had given evidence on Mordaunt's behalf was Alexander Cummings, FRS, a native of Edinburgh, who after having served his apprenticeship as a watchmaker made a great reputation in Bond Street, London. Like More he had, in 1781, felt himself 'not authorised to derive any information from any thing else, than the specification', from which he believed the machine displayed in court to be a separate and distinct invention and not an addition to the specification. Cross-examined by Adair as to whether he considered it impossible for any man with a knowledge of the former machine and specification to construct the model then on display, his reply might almost have come from Watt: 'That is a question I am not competent to answer; a thing may be seen clear by another person, that I do not see.'

Further evidence unfavourable to Arkwright was given by another FRS, William Harrison, the son of John Harrison, inventor of the marine chronometer. It was later to come out that by strange coincidence Erskine had sailed as a midshipman on HMS *Tartar* from Scotland for Barbados in March 1764, when the Harrisons were also on board testing the marine chronometer.[73] Harrison now testified that from his knowledge of the old machine and the specification and drawings he could not have made the new machine and, further, that from the specification 'It does not appear to me that the secret was intended to be disclosed.'

Amongst the most interesting of Arkwright's witnesses was Charles Wilkinson, who said that although he was not a 'practical mechanic' Arkwright had asked him to draw up and to describe the specification, a task which had taken him 'the greatest part of two days'. At the time Arkwright had produced the crank and roving box 'and perhaps more parts' and had made sketches of the cylinder and other sections. The remainder of the work he had completed with the aid of Arkwright's verbal descriptions 'and by the help of little sketches he made'. He had, he maintained, no instruction 'to obscure or render any thing difficult to be found out', indeed, 'very far from it'. Wilkinson, who 'frequently had access to Mr. Arkwright's works', was 'pretty certain' that he could have constructed the machine from the specification had he had the old machine before him and seen it worked. This evidence was in part controverted by W. D. Crofts,[74] who as clerk to Francis Evans, a Nottingham attorney, had been employed by Arkwright to write the formal part of the specification after the drawings had been prepared by Wilkinson. At the time, Crofts recalled:

> I observed to him that it was not specified so perfectly as I thought it might have been, from the opinion I had of Mr. Evans, as a draftsman, they [the various parts] not being connected together as a machine; and Mr. Arkwright said, he looked upon the specifications rather as a matter of form, and that for some time past, they had not specified them so perfectly as they should do, and for this reason, that, in his opinion, the invention might be taken abroad, as the specifications were not locked up; and that he wished it to appear as obscure as the nature of the case would admit, and he did not doubt but that it was sufficient to answer his purpose.[75]

The case against Arkwright is, however, perhaps best summarised in the sharp responses of Joshua Wrigley,[76] a Manchester millwright, to questions put to him by Bearcroft:

Q Then from your knowledge of the old machine and that specification, could you, taking due pains, and setting about, make the new machine?
A No, not from that.
Q It is not sufficiently described?
A It is not.
Q Is it easy to describe it sufficiently?
A Yes.
Q Could you, now you do see it, sit down and describe it easily on paper?

A I could.

Q Are you of opinion, reading that description as a man of skill, that Mr. Arkwright meant to describe it sufficiently?

A No, he might have given a better description a great deal.

Arkwright's trump card turned out to be those five of his witnesses each of whom testified that he had actually built the machine from the drawings and specification. One of the earliest to have done this was Thomas Wood, who had first seen the drawings and description 'as much as eight years ago' and had made the machines in 1782 or 1783. It was not, he said, until September 1784 that he had visited Arkwright's mill.

Samuel Wise[77] testified that Arkwright had called upon him on 23 December 1784, had asked him to make a model and that a workman following the specification had done so inside three weeks. This machine 'produced the work extremely well'. Wise's sole knowledge of the Cromford mills had been obtained 'About 8 or 10 years ago, I was at Matlock and I prevailed, with some difficulty, upon Mr. Arkwright to let me see his works there. He took me through a room hastily. I saw the spinning cotton, and the carding; but I had such a cursory view, that I could not from that have done any thing.'

John Stead, a Quaker who had served his apprenticeship as a millwright and was now an engineer at Birmingham, testified that about three and a half years earlier he had seen Arkwright's drawings but not his specification. The 'drawing was put in my hand' by John Watson of Bromsgrove, whose 'cotton works at that time ... did not succeed so well as he could wish' and who had asked him 'to evade the patent to endeavour to steer clear of it'. In accordance with Watson's wishes Stead had made a part of the machine but had not gone further by the time Watson 'agreed with Richard Arkwright for a licence to make his mill ... so he did not wish for my farther services'.[78]

Arkwright had told Watt of the agreement in a letter of 'Sunday morning Jany 30th 1785':

Mr. Arkwright's Compts to Mr. Watt, is very Sorry he was prevented waiting on him yesterday afternoon, by some unforeseen Engagement & being under the necessity of going off for London this morning prevents his waiting upon him again as he intended, has sent him 10£ to defray any Expence he may be at on my acct. & will settle any thing further with him when have the pleasr. of seeing him again. R. A. has spoke to Mr. Watson, who will shew him any thing that is necessary at Bromsgrove & as R. A. intends being at Cromford on Saturday or Sunday next, would be much obliged to Mr. Watt after he returns from Bromsgrove if he would meet him with a Letter with his Sentiments & remarks.

please to direct for R. A.

Cromford
near Wirksworth
(private) —— Derbyshire[79]

this private prevents it being opened by my Servts.

Stead, who had 'no doubt' that from the specification he could have given directions for making the new machine, said that he had met Arkwright for the first time in London six weeks before the trial and had been told that he was likely to be subpoenaed, now approached William Allen, a turner and model maker of Birmingham, and William Whitmore, a clock and watch tool maker, to make from Arkwright's drawings and specification models of his machine. This they swore they had done without further assistance inside two and three weeks respectively.

Erskine, not a little disturbed by this kind of evidence, repeatedly pressed the verbally hesitant Whitmore to describe the working of his model. This brought interjections from Samuel More ('I know this man to be a very ingenious mechanic') and from Lord Loughborough:

> If he cannot describe it, the consequence will be that the man can't speak, not that he can't work.
>
> *Erskine.* I think that it will go to the credit of the witness.
>
> *Lord Loughborough.* Not the least in the world, he never undertook to make an argument; a description, or a speech, would cost him much more trouble than to make a machine, the ablest mechanic that I believe the country ever produced, that is Mr. Brindley, to my certain knowledge never could explain any thing.

And at the end of the evidence for Arkwright Stead's further examination about his instructions to Whitmore again drew comment from Lord Loughborough:

> Mr. Bearcroft, will any number of witnesses prove that the machine cannot be made from the specification; I fancy you was not aware of this evidene, that it has been made from the specification.

The evidence of those five witnesses formed the crux and the conclusion of Lord Loughborough's summing up:

> Gentlemen, having stated the whole of the evidence, as it was my duty to do, upon a cause of great expectation, and as I am told, of considerable importance ... I cannot help concluding with saying it is one of those causes, that I have had the opportunity of trying lately, that turns upon the shortest point; there is no matter of argument in it, there is no reasoning, it is simply thus, Whether you believe five witnesses who have sworn to a positive fact, for it is undoubtedly true, there is no palliating it, that if their testimony does not obtain effect with you, it can only be upon a supposition that they are every one of them perjured;

because the reasoning is only this, that that which five men have done is possible to be done; that is the only proposition in reason, which no man can make a dispute about; therefore the only question for your consideration is, Whether these five men have made the machine; the evidence you have of that is, that each of them come and positively swear they have done it, and if they have not done it from such information as they state themselves to have received, they are each of them perjured; therefore the single question is, Whether you believe these five persons are perjured, or that they speak the truth; according as you are of opinion, one way or the other, you will find your verdict for the plaintiff or for the defendant.

The trial, which had lasted from eleven in the morning until nine at night, ended abruptly when the jury, without leaving the court, brought in a verdict for Arkwright, who was awarded the 1s damages for which he had asked.[80] Altogether the proceedings had cost him £1,049 3s 8d (£946 8s 4d of which was owing to Goodwin and the remainder to Ince). This was, indeed, a remarkable sum if, as was suspected at the time, the trial was in some way collusive.

The verdict obtained, Arkwright returned to Derbyshire and shortly afterwards (26 and 27 February) visited Howarth & Peel's mill at Burton on Trent with Goodwin who on 28 February called at Lums mills, Matlock, 'to give Notice to the Proprietors of the Cotton Mills there not to work'. Goodwin then went on to Cromford 'to draw Case, Advertizements &c.'. The same day Ince was with Arkwright:

Attending at Cromford this Day by your Desire to consider the Propriety of advertising in the Publick Prints that you were willing to agree with Persons for the Priviledge to use your Machines & also to consider settle a Case for Serjt Adairs Opinion & Directions as to the Proceedings against such as refused to agree & persisted in making use of your Machines.

On 3 March Goodwin was again at Cromford '& from thence to discharge Mr. Bradley [of Mayfield, near Ashbourne][81] & others from working with Patent Machines'. After four more consultations with Arkwright he was at Cromford 'all day' on 6 April, when, Ince noted, 'Mr Goodwin recd Serjt Adairs Opinion on your Cause attendg you & Mr Goodwin ... on the subject.'

On 12 April, after yet another visit to Cromford, Goodwin went on to Nightingale's mill, a journey perhaps not unconnected with Ince's note of 25 April: 'Attending you [Arkwright] & Mr Goodwin at Cromford when you determined to file a Bill for an Injunction against Mr Nightingale & Mr Goodwin & myself prepared Instructions for such a Bill.' And it was about this time that Ince was busy 'Drawing the several Different fforms of Articles as prepared by Mr Goodwin for sale of machines to the several Persons with whom you had agreed in order that the same might not interfere with the Terms of the Patent.' Arkwright's charges, the regained patent having almost five years still to run, were said to be 'at the Rate of 5s. per Spindle per Annum[82] ... if they confine themselves [to spinning] by the Day, and 5s. more if by Night'.[83]

NOTES

1 Page 183.
2 *The Case of Richard Arkwright and Company*, 1782, pp. 2–3.
3 For a full account of the affairs of Gardom Pares & Co. see Miss M. H. Mackenzie, 'Calver Mill and its owners', *D.A.J.*, LXXXIII, 1963, and LXXXIV, 1964.
4 A.F. MSS.
5 Signed also by John Dunning.
6 A.F. MSS.
7 They had by this time paid out £2,000 for the use of the water frame, a further £5,000 for that of the carding machine, and also an unknown sum as 'the Penalty on Account of the Extra Hours' (that is, for spinning beyond an agreed amount). See also Fitton and Wadsworth, pp. 93–4, and House of Lords Papers, 1781–82 to 1786.
8 D.P.L., Pares MSS., Thomas Pares to his son Thomas, 31 May 1783.
9 Alexander Bossley, attorney, of Bakewell (*Bailey's Northern Directory*, 1781).
10 *An Impartial Representation of the Case of the Poor Cotton Spinners in Lancashire*, 1780, p. 2.
11 *House of Commons Papers of the Eighteenth Century*, LI, p. 17.
12 Arkwright's Scottish patent is recorded in the Register of the Great Seal, Scottish R.O., C3/20 No. 101, dated 31 May 1771. Until the Patent Law Amendment Act, 1852, separate patents were issued under the Great Seals for each of the three kingdoms of England, Scotland and Ireland. See State Paper Office, Dublin Castle, OP 884/5, 'A list of patents issued between 1696 and 1814', which contains a reference to a patent granted to Richard Arkwright on 23 January 1772 for a machine for making yarn from cotton, flax or wool.
13 *Manchester Mercury*, 13–20 February 1781; *Derby Mercury*, 2 March 1781.
14 *Manchester Mecury*, 3 March 1781.
15 *Machester Mercury*, 20 March 1781.
16 A.F. MSS.
17 *English Law Reports*, Index 178, Jn. Barnet, Bentley Brooke, Wm. Clegg, Robert Ellison & Relp Whitehead, Thomas Leemin, Jn Taylor & Joseph Smith, Jn Whitehead and Jn. Phillips.
18 *Manchester Mercury*, 14 May 1805, 'Store containing large quantity of timber belonging to Mr. Leeming, machine-maker, Bury St., Salford, a fire'.
19 John Philips was a member of the Committee of Trade in Manchester, along with (among others) Daniel Whittaker. *Manchester Mercury*, 7 May 1782.
20 L.G., 1794, p. 207.
21 MP for Horsham and Attorney General.
22 G.M., 1783, p. 717, 'his wit always at command ... His industry and zeal for the interest of his clients were equal to his abilities, and in cases where the fees were small, he was never known to show less ardour than when they were considerable.'
23 Baines, *Cotton Manufacture*, p. 162 n.
24 F. Elrington Hall, *The Judges in Ireland, 1221–1421*, II, London, 1926, pp. 164, 218. Hamilton was 'a promoter of the material resources of Ireland, especially near his own seat at Balbriggen ... appointed a baron of the Exchequer, 1776; ... resided in Dublin ... and in county Dublin at Hampton Hall, near Balbriggen; died at Oswestry 1793.
25 *Manchester Mercury*, 25 January and 5 February 1791.

26 Guest, *Compendious History*, pp. 104–5, 129, 206.
27 Historical Manuscripts Commission, Rutland MSS iii (1894), 58. For Mordaunt see Fitton and Wadsworth, p. 83.
28 *Derby Mercury*, 19 July 1781; *Manchester Mercury* 24 July 1781.
29 *S.F.*, pp. 22–3.
30 24 July 1781.
31 B. & W. MSS.
32 M.C.R.L., MF 902, for microfilm copy of material in the Special Collections, Columbia University Library. *The Case of Richard Arkwright and Company*, 1782.
33 *C.J.*, XXXVIII, pp. 687, 865, 882.
34 Special Collections, Columbia Univesity.
35 *Manchester Mercury*, 12 February 1782.
36 *Manchester Mercury*, 7 May 1782.
37 *Manchester Mercury*, 31 December 1782.
38 W. H. Chaloner introduces the letter in *Bulletin of the John Rylands Library*, XLVIII, 1965.
39 *C.J.*, XXXIX, p. 147.
40 *Mancheser Mercury*, 11, 18, 25 February 1783.
41 *C.J.*, XXXIX, pp. 147–8, 158, 263–4, 269, 280.
42 G. W. Daniels, *The Early English Cotton Industry*, Manchester, 1920, p. 103.
43 *D.N.B.*; *G.M.*, 1793, p. 965; like Chambré, buried at Kendal.
44 On Evans and Middlemore see *G.M.*, 1815, p. 381.
45 Taplow *L.G.*, 10–13 March, 18–22 September, 6–9 October 1781, 6–8 January 1782, 10–13 January 1784. *Manchester Mercury*, 24 September, 8 October 1782.
46 *G.M.*, 1821, p. 572.
47 *G.M.*, 1813, pp. 406, 703.
48 *Manchester Mercury*, 31 December 1781, 14 January 1783.
49 Brother of Ichabod Wright.
50 Thomas Bell, joiner, mentioned in 1772 in Arkwright's letter.
51 *G.M.*, 1786, p. 1002.
52 *G.M.*, 1783, p. 453.
53 *D.N.B.*
54 *G.M.*, 1798, p. 815.
55 *G.M.*, 1790, p. 372.
56 G. E. Mercer, 'Mr. More of the Adelphi', *Journal of the Royal Society of Arts*, 1979; *Transactions of Society of Arts* XVIII, 1800, p. viii; *Times*, 22 October 1799; *G.M.*, 1799, p. 909.
57 Details of patents and business, *House of Lords Papers*, 1781–82 *to* 1786, pp. 82–6.
58 *G.M.*, 1795, p. 621. Only son of John Jortin, DD, (1698–1776), ecclesiastical historical critic and editor of his father's posthumous sermons. He had a very considerably practice in the Court of Exchequer as one of the principal clerks. He married Louisa, daughter of Dr. Maty, who was Principal Librarian of the British Museum. Roger Jortin died 9 July 1795.
59 *Bailey's Northern Directory*, 1781; *Derby Mercury*, 18 November 1784, 3 May 1792.
60 Cecil Woodham-Smith, *Florence Nightingale*, 1820–1910, London, 1950, p. 4.
61 *Manchester Mercury*, 1 June 1784. The manufacturer was probably Benjamin Pearson, who, according to *S.F.*, p. 34, had worked for Arkwright for some seven years up to 1782, and whose partnership with Nightingale ended on 28 March 1785. *L.G.*, 1785, p. 179.
62 Probably William Lawson, attorney, of 5 Holborn Court, Gray's Inn; died 20 June 1800 (*G.M.*, 1800, p. 596).
63 *G.M.*, 1798, pp. 720–1.
64 B. & W. MSS.
65 Musson and Robinson, *Science and Technology*, p. 158.

66 Later Sir John (*G.M.*, 1811, p. 683).

67 M. P. Hinden, 'respectable veteran of the Bar' (*G.M.*, 1796, p. 972).

68 A future Lord Chancellor (*G.M.*, 1823, pp. 553–8).

69 Musson and Robinson, *Science and Technology*, p. 81 n. 2, write that Adair's view may be contrasted with that of the defending counsel in the Tennant bleaching patent case of 1802, that 'most of these discoveries arise from scientific men engaging in them, for the purpose of science and speculation in their closet'. *Richard Arkwright, Esquire; Versus Peter Nightingale, Esquire. Proceedings on the Trial of this Cause*, 1785 (henceforth *Nightingale*).

70 All quotations in this section (except where stated) are from *Nightingale*.

71 A. F. MSS.

72 Morris against Branson. An action for the infringement of Morris's patent of 1764 for a machine with a set of working needles to be applied to a stocking frame for making oilet holes. Tried at Westminster after Easter term 1776 before Lord Mansfield; verdict for the patentee. P.P. 1829 (332) III, *Select Committee on the Law relative to Patents for Inventions*, p. 183. For an earlier Morris trial see Fitton and Wadsworth, pp. 43, 46.

73 *S.F.*, p. 92.

74 For Crofts see *G.M.*, 1810, p. 500.

75 'answer his purpose'. See also *S.F.*, pp. 74–5. Espinasse, *Lancashire Worthies*, I, p. 437, writes, 'Croft's evidence would have been corroborated had Nightingale's counsel been allowed to "put in" and to read published *case* in which somewhat the same admission was made by Arkwright himself'. But they were baffled in the attempt by a legal technicality.

76 For further information about Wrigley (sometimes spelt Rickley or Rigley) see Musson and Robinson, *Science and Technology*, pp. 396–406, 443–5.

77 Samuel Wise, musician, of the town and county of Nottingham, had taken out patent No. 897 (14 March 1768), a machine or engine for raising water out of mines and wells, and for draining lands, and patent No 925 (11 May 1769), a machine which, it was claimed, when fixed to a stocking frame, would make any sort of work usually manufactured on such frames.

78 For their expenses at the trial John Stead and Thomas Wood respectively received £52 10s and £21. For their expenses in London and for making models William Allen received £21 and £15 15s, William Whitmore £21 and £21 and Samuel Wise £23 12s 6d and £12 12s.

79 B. & W. MSS, Arkwright to Watt, 30 January 1785.

80 *Derby Mercury*, 24 February 1785; *Manchester Mercury*, 1 March 1785.

81 S. D. Chapman, *The Early Factory Masters*, Newton Abbot, 1967, p. 232.

82 *House of Commons Papers*, LI, p. 43.

83 *House of Lords Papers*, 1781–82, *to* 1786, p. 243, for evidence of Joseph Smith, 'A Callicoe Manufacturer & Printer. (S. D. Chapman, 'The Peels in the early English cotton industry,' *Business History*, XI, 1969, p. 65 n. 1, says Joseph Smith was a London partner of Livesey Hargreaves & Co., calico printers, until their bankruptcy in 1788.)

CHAPTER V

The great patent trials:
Rex v. Arkwright

ARKWRIGHT'S PLAN to sell his machines under whatever 'fforms of Articles' was short-lived. His victory over Nightingale interfered with so many vested interests that it was bound to be contested. Predictably, the Lancashire spinners soon rallied, and combined to oppose him in larger numbers and in greater strength than ever before. To the Manchester men it was a matter of the greatest consequence that the judgement for Mordaunt had been reversed, for, as the *Manchester Mercury* of 1 March 1785 put it:

> this great Manufactory, the Envy of *Europe*, will in a great degree lay at the Mercy of one Man, who has already received by far, greater Emoluments than any Individual, or any united Body of Discoverers ever did ... During almost four Year's Liberation from the destructive Monopoly, the Cotton Manufactory has flourished to an extent beyond Example, many Individuals having erected large Works at a very great Expence during that Period, which increased the Supply of Manufacturers, and enabled them, by obvious means, to extend their Manufactures to a great degree, inasmuch as to become an object of Taxation to the Minister. But now having fallen again under the Monopoly, if not publicly relieved, the Trade must emigrate more than gradually to Ireland, Scotland, and other Countries, the fatal Consequences of which need not be explained.

Since 1781, when the use of the inventions that together had gone to make up the carding patent had been thrown open to all, an estimated £300,000 had been invested in buildings and Arkwright machines, an industry which provided employment for some 30,000 men, women and children. All those manufactuers who wanted to keep their mills running would now have to become Arkwright licensees at whatever price he decided to charge. No effort or cost could be too high to avert such a disaster. The Manchester spinners determined to attack the patent on all possible grounds, and successfully applied for a writ of *scire facias*[1] to have the verdict annulled. So began the case of Rex *v.* Arkwright.

Arkwright was not slow to respond. 'Agent attend you in Town [on your] being Served wth Scire Facias,' Goodwin recorded, and the agent at once went on to the Petty Bag Office to make a search. On 24 April Goodwin was summoned to Cromford to discuss the new situation, and was joined there by

Ince the following day. The outcome was that a copy of the *scire facias* was sent to Baldwin 'on settling plea' and shortly afterwards another copy was sent to Chambré, whom Baldwin had asked to consult.

Goodwin visited Arkwright on 25 and 30 May, and on the latter occasion went on to Wirksworth to talk matters over with Ince. A point raised, it seems, was the desirability of having Gurney's notes of the Nightingale trial printed, for by 2 June Arkwright had directed Ince to send them to Dr Darwin, 'requesting him to correct the Press at Derby'. Dispatch, at a cost of 3s 4d, was by the hand of a 'special Messenger ... who waited all Night Dr. Darwin being out'. Two days later Ince, acting on Arkwright's instructions, went to Derby 'to confer with Dr. Darwin respecting the Cause & to give Directions about the Printing of Gurneys Notes'. Notice of the trial having been given for 16 June, Arkwright spent the whole of 5 June consulting Goodwin and Ince. Letters were sent off to several witnesses requesting their attendance at the trial, and it was then agreed that both attorneys should set out for London on Wednesday 8 June. (For his twenty-day stay Ince was to charge £42, while 'Chaise-hire and Expences to London' for himself and Goodwin cost Ark-wright a further £10 12s 6d.)

The great trial, which was to have important implications for the patent law, came on in the Court of King's Bench in Westminster Hall before Mr Justice Buller and a special jury on Saturday 25 June 1785, little more than four months after the verdict in the Common Pleas. The case for the Crown was led by Mr Edward Bearcroft, who was assisted by John Lee, Thomas Erskine, Mr Serjeant Bolton and Mr (later Sir) George Wood. Mr Serjeant Adair again led for Arkwright, assisted, as in the Common Pleas, by Wilson, Chambré, Baldwin and Anstruther. Also retained was forty-one-year-old Thomas Cowper, who two years later was to be elected Recorder of Chester.

In his opening address for the Crown, Bearcroft ('a case of greater impor-tance, of greater value to the individuals disputing it, and to the public in general, was never yet tried in this or any other Court') launched a powerful and wide-ranging attack on the validity of the 1775 patent. The first and most serious objection, 'not to the parties, but to the public', was that the patent 'is prejudicial and inconvenient to the public in general', in that 'if this patent remains good in point of law, it prevents every individual from the preparation of cotton for all the cotton manufactures of this country'. It was an objection the judge refused to allow, on the ground that the 'issue should not be in general terms, prejudicial to the country, but you should state how? and then the party comes prepared to answer it'. But this was only the start of the assault.

This time the attack was launched not only on the insufficiency, obscurity and mystifying nature of the several parts of the patent specification (the sole issue on which the Mordaunt and Nightingale verdicts had been reached); it was also contended that the roving operation patented in 1775 was merely a repetition of the spinning process patented in 1769, Arkwright's exclusive right to which had lapsed with the expiry of his first patent in 1783. Allied to this was Bearcroft's contention that the remainder of the processes making up the carding patent had been invented or used by others before 1775. Further, Arkwright's claim to be the inventor of the machine for which he had obtained the 1769 patent was disputed. He had, the Crown asserted, stolen the roller-spinning invention from Thomas Highs through the agency of Highs's workman John Kay. Finally, the crank and comb which had played so important a part in the Nightingale trial were held to have been the invention of James Hargreaves. In short, not a stone was to be left unturned to quash for good Arkwright's claim to the carding machine.

Early on, Bearcroft had worked in court models of both the 1769 and 1775 patents to demonstrate to the jury the complete process of cotton spinning as it stood when the spinning patent was granted and as it had become six years later under the carding machine, or, rather, the series of machines which prepared the cotton by carding, roved it, and finally turned it into marketable thread. For the spinning machine the cotton had to be carded and roved by hand, at considerable expense, before being spun by the rollers. In the series of machines patented in 1775 the cotton was carded by machinery and roved by the rollers and dependent can, after which another set of rollers with the aid of the spindles made it into yarn.

Before having the old and the new methods of spinning demonstrated Bearcroft addressed the court as to Arkwright's motives for taking out the second patent. His case was misleading, perhaps intentionally so, in implying that Arkwright had obtained his carding patent after the 1769 patent had expired, whereas in fact it then had more than seven years to run:

> Gentlemen, Having given you the idea of the [1769] machine for spinning, and shewn you it will operate to spin either a coarse or a fine thread, I come now to shew you the sort of patent which is in question, and which machine Mr. *Arkwright* does not sell ready made, but gives the permission to use, at a price that produces a princely income into his pocket.
>
> Now the patent for *spinning* expired in *July* 1783; Mr. *Arkwright* therefore had lost a glorious and profitable monopoly. He was, like any other man, unwilling to part with his term and with his profit, because the term was expired, if by any means he could contrive by another kind of ingenuity than that which invents machines, to keep up the enjoyment of that monopoly in another shape. It was not however right or just to do it, and I pledge myself to satisfy you, that such was the idea which Mr. *Arkwright* had in his mind. Upon that idea he took every step in the business, from that moment to this. I will trace his footsteps from time to time all in that line. Because he was unwilling to part with the benefit he was intitled to of fourteen years, he chose to have it as long as he could. Before this cause is at an end, you will see that this was in truth what passed in Mr. *Arkwright's* mind. Then Mr. *Arkwright*, upon the expiration of this patent for

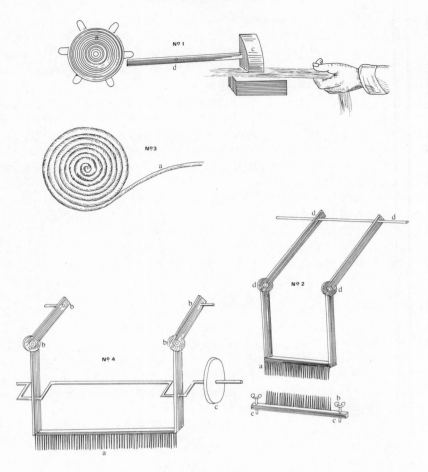

Carding engine patent specification, 1775

The specification (which includes the carding engine among other preparatory machines) in the petition for royal letters patent reads: 'NOW KNOW YE, that I, the said Richard Arkwright, in compliance with the said proviso, do hereby describe and ascertain the nature of my said Invention, and declare that the Plan thereof drawn in the margin of these Presents is composed of the following particulars, (that is to say):- No. 1: a beater or breaker of seeds, husks, &c., and a finer of the flax, hemp, and other articles which are to be prepared for dressing, in which *a* is a wheel with teeth, which, by acting upon a lever, raises the hammer *c*, the lever being movable upon the centre *d*. No. 2: an iron frame with teeth at *a* working against a lower frame with like teeth at *b*; this lower frame is firmly connected to a wooden frame by means of the screws *c, c*. The upper teeth are made to act against the lower by means of the joints *d, d, d, d*. No. 3 is a piece of cloth, with wool, flax, hemp, or any other such materials spread thereon, as at *a*. No. 4 is a crank and a frame of iron with teeth at *a*, being movable at the joints *b, b, b, b*, by means of cranks and by a cord turning the pulley of wheel *c*. This motion of the teeth *a* works them backwards and forwards upon the cylinder No. 5, and dischargeth the cotton,

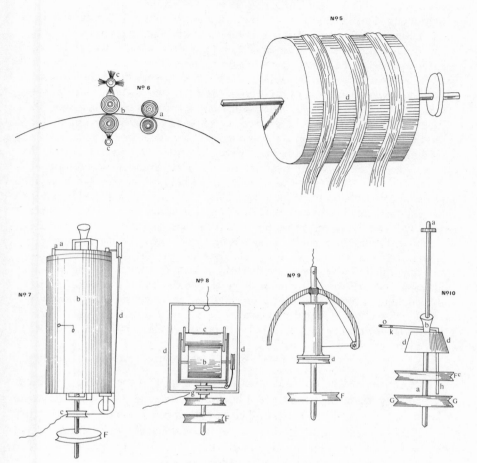

wool, &c. from it at *d*. No. 5 is the last-mentioned cylinder, which hath fillet cards; behind this cylinder No. 3 delivereth its contents upon another cylinder. No. 6 consists of rollers fixed to a wooden frame, the contents of No. 5 being brought to it at *a*, and going through at *b*, produceth it a proper size *f*, *c*, *c*, are brushes for clearing the machine. No. 7, a cylindrical box for twisting the contents of No. 6 at *b*; *a*, *a*, are two rollers, one moving the other, between which the contents of No. 6 passeth into the cylinder *b*; *c* is a dead pulley fixed to the frame; *d* a cord, which, passing from the pulley *c*, moves the rollers *a*, *a*; F, a wheel, the movement of which is brought from F, No. 10, and is fixed to No. 6. No. 8, a machine for twisting the contents of No. 6, in which *d*, *d*, is a frame of iron; *b*, a roller on which a bobbin *c*, is fixed; this is turned the same as No. 7, that is by a dead pulley or wheel fixed to a wooden frame at *g*. No. 9, a spindle and flyer, being fixed to No. 6, for twisting the contents from *b* in No. 6; *d* is pulley under the bobbin, which hath a communication by a band to No. 10 at *d*, *d*, it being a conical or regulating wheel, which moves the bobbin quicker or slower as required. No. 10, a spindle, which being fixed to No. 6 at *a*, worketh No. 7, No. 8, or No. 9, at F, F, F, by the pulley F*c*; *d*, a regulator for No. 9; *b*, a socket having a bolt going through *d*, *d* and F*c* to G, stops or sets the whole going by means of a catch *a*; for the pulley G, G, being loose upon the spindle, *o*, a lever movable about *k*, raiseth or falleth the bolt *h*.'

spinning the fine thread, could no longer in those words enjoy that thing at all: but inasmuch as the cotton manufactory depends upon all the several things that are already stated to you, the *carding*, the *roving*, and the *spinning*; though he had lost the patent for the spinning, if he could contrive to get a patent, and to gull the world to submit to that patent as a new invention for the roving and the carding, it would answer all his purposes; for still he would be in possession of a monopoly of two thirds, and that of the important parts of the spinning. In the name, therefore, he would not have the spinning; but if he got a patent for the carding and the roving, the spinning would follow: in truth, the whole operation would be his, and he would keep possession of it against the world.

Gentlemen, Suppose any two men struggling for a yard which consists of three feet; if Mr. *Arkwright*, with one hand, got hold of one foot, which he is forced to part with, yet contrives to get hold of the other two feet with his other hand, he certainly would have the better hold. I have lost the spinning, says he; but I will contrive to get the carding and the roving, and then I shall keep the spinning. For that purpose, he procures the present patent. What is it for? For spinning? No: that would be too gross. The same word is very apt to describe the same thing; and you will see that Mr. *Arkwright*, both in writing and in drawing this specification has most diligently avoided any words, or any thing that could too plainly strike the imagination, and shew that his new patent was in effect his old one. For the foundation of his new patent, he says 'I have invented machines of great public utility in preparing silk, cotton, flax and wool for spinning.'

What are the preparations for it? What I told you; the carding and roving.

There can indeed be no doubt that the spinning and the roving operations were basically the same, since the application of the rollers to carded cotton to make roving was but a repetition of their application to roving to produce yarn. But whether the new application was sufficient to justify an extension of the patent was secondary to the question as to whether Arkwright could be regarded as the inventor of the rollers, a matter which was to come up later.

Many of the witnesses who had appeared at the Nightingale trial were again examined, only to repeat their evidence. Arkwright's witnesses were, however, cross-examined more rigorously than before, in an attempt to prove that those who had claimed to have made the machinery solely from the specification had nevertheless received some hint or guidance from his friends or agents, while those who earlier had testified that they believed that the machinery could be made from the specification alone were stringently cross-examined in an effort to show that it could not in fact be done without a knowledge of the first patent, in which case the 1775 specification could, of course, be held to be defective.

Each of the ten parts of the carding specification was examined in the Crown's attempt to show that it was the same as in the 1769 patent or had been invented or used by others before 1775 or had been included solely to mislead or confuse and was, therefore, at best useless.

Five of the ten parts fell into the last category. The first, a beating hammer, which John Immison testified was described in the 1773 edition of William Emerson's *Principles of Mechanicks*,[2] was, said Bearcroft, 'never used, and is put in front of the specification for no other purpose but to puzzle and confound ... So it begins; this is the Alpha, and I promise you the Omega will be exactly like it; this is not all, this hammer not only is useless, but I will prove to you, by witnesses, it is mischievous.' And he went on to call Benjamin Pearson, who maintained, 'It would beat the seeds so small, they could not be picked out; it could not be picked clean; the cotton could not work without more expence.' To this Adair could only reply that the patent was not confined to cotton and that the hammer had been intended for the beating of hemp.

Pearson had never seen Arkwright make use of the second part, an iron frame with teeth. Joshua Wrigley had not come across it at all, while Samuel More, cross-examined by Erskine — 'How would you get over No. 2; where have you got a place for that?' — merely replied, 'I have always considered this machine as adopted for spinning of cotton; I don't believe No. 2. was meant to allude to cotton.' Adair countered that 'It was a machine separate and distinct in its nature from the other. It occurred to Mr. *Arkwright*, it might be made useful in drawing out and stretching the fibres of the flax, hemp, and so on, previous to being carded; but the card is afterwards found to answer every purpose intended for that ... and it is not now in use.' But this did not convince Mr Justice Buller: 'If it had nothing to do with the machine, it is very difficult to say, how, with a good motive, it could ever come into the specification or plan.'

Nos. 8, 9 and 10, 'instruments used in spinning', as Bearcroft described them, came under a similar attack. Towards the end of his opening address he had observed:

> You will now be very much surprised to find I have gone through all the specification, and yet you find No. 8, 9, and 10. remain; look at one of those spindles that turn round, that is No. 9, that is no new invention; but No. 9. and 10 are exactly like No. 1. and 2, that is to say, have no relation to the subject, and never were used at all. No. 8. to be perfectly correct, is not used at all, you will have that from the witnesses.

Adair's reply was merely to read out the relevant parts of the specification. The end of the day found Buller in agreement with Bearcroft:

> This is the evidence upon the part of the prosecutor against the specification, and it is material to see a little, how the defendant's counsel endeavour to support him. Here is a specification that states ten different instruments; it is admitted by them, that as to No. 8. it is of no use, and never was made use of by the defendant in his machine. It is also admitted, No. 9. stands exactly in the same situation, as these could not be put into the machine. This is a little extraordinary, for if

he meant to make a fair discovery disclosure why load it thus with things that they make no use of, and which are totally unnecessary? That could answer no purpose but to perplex ... As to No. 10. nothing is said about it for the defendant. First Mr. *Moore* said, it was not difficult to conceive; but there is no witness that says at all what the use of it is — So this seems to stand without any evidence at all.

As to No. 3, the feeder (said by Bearcroft to look 'more like a worm, or a curl, than any thing else. But this is beginning to talk in a dark way, about something that really does belong to the machine'), Adair's first witness, Richard Briddon,[3] asserted that it was as described in the patent. Further, it was not more inconvenient than the old feeder. More admitted that the cylinder roller or axis upon which the feeder turned was not described in the drawing but contended, 'it would very easily have occurred to any man deserving the name of a mechanic, putting a cylinder or a roller in any thing that wants to be rolled up; there don't seem to me to be any great want of ingenuity to describe that'. Watt believed the feeder would work without a roller, but 'It stands to reason, in rolling up a piece of cloth or paper, to take a roller to roll it upon.' Joshua Wrigley, who had seen the feeder used by Arkwright, thought it not properly specified and inferior to the old, which the Crown displayed, as Erskine put it, 'to shew ... the feeder described at No. 3. or rather not described at No. 3. involves in fact no new principle'. John Lees, a Quaker, claimed that he had invented the feeder in the summer of 1772 and that he had never seen Arkwright's used, while Henry Marsland said that Arkwright had seen the feeder in operation at his mill in 1771 or 1772 and had raised no objection. Nor had he after he had obtained the carding patent.

All this, Buller held, went to show that the feeder was 'no new invention' and was 'not invented by the defendant, for this invention is spoken of as used before the time of the patent'.

A vigorous attack was launched on Arkwright's claim to the crank, a device enabling carded cotton to be taken from the cylinder in a continuous sheet. This was almost a point of honour to Bearcroft:

> I ... shall die with the belief of it, [that this] ran away with the verdict in the Common Pleas ... [where] My learned friend shewed the machinery with such skill and address, and performed the operation so well, he tickled the fancy of the jury like so many children, that it was impossible to put them out of love with their plaything to the end of the cause, till they finally decided in its favor.

An important witness for the Crown was Elizabeth, the widow of James Hargreaves, who testified that in 1771 or 1772 her husband, then in partnership with Thomas James, had taken 'a deal of pains' in making a crank. In this he had been assisted by George Whitaker, a smith and frameworker, who when called confirmed that he made one for Hargreaves in 1772: 'he told me he wanted a machine, and he told me the purpose he wanted it for: I set to work with his directions and my own judgment, we set about and made one.' Among 'a great many' he had made in 1773 and 1774 were one for James in September 1773, 'a good many' for James Hudson of Nottingham (the first on 28 May 1774) and three for John Grimshaw, also of Nottingham. Thomas Ragg, Whitaker's former apprentice, said that he had first made cranks in 1773 and that they were in public use before 1775. John Bird, Hargreaves's son-in-law, claimed to have made one of his own in his Nottingham mill in 1773, while Henry Marsland testified that Arkwright 'called upon me very often' and had objected to his using the crank, which 'at that time [1781] I believed to be his, and so I gave it up'.

On the Arkwright side were two of the workmen who had helped him to perfect the carding machine, Thomas Bell and John Hacket. According to Bell the machine had been made 'From time to time, and sometimes it would be pulled all to pieces and new ones supply their places'. Like Hacket, who had known Arkwright for almost fourteen years and who about the beginning of 1772 ('I cannot be quite sure') had been employed in making a crank, he had not then heard of it being already in use. 'Mr. *Arkwright*, in making these discoveries, employed me,' said Hacket. 'I was employed by Mr. *Arkwright* from the first beginning of those machines, for which this was obtained, and in trying experiments from the directions I got from him ... He gave me directions by chalking upon the board sometimes and crooking of lead and wire and things in that shape.' A further witness, Thomas Wood, confessed that he had evaded the crank 'by another method that answered' but 'I think it rather injures the cards worse than the crank does — They don't stand so well.' He had seen no crank before Arkwright's.

Mr Justice Buller's summing up on the crank gave Bearcroft what he wanted: 'Some of the witnesses have proved them made in great numbers, and used in different factories publicly, and they have proved it by the persons who made them. Upon the part of the defendant, the witnesses never having heard of it may be perfectly true, and yet no contradiction to the evidence for the prosecu-tion.'

In that part of the examination relating to No. 5, the fillet cards which enabled the cylinder to give off the cotton in a continuous fleece, the Crown sought to demonstrate that it had been invented before Arkwright had taken out his patent. The first cylinder with fillet cards, claimed Robert Pilkington, had been made in 1770 by Richard Livesay and himself. The story was continued by Thomas Wood, who maintained that in 1773 it had occurred to him that the cylinder might be entirely carded and that at the end of 1774 or the beginning of 1775 he had a full trial of it.

Cross-examined by Adair, Pilkington said that after working the machine privately Wood had obtained a patent in 1776, the year after Arkwright's was granted. It was then that Pilkington, accompanied by William Cockshott

shewed Mr. *Arkwright* our plan and he asked us in what method we meant to keep it a secret, how we designed to proceed upon it, to keep it a secret; we told him that we proposed swearing the hands we employed, that they should keep it a secret, and he told us we might swear them as we pleased, but if any body would give them a penny more they would divulge it, and he advised us it was the best means to get a patent ... because if the country got hold of it, neither we nor he would have any advantage from it.

'A word more as to this conversation with Mr. *Arkwright*; Was this the whole conversation?' Adair went on. And further, 'Do you recollect nothing else material that passed between you and *Arkwright* at the time?'

Q I do not at present?'
A Now I will put you in mind; Do you recollect Mr. *Arkwright* telling you, it was upon the same principle with his invention, and that he would bring an action against you if you used it?
Q He said, if he found we were upon his principle, he should enter an action against us.
A Do you conceive *that*, as an immaterial part of the conversation, or for what reason do you leave it out?
Q I did not recollect it then.
A That was a little unlucky, 'till I put you in mind of it; Now, Sir, did not he repeatedly send persons, in order to see what invention you had and were not his people refused admittance?
Q They were.

Pilkington's use of the filleted cylinder was taken up by Bearcroft in his final address:

It is not in public use, says my learned friend! I don't know what he means by not being in public use; it was used by this man in the presence of *Arkwright*, he used it for the purpose of his trade, it was used in the presence of all his servants that were employed about him, and I should be glad to know whether that is not in public use, if my learned friend did not give some definition or clear line of what was public use, to shew you this was not so. — Oh! says my learned friend, it is clear, that was all stolen from Mr. *Arkwright* — Why? — Because, after Mr. *Arkwright* threatened him, he never suffered Mr. *Arkwright* to come there again, nor would he suffer any strangers or any body else to know what was going forwards. Has it not been proved, that was Mr. *Arkwright's* course, and the course of all the great manufacturers of the kingdom; and if you happen not to know it, I must inform you it is of great importance they should shut up their doors and not admit people, and I wish they would learn to keep all foreigners out of their manufactories; I have heard say that some foreigners of rank have done, what is hardly justifiable, availed themselves of admission conceded to their quality, and carried away the secret of some valuable machines in this country. But the shutting it up, they say is a proof he was afraid of Mr. *Arkwright*. Surely, my friend forgot the conversation between *Pilkington* and Mr. *Arkwright*! It is proved out of Mr. *Arkwright's* own mouth — he said, 'You had better get a patent for it; as to swearing the men, it does not signify a farthing for if they can get a penny more, they will tell any-body.' Have you any doubt, upon the evidence, if Mr. *Arkwright* thought this *Pilkington* was invading his patent, he could not have got some of the various servants that assisted in that operation to have given evidence against him? — That Mr. *Arkwright* can get witnesses to speak out, the whole defence to-day has amply demonstrated.

Gentlemen, what could be the reason that Mr. *Arkwright* did not commence an action against him? Mr. *Arkwright* is ready enough with his actions — God knows he would have brought his action against Mr. *Pilkington*, if he had dared; and the true reason why he did not, was that which appeared in Court to-day, that is, they invented, and were in the exercise and enjoyment of it before him; that is the only and true reason that operated with Mr. *Arkwright*, to prevent his bringing an action.

The Crown also called upon witnesses to show that No. 7, the revolving can, 'an ingenious part of the machinery',[4] had in fact been used by others before 1775. Most spectacular was Benjamin Butler's improbable boast that he had used a similar can as early as 1759. More likely was Neddy Holt's claim to have used a can in 1774, although it turned out to have been made for him by two of Arkwright's former workmen. Small wonder Arkwright told Holt that he was infinging his patent ('because he said it was the same as spinning') and threatened to prosecute if he continued. Another witness, Betty Kennion (formerly Mrs Bickerstaff) testified that until his death in December 1774 her husband had worked for a Mr Binyon at whose factory the can was in use, and in this she was supported by Joseph Wolley, who had been at Binyon's in 1773 or early 1774.

The trial took a dramatic turn with the appearance for the Crown of Thomas Highs and his former workman, John Kay, through whom Arkwright was accused of having stolen Highs's machine for roller spinning.[5] The Crown's aim here was to show not only that Arkwright was not the inventor of the rollers (No. 6) but that in their more important aspects the 1769 and 1775 patents were one and the same.

Examined by Mr Serjeant Bolton for the Crown, Highs claimed, 'I made rollers myself in 1767'. This was 'In the town of *Leigh*. I did not follow the new manufacture; I was only improving myself, as I had a large family at that time, and was not able to follow it. I thought, when I came a little abler, when I could get a friend to assist me, being poor, and having a large family I was not willing and-body should steal it from me.' Two years later, he maintained, he had made rollers similar to those now displayed in court. They had 'fluted work, fluted wood, upon an iron axis; but the other roller was the same, only it was covered with shoe leather, instead of that leather; I am informed it is such as they make shoes of.'

At the outset, Highs recalled, 'I employed one *Kay*, who came from *Warrington*' and 'followed clock-making, at that time ... I employed him to make a small model, with four wheels of wood, to shew the method it was to work in and desired him, at the same time, to make me brass wheels, that would multiply it to about five to one' for the purpose of drawing the thread finer.[6]

Highs now went on to describe a remarkable encounter with Arkwright in Manchester in 1771,[7] when, through Thomas Rothwell[8], a mutual acquaintance of Bolton, they met in the parlour of Widow Deborah Jackson's Windmill Tavern in Deansgate:

> we fell into some conversation about engines; at that time I was making another engine for a gentleman in *Manchester*,[9] that they gave me a premium for. It happended I was there at that time, and Mr. *Arkwright*; and accordingly we fell into conversation, and I began to tell him he had got my invention. I told him, I had shewn the model of it to *John Kay*, the method I intended to use the rollers, because *John Kay's* wife had told me that before, how it happened, and Mr. *Arkwright* and them could never deny it. I told him, I had been informed that he had hired *Kay*, for twenty or twenty-one years[10] for about half a guinea a week, or something more, I don't know what; but however, I should go on, if I would. I told him which way she told me he came by it. He said very little about it: when I told him, he never would have had the rollers but through me, he put his hand down in this way, and never said a word.

Asked to repeat a part of his evidence, Highs elaborated:

> We were in some discourse about the rollers: I told him, he would never have known them but for me; and he put his hand in this manner, I remember very well in this manner, to his knee, and that was the answer he gave; also he told me, when I told him it was my invention, Suppose it was, he says, if it was, he says, if any man has found out a thing, and begun a thing, and does not go forwards, he lays it aside, and any other man has a right in so many weeks or months (I forget now) another man has a right to take it up, and get a patent for it.

And later cross-examined by Adair, attempting to offset his evidence:

Q Now what knowledge have you, how came you to suppose, Mr. *Arkwright* ever got that from you?

A I have no further knowledge than what I told you; *Kay's* wife told me.

Q You, yourself don't know?

A I cannot tell which way he got it.

Whereupon Mr Serjeant Bolton interjected, 'We have that *Kay*, a clockmaker, that will tell your Lordship how this *Arkwright* got it from him.'

Examined by Lee for the Crown, Kay recalled how in September 1767[11] he had met Arkwright at a Warrington public house (whether by chance or design is not clear) and in the course of conversation agreed to turn several pieces of brass for him. A further order followed the next day, and yet another within three or four days, when Arkwright asked if he 'would drink a glass of wine with him in *Dale street*'. Here, having learned that Kay made 14*s* a week, Arkwright told him that he did better. 'I was a barber, but I have left it off, and I and another are going up and down the country buying hair and can make more of it.' And, Kay went on:

> We were talking of different things, and this thing came up, of spinning by rollers — he said, that will never be brought to bear, several gentlemen have almost broke themselves by it.[12] I said, I think I could bring that to bear; that was all that passed that night. The next morning he comes to my bedside, and says, Do you remember what I told you last night, and asked whether I could make him a small model, at a small expence? Yes, says I, I believe I can; says he, if you will, I will pay you. I went and bought a few articles, and made a small wooden model, and he took it with him to *Manchester*, and in a week or fortnight's time, I cannot say which, he comes back again, and I made him another.

Lee continued with his examination:

Q Before you go farther, who did you get the method of making these models from?
A From Mr. *Hayes*, the last witness.
Q Did you tell Mr. *Arkwright* so?
A I told him, I and another man had tried that method at *Warrington*.
Q You made him a model?
A I made him two models, and he took one to *Preston*;[13] *Burgoyne's* election was about that time.

And when Arkwright obtained the carding patent:

Q You know very well he did not invent the rollers?
A No.
Q On the contrary you know he had them from you?
A Yes.
Q And you had them from this poor *Hayes*?
A Yes.
Q And you told him so?
A Yes, I told him so many a time.

In all, Kay maintained, he had spent 'about thirteen weeks' with Arkwright in Preston at the time of the Burgoyne election. 'I went there to make a clock for him.' A somewhat different story, it will be remembered, from the one he had told at the inquiry into the right to vote in the election.[14]

In April 1768 ('As soon as the election was over') Kay accompanied Arkwright to Nottingham for 'four or five years perhaps'. Asked how he had heard of Arkwright's 1775 patent, he replied that '*James Hargrave* came and told me he had got his patent ... you see I did not know any thing at all about it.' Further, 'James Hargrave told me I should have lodged a *caveat*.' (Kay, one is tempted to suspect, had led Hargreaves to believe that he was the inventor.)[15]

Cowper did his best to counter this damaging evidence by attempting to show that Kay (who, it came out, had unsuccessfully sought a partnership with Arkwright) was hardly a man whose word was to be trusted:

Q You lived with him before he gained his patent?
A Yes.
Q Parted with him upon very good terms?
A I don't know upon what terms I parted with him.
Q I don't know whether I have a right to ask you, Did you leave his house without his knowledge?
A Yes.
Q I must not ask you, whether any thing else left his house at that time: You fled from his service?
A Yes.
Q By what apprehension did you leave him, whether well, or ill-founded I will ask you this, Was there not at least a charge of felony against you?
A They pretended so, but they could not find any thing against me.

A little later Mr Justice Buller intervened:

Q *Kay* What were the things Mr. *Arkwright* had taken out of your house?
A Several tools.
Q Were they tools respecting this business?
A Yes.
Q Was that the subject of the charge against you?
A Why, I was making another machine in my house to spin jersey, which I thought of while I was at *Nottingham*, I might compleat it, I believe he thought I was making this machine, and that was his intent.
Q You was making a spinning machine?
A I was making a thing, to spin jersey; before I went to *Nottingham* I pulled that thing to pieces.
Q You don't understand my question, Were the tools, which Mr. *Arkwright* had taken out of your house, the subject of the charge of felony against you, was it upon that account, he said you was to be charged with felony?
A I believe he did, he told my wife, I had stole things from him.
Q Did he take those things, as the things stolen?
A No; I brought them out of *Lancashire*.

[130]

Q Tell what it was Mr. *Arkwright* took away.

A Several tools, compasses, pliers, and vice, and other things.

Q Did he take any thing besides tools?

A Yes, a pair of sleeves, a spying glass I had, and locks and brass wheels, I had brought with me, to make a movement with, from *Lancashire*, I had not time to make it, and I brought them with me.

Q What was the spying glass?

A That was a small spying-glass which drew into four joints, that was mine, I brought it from [to?] *Nottingham*.

After a brief but sharp exchange about the admissibility of evidence as to why Kay was not called at the Mordaunt trial, Lee continued his examination:

Q It is suggested to me; Did Mr. *Arkwright* require you to enter into any obligation or bond, not to do any thing in this way of business?

A Yes, at the time I was at *Preston* with him.

Q In the year 1768?

A Yes.

Q After you had given him that model?

A Yes.

Q Was he then well to live, or in a situation not much better than you were?

A He was a poor working man.

Q He was?

A He was, and I too, he got assistance[16] to join him in this affair, and I agreed to work for him as a servant.

Q He got a bond, did he?

A Yes.

Q What was it for?

A To serve him so many years.

The case for the Crown ended with the reading of *The Case of Mr. Richard Arkwright and Co.*, a copy of which Pilkington testified had been given to him by Arkwright in 1782, soon after the verdict in the King's Bench: 'He gave me one, and I desired he would be kind enough to let me put it in my pocket, and read it at my leisure; he said, I might by all means; and likewise said, he would send me some more by his servant; which he did ... I don't recollect that he mentioned any thing, for what purpose, or for what effect they were drawn up.'

The inclusion of this evidence, all-important in that the *Case* contained Arkwright's own admission of the obscurity of the specification, had been denied to Nightingale's counsel four months earlier by a legal technicality, and witnesses had then given evasive answers when questioned as to the authorship of the *Case*.[17] Thus one maintained that 'I was attorney for Mr. Arkwright, I know nothing of it but in the character of an attorney', another that he knew nothing 'but as solicitor', while Thomas Ince, who was 'not at that time [1782] concerned for Mr. Arkwright', added that he had 'heard it mentioned' that Arkwright had distributed the *Case*. Mentioned 'By Mr. Arkwright?' queried Erskine. 'I heard the other day of it in company,' replied Ince. 'Mr. Arkwright said he never gave any directions for the particular part of the case that you are referring to.'[18]

Bearcroft can then hardly have accepted Ince's testimony, nor did he now when Arkwright's *Case* was admissible evidence. He moved to exploit the changed situation:

> Gentlemen, ... I said, I remember, before the court of Common Pleas, and I repeat it now, 'Oh that mine enemy would write a book!' Mr. *Arkwright* has written a book, and out of his own mouth will I condemn him; and without all doubt he himself was conscious, that, instead of complying with that essential condition of the patent — instead of complying with the condition of the act of parliament, and fairly disclosing his knowledge of the manner of carrying the invention into effect, that other people might have it at the end of the term, he had purposely secreted it ... This evidence I will read to you, for it states in terms, his design of secreting the invention, for those are the words; 'At the time Mr. *Arkwright* obtained his last patent,' (this patent that is here) 'he justly concluded, that his inventions were if great national importance' (I have argued they are) 'and conceived they would be sought after by foreigners to introduce it into other countries.' He therefore purposely, in prevention of that evil, he had almost himself said, national injury 'omitted to give so full and particular a description of his inventions in his specification, attendant on his last patent as he otherwise would have done; and, in order the more effectually to guard against foreigners, it has been Mr. *Arkwright's* uniform rule to forbid the admission of them into any of his works. Other gentlemen, natives of this kingdom, were most generally admitted upon proper application. Mr. *Arkwright* was the more inclined to omit so full a description of his inventions, as by a clause in the said letters patent, he was led to believe it was not essentially necessary because it is therein said, that the said letters patent should be good and effectual in the law, according to the true intent and meaning thereof, notwithstanding the not full and certain describing the nature and quality of the said invention, or of the materials thereunto conducing and belonging.'

Adair found himself faced by an almost impossible task, since if his case broke down on even a single point the verdict would of necessity go to the Crown. His reply to Bearcroft's contention that Arkwright had taken out his second patent 'to gull the world to submit to that patent as a new invention for the roving and the carding' and that 'his new patent was in effect his old one' is worth noting on account of the allegation — very properly denied by Bearcroft — that his client was actually losing money when operating his first patent alone:

> Gentlemen, it is very natural Mr. *Arkwright* should be desirous of having the

benefit of the [1775] patent obtained; in the state in which it then stood; he was undoubtedly a loser; it is a most undoubted fact, the [1769] spinning patent never paid for itself, nor indemnified Mr. *Arkwright* for the construction of those ingenious machines. But why did it not? Because of the modes in use at that time, during greater part of the continuance of Mr. *Arkwright's* spinning patent, for preparing the cotton from the coarse state; first, the operation of the spinning was so tedious and imperfect, and subject to those difficulties, it is impossible to derive any benefit from the exercise of the spinning machine, for so much time, and so many hands were employed in carding, sizing, and roving the cotton to prepare it for spinning.[19]

On the important question as to whether the invention was new Adair contended that 'the more important part of the mechanical powers have been discovered, rather than invented, many centuries ago, many thousand years ago' and 'that is a new invention in a machine, which consists of a new combination of old parts'. In order to show that the carding machine was not a new invention the Crown had produced witnesses to prove that each separate part had been in use before Arkwright took out his patent; but, argued Adair, 'have they ventured to produce any one witness, to say, before the date of Mr. *Arkwright's* patent, he ever saw such a machine as we shall now produce to you? ... The man who first brings his invention to that degree of maturity and perfection, as to make it capable of general use, for the sake of improvement of the manufactures of his country, he alone is the man intitled to the patent'.

As to whether Arkwright had made a sufficient disclosure of the invention to secure its benefit to the public after the lapse of the patent, Adair contended that a specification 'ought to be such, as to enable a mechanic, of reasonable general knowledge in his profession, and thoroughly acquainted with the machines before in use, to produce the same purposes, and all the prior improvements of them; he should, with that previous knowledge, and assistance from the specification together, be able to form that from the specification, and make that machine'. And Arkwright's specification, he maintained, fully satisfied these requirements, as he would demonstrate by calling 'some of the most eminent mechanics in this country or the world'.

Confronted with the testimony of Thomas Highs and John and Sarah Kay to the effect that 'Mr. *Arkwright*, in the language which has been so liberally used to-day, stole that invention [the rollers] from Mr. *Hayes*, by the medium of Mr. *Kay*,' Adair could well have cross-examined Highs as to why he had delayed so long in putting forward his claims when as early as 1771 the Manchester men who had awarded him a 200 guinea prize for the double jenny he had exhibited at the Exchange would presumably have been ready, even eager, to back him against Arkwright.[20] Nor in his address did Adair refer to the evidence Hacket would give to the effect that under Arkwright's direction he had worked with Kay 'in the same shop ... making rollers, and things in different parts of the machinery' and that he had never heard Kay mention that he had received instructions from anyone before that time.

Instead Adair tried to cast doubt on Highs's character through his association with Kay:

> I know nothing of *Hayes*, you know nothing of him but from his evidence, and the light that he appears in to-day: all I ask of you in respect of Mr. *Hayes*, is to judge of him from his company, his friends, his acquantance, and his associate, Kay; in what situation does *Kay* stand, the servant of Mr. *Arkwright*, worked for him, was possessed of all his secrets, and running away from his master's service upon a charge of felony, which charge, appeared to himself to be so well founded, that he has never dared to return to *Nottingham* to this hour; *that* servant, so trusted with Mr. *Arkwright's* secrets, running from him upon a charge of felony, and now coming into a Court of Justice, to swear, he and his associates were the authors of Mr. *Arkwright's* invention.

Bearcroft's concluding address, less than half the length of Adair's, was that of a man sensing the verdict was his. Before long he was citing the case of Williams *v.* Brodie, which had determined that 'if a new invention, which is the ground of a patent, is the addition of a new application to an old machine, they should so describe it in their patent'. And Arkwright, Bearcroft contended, had not done so.

As for the rollers 'now called a new invention, and made the foundation of this patent', they had been invented by Highs, whose workman, Kay, had passed the secret on to Arkwright, whose servant he had become:

> How is all this evidence to be got rid of? — By a cool observation of the Counsel at the bar: Pardon me, Gentlemen, for using the expression, when it comes to be examined, it is perfectly rediculous; there is this *Hayes*, and *Kay* and his wife, three in all to confirm each other in this — What is the answer to it that is given by the Counsel? — Oh! Mr. *Hayes* is a good honest man, says the Serjeant; if he stood by himself, we could not attack his credit, but *noscitur ex sociis*, says my learned friend, but he keeps such horrid company — That company Mr. *Arkwright* was glad to borrow from him and keep two years — My learned friend, says, Oh! he is a sad man, a felon that committed larceny, and fled from prosecution for fear of Mr. *Arkwright*. They chose to use that weapon, that two-edged sword, Mr. *Arkwright* frightened this fellow out of the country, I doubt it not. There is not a more miserable or dangerous situation for a poor man, than to be in possession of a secret, of which a powerful and rich man dreads the discovery ...
>
> Gentlemen, Three witnesses have positively sworn to a fact which I trust they have a right to be believed in.
>
> Gentlemen, I don't find the learned Serjeant was surprised by this evidence, no man of common sense will believe Mr. *Arkwright* is the only man *in England*, that never heard the accounts spread abroad by every *man* that speaks upon the subject, that he did get this from *Hayes*, by means of *Kay*, it is a notorious story

in the manufacturing counties, all men that have seen Mr. *Arkwright* in a state of opulence, have shaken their heads, and thought of these poor men, *Hayes* and *Kay*, and have thought too, that they were entitled to some participation of the profits, What is the consequence of this? Mr. *Arkwright* must have expected this evidence, Where are the witnesses that tell you Mr. *Hayes* has a bad character? Where are the witnesses that tell you *Kay* and his wife are of bad character? or that either of the three is not intitled to belief upon their oaths.

And finally, on the already twice tried question of the sufficiency of the specification:

That point is, that Mr. *Arkwright*, by this specification, not only did not make a fair disclosure, but purposely intend to puzzle and confound the secret, to prevent its being understood. Is there any doubt, Mr. *Arkwright*, this great mechanic as he is called for certain purposes, was perfectly equal to the description? he could have done it fairly, if he had been fairly disposed to do it.

Gentlemen, I will convince you, when he has to explain he has the ability to do so. You heard at the beginning of the day read, at my desire, his specification unde the first patent for the rollers for spinning, Was not that a discovery of importance? — Has not he found it so? — Was there any reason why he should be more willing to part with *that* to the French than the new patent? if there is, let Mr. *Arkwright* or his friends, or his Counsel (if they are not all gone — no, they are not all gone, one still remains I see.) Let any man still get up and interrupt me, I challenge him to say why he should be more disposed to let the French run away with *that* than the present ... To sum up the whole, Mr. *Arkwright* has been too clever; he has been too careful to conceal it; he has sailed too near the wind, and must abide the legal consequence.

Mr Justice Buller's careful and thorough summing-up was from the begin-ning unfavourable to Arkwright. There were, he told the jury, three questions for them to decide upon. First, was the invention new? Second, if so was it invented by the defendant? Third, was it sufficiently described in the specifica-tion?

This last question, he maintained, was of the greatest importance, since if the jury decided against Arkwright:

it may have the effect of inducing people who apply for patents in future times, to be more explicit in their specifications, and consequently, the public will derive a great benefit from it ...

Upon this point it is clearly settled at law, that a man, to intitle himself to the benefit of a patent for a monopoly, must disclose his secret, and specify his invention in such a way, that others may be taught by it to do the thing for for which the patent is granted; for the end and meaning of the specification is, to teach the public, after the term for which the patent is granted, what the art is; and it must put the public in possession of the secret in an ample and beneficial a way as the patentee himself uses it. This I take to be clear law, as far as respects the specification; for the patent is the reward, which, under an Act of Parliament, is held out for a discovery, and therefore, unless the discovery by true and fair, the patent is void. — If the specification, in any part of it, be materially false or defective, the patent is against law, and cannot be supported.

It has been truly said by the counsel, that if the specification be such, that mechanical men of common understanding can comprehend it, to make a machine by it, it is sufficient; but then it must be such, that the mechanics may be able to make the machine by following the directions of the specification, without any new inventions or additions of their own. The question is, Whether, upon the evidence, this specification comes within what I have stated to you to be necessary by law, in order to support it?

The prosecutors have attacked it in almost every part.

As to those parts of the specification claimed by the Crown to have 'no relation to the subject':

If those are of no use but to be thrown in merely to puzzle, I have no difficulty to say upon that ground alone, the patent is void, for it is not that fair, full, true discovery which the public have a right to demand from an individual, who, under the sanction of the Parliament, gets so great a reward as a monopoly for fourteen years together.

Further, should the jury consider the specification not sufficiently described, 'that alone puts a compleat end to this cause, and then it will be unnecessary to trouble you with any other'.

Mr Justice Buller concluded:

Gentlemen, thus the case stands as to the several component parts of this machine; and if, upon them, you are satisfied none of them were inventions unknown at the time this patent was granted, or, that they were not invented by the defendant; upon either of these points the prosecutor is intitled to your verdict.

If upon any point you are of opinion with the presecutor, you will find a verdict for him.

If upon all the points you are of opinion for the defendant, you will find a verdict for him.

The Jury, without a minute's hesitation, brought in their verdict for the Crown.

Arkwright at once instructed John Kinderley, attorney, of Chancery Lane, to find out what could be done to reverse the judgement. Kinderley thereupon conferred with 'M^r. Lister[21] on his coming to Town . . . as to Moving the Court for a New Tryal'. It was decided to seek the opinion of counsel, and soon afterwards Kinderley, Baldwin and Mansfield were in 'Consultation with M^r. Lister Conferring as to an Application to be made for a New Tryal or an Arrest of Judgment And whether the Application sho^d. be made in the Court of Chancery or in the Court of Kings Bench when they desired me [Kinderley] to search the Petty Bag Office for Precedents and the form of the Judgment to be Entered on the Scire Facias.'

[136]

By the beginning of the Michaelmas Term Chambré, Adair, Wilson and Cooper (probably Samuel of Chancery Lane or James of Holborn Court) had been retained and, acting on Chambré's instructions, Kinderley drew up affidavits from Arkwright, Sarah, the widow of Thomas James, 'and others ... in support of the intended Application for a New Tryal'.

On 9 November Kinderley met Arkwright's counsel 'till between 11 & 12 at Night' and the following day Adair moved in the Court of King's Bench for a rule to show cause why there should not be a new trial. The Mordaunt and Nightingale trials, he contended, had both turned on the sufficiency or otherwise of the patent specification but at the recent trial, 'contrary to the expectations of Mr. *Arkwright* ... the chief force of the evidence was then against the originality of the invention' and the verdict 'was principally founded upon that kind of evidence'.

At this stage Mr Justice Buller intervened:

> I cannot say that, nor can I say, if you ask now, which point it was, they were all so strong ... it appeared to me, after we had been four or five hours in the cause, the defendant had not a leg to stand upon; I thought it a point of duty and decency in me, in such a cause, and of that consequence, and where it had been tried before two respectable judges, who held a difference in sentiments, that I should hear it fully out. I began with directing the idea of the jury, to that point, and I believe it occurred to the jury, that if it was ever so clear, it was better they should hear it all out.

Adair went on to speak of affidavits 'to contradict the evidence of *Kay* and Mrs. *Hargrave*, and some others that were material witnesses upon that part of the case' as well as those of Sarah James, of her son, and of 'one or two' of the workmen of Hargreaves and James to the effect that the crank did not come into use until later than they had testified and that 'they were informed from *Hargrave* himself, that the invention had been surreptitiously obtained from a workman of Mr. *Arkwright's* himself'.[22]

As to Arkwright's alleged insertion into the specification of articles that were of use only 'for the purpose of puzzling and perplexing', it was now argued that 'some or most' had been included for such time 'when the machine came to be applied to wool instead of cotton, and the others had actually been used by Mr. *Arkwright* himself and his workmen'.

Adair's pleading failed to impress Lord Mansfield:

> It is very clear to me, upon your own shewing, there is no colour for the rule; the ground of it is, if there is another trial, you may have more evidence. There is no surprise stated, no new discovery, but upon the material points in question, you can give more evidence. — There were two questions to be tried, that is, the specification, and the originality of the invention; there has been one trial in this Court, another trial in the Common Pleas, where this patent has been questioned, and this proceeding is brought finally to conclude the matter — for

[137]

it is a *Scire Facias* to repeal the letters patent. The questions to be tried, are stated upon Record — there is not a child but must know they were to try the questions there stated; they come prepared to try them, they have tried them, and a verdict has been found, which is satisfactory to the Judge, and now you desire to try the cause again, only that you may bring more evidence. There is not a colour for it.

The rule was refused and on 14 November 1785 the Court of King's Bench gave judgement to cancel the letters patent.

Even so, Arkwright was unwilling to accept defeat. Chambré advised that an application might be made to the Court of Chancery for a writ of *certiorari*, and after 'Altering and Redrawing' Arkwright's affidavit and those of Sarah James and her son Thomas, Kinderley sent copies to Chambré, Mansfield and Cooper. But after consulting Arkwright's counsel Kinderley reported them to be 'of Opinion that no Motion co^d. be done'.[23] The patent was lost for ever. Its final defence had cost Arkwright £861 15s 9d.[24]

Arkwright's defeat was looked at in two lights. News of the verdict in the trial before Mr Justice Buller had reached Manchester early in the morning of Monday 27 June with the arrival at the Bull's Head of an express from London. A hastily composed broadsheet[25] was soon on the streets. Arkwright's counsel, it recounted:

> during the course of the trial, which continued till one o'clock on Sunday morning, strained every nerve, that if possible, Mr. A. might ride his hobby-horse in triumph, in this town and neighbourhood, and thereby make his assertion good, which was, 'that he would procure a razor that should shave Manchester, &c.' But, it appears, to the great joy of thousands, that the old Fox is at last caught by his over-grown beard in his own trap, and that keen weapon he intended for the use of a set of humane and generous men, he may now scrape his own assylums of purgatory with.
>
> 'Tis pity, that any man, tho' of ever so bright parts, should engross and enjoy and fruits of the labour and ingenuity of other industrious mechanics; but, it is hoped, the dose that has now been administered to him, will entirely purge him from all his hatefulness and tyrany, and from his every unjustifiable claim and demand, whereby he has amassed such an immoderate sum of money.

On the other hand there were those sympathetic to Arkwright, like James Watt and Josiah Wedgwood, who saw their own interests threatened. 'Though I do not love Arkwright, I don't like the precedent of setting aside patents through default of specification. I fear for our own,' Watt had confided to Boulton on 30 July 1781, less than a fortnight after the Mordaunt trial, and on 13 August he elaborated:

> I am tired of making improvements which be some quirk or wresting of the law may be taken from us, as I think has been done in the case of Arkwright,

who has been condemned merely because he did not specify quite clearly. This was injustice, because it is plain that he has given this trade a being — has brought his invention into use and made it of great public utility. Wherefore he deserved all the money he has got. In my opinion his patent should not have been invalidated without it had clearly appeared that he did not invent the things in question. I fear we shall be served with the same sauce *for the good of the public*! and in that case I shall certainly do what he threatens, This you may be assured of, that we are as much envied here as he is at Manchester, and all the bells in Cornwall would be rung at our overthrow.[26]

Juſt arrived, by Expreſs, from London, an Account of the

Law Suit betwixt A------ht and the Gentlemen of the Cotton Factories,

In and about the Town and Neighbourhood of Mancheſter.

ON Monday, June 27, 1785, early in the morning, an expreſs arrived from London, at the Bull's Head, in Mancheſter, which gives an account, that on Saturday morning, at 8 o'clock, came on, the cauſe betwixt a Mr. A. and the Gentlemen belonging to the cotton factories of this town and neighbourhood. He claimed the right of his patent, which he had enjoyed ten years, to the great detriment of this populous town, &c. After the examination of great a number of witneſſes on both ſides, but particularly on that of the Gentlemen, it appeared in the moſt conſpicuous manner, that the far greater part of the works belonging to the cotton factories, were the inventions of ſeveral ingenious men, in and about this town, before Mr. A. got his patent. Nevertheleſs, his counſel, during the courſe of the trial, which continued till one o'clock on Sunday morning, ſtrained every nerve,

that if poſſible, Mr. A. might ride his hobby-horſe in triumph, in this town and neighbourhood, and thereby make his aſſertion good, which was, " that he would procure a razor that ſhould ſhave Mancheſter, &c. But, it appears, to the great joy of thouſands, that the old Fox is a laſt caught by his over-grown beard in his own trap, and that keen weapon he intended for the uſe of a ſet of humane and generous men, he may now ſcrape his own aſſylums of purgatory with.

'Tis pity, that any man, tho' of ever ſo bright parts, ſhould engroſs and enjoy the fruits of the labour and ingenuity of other induſtrious mechanics; but, it is hoped, the doſe that has now been adminiſtered to him, will entirely purge him from all his hatefulneſs and tyrrany, and from his every unjuſtifiable claim and demand, whereby he has amaſſed ſuch an immoderate ſum of money.

The broadsheet distributed in Leigh

And Boulton, who on 28 July 1781 had been reassuring Watt ('You have not done as Arkwright did but you have delivered a clear specification of the principles & you have illustrated those principles by the erection of 50 Engines which are all exposed to publick inspection & not kept secret like the Cotton Mills') was soon afterwards preparing to marshal resources to defend Watt's own patent. He wrote to him on 7 August:

As to ourselves I shall make myself easy untill I find the God of nature hath revaild to mankind some new knowledge which we are not yet possessed of, but at the same time I suppose we shall find it necessary to defend our property since there are men who are fools & Rogues enough to invade it, but our case is not singularly hard, therefore dont let us vex ourselves but as we are emboldened by good conscience let us calmly determine to assert our right to lay a rational plan for a law suit, & lay acc^t for spending one Thousand £ if necessary & thereby make an example of proud, conceited, ignorant, rascaly, ingrates: nothing can be done untill they have committed some ouvert act, but if they attempt to erect a large Engine we should give them & the proprietors of it proper notice, that they may not plead ignorance & if they persevere we should fix upon some London attorney that w^d. not neglect our business & we should retain silently 3 or 4 of the best Council in Eng^d. Dunning is '[a] good Lawyer, M^r. Lee D^o + firmness, good lungs, & some philosophical knowledge, there is also a Councilor that Cummins recommended (I forget his name) as a good Pleader & a very good mechanick & philosopher. We must also summon various witnesses without regard to ye expence, for the thing well done is perhaps done for ever.

'I hear Arkwright is bringing on a new trial I wish him success though I don't like him,' Watt wrote to Boulton on hearing of Arkwright's preparations for the forthcoming trial against James.[27] It was not, however, until the Nightingale trial that a reluctant Watt agreed to Darwin's request that he assist Arkwright to regain his carding patent. Darwin had written to Boulton from Derby on 26 January 1785:

> I believe some shyness has existed between you & M^r. Arkwright, but is it not your interest to assist him with your evidence on his trial? which also may make good humour between you, & you make fire-engines for cotton-works in future; which I understand for spinning wool also, will increase tenfold.
>
> If yourself or M^r. Watt think as I do on this affair, & that your own interest is much concern'd in establishing the operation of patents, pray give me a line that I may advise M^r. Arkwright to apply to you, & send you a drawing & specification & model ...
>
> I think it hard, that an inventor of machines has not his property in the invention secured to him for 14 years without paying £100 for a patent; as a writer of books has; much more so, that his right to his invention should be so easily infringed for want of an intelligent or mechanic jury.
>
> Tho your inventions, by draining Cornwal, have supply'd work to ten thousands — M^r. Arkwright has employed his thousands — I think you should defend each other from the ingratitude of mankind. His case comes on the 14th. of February, that the time is urgent, pray let me soon hear from yourself or M^r. Watt on this affair.[28]

Almost eight months later came a plea from Wedgwood to Watt that he join forces with Arkwright in an attempt to secure better the rights of patentees. Wedgwood's letter of 17 September 1785, written from Matlock after a visit to Arkwright, reads, 'He will be in Birmingham in a few days and I will ask him to call upon you. I told him you were considering the subject of patents, and you two great genius's may probably strike out some new lights together, which neither of you might think of separately.'[29]

It must have been about this time that Watt and Arkwright got together and drew up the 'Heads of a Bill'[30] for the drastic amendment of the patent law which would have avoided the necessity for the public disclosure of a detailed specification. The draft in Watt's handwriting has corrections and additons by Arkwright, who queried 'Whether it might not be better to require the Patentee [instead of the Attorney General] to tender proper persons to be examined by the Atty General?' He also suggested that the 'three or more persons of probity skilled in the art or science to which the ... Inv[n] shall more particularly relate' to be called by the Attorney General should be referred to as witnesses rather than as commissioners. Arkwright also felt that a patentee seeking an 'alternative or addition' to his specification should petition the Attorney General and not, as Watt had proposed, the Lord Chancellor.

Annotations by Arkwright are also to be found on the more finished draft of Watt's 'Thoughts upon Patents, or exclusive Privileges for new Inventions', a document in which it is argued that *'if one Capital & meritorious invention such as S[r]. Rich[d]. Arkwrights Cotton machine shou'd be brought forth in a Century in consequence of them* [patents] *it should justify the measure of granting them'.* Arkwright suggested that, instead of being available only in the Chancery Records, the general patent specifications should be 'printed annualy by the Kings printer, on the same size letter & price as acts of Parliament each year making a volume of all his specif[n] in that year'. And to Watt's proposal that 'after the patent is expired the particular & past specifications shall be still kept locked up, but the lord Chan[r]. shall be impowered to grant copies thereof to be given to persons natives of Great Britain & residing therein petitioning for such copies & making affidavit that they intend to practise the s[d]. art or invention within the realm' Arkwright rather surprisingly commented, 'Perhaps the most liberal way will be found the most advantageous for the public viz. the printing all the specifcations as soon as the patent is expired.'[31]

Wedwood's meeting with Arkwright had a further curious sequel, nothing less than the proposal that Arkwright be granted a statutory monopoly of wool spinning. Wedgwood set out the scheme in his common place book:

Sept[r]. 1785
Some Outlines of a plan for spinning Wool by Machinery

Proposed,
    That Mr. Arkwright should engage to spin wool by machinery, at certain prices hereafter to be agreed upon.
    To make the machinery known when it is completed, and to instruct any one in the use of it, upon certain conditions contained in an Act of Parliament to be made upon this subject.

To accomplish the machinery, & complete the art for this purpose in —— years after the passing of the said Act.

In consideration of the above engagements on the part of Mr. Arkwright the legislature shall be petitioned to pass an Act of Parliamt to secure to Mr. A. his heirs &c. the sole spinning of wool in Great Britain by machinery, for the space of —— years after passing the said Act.

A clause to be inserted in the said Act to give compensation to such persons as have at this time mills or machines employed in spinning wool, they giving up all right or claim to spin wool by machinery otherwise than as it is provided for by the said Act.

To obviate any objection which may be made, viz. that this Act will preclude any better method of spinning wool, which may possibly be invented during the time of the said Act, ——

It is proposed to name a committee of mechanics to decide upon the originality and merit of such invention or inventions.

In case of death of any of the committee, the survivors to nominate others in their stead.

Mr. Arkwright engages further to spin wool 50 per cent. cheaper than it is now spun, which 50 per cent. will be an entire gain to the public; —— and so much cheaper still, that he will himself be content with one half of the surplus profit above the 50 per cent. —— the other half to belong to the person whom he instructs in the business.

There will be a further advantage to the public for this invention, that one pound of wool will go as far as two pounds do now, on account of the greater fineness of the thread: —— And that in virtue of this fineness, and evenness, new species of cloth will be produced, by which the wear and consumption of woollen cloths will be increased, and we shall regain the Levant, Turkey & other foreign markets which we have lost on account of the French spinning a finer species of woolen cloth than we now do.

Wedgwood then went on to set out the history of the scheme:

The first time of meeting Mr. Arkwright was in London, on the business of the Irish propositions; and after he had lost his patent trial, I attended a meeting of patent holders at his lodgings. Upon my mentioning to Sir Joseph Banks some conversation which I had had with this extraordinary man, Sir Joseph was desirous of an interview with him, and requested I would bring him to his house; but this I could not accomplish.

In the beginning of September following (1785) being at Matlock for two or three weeks, I had frequent opportunities of conversation with Mr. Arkwright, and found him a very sensible intelligent man, but his views confined chiefly to mechanics. He was much disgusted with the treatment he had met with in his trial; and threatened, as they *would* have his machinery made public, to publish descriptions and copper plates of all the parts, that it might be known to foreign nations as well as our own. I strongly dissuaded him from such a step, representing how unjust it would be, that a whole nation should suffer for the

imprudent conduct of a few, for his opponents were few indeed in comparison
with the great body of people who would be benefited by having his admirable
inventions confined to ourselves.

I afterwards found an opportunity of bringing Sir Joseph Banks & Mr
Arkwright together; when I drew up the above proposals. Mr Arkwright agreed
to prepare machinery for making an experiment to ascertain the practicability of
spinning wool on his plan; and Sir Joseph agreed to consult his friends in the
mean time relative to the obtaining of the Act of Parliament above alluded to.[32]

On 21 February 1786 Wedgwood wrote to Arkwright from London:

Having had the pleasure of bringing S[r]. Joseph Banks and you together the
last summer at Matlock upon the subject of spinning wool by machinery, S[r].
Joseph told me the other day that he had taken a good deal of pains to prepare
matters on his part, & would gladly proceed, but wished to know if you had
taken any steps in preparing machinery &c. that he might have something certain
to lay before his parliamentary friends. Being my self fully convinced that this is
a subject of the first magnitude I should be happy to contribute any thing in my
power towards promoting so great & usefull a work.[33]

How far Arkwright got with his experiments we do not know. In January
1779 Robert and Thomas Barber had announced in the *Derby Mercury*[34] that
they had been 'informed by their Friends, that they would certainly be prosecuted by the Cromford Company, for infringing upon their Patent: but that
they were 'determined to prevent any Infringement that may be made on their
own Patents'. It was apparently these activities that are referred to by George
Dempster in a letter of 16 December 1786 to the Earl of Buchan from
Knightsbridge:[35]

It is long since a M[r] Barber at Derby applied M[r] Arkwrights machinery to
the spinning of the coarser kinds of woolen yarn. There is a mill constructed by
him or by his consent on Lord Bathurst property at Cirencester & another I
believe at Glasgow. Such a mill would suit your Country well where the sheep
would bring the wool to the Mill on their backs whereas Cotton could only come
by a long Land Carriage after a Couple of Long Voyages by sea.

Meanwhile the water frame had come to be applied to worsted spinning (as
Arkwright had suggested in 1772) at Dolphinholme on the river Wyre in 1784
and at Addingham on the river Wharfe, near Ilkley, three years later.[36] But there
was to be no application to wool, which kept to hand-worked jennies until the
mule came in slowly twenty years later, even then not widely adopted until it
became self-acting.[37]

NOTES

1 The quotations in this section are all taken from *S.F.* unless otherwise stated. The full title
of the presented case is *The Trial of a Cause instituted by ... his Majesty's Attorney General ...*

to Repeal a Patent granted on the Sixteenth of December 1775, to Mr. Richard Arkwright, London, 1785.

2 First published in London in 1758.

3 In *Nightingale*, p. 1, he is referred to as Breddon; incorrectly printed in *S.F.* as Pridden.

3 Adair, *Nightingale*, p. 10.

5 Fitton and Wadsworth, p. 62.

6 'Multiplying five to one,' he explained, meant 'making the different rollers go, one faster than the other'. (*S.F.*, p. 58.)

7 Guest, *Compendious History*, pp. 203–4. 'In 1772 [should be 1771] he exhibited a double jenny with fifty-six spindles, for which he won a two hundred guinea prize'. (P. Mantoux, *The Industrial Revolution in the Eighteenth Century*, London, 1948, p. 235.)

8 A Rothwell had a public house opposite the Man and Scythe in Bolton.

9 *Manchester Mercury*, 2 July 1771.

10 See the information that Arkwright gave to lawyers at the Mordaunt trial, chapter IV, p. 124.

11 Kay says that this was at the time of Warrington races (8–10 September 1767).

12 A reference to Paul and Wyatt?

13 L.C.R.O., DDPr 138/7, says Arkwright came to Preston from Manchester. See above, chapter I, p. 20.

14 See above chapter I, p. 20.

15 *S.F.*, p. 65. Kay: 'I was at Nottingham, and he took my property away'. Cowper: 'You heard soon after, of this (1775) patent which you knew to by yours, or *Hayes's* invention, and not Arkwright's? Kay: 'Yes.'

16 I.e. Smalley.

17 Even before then its (legal) significance had not been lost on the attorney Thomas Pares, of Hopwell, who on 10 February 1783 had written to his son Thomas at Gray's Inn, 'I think his (Arkwright's) printed case sufficiently admits it (the 1775 patent) invalid & I should imagine Evidence might be obtained of his having published it.' Arkwright (as we have seen) was then threatening Gardom & Pares, his earliest licensees with action to recover royalties which they held to be no longer payable on account of the decision for Mordaunt in 1781.

18 *Nightingale*, pp. 24, 32, 33.

19 See Chapter VII, p. 182.

20 Guest, *Compendious History*, pp. 203–4, *Manchester Mercury*, 2 July 1771.

21 Of Travis and Lister, attorneys, of Scarborough?

22 It is perhaps interesting to note that Adair had not elaborated on the contents and authorship of the affidavit said to rebut the evidence of Kay. Half a century later, when Baines had almost completed his *Cotton Manufacture*, he received important evidence from the son of Thomas James, Hargreaves's partner. It reads: 'He [James Hargreaves] was not the inventor of the crank and comb. We had a pattern chalked out upon a table by one of the Lancashire men in the employ of Mr. Arkwright; and I went to a framesmith of the name of Young to have one made. Of this Mr. Arkwright was continually complaining, and it occasioned some angry feelings between the parties'. (Baines, *Cotton Manufacture*, p. 178.)

23 See 'Application for a New Trial'.

24 A.F. MSS., Mr Goodwin's bill.

25 Broadsheet distributed in Leigh and in and around Manchester, (according to J. Lunn, *Leigh*, published for the Borough Council; the broadsheet is reproduced facing p. 68). A copy of the anonymous broadsheet was preserved among the papers of Richard Guest II, the vindicator of High's claim. It is reproduced and in the margin, 'inserted by an old hand in pencil', is: 'Piece said to Thomas Highs this is the peculiar phrase Sir Richard used'.

26 Samuel Smiles, *Lives of the Engineers, Boulton and Watt*, London, 1904 edition, p. 274.

27 B & W. MSS., Watt to Boulton, Tuesday 18 (February) 1783.
Watt to James McGrigor, 30 October 1784. 'As to Mr. Arkwright he is to say no worse

one of the most self sufficient Ignorant men I have ever met with. Yet by all I can learn he is certainly a man of merit in his way, and one to whom Britain is much indebted and whom she should honour & reward, for whoever the Spinning, Arkwright certainly had the merit of performing the most difficult part, which was the making it usefull.'

28 B. & W. MSS.
29 B. & W. MSS.
30 'Heads of a Bill to explain and amend the laws relative to the Letters Patents & grants or privilege for new Inventions' (B. & W. MSS). For the best account see Eric Robinson, 'James Watt and the law of patents', *Technology and Culture*, 13, 1972, pp. 128–30.
31 B. & W. MSS.
32 Wedgwood's Common Place Book, 325–6 (at Etruria Museum).
33 Lady K. E. Farrer (ed.), *Correspondence of Josiah Wedgwood*, London, 1906, p. 35. Sir Joseph Banks had been President of the Royal Society of Arts since 1778. Sir Joseph Bank's friends George Dempster and Charles, Lord Hawkesbury, received from Samuel More in 1785 and 1787 respectively copies of 'Considerations of the Improvement of the Manufacture of Wool in Great Britain', a paper of unknown authorship. It proposed a national reward for mechanical wool spinning, but neither the committee of the Privy Council for Trade, nor Parliament, nor the Society of Arts acted upon its recommendations. (D. G. C Allan 'A proposed national reward for mechanical wool spinning, 1785–9', *Journal of the Royal Society of Arts*, CX, 1962, pp. 529–33.) *Derby Mercury*, 24 March 1791 (commenting on and praising Arkwright's machinery, part of a much more general comment), 'It is surprising that manufacturers should have been so backward in applying this machinery to the spinning of woollen yarn. This however is now coming into practice. One machine of this sort is already established in the west of Scotland, others will soon follow the example.'
34 15–22 January 1779.
35 University of Edinburgh, Laing MSS, II, 588/1 (cited by Cooke, 'Richard Arkwright and the Scottish cotton industry', p. 202 n. 28).
36 John James, *History of the Worsted Manufacture in England from the earliest Times*, London, 1857, pp. 327–8.
37 Crump (ed.), *Leeds Woollen Industry*, pp. 24–5.

CHAPTER VI

The Arkwright system

JUDGED BY THE NUMBERS employed, the Arkwright empire was the largest in the country, having soon after the turn of the century between 1,800 and 1,900 workpeople.[1] Of these Cromford's two mills, together with Masson, accounted for 1,150.[2] Only the Strutts, with 1,494[3] workpeople in 1815 and 1,613[4] three years later, and Robert Owen's New Lanark, with a claimed 'sixteen or seventeen hundred',[5] could approach this total. Among other large country water-driven establishments John Smalley's foundation, the Holywell Twist Company,[6] had 840 in 1818;[7] it was at this time owned by William Douglas, whose mills at Pendleton, near Manchester, employed 531.[8] Catrine had 875 in 1816,[9] and Monteith & Bogle at Blantyre, Lanarkshire, where David Livingstone, the Victorian missionary, was to work as a piecer, 750.[10] Deanston had, however, contracted from 600 to 800 in the late 1780s to about 500 in 1800 and 377 in 1819.[11]

Mills of this size were nevertheless the exception, and below the handful of cotton lords were ranged a whole army of smaller competitors. Some idea of the variation in size is given in the evidence on Peel's factory legislation between 1816 and 1819 — the Commons (Peel's) committee of 1816 and the Lords committees of 1818 and 1819. At the bottom end of the scale were those who struggled at home with a carding engine and a few jennies or perhaps with hand-operated mules. John Saxon, in 1819 a spinning overlooker at Birley & Hornby's Manchester mill, recalled how about 1780 he had begun work 'In my Father's House; my Father had a little Cotton Concern of his own in a Garret, a Carding House; I was employed first at eleven Years of Age.' As to the hours of work, 'Sometimes none at all for a Day or two at the beginning of the Week, and then at the latter End of the Week they made long Days.' Work, he remembered, was carried on 'very irregularly', so much so that 'Sometimes the Masters would send the Piecers after the Spinners to the Public Houses.'[12] And Thomas Welsh, who began work as a piecer in 1788, said of the finer counts, 'It was all spun by small Mules of from Forty ot Sixty Spindles, and sometimes from Sixty to Eighty; they were kept in Garrets and Bed-rooms . . . They were not regular Mills then, they were private Rooms in Dwelling Houses, which was the only Way in which Mule Spinning was carried on'.[13]

Midway between the private house or garret and the smaller purpose-built mills were the converted cottages in villages and towns, as at Oldham, where 'many are made from cottages, a steam-engine attached to them, and the rooms laid together',[14] while at Accrington, noted John Byng (later fifth Viscount Torrington) in his diary for 24 June 1792, 'every vale swarms with cotton mills; some not bigger than cottages — for any little stream, by means of a reservoir will supply them'.[15] And not only in Lancashire. Keighley had 'from twenty to thirty mills upon one little brook',[16] among them Yorkshire's earliest on the Arkwright system, the Low Mill, completed and equipped in 1780 by the brothers George and William Clayton and Thomas Walshman (one of the Birkacre partners) and powered by the Highley beck. The first workpeople were sent to Cromford for training.[17]

Another mill, small by Arkwright standards and accused by him in 1781 of having infringed his carding patent, was that of John Taylor and Joseph Smith, which was advertised for sale by auction at the Unicorn, Altrincham, in the *Manchester Mercury* of 14 May 1782:

> All that large new-erected BRICK BUILDING, situate in *Altrincham*...being four Stories high, with a Cellar under, and containing in the Inside, 46 Feet in length, and 25 Feet in breadth, laid out into proper Rooms and Apartments, for the Spinning, Carding and manufacturing Cotton, with a Washhouse and Stove at one End of the Building, containing in the Inside 25 Feet and a half in length, and 18 Feet in breadth, and two Rooms over the same, with a Stable and Smithy at the other End of the Building, containing in the Inside 25 Feet and a half in length, and 18 Feet in breadth, and two Rooms over the same, used for a Turner's Shop and a Joiner's Shop. Also the Close of Land in which the said Buildings are erected, called the Higher Reeding Pit Field, containing about one Acre of Land of *Cheshire* Measure.
>
> There is a very good Water Wheel fixt in the above Buildings, which is plentifully supplied with Water, sufficient to work a great Number of Machines, and there are Plenty of Hands to be procured in *Altrincham*, for carrying on the Cotton Manufactory, and on very reasonable Terms.

Almost a year later the *Manchester Mercury*[18] carried notice of another concern that Arkwright had claimed to have violated his 1775 patent, John Barnes & Co. of Congleton. It was advertised for sale by auction at the Black Lion and Swan, Congleton, on 22 May 1783 as:

> A Cotton mill, with all the Machines as they now stand . . . very desirably situated for the Manufacturing of Cotton Twist, being in a Country where Labour is cheap, and Plenty of Hands may be readily got. The Mill never wants Water in the dryest Seasons, and is never in back Water but in the highest Floods; and even then, not in Flood above an Hour or Two. There is a very good Turnpike Road from *Manchester* to *Congleton*, lately made, and regular Carriers upon the Road. The above Premises did belong to the Firm of *Thomas*

Morriss of Congleton, James Robinson, Henry Mather, and *John Barnes* all of *Warrington.*

As mule spinning came in, and as steam became auxiliary to, then super-seded, water as power, the same variations in scale persisted. On the one hand there were by the end of the Napoleonic Wars five spinners in Manchester and its neighbourhood employing more than 600 workpeople each: Adam & George Murray (1,215), M'Connel & Kennedy (1,020), Philips & Lee (937), Thomas Marriott (649) and Thomas Houldsworth (622). Below these were such well known concerns as Birley & Hornby (549), James Kennedy (490), Peter Marsland (465), the Ancoats Twist Company (376), John & Richard Simpson (334), David Holt (320), Peter Appleton & Co. (258), Peter Ewart & Co. (192) and B. & W. Sandford (178).[19]

The usual layout of this type of mill is given in Rees's *Cyclopaedia* (November 1812) in an article entitled 'Manufacture of Cotton':

> A large cotton mill is generally a building of five or six stories high: the two lowest are usually for the spinning frames, if they are for water twist, because of the great weight and vibration caused by these machines. The third and fourth floors contain the carding, drawing, and roving machines. The fifth story is appropriated to the reeling, doubling, twisting, and other operations performed on the finished thread. The sixth, which is usually in the roof, is for the batting machine, or opening machine, and for the cotton pickers, who for a large mill are very numerous. This last is not always so occupied, many manufacturers thinking it better to have out-buildings for these parts of the process, and only to have such parts in the mill as require the aid of the large water-wheel, or steam-engine, which turns the whole mill. If the mule is used for spinning instead of the water frame, then the cards are usually put below, because they are then the heaviest and most powerful machinery.[20]

But in urban as in country establishments the small firm was predominant. Twenty-four of the forty-nine Manchester concerns for which figures were supplied to Peel's committee had fewer than 200 workpeople, as had sixteen out of eighteen in Preston (one of the exceptions was Horrocks's, with 704) and six out of seven in Oldham.[21] And in this category must also be included 'some large Mills, whose respective Stories are let off to different Occupiers'.[22] This room- or floor-letting system was especially common in Manchester, where Samuel Baker's factory in Newton Street had twenty-six or twenty-seven different tenants, not all of them spinners ('the Appearance of this Place is extremely bad'),[23] and in Stockport, where the Lower Carr Factory had twenty-seven 'Masters' in it employing in all 250 people.[24]

Manchester's earliest mills dated from the beginning of the '80s. In 1786 'a stranger approaching the town only saw one high chimney, which was of Mr. Arkwright's mill'.[25] Three years before, this was said to be 'on a small scale'[26] but at the time only two others, those of Joseph Thackeray at Garratt on the river Medlock and William Douglas on the river Irwell at Pendleton, could approach it.[27] Both had begun as fustian manufacturers, as had Peter Drink-water, who by 1781 had left Bolton for Manchester, where Elizabeth Raffald's *Directory* for that year records him as being of Spring Garden.[28] The following year Drinkwater turned to spinning when he bought from his old Bolton partner William Cockshott (now of Macclesfield), his son John and Thomas Bromfield a 'New-erected' cotton mill 'in the Center of Northwich on the River Weaver . . . a Situation, which for Water and Hands cannot be exceeded by any in the Kingdom'.[29]

In 1789 Drinkwater built just off the London Road in Manchester the Piccadilly Factory,[30] a concern managed by Richard Slack, on whose death early in 1791 George Augustus Lee, a clerk at the Northwich mill, was promoted to the position. A year later, however, Lee left to become a partner with George and John Philips, Peter Atherton and Charles Wood in the Salford Engine Twist Company (later Philips & Lee).

Lee was succeeded as manager of Drinkwater's 'extensive Mule Factory', a post advertised in the Manchester newspapers in April 1792, by Robert Owen, whose own short-lived partnership with John Jones in machine making and cotton spinning had ended the previous September. Owen had then rented 'a large newly erected building, or factory, as such places were then beginning to be called' in Ancoats Lane. Here, with three men to work the mules he had received as compensation for his share in the partnership with Jones, he set up on his own 'in a small part of one of the large rooms in this large building' and was making £300 a year when interviewed by Drinkwater and, to the astonishment of Manchester, appointed manager of the Piccadilly Factory.[31]

While employed on his own account Owen had bought rovings from the recently established firm of Sandfords M'Connel & Kennedy. Benjamin Sandford had previously been in business as a lapboard manufacturer of Shudehill[32] and, at the same time, in partnership with his brother, William, as fustian warehousemen. James M'Connel and John Kennedy, both of Kir-cudbrightshire, were among a remarkable incursion of Highlanders and Low-landers who were to play an important part in the development of the Lan-cashire cotton-spinning industry. In 1781 nineteen-year-old M'Connel had moved to Chowbent, near Leigh, to become an apprentice machine maker with his uncle, William Cannon, who had learnt his trade of carpenter near New Galloway. On coming out of his time seven years later M'Connel had worked for a short period for Alexander Egelsom, a dealer in cotton twist and weft, of 48 Newton Street,[33] Manchester, before setting up on his own as a machine maker. Meanwhile in February 1784 the fourteen-year-old Kennedy had also been apprenticed by his widowed mother to William Cannon and, accompa-nied by James Smith, Cannon's partner, travelled to Chowbent by pony

— a journey which took six days.[34]

The beginnings of the great spinning concerns of B. & W. Sandford and of M'Connel & Kennedy are recalled by John Kennedy in *My Early Recollections*, written in 1827:

> My apprenticeship being ended, which lasted seven years, all which time I spent at Chowbent, I came to Manchester. This was on the 13th or 14th of February, 1791. I there formed a partnership with Benjamin and William Sandford, who were fustian warehousemen, and James M'Connel, under the firm of Sandfords, M'Connel, and Kennedy; and we immediately commenced business as Machine-makers and Mule Spinners: I taking the direction of the machine department. Our first shop was in Stable-street, or Back Oldham-street; and our capital was not more than £600 to £700. Here we made machines for others as well as ourselves, putting up our own mules in any convenient garrets we could find. After some time we removed to a building in Canal-street, called Salvin's Factory — from the name of the owner, who occupied a portion of it himself, letting off the remainder to us. This building is now a cholera-hospital. Here we continued to the end of our partnership which lasted four years, terminating in 1795.[35] The Sandfords choosing to remain in Salvin's Factory, James M'Connel and myself now removed to a little factory in the same street, where Mr. Fairbairn's machine-shop now stands. Here we continued to make machines for ourselves and others — the cards being turned by horse or by hand. These premises we occupied about six or seven years, when we began to build our first mill in Union-street. We subsequently built two others, adjoining the first — the Long Mill, begun in 1804 — and the Fireproof Mill.[36]

Several of the leading Manchester spinners had family connections with M'Connel & Kennedy. James Kennedy, a brother of John, began business in German Street about the turn of the century. His factory, 'reduced to a mere shell'[37] by fire in February 1803, was quickly rebuilt in nearby Gun Street, and a decade or so later another was added in Pickford Street.[38]

Alongside M'Connel & Kennedy's Union Street mills were those of Kennedy's childhood friends Adam & George Murray,[39] Manchester's largest spinners[40] by the end of the Napoleonic Wars. Fourteen-year-old Adam Murray had left New Galloway in 1780[41] to serve his apprenticeship with William Cannon and was followed, probably in 1786, by his brother George, who was to marry Cannon's daughter, Jane.[42] In 1794, or a little earlier, Adam set up a small concern employing about twenty hand spinners[43] as well as machine makers at 12 Newton Street,[44] and in partnership with his brother built in 1798[45] a factory in Union Street.

George Murray's daughters Catherine and Isabella[46] married James M'Connel's sons Thomas and Henry respectively. (Henry's first wife had been Margaret,[47] the eldest daughter of John Kennedy.) James M'Connel himself had in 1799, when almost thirty-seven, married Margaret, the twenty-year-old daughter of Henry Houldsworth, of Gonalston Hagg farm, near Gonalston, Nottinghamshire.[48] Margaret was then living in Manchester, where in 1795[49] her twenty one-year-old brother Henry had begun as a spinner in Little Lever Street.[50] The machines were worked by hand until the following year, when, as in several other Manchester mills about that time, a steam engine was installed.[51] Henry was soon joined by his brothers Thomas and William in a partnership which lasted until 21 January 1800.[52] The business was retained by Thomas, and by 1816 employed 622 workpeople. Henry meanwhile had moved in 1799 to Glasgow, where he took over the mill William Gillespie, a former Nottingham draper,[53] had built in 1784[54] at Woodside on the river Kelvin. In 1801 and 1805 he built mills at Anderston which, with Woodside, employed 635 workpeople by 1816.[55]

The work force of these early years was young and volatile. Questioned before Peel's committee as to 'the general habits of the operative spinners' in Manchester shortly before the turn of the century, Henry Houldsworth described them as

> very irregular, as the business at that time was done mostly by hand, and it was too generally the practice to drink the first day or two of the week and attempt to make it up by working very long hours towards the close of the week . . . I have seen them work all night on a Friday night . . . And, he went on, It must always be of importance that work-people should be steady and attentive to their work, but the capital occupied by a hand-spinner was so much less than that which is now occupied by a power-spinner, it of course was not of the same importance, and particularly when upon the whole he was able to make it up by working extra hours, which he now cannot do.[56]

In short, as John Saxon put it, work was now carried out with greater 'regularity' than in the pre-war years.[57] Even so A. & G. Murray, a concern generally regarded as being one of the best employers, were said in 1819 to have a labour turnover of almost 42 per cent. This figure was probably not untypical of the industry as a whole. By now, maintained William Simmons, a Manchester doctor, it was the 'general Practice' that workpeople 'are engaged from Week to Week, and they may leave at the End of every Week'.[58] His assertion was supported by Thomas Scott, an overlooker at M'Connel & Kennedy's, who told the 1818 committee, 'there is no Person about the Building who is employed beyond the Week, not of Spinners'. Further, workpeople need not give a week's notice, 'they frequently go away on Saturday Night, and do not come on Monday Morning'. Nor did M'Connel & Kennedy look for them; spinners, unlike weavers, did not keep Saint Monday and 'unless they appear by Eight or Nine o'Clock on Monday Morning, we get fresh ones' and 'they lose their Chance of a Week's Work'. It was much the same with piecers, who 'very often keep away Monday Morning for two or Three Hours for Play, and then go and get another Place'.[59] Workpeople at William Douglas's Pendleton mills were 'at Liberty to go at any Week End if they do not like their Place',[60] while at the Ancoats Twist Company anyone absent from work for two days was 'by the Rules of the Factory . . . liable to be discharged'.[61] 'Perhaps it may not be generally known,' said G. A. Lee, 'that there is really a place for hiring children; that is, that on a particular Monday moring there are a number of children that you can find at a particular place; their parents may perhaps attend, but it is rare; I think they are generally those independent children without parents'.[62]

In the early decades production was carried on round the clock. The Arkwright mills, it was said in 1784, 'are worked night and day or at least 23 of the 24 hours one hour is allowed for examining oiling and cleaning. There is as regular a relief of hands watch and watch about as in a ship.'[63] 'At that time,' said Sir Robert Peel, 'the profits arising from the machinery of Sir Richard Arkwright were so considerable, that it frequently happened, in different parts of the country, that the machinery was employed for the whole four-and-twenty hours.'[64] The Peels' own mills had been no exception. In the 1780s that at Radcliffe, near Manchester, worked its children eleven hours each night, including (a critic maintained) 'half an Hour at Dinner, as they call it'. And when during an outbreak of 'putrid fever' Peel was asked to stop night work he considered it 'so unprecedented a Requisition, to deprive one House of Privileges which are common to every other Person in the Business) that, I am persuaded, no man in his senses would have complied with it'.[65]

William Bray, a visitor to Cromford in 1776, recorded that the mill hands worked 'by turns, night and day', the spinning being done at night and the preparatory processes during the day.[66] Cromford had, indeed, worked these hours 'for about twenty-two years',[67] the greatest number of night workers, 164 boys, having been employed in 1781. The younger Arkwright, testifying before Peel's committee, remembered them as having 'got extravagant wages, and were extremely dissipated, and many of them had seldom more than a few hours sleep'.[68] In 1790 John Byng witnessed the change-over of the shifts: 'I saw the workers issue forth at 7'oClock, a wonderful crowd of young people, made as familiar as eternal intercourse can make them; a new set then goes in for the night, for the mills never leave off working . . . These cotton mills, seven stories high, and fill'd with inhabitants, remind me of a first rate man or war; and when they are lighted up, on a dark night, look most luminously beautiful.'[69] It was a scene caught in moonlight about 1783 by Joseph Wright, who revealed every window blazing from the light of candles or oil lamps.[70] Eight boys were at work in 1792, when night work was ended. Bakewell, the earliest records reveal, had ninety to a hundred night workers in 1787 but only twenty when, eight years later, round the clock working was abandoned.[71]

A writer in the *Gentleman's Magazine*[72] estimated that in Manchester in 1803 only one spinner in ten worked at night, and by 1819 the only reported instance was at William Douglas's, where forty-two[73] were employed, all but one aged over sixteen, out of a total work force of 531.[74] 'I can hardly think it would be to the interest of any manufacturer, at any time, to work in the night,' Arkwright told the 1816 committee. 'When two sets of hands come to the same machine they each will put the cleaning of it to the other, from which circumstance it is never clean.'[75]

The year 1781 saw Cromford with not only its largest number of night workers but also its greatest number of apprentices, fifty-four. According to the younger Arkwright, 'Apprentices first came, 8 in number, in 1777',[76] following close upon the completion of the second mill. Some few, like John Thomson, upon whose behalf the elder Arkwright in October 1783 engaged Thomas Ince to defend 'against the Charge of bastardy of Sarah Stanhope of Alfreton' (he was ordered to pay 'only eight pence per Week'), were parish apprentices. Two years earlier Ince had been called upon to write to the magistrate, Dr Joseph Denman, 'with respect to the behaviour of Thomas Stonehouse and Joseph Pearson'. Both were Arkwright apprentices, as was John Flint, a runaway from Cromford, 'by Trade a Joiner; he is a stout young Man, about 20 Years of Age, Red Hair, and has a mole on his Face'. Arkwright advertised in the *Derby Mercury* of 6 December 1781, offering a handsome reward for information as to his whereabouts.

By this time Bakewell also had its apprentices. Among the earliest was Simeon Cundy, who told the Factories Inquiry Commission of 1833[77] how in 1782, at the age of six years and two months, he had 'Entered Mr. Arkwright's factory . . . as a worker in the card-room; four years after [he] became an apprentice for seven years, to learn the turning, filing, and fitting up of wood, brass, iron, steel, and every branch of machinery.' His statement (he had left Bakewell for Manchester in 1793 to become a manager at William Young's mill) brings to mind Samuel More's description of 'those stupendous works the Cotton Mills at Crumford',[78] which he visited in 1783 and the machine shop described in Rees's *Cyclopaedia* some thirty years later:

> Curious lathes for turning spindles, and various other circular work, are used in the workshops of the cotton mills and fluting machines, for cutting the flutes in the lengths of the rollers of the drawing and spinning frames: in short, such works as Messrs. Strutts' at Belper, Mr. Arkwright at Cromford, in Derbyshire, Messrs. Phillips and Lees at Manchester, Mr. Peeles' and many others, are schools for mechanics in almost every department of that science; and good ones too, as the cotton manufacturers in general are convinced, that it is their interest to attend to every minutia in the construction of their machines, which may render them more durable or their operations more perfect.[79]

In his evidence before Peel's committee the younger Arkwright stated that he himself had never employed a single parish apprentice at Cromford but that

Samuel Oldknow, in whose concerns he had been a partner during the years 1800 to 1805, then had 'about fifty or sixty at the most'.[80] Arkwright's estimate is confirmed by Oldknow's accounts. The earliest apprentices (two boys) had come to Mellor in 1791. Seven years later there were about a hundred apprentices, for each of whom 4s a week was allowed for maintenance; by February 1804 the number had declined to sixty and the cost of maintenance increased to 6s a week.[81]

In a letter to the *Gentleman's Magazine*[82] James Neild estimated that in 1803 only one in ten of the children employed in the Manchester cotton mills were apprentices. And, he went on, 'it is not uncommon to hire *four* or *five* out of one family, by whose earnings alone (about 25s *per* week) their parents are supported in idleness and profligacy. I was informed none of the children could read, but those who were apprenticed out by the parishes of London, &c.'.

Another, and significant, aspect of child labour was noted by Robert Southey during his visit to Manchester in 1802:

> Mr. —— remarked that nothing could be so beneficial to a country as manufactures. 'You see these children, sir,' said he. 'In most parts of England poor children are a burthen to their parents and to the parish; here the parish, which would else have to support them, is rid of the expense; they get their bread almost as soon as they can run about, and by the time they are seven or eight years old bring in money. There is no idleness among us: — they come at five in the morning; we allow them half an hour for breakfast, and an hour for dinner; they leave work at six, and another set relieves them for the night; the wheels never stand still.'[83]

In 1802 Peel, influenced by a report published on 25 January 1796 by Dr Thomas Percival for the newly formed Manchester Board of Health, and 'struck with the uniform appearance of bad health, and in many cases, stunted growth of the children'[84] in his own mills, persuaded Parliament to pass the Health and Morals of Apprentices Act, a measure that applied to all mills and factories having three or more apprentices or twenty or more other workpeople. The Act prohibited the employment of apprentices for more than twelve hours a day (exclusive of the time allowed for meals), and from 1 June 1803 night work (between the hours of 9 p.m. and 6 a.m.) was forbidden. Other provisions related to sanitary conditions, general welfare, education and religious instruction. A printed copy of the Act was to be put in every mill or workshop and visits were to be made by clergymen and magistrates to ensure that its provisions were being carried out.

Almost a year before Peel's Act became law conditions at Cromford were described by Joseph Farington in his diary:

Saturday August 22d. [1801.]

In the evening I walked to Cromford, and saw the Children coming from their work out of one of Mr. Arkwright's manufactories. I was glad to see them look in general very healthy and many with fine, rosy, complexions. — These Children had been at work from 6 or 7 o'Clock this morning & it was now near or abt. 7 in the evening. The time for resting allowed them is at 12 o'Clock *40 minutes*, during which time they dine. One of them, a Boy of 10 or 11 years of age told me his Wages were 3s. 6d. a Week, — & a little Girl said Her wages were *2s 3d* a week.

Sunday August 23rd.

We went to Church at Cromford where is a Chapel built abt. 3 years and ½ ago by Mr. Arkwright . . . On each side the Organ is a gallery in which about 50 Boys were seated. These Children are employed in Mr. Arkwrights works in the week days, and on Sundays attend a School where they receive education. They came to Chapel in regular order and looked healthy & well & were decently cloathed & clean. They were attended by an Old Man their School Master. — To this School girls also go for the same purpose, and alternately with the Boys go to Church they Boys on one Sunday, — the Girls on the next following. — whichever are not at Chapel are at the School, which they both go to every Sunday both morning & afternoon. — The whole Plan appears to be such as to do Mr. Arkwright great credit.[85]

It was an impression of Cromford supported by Britton and Brayley in 1802. 'Proper attention,' they observed, 'is paid to the health and morals of the children, who are not admitted into the mills till they have been some time at school; and the sunday-schools are supported by Mr. Arkwright for their instruction afterwards. The mills are not worked by night, and are constantly kept very clean and neat.'[86]

At this time, Arkwright told Peel's committee, the Cromford mills were 'clean, and in very good order, and well ventilated . . . With respect to cleanlinesss and ventilation, they were matters that I had thought about, I think I may say, more than any other person, and on these points I certainly did not think it necessary to look over the works.'

All the same, he had found 'some rules in the Act which were troublesome, and could answer no purpose'.[87] Especially so was the requirement that all rooms be whitewashed at least twice a year: 'Now there are a great many rooms and apartments belonging to a large manufactory . . . and it was necessary to see that all those were done, or I should be liable to the penalties of the Act.'[88]

Arkwright had been 'very glad'[89] to receive visiting magistrates but agreed that 'it would be rather an invidious task for magistrates to inspect the mills of their neighbours and friends'.[90] The observation was not without point. Between 1803 and 1808 Philip Gell, from whose father the elder Arkwright had leased land upon which to build the Bakewell and Wirksworth mills, had inspected the Cromford and Masson mills on six occasions. The Wirksworth hundred's cotton mills, he reported, were 'in such State and Condition and regulated in such Manner as is required by the Directors of the said Act'. The report on Bakewell was even shorter: 'No apprentices. Every thing in great Order.'[91] The visiting magistrate here was Joseph Denman, who had been the elder Arkwright's physician.

The discussion that resulted from Peel's Act, Arkwright believed, had been of greater value than the law itself in bettering working conditions: 'Great improvements have been made in the management of the machinery since that Act was passed',[92] 'particularly with respect to ventilation and cleanliness.'[93] The Act, he contended, 'only speaks of there being sufficient windows for the admission of air, but nothing about ventilation'.[94] In short 'there are not so many ill conducted mills as there were'.[95] It was a view shared by Thomas Scott, who had eighteen years' experience of mill work. 'They are very much improved, both in Cleanliness and Commodiousness of the Rooms.'[96]

Even so, the earliest report of any length, that by Ralph Wright and Thomas Beard, the Justices of the Peace appointed to visit the Manchester mills, is worth reproducing as showing the state of the eleven concerns inspected by them in the course of a single day:

That on the 21st Day of September 1810, we visited the Weaving Factory of George Merryweather, situated near Ancoat's Lane in Manchester; we found the Rooms in general tolerable, but crowded with too many Looms; that there were no Rules put up in this Factory. In one of the Boys Rooms there were Seventeen Beds, in another Seventeen Beds, in another Eighteen Beds, and Two in the Sick Room; in the Girls Room there were Forty-two Beds; there is a great want of Ventilation in this Factory.

The Potatoes for Dinner were boiling with the Skins on, in a State of Great Dirtiness, and Eight Cow Heads boiling in another Pot for Dinner; a great Portion of the Food we were told was of a liquid Nature; the Privies were too offensive to be approached by us; some of the Apprentices complained of being overworked.

That on the same Day we visited the Factory of Adam and George Murray, accompanied by the said George Murray.

That there were no Rules put up; that Two Rooms were not whitewashed; that there was not sufficient Ventilation in a large Room 13 to 14 Yards wide, and 66 Yards long; that this Room had not been whitewashed of upwards of a Year; that the Part called the New Mill, had lately been whitewashed; that in the Fourth Room the Thermometer stood at 74 after an Exhibition of Ten Minutes, and that Mr. George Murray said he conceived the general Average 75.

That on the same Day we visited the Factory of Archibald Crowther, in which there were no Rules, no Ventilation; that it was whitewashed about Three Months before our Visit; and that the Thermometer stood at 75.

That on the same Day we visited the Factory of James Gratrix, in which no Rules were put up; not sufficient Ventilation; that the new Part was about Twelve Months ago whitewashed.

That on the same Day we visited the Factory of Messrs. William Mitchell and Co.; that there are 36 Apprentices; that there are from 4 to 500 Persons employed in the Factory; that there were no Rules put up; and that the New Mill was greatly in Want of Ventilation; that it wants Whitewashing; only whitewashed Once a Year. The Apprentices appeared to us to be well-fed and clothed, and in a most comfortable Situation.

That on the same Day we visited the Factory of Jonathan Pollard; in this Factory about 600 Persons are employed; there were no Rules up; that it is whitewashed Once a Year only; that the Thermometer was about 70.

That on the same Day we visited the Factory of James Kennedy, in which there were no Rules put up; that it had not been whitewashed of Twelve Months; that the Thermometer was at 75, and that the Rooms are 55 Yards long, and $13\frac{1}{2}$ wide; there is Want of Ventilation.

That on the same Day we visited the Factory of Lawrence Buchan and James Shaw, which we found had not been whitewashed for a Year; that there were no Rules up; that there was not sufficient Ventilation; that the Thermometer was about 70; and that all the Spinning done here is coarse, being Nos. 18 and 20 only.

That on the same Day we visited the Factory of Messrs. H. H. Birley and Co. which appears to have been whitewashed Twice in the present Year; that there were no Rules up in this Factory; that in the Old Mill the Thermometer was at 73, where they spin No. 40, and that in the New Mill it was at 72, where they also spin No. 40.

That on the same Day we visited the Factory of John Marsland, in which we found the Rules up; there was not sufficient Ventilation; the Thermometer was about 80.

That on the same Day we visited the Factory of Joseph Wilson, John Fairweather, and John Jones; that there were no Rules up in this Factory; that it is whitewashed Once a Year only, the last Time in the Race Week; that about 300 Persons are employed in this Factory; they spin about No. 30; the Thermometer was about 75.[97]

On this kind of report it is hardly surprising that the large spinners who gave most of the evidence during the hearings of the parliamentary committees that preceded the Factory Act of 1819 considered it necessary to go to some pains to present a case. Highly critical,[98] as for a generation afterwards, of their small uncouth competitors, not a few felt constrained to take positive steps to prepare for the visits of the medical men called in, sometimes by themselves, sometimes by John Douglas, chairman of the Committee of Master Cotton Spinners, to inspect their mills.

Preparations, indeed, were such as to lend weight to the views of the anonymous author of *Answers to certain objections made to Sir Robert Peel's Bill,* a tract published in Manchester in 1819. 'The labors of the Master-spinners in organizing opposition to this Bill [the writer maintained] are co-extensive with their influence, and as inexhaustable almost as their funds.' And, further, the 'Master-Spinners and their philosophical friends . . . seemed disposed to think, that employment in a Cotton Mill has the nature of a *privilege*, that the working classes can only then be happy, peaceable, and healthy whilst they are spinning cotton'.[99] In short, as Owen put it, 'the Factory Bill . . . was strongly opposed, and often by the most unfair means, by almost all the cotton spinners and manufacturers in the kingdom, except Messrs. Arkwright, the Strutts, and the Fieldens'.[100] (And even the Strutts admitted themselves opposed to Peel's Bill in that 'interference is bad in principle'.[101])

Present and recent workpeople (some had been dismissed for going up to London to give evidence before the Lords committee of 1818) contended that before the visits of medical men the master spinners had shortened hours of work, dismissed sick and deformed workpeople, lowered room temperatures, reduced the speed of machinery, ordered the cleaning of mill work rooms as never before, and told workpeople to tidy themselves.

Not a few of these charges were admitted by the mill owners or by their representatives. Both the manager and spinning overlooker of Birley & Hornby confirmed that hours had been reduced by twenty minutes each day, although they differed by as much as nine months as to when this had taken place.[102] Appleton & Plant (now the owners of Drinkwater's Piccadilly Factory) testified that they had shortened hours by the same amount 'About Five or Six Months since'.[103] The Ancoats Cotton Twist Company (a concern owned by Reid Irving & Co. of London and Benjamin Gray[104] of Manchester) said that at the end of 1818 they had cut their hours by two and a half a week. The firm's superintendent, James Frost, was somewhat evasive as to his personal responsibility for this sudden conversion. 'I cannot state the exact Reason why they were shortened. It was an Order given to me by my Employer; what his Reason was I do not enter into.'[105] In October 1818 M'Connel & Kennedy also shortened hours by the same amount. 'I do not know that I gave any Opinion to my Brother in favour of shortening the Hours,' edged John M'Connel, superintendent and half-brother of the owner; ' . . . my Employers, if they form a Resolution, do not always consult me upon the Propriety of it'.[106]

Between the publication of an article about conditions at M'Connel & Kennedy in *The Times* of 8 April 1818 and the visit of the doctors, the owner, M'Connel testified, dismissed three lame workpeople — Thomas Wilson, Edward Worsley, a piecer, and William Hawkesworth.[107] Worsley, aged eighteen, took up work at A. & G. Murray.[108] Wilson, also eighteen, said that he had been 'turned away' a fortnight before the doctors' visit, 'Mr. M'Connel told me, it was killing me by Inches, and that my Parents must get me some other Trade.'[109] He became a tailor.[110] At Sandfords' Peter Manning, a sixteen-year-old cardroom worker dismissed after the visit — 'My Master came himself and turned me away' — testified that six or seven cripples had earlier been given their notice. 'The Hue and Cry went through our Rooms, that any who complained of bad Health would be turned away.'[111]

Joseph Tavner, a thirty-four-year-old spinner,[112] was discharged from the Ancoats Cotton Twist Company because (said the superintendent[113] who had been present when the doctors had questioned the child workers) of what he had said about preparations for the visit. He had, he maintained, been 'ordered to clean up and wash and shave' and the steam-heated rooms 'were much colder than they had ever been before'.[114] According to the superintendent the thermometer had stood at $73\frac{1}{2}°F$, and washing and cleaning on the day in question were 'no more than common'.[115] 'I think, in Mr. Gray's Factory,' said Dr Edward Carbutt, a physician at the Manchester Infirmary and an opponent of reform, ' the Children had made themselves a little cleaner than usual'.[116]

Despite the absence of thermometers workpeople at David Holt's and at Sandfords' were not at a loss to advance reasons for their belief that temperatures had been lowered for the doctors' visits. 'The Rooms seemed to be colder than usual,' said George Brennan, a twenty nine-year-old 'Working Spinner' at Holt's. 'I worked near the driving Pipe, where the main Steam comes; it leaks, and I have a Jug under it; I put my Hand to it, there was no Water coming, and it was cold.'[117] The rooms at Sandfords', said Peter Manning, were 'a deal colder . . . before the Doctors came I never used to work in anything but my Breeches and Shirt; and after they came, I had my Shoes and Stockings on, and could abide to have my Waistcoat on'.[118]

Spinners at Birley & Hornby contended that the speed of machinery had been reduced: 'the Spinner next to me [testified twenty-year-old John Mellor] was saying something was amiss with the Engine, and I said the same to him, but we did not know what was happening 'till the Middle of the Day, when the Doctors happened to appear, and then we judged it was that that caused the Engine to go slower'.[119] This was denied by the manager, who gave figures of output in an attempt to support his case.[120]

The most elaborate preparations were said to have taken place at the mills of John Pooley, a concern well known to the visiting Dr Edward Holme, the family's physician. According to Matthew Carter, a spinner now employed at Ralph Walley's,[121] Pooley had ordered his workpeople to take their dinner break not in the room in which they worked but in a field opposite the mill,[122] and that, further:

we received orders . . . to stop the Machinery, and wash the Rooms with Sand and Water . . . the Spinners received Orders to tell their Piecers to wash and clean themselves very well before they came in the Morning; and on the 18th [April] there was a Barber employed to cut the Hair of the Children or any

Person that stood in need of it . . . the Manager and Overlooker came into my Room, and the Manager opened the Window himself with the Assistance of the Overlooker . . . and we have every Reason to believe they were kept open all Night; there were People who went early in the Morning and found them open and the Doors too.[123]

And finally, one hour before the doctors arrived, the speed of the machinery was reduced by about a fifth.[124]

All this was denied by Pooley's overlooker, Joseph Hassel, although at times he came close to a partial admission:

Q Were you present when the Mill was inspected by the Doctors last Year?
A I was in the Mill.
Q Was there any extraordinary Preparation made for them?
A No, I had no Orders whatever.
Q Was the Mill more cleaned upon that Occasion than at any other Time or in any other Manner?
A No.
Q Was the Machinery stopped on that Morning in any unusual Manner, or for more Time than common?
A No.
Q And no extraordinary Cleaning took place?
A No.
Q Were there any Orders given to have the Spinners or Piecers in the Mill washed or dressed, or to appear in any other way than usual on the Day?
A I do not recollect having heard of any.
Q What Orders had you from Mr. Pooley about cutting the Children's Hair, and when?
A Mr. Pooley told me he would have their Hairs cut in the [Sunday] School about a Month or Six Weeks before the Medical Men came into the Mill; he said he would have their Hairs cut, and that they would look much better and cleaner.
Q What did you do accordingly?
A I think it was done the Week following, and part of the Week after that; I think they were finished about a Fortnight before the Doctors came.[125]

Hours of work in the Manchester mills at this time averaged fourteen a day (meal times excluded), according to a list of twenty-two concerns presented to the 1816 committee by George Gould, an active supporter of Peel's Bill.[126] Another list, compiled by Dr W. J. Wilson, named fifteen mills at which the average actual weekly hours came to seventy-three.[127] Benjamin Potter's, at eighty hours a week, was said to have worked longer than any other Manchester mill;[128] John Birch junior's, at seventy-five, was not far behind.[129] Thackeray's worked 'fourteen hours in a day without intermission, no time being allowed for meals'.[130] G. A. Lee told the committee that Manchester's hours were only half an hour longer than in Sir Richard Arkwright's time.[131]

From its beginnings, the early indentures reveal, Cromford had put in thirteen hours a day, including the one-hour break allowed for dinner.[132] This had been the invariable practice at the Derby Silk Mill since its foundation in 1717 and had thus a venerable antiquity.[133] Work began at 6 a.m. in summer and an hour later in winter.[134] Spinners, it is true, now, as perhaps always, shortened the day by taking 'some minutes' to 'set the whole of the machinery to work' in the mornings and by 'preparing to go away' fifteen or twenty minutes before the machinery stopped working at the end of the day.[135] On the other hand some attempt was made to make up for time lost through floods, droughts and breakdowns of machinery to 'fractions of a quarter of a day; not more . . . When the works are stopped a quarter of a day or more the wages are deducted in proportion to the time.'[136] On average the mills lost six days a year through floods but only about twelve hours of that time was made up.[137] There was also a loss through sickness. 'Upon the average of two years,' Arkwright told the 1816 committee, 'there have been seven [our of 727] upon the sick-list . . . when they are ill they receive half wages, so that they are sure to be put on the sick-list if they have the least complaint.'[138]

Whether Cromford's week ended at 3.30 p.m. on Saturdays as was usual in Manchester[139] is not clear, but its normal working day was shorter, a fact that supporters of Peel's Bill were not slow to point out: 'in the Mills of Mr. Arkwright . . . the customary time of labor is from one to two hours a day less than in many other Cotton Factories, and yet the owner of these Mills is not aware, that others whose hours of employment are longer than his own, have any advantage over him in the trade on that account'.[140]

Except for the dinner break Cromford's water-powered machinery never stopped. Arkwright described how breakfast and tea were taken:

> As to breakfast, it is very irregular. In the summer-time the bell rings for breakfast as half past eight; those who go to breakfast, which includes the workmen, but not the spinners, go and stay half an hour. There is a room called the dinner-house, in which there is a range of hot plates or stoves, much the same as in gentlemens kitchens; the mothers, or the younger sisters of the hands employed, bring the breakfasts into this room; they bring them probably a quarter of an hour before the bell rings. As soon as the bell rings, a number of boys, perhaps eight, carry those breakfasts into the different rooms in the factory; those who come first may receive their breakfasts probably in two minutes those who come later may not receive it for a quarter of an hour; so that possibly some of the hands may have eight-and-twenty minutes at breakfast, others cannot have more than fifteen, they cannot have less. In the afternoon the bell rings at four, and they are served in like manner; but very few have their refreshment, probably not one in five, I should think . . . there may be from forty to forty-five minutes allowed in the whole in the morning and afternoon.[141]

Manchester's breakfast and tea arrangements — except perhaps for the provision of the 'dinner-house' — were in line. At M'Connel & Kennedy, which worked from 5 a.m. to 7 p.m. in summer and from 6 a.m. to 8 p.m. in winter[142] (including a break of an hour for dinner)[143] the engine did not stop while workpeople took breakfast and tea.[144] The mechanics, Thomas Scott told the Lords committee of 1818, went out to their meals. 'The Spinner generally sits down to his Breakfast, the Piecers keeping the Machinery on, and then one of the Piecers sits down.'[145] 'I sometimes leave them sitting when I go to my [half-hour] Breakfast, and return and find them still at it; then I check them for it.'[146] Workpeople, he went on, 'Sometimes boiled Milk in a Morning, sometimes Tea'.[147]

Asked, 'How do the Children get their Breakfast and Afternoon Meal?' John Reid, manager of Birley & Hornby, replied, 'The Scavengers and Creel Fillers sit down; the Piecers take it as the Machinery is going, between Stretches.'[148] At Pooley's, where there were two piecers to every spinner, 'One generally gets its Breakfast, and the other keeps the Ends up for both.'[149] Holt's, said fifty-two-year-old superintendent Joseph Gosling, allowed 'One Hour for Dinner; as to the other Refreshment, all that goes by Steam do not go out; the others do'. Spinners did not leave their machines for breakfast; piecers breakfasted in their rooms, spared from work 'By others assisting in their Place'.[150]

A detailed picture was presented by Lawrence Gardner, an overlooker at William Douglas & Co.:

Q How do the Children in that Factory get their Breakfast or Afternoon Meal?
A They get it how they can; they never have any Stoppages.
Q Can they sit down to get it?
A If their Ends are up, they can sit down and get it; they must not neglect their Work.
Q How often have they to piece the Ends?
A They are continually breaking down; they break faster sometimes than they can piece them, and if the Overlooker comes, he chastises them if he finds that, and asks them how it is; they say they can do no more.
Q If he finds them getting their Breakfast, and their Ends down, what will he say?
A He dare not strike them; he will jaw them.[151]

It would, Arkwright believed, be 'extremely inconvenient'[152] if Parliament decreed that workpeople must leave the mill for breakfast and tea. Of his 725 workpeople in 1816 373 lived in Cromford (at a distance, he calculated, of 970 yards), 147 in Bonsall, ninety-five in Matlock, sixty-three in Middleton, twenty-five in Wirksworth (at two miles the farthest point) and the remaining twenty-two in other places; he had found 'upon experiment' that forty-five minutes 'too little for their going to dinner', fifty minutes was more realistic. Further, 'two thirds of these 725 are working in effect by the piece; if the doors were thrown open to them very few would go out'.[153]

If Cromford's workpeople were able to enjoy a full hour for dinner it was an unusual state of affairs. In Manchester only James Kennedy's, where there was a complete halt (except that once a Fortnight they [the piecers] stop a short Time to clean the Machine, to assist the Spinner in cleaning through the Machine'), could approach it.[154]

John M'Connel said that during the dinner hour the men spinners, assisted by their piecers, 'usually clean on Friday and Saturday, on Friday from Half an Hour to Forty Minutes, and on Saturday from Half an Hour to the whole Hour, just as it may happen'. On Saturdays 'the Engine stops at Four, the Spinners usually stop a Quarter of an Hour or twenty Minutes before that Time, in order to finish any cleaning that has been left undone before'.[155]

At Pooley's, which worked a twelve-and-a-half-hour day, the dinner break excluded, children spent ten to fifteen minutes of their break cleaning machinery on four days of each week. On Wednesdays all were detained to clean the mill, dinner — upon which they were able to spend fifteen to twenty minutes — being brought to them.[156] The position was similar at Holt's. Although the engine stopped for an hour, children were unable to go to dinner, Mondays excepted, until they had finished cleaning and oiling the machinery, a task which took up an increasing amount of time as the week went on — fifteen minutes on Tuesdays to a maximum of forty-five minutes on Fridays. On Saturday forty minutes were spent in this way.[157]

At William Douglas's, said Hugh Batho,[158] the manager, piecers were not responsible for cleaning the mill, 'They clean as they go, many of them; some Jobbers stop during the Dinner Hour to clean.' They were paid extra for 'every Hour they work'.[159] Isaac Hodgson,[160] a prominent member of the Committee of Master Cotton Spinners, employed children, usually over sixteen, to clean his mill at Caton, near Lancaster, for twenty to thirty minutes of each dinner hour at 6d a week. 'It is,' he said, 'rather a favour to them to stay ... they are desirous of it; and if they behave ill they are not allowed to do it.'[161]

From about 1806 — Arkwright was not certain as to the exact time — Cromford stopped taking on children under ten.[162] The 'principal reason was, that they might learn to read before they came; I do not think their health was taken into consideration, as no injury ever appeared to me to arise to it.'[163] All the same, 'I should think if boys were taken at nine it would be better: I see them often running about, and in mischief.' The girls 'have to nurse their younger brothers and sisters, or they work at home, or they do something; but boys have nothing to do unless they go to school'.[164]

As to Peel's proposed legislation, Arkwright thought that it would be impracticable in water spinning for the minimum age to rise much above ten: 'in that particular part that requires the best hands it requires some years to learn the business, and if they were not to go till they were twelve or thirteen, they would be leaving when they became useful. According to the statement I have made the greatest number are at fifteen, after that the number decreases.' Cromford, Arkwright maintained, employed no child under ten and only four of that age.[165] He had, he said, 'never heard of any chidren being employed so young as five till I came into this room', although he had 'heard of their being taken in at six'.[166] He may well have had in mind Robert Owen's testimony that he had been told of a girl of three being employed at Stockport and that 'it was a very common practice to employ children at the ages of five or six'. David Dale's pauper apprentices at New Lanark were 'generally from the age of five and six, to seven and eight'. Owen admitted that he had taken on children of from six to eight as scavengers but now employed them at ten to twelve.[167]

Children of five and six were still said to be employed at Manchester and Bolton, while at Preston twenty-two of Horrocks's 704 workpeople were under eight and a further seventy-one under ten.[168] Out of their work force of 531 William Douglas admitted to employing five under nine:[169] 'Ten is the general Age, and not younger, unless by the Desire of the Parents,' said the firm's manager,[170] and this was confirmed by John Saxon: 'I never knew any taken under Ten, unless at the Desire of their Parents, who are poor People.'[171] It was an attitude similar to that of M'Connel & Kennedy, who admitted to having had seventeen children under nine in 1818 but none a year later. 'We do not wish to have them [under nine] from Choice quite so young as that; Part of them are working with their Parents, and they wish to introduce them as soon as they can, but it is not from Choice we take them.'[172] Of the medical men called in to examine workpeople Dr Gavin Hamilton found 'Very few indeed' as young as eight,[173] Dr Wilson forty-one under nine[174] and Dr James Ainsworth eighteen under nine out of a total work force of 992 in the mills he had visited.[175]

At Cromford, where children were not admitted until they were able to read, Arkwright conceded that the pressure of parents to get their children into the mills had resulted in a lowering of standards, and children were in fact taken on 'if they could read at all . . . Any small words.' 'And in general,' he elaborated, 'the parents are so anxious to get their children to work, that the man appointed to hear them read will sometimes examine them very little, and probably they can scarcely read; that is a matter that has been obliged to be attended to sometimes, to make them adhere to the rules.'[176]

The youngest children began work as scavengers. 'The way in which many of these infants are first employed,' Owen told Peel's committee, 'is to pick up the waste cotton from the floor; to go under the machines, where bigger people cannot creep, and the smaller they are the more conveniently they can go under the machines.'[177] At the same time they wiped the dust and dirt from the machinery. More than a few doubtless began in the manner described by Henry Houldsworth: 'I have known children that carry up their parents' tea in the afternoon, kept by their parents for half an hour or an hour, to do a job of that kind, and perhaps to go up for half an hour, as much as four times a day, to assist in what they call wiping down, which is generally done in the course of fiteen minutes.' These children, he said, were employed not by the mill owner but by their own parents.[178]

'Are not the young Children, taken in as Scavengers, gradually learning the Art of Piecing?' John Stewart, until recently manager of James Kennedy, was asked by the Lords committee of 1818. 'Yes,' came the reply, 'they gradually learn; every now and then they will put up a Thread . . . as they get bigger to reach to the Piecing.'[179] In fine spinning, he maintained, it was 'very difficult' for children under nine to become piecers and he had not considered them until they were a year older.[180]

At James Kennedy's, Stewart went on, 'the Master pays the Piecers', who, unlike the spinners, were 'paid by the Week'.[181] At M'Connel & Kennedy, on the other hand, some of the scavengers and piecers were paid by the firm and the remainder by the spinners, all of whom worked by piece;[182] male spinners engaged and paid their own piecers, while those working for female spinners were usually taken on by the overlookers in charge of the rooms in which they worked.[183] In general, Dr Carbutt agreed, 'the Spinners only are employed by the Master Manufacturers, and . . . they employ the Piecers and Scavengers themselves'.[184] And, according to George Gould, the younger the better: 'The spinning men or women, whichever they are, have the privilege, I understand, generally to employ children of their own selecting; and if they can get a child to do their business for one shilling, or one shilling and sixpence, they will take that child before they will give three, four, five, siz, or seven shillings, to an older one.'[185]

It was widely held that water powered mills were healthier places in which to work than those driven by steam. 'It is an unquestionable Truth,' said James Watkins, of Bolton, 'that Children in Cotton Factories that have fallen under my Observation are generally puny and squalid, especially those who work in Mills where Steam Engines are used; but in Establishments where the Machinery be worked by Water Wheels, the Climate of the Rooms is more wholesome, and the Appearance of the Children better.'[186]

In the eyes of contemporaries room temperature was, perhaps, the most important of 'the Climate of the Rooms'. And, it was said, the finer the spinning the greater the temperature required. 'Nothing can be more pleasant than the Temperature of the Factories,' Major General Gabriel Doveton, MP for Lancaster, told the Lords committee of 1818, comparing mill conditions with those of barracks in India. Altogether he had spent 'About an Hour' at Horrocks's, where the 'average heat' was said to be in the low sixties.[187]

Not everyone shared the opinion of this former official of the East India Company. And among these was Robert Hyde, a spinner at Appleton &

Plant, a concern spinning counts from 110 to 240: 'In the Coarse Mills, People generally complain of the long Hours and hard Work; and in the Fine Mills they complain of the long Hours and the intense Heat; for my own Part, I have worked to that Degree in the Coarse Mills, I have been so, that I could not sleep in my Bed; and it is the Case too often in Manchester, and other Places.'[188]

In mills spinning low counts temperatures of 60°F to 65°F seem to have been sufficient, although in the summer months they were likely to be exceeded. Cromford, water-driven and spinning low counts of 'Perhaps twenty, or five-and-twenty', tried to maintain its rooms at 60°F, the temperature Dr Darwin advised was 'the best heat', but, said Arkwright, 'In summer it must be higher than that; it is kept as cool as it can be in summer.'[189] The person responsible for inspecting the rooms, he went on, carried a thermometer 'which he uses when the rooms are complained of as being too cold; never for being too hot'. There was at the time no method of preventing this but by 'making less fires, or admitting less warm air; something of that kind is in use in almost all well regulated manufactories'.[190]

Fine spinners freely admitted mill-room temperatures up to the mid-seventies, while workpeople protested that they worked in temperatures up into the eighties. At Thomas Houldsworth's, a firm said to produce the finest twist for the Nottingham lace industry, Dr Henry Hardie of the Manchester Infirmary noted a temperature of 74°F a figure, he said, confirmed by the enquiries he had made of workpeople: temperature was 'seldom or never above 74°F.; and when it was, that extra Degree of Heat was not necessary'.[191]

Thomas Scott of M'Connel & Kennedy maintained that 75°F was needed to produce the finest yarn, 220; 'it is apt to stick to the Rollers in a lower Temperature'.[192] John M'Connel said the card-room temperature was 'Seldom ever above 70',[193] while in the spinning rooms 'We do not wish it more than 75 or 76 at the outside for the finest.'[194] 'Eighty or upwards,' he added, 'I should call an excessive Heat . . . I probably may have seen it a little above 80 on some Occasions, when the Windows were closed, or under some particular Circumstances, but very rarely.'[195] James Johnson, a thirty-seven-year-old spinner, claimed that counts of 160 to 250 needed temperatures of 77°F to 80°F and that the highest he had known was 89°F.[196]

Spinners, M'Connel contended, were 'usually very desirous' of having it hotter[197] and in this he was supported by Johnson, who testified to having heard of spinners who liked a temperature of 80°F, 'bribing the Man to keep the Heat higher' or 'at least they give the Man a Penny a week to keep the Heat up, at least to take care that they have Heat'.[198] A more orthodox version of the way in which the temperature was regulated was given by M'Connel: 'There are Two Men Spinners, who work adjoining where the Thermometer is hung up, order the Engineer when to admit or stop the Steam; and in case I was to find it excessively hot at any Time, I should complain of it, and order it to be lowered.'[199]

In this he was supported by Dr. Hardie:

> I ascertained, [from the engineer] at Mr. Murray's, and at other Factories . . . that if . . . I were a Spinner, and sent down to the Engine Man to tell him to turn his Steam off, he was obliged to do so; and that it was turned off, not only for the individual Room, but for all the Rooms in the Factory; so that one Person, finding the Heat oppressive, could immediately order the whole of the Rooms to be cooled, by having the Steam, which ascends in the hollow Tubes, let off at the Engine . . . and in consideration for the Trouble the Engine Man took in so doing, he had a Penny a Week allowed to him by every Spinner in the Factory.[200]

Whatever the attitude of spinners towards the temperature of the rooms in which they worked, it was often inconvenient or well nigh impossible for windows to be opened, especially when spinning high numbers.

At M'Connel & Kennedy ('There is Part of every Window which opens, and they have the Liberty of opening it whenever they please, to let in fresh Air')[201] spinners working by piece preferred high temperatures to a more comfortable atmosphere. With windows on 'both Sides' of their factories[202] 'when there is a Wind it will blow one Thread upon another, and that is a Loss to the Spinner', said Thomas Scott.[203] At William Mitchell's a spinner confirmed that windows were opened 'Very seldom; they cannot do with any Wind, it blows the Yarn down',[204] while at Appleton & Plant's a fine spinner, when asked, 'It is the Wish of the Owner of that Factory, that Air should be admitted if the Work-People will allow it?' replied, 'Yes; but he is as conscious as I am that it will not do.'[205] Pooley's were said to have ordered windows to be opened every day except when the wind was too high.[206] 'It would not do to open the Windows of a fine Cotton Room on a very stormy Day,' said John Stewart, until recently of James Kennedy's, 'it would blow the Ends down; but we have another Means of ventilating the Rooms, by a Funnel from the Top to the Bottom of the Factory.'[207]

How, whatever the state of the weather, Cromford was kept in 'a constant state of ventilation as well as warmth' was described by Arkwright:

> It is by the admission of a current of warm air; it is admitted into the mill, in a column of probably four feet square in general, but there are different constructions: an aperture out of this column is made into each room, that aperture is more or less, as circumstances may require, and in consequence, a regular flow of air goes into each room; an outlet is made at the greatest distance from this inlet, which allows the foul air to escape.[208]

Some method of ventilation and dust extraction was especially needed in the scutching rooms. The beating, opening and cleaning of newly arrived raw cotton had usually been done by women, sometimes working in their own homes (as would appear to have been the case in the mid-1780s with the fifty or so workpeople at Youlgreave[209] employed by Arkwright's Bakewell mill), until, in 1797, a scutching or blowing machine was constructed by Neil Snodgrass and first used at Houston's mill at Johnstone, near Paisley. Eleven or twelve years later it was introduced into Manchester and became generally adopted for the cleaning of cotton. 'The labor of that operation,' we are told by John Kennedy in his paper on the early cotton industry, 'formerly performed by women, in a most fatiguing manner, and always considered as degrading; has been reduced by this machine to about one twentieth of what it used to be.'[210] Arkwright and William Strutt, he added, had made 'most useful improvements'.

A description of the machine in use at Cromford was supplied to the 1816 committee by Arkwright:

> The scutching machine most in use, is a machine for cleaning cotton from the seeds and other impurities, and is in principle similar to the thrashing machine. The cotton passes through a pair of rollers, and is struck by bars of iron or steel called beaters, which revolve with great velocity, striking the cotton with considerable force over a number of parallel bars so placed as to allow the seeds to fall through, the current of air passing over the bars, and carrying the cotton fly and dust forward into an apartment called the cotton chamber. It is necessary this air should be got rid of, and it is effected by a large opening, in which is placed a fine wire-grating; the air either returns into the room or is suffered to escape externally. But even by this latter mode considerable inconveniency arises to the persons employed, from the dust and fly, as it is impossible to close up every aperture and crevice so as to prevent some portion of it from coming into the working-room. This inconveniency is now completely remedied, by the adoption of a very simple plan: a fan is placed on the outside of the wire-grating before-mentioned, which by a quick rotary motion rarefies or exhausts in some degree the cotton-chamber; consequently the air in the working-room presses in at every opening to restore the equilibrium, carrying with it all the fly and dust created by the working of the scutcher.[211]

Arkwright maintained that there was no more dust to be found in the scutching room at Cromford than in the room in which the committee was meeting,[212] and he might well have supported his assertion by reading from the notes he had prepared concerning the health of his workpeople: 'Fly & dust — Old Joseph Stundall aged 80 years worked at dust Machine 20 years. At Cromford 42 Males and Females have worked 25 years & upwards, none are asthmatic.'

Yet there remained great variations in the conditions of work in this as indeed in other stages of manufacture. An overlooker at M'Connel & Kennedy claimed that there was no dust in any of the rooms;[213] another at Pooley's testified that he had never seen workpeople's breakfasts 'spoiled or covered with the Flyings'[214] as was said to be common in many mills.[215] Peter Leigh, 'Master in one Part'[216] of the Lower Carr Factory, Stockport, said that apart from opening windows the only method of dust prevention was 'by the Engines being covered, some with Wood and some with Tin, to prevent the Dust rising as much as they can'. But workpeople, he held, had no ground for complaint: 'I never had any Reason to complain when I was a Spinner, and I have worked in one of the dirtiest Rooms I ever saw.'[217]

Joseph Dutton, of Liverpool, said that the scutching room at Ainsworth & Catterall of Preston contained 'so much [dust] that I could scarcely see the women who worked at the engine',[218] yet at Robert Davis's of Ashton-under-Lyne he found 'the scutching machine. . . was upon a most admirable plan indeed; there was no dust whatever came to the people that worked at it . . . It was completely insulated from the other part of the factory, in a separate room, and all the dust was carried by tubes into the air, and the cotton fell into a room below, so that there was no inconvenience to the people whatever.' Dutton believed this machine to be upon the same plan as the one at Horrocks's 'but I did not see it'.[219] He had, however, visited Horrocks's carding room and believed it to be 'the completest one I saw, but it certainly was not free from dust; the carding machinery was covered, but still there was dust; in other places, where they were not covered, the dust was astonishing'.[220]

Seventeen years later Masson, now employing some 350 workpeople, was not without its problems. Ventilation was described as 'Indifferent' and cleanliness as 'Moderate'. Of the forty boys and seventy girls under the age of eighteen medically examined in June 1833 six boys, all carders, were said to have coughs, inflamed eyes or, more generally, to 'suffer from carding'. One is listed as having 'good' and the remaining five 'middling' health. Of the girls the work of only two, both of them thirteen-year-old carders, is given. One was of 'good' and the other of 'bad' general health and both were said to suffer 'Cough from [working in] the card-room'.[221]

A somewhat more detailed report on the health of Arkwright's workpeople as well a the general conditions in the mills was sent to the factory inspector on 20 February 1834 by Thomas Poyser,[222] a surgeon, of Wirksworth:

> Having been employed the greater part of yesterday and to-day in examining the work-people of Cromford and Masson mills, between the ages of 11 and 18 years, I cannot omit this opportunity of remarking generally on their clean, healthy, and comfortable appearance. There was not an individual employed under the age of 11 years; and among 302 (the number between 11 and 18 years) there were only 24 who were suffering from any ailments. Of these, 17 had some trifling local maladies . . . and the rest had scrofula or some other constitutional disease.
>
> Having likewise visited most of the rooms to make this examination I cannot avoid noticing the attention that has been paid to the health and comfort of the inmates, by free ventilation, a regulated temperature, and cleanliness. There was

but little dust, no noxious or unpleasant smell, or other impurity.

It may not be improper also to add that having professionally attended the whole of Messrs. Arkwright's mill-hands for several years, that their general health is usually good that they are subject to fewer and less severe diseases than those individuals of the same class of society who are unemployed, and whose means of subsistence are consequent more precarious and scanty' and that they are not liable to any endemic disease, or such as is peculiar to their employment.

From pretty accurate and careful investigation, I should also say that the ratio of mortality is less in this class of people than in that of the poor who have no fixed employment, or whose occupation exposes them to the inclemency of the weather. And this I apprehend may be accounted for, not only from the causes above-mentioned, but also from their wages enabling them to have uniformly better food and clothing, and from the attention they receive as soon as they are sick.

Having gratuitous medical assistance, they apply for it at the very commence-ment of their diseases, and receiving half-pay during their illness, as well as such food and wine, &c. from Messrs. Arkwright, as their medical attendant may think necessary, their cases are more manageable and the recoveries more rapid, than in those who have not the means of obtaining these important auxiliaries.[223]

As to the physical strain of factory work, opinions were divided even among opponents of Peel's Bill, but Dr Carbutt, a Quaker who had refused to sign the petition organised by the reformers Nathaniel Gould, Nathaniel Shelmer-dine and Charles Augustus Tulk and who had examined 'with Minuteness'[224] workpeople at four Manchester mills, perhaps best summed up the majority view of opponents of further regulation:

Q Did it [child labour] appear to you to be of a light or laborious Kind?
A Of the lightest Kind that can be given to a Person to perform.
Q Did the Children appear to go through it as a Matter of Labour or Drudgery, or otherwise?
A They appeared very attentive to it.
Q Were they at the same Time playful and in good Spirits, or did they appear to be dull and depressed by their Work?
A In some Instances I observed them what I may call arch about it; what I mean by that is, that they were performing something like Tricks while they were about it.
Q That they were amusing themselves like Children while they were performing this Occupation?
A Yes.[225]

And later:

Q You have seen those Children work?
A Yes, I have.

Q Did it not strike you more in the Nature of an Occupation that requires Attention, than of Labour that could fatigue?
A Certainly the Occupation of a Spinner requires Attention, but is accompanied with very little Fatigue; the Piecers are under nearly the same Circumstances as the Spinners on that Point; the Scavengers seem to require very little either of Attention or Exertion.[226]

Dr. Carbutt was supported by Major General Doveton in the case of Horrocks's seven-to-nine-year-old piecers:

Q Did you happen to take Notice whether the Threads often broke?
A I think not very frequently; the Children appeared to be running about, and to be playful: it appeared to me to be absolutely an Amusement.[227]

But Archibald Buchanan, speaking of his own twelve- and thirteen-year-old piecers at Catrine,[228] thought otherwise:

Q Have they an Opportunity of lying down or sitting down, if they should choose it?
A Not at any time.
Q How frequently does their Work require their Attention?
A Every Minute almost, I should think.[229]

And Dr Samuel Barton, a surgeon at the Manchester Eye Institution who had carried out examinations at the request of John Douglas, agreed:

Q How often did they walk?
A They were constantly in Motion nearly; probably they might stand Half a Minute or so.
Q Did you see any of them sitting down at all?
A Not except when they were eating, in the Middle of the Afternoon, at the Time of their Meal.[230]

According to Dr Hardie scavengers 'sometimes . . . sweep merely once an Hour', a task taking five or six minutes and not repeated for at least half an hour. During the break, he testified, 'They are employed in Play.'[231] But, speaking of scavengers and creel fillers, Birley & Hornby's manager put their 'actual Labour' at 'not more than Two-thirds of a Day'.[232]

James Kennedy's former manager believed that young people's work had 'nothing that requires bodily Exertion about it, except the Pickers'.[233] Of the carding-room children ('They carry the Cotton, wrapped up in Cloths, to and from the Carding Engines') Thomas Scott maintained, 'It is not hard Labour at all; it is only Attention to keep it regular,' and of scavengers, spinners and piecers, 'The Spinners is the hardest Labour in their Rooms, having to put the

[171]

Machines into Gear.' But, he added, it was not difficult work for an adult and M'Connel & Kennedy did not employ spinners under eighteen or twenty.[234]

Of Cromford's 725 workpeople in 1816 507, Arkwright noted, '*may* and in general do sit down'.[235] 'I never saw the children affected at all by the work,' he went on, 'and it is very extraordinary, from my house, I see the children playing in groups in the summer time till it is dark. I do not think the hours of labour have any injurious effect.' But, he was careful to add, 'I speak of the labour at Cromford'.[236] It was a view apparently shared by James Ainsworth, surgeon to the Manchester Infirmary and Workhouse and a trustee of the will of Jonathan Pollard, at whose mill he had seen children at work. 'Is it not an Occupation which requires Attention more than Labour which can create Fatigue?' he was asked by the Lords committee of 1818. 'Oh! in that Factory it certainly is; the Labour they undergo, and the Exercise they take, would, I think, be more of a Relief, and more conducive to Health, than if they stood still.' Yet, he had the grace to concede, 'It must have a Limit.'[237] Isaac Hodgson, asked whether workpeople were 'kept principally standing', replied, 'Yes, chiefly so; it is their Business to be standing; I do not say that they do not sit down, but when they are not standing they cannot be doing their Business.'[238]

Evidence given on Philips & Lee by the Rev. W. W. Davis, an Anglican clergyman, was in parts somewhat contradictory. 'I do not know that I have not seen School Boys on a Holiday more joyous, but there appeared to be no Lassitude at all,' he told a questioner. But, a little later: 'It appeared to me to be a constant Occupation, moving backwards and forwards Three or Four Yards, attending to the Bobbins each had under his Inspection; they did not seem to me to have any Rest; but I cannot recollect that it was so; they appeared to me to be constantly on the Foot.'[239]

Dr Thomas Turner, of the Manchester Poor House, when asked, 'Do you think it more fatiguing for a Boy of Twelve Years old to work in those Factories for Twelve Hours, or to drive a Team in a ploughed Field for Twelve Hours?' replied, 'It is much more laborious, I conceive, to drive a Team for Twelve Hours in a Field.' He was not prepared to say whether 'one [occupation was] as little likely to be injurious to Health as another' but believed it 'probable that the Employment in the open Air is more salutary than Confinement in a Room'.[240]

If the witnesses before the parliamentary committees were truthful a change had come over the cotton trade, for ten was now considered a reasonable starting age. 'Thirty years ago they were almost all children, and at least five times as many under ten years of age as at present,' G. A. Lee told Peel's committee.[241] This may have come about from educational motives (the discovery that factory methods could be applied to education under the Bell and Lancaster systems) but there was also the threat in Peel's draft Bill of June 1815 of a statutory minimum age of ten and no night work. And undoubtedly the number of small children had been lessened by changes in machinery. 'Certainly there is a greater proportion of adults . . . young children cannot so well be employed in water-spinning as they could formerly, and as they can, I understand, be employed in mule-spinning,'[242] Arkwright told the 1816 committee, and his view was supported by Isaac Hodgson, who testified that it took two or three years to learn water-spinning.[243] But, said Hodgson:

> In all the Water Spinning, Spinning by Water Frames, whether turned by Steam or by Water, a very small Number of Adults are required; I have not Occasion, including Joiners and Smiths, for more than Eleven or Twelve Men altogether; the Remainder may be Children and young Women. It is the Case with me that they begin to go away at the Age of Fourteen and upwards; they keep flowing off in a regular Stream, as they can get Employment; the boys go to Handicraft or agricultural Employments, and the Girls to Service, or other Employments.[244]

At M'Connel & Kennedy, said Thomas Scott, 'several Lads have left to go to Apprenticeships, but not to Employments more healthy'. They had gone 'To Shoemakers and Tailors, and such Branches, when they have been young'. Some became calenderers ('a Trade by which they can get a Living afterwards; when they go to be Apprentices they have very little Wages; but they reckon it a better Trade when they have grown up') but for many years none had left to become weavers.[245]

'According to the statement I have made the greatest number [fifty-eight workpeople] are at fifteen, after that the number decreases,' Arkwright told the 1816 committee.[246] But as to the 159 Cromford spinners nineteen were under fourteen, thirty-four between fourteen and eighteen, twenty-eight between eighteen and twenty-one, sixty-eight between twenty-one and thirty and ten between thirty and forty.[247] None was above forty, the commonly supposed upper age limit for spinners.

Yet M'Connel & Kennedy's seventy-two male spinners were said to include twenty-six above forty and six above fifty.[248] John M'Connel had no reason to believe that workpeople over forty were unable to carry on as spinners, nor had he known 'any Persons leave their Work on account of Age and being worn out'.[249] And of those who had left, 'I presume they thought they were bettering themselves; we have parted with none from old Age.' James Johnson, a spinner with them ('Very kind they have always been to me'), confirmed that work-people 'are not discharge in our Place through Age' but added that many left at forty 'or upwards' owing to their being 'not so active as the younger Hands', to become 'Book-keepers, and Sweepers of the Rooms, and Joiners, and Mechanics'. 'There are very few better themselves. I rather think they do not quit it of their own Will and Pleasure.'[250]

Robert Hyde, a thirty-six-year-old spinner who had entered the mills at seven, told a similar story:

[173]

Q You said the People left the Factory generally about Forty' is their leaving at that
   Time owing to their feeble State of Health, or merely from their Age?
A Sometimes from both; sometimes one is the Case and sometimes the other.
Q Do you happen to know what has become afterwards of many of them who have
   quitted the Factory?
A I do.
Q Give the Committee an Account of what they have done, those you know?
A I have known some go to Weaving, some to the Trade of Dying; sometimes in
   Manchester, I could shew some of them standing in the Street Row, selling
   Oranges and Apples, and others driving Sand Carts.
Q Are there not many of them who have not lived a long Time?
A Leaving the Factory and being in the open Air has prolonged their Life much
   longer.[251]

Robert Thornely, a spinner at Appleton & Ogden, who had started his
factory career 'laying Roves in a common Slubber Billy', agreed that it was
unusual 'the People as far advanced as the Age of Forty' should continue as
spinners. 'Some go [as] Scavengers in the Street, and some to one thing and
some to another, and some as Watchmen, and some to the Parish.'[252]

Fifty-eight-year-old Samuel Lee, a 'Nobleman's Servant' who at thirty had
become a Manchester spinner and was now a gardener, contended that many
entered the mills 'as nice healthy stout Men, but they may not work there above
Four or Five Years before they are destroyed, and others will stand it Ten or
Twenty'. And as to the number over forty: 'Very few, there may be some few;
if they are in other Departments than the Spinning Concern; their Masters may
put them into different Branches, such as making Sweepers, or something of
that; but to stand to spinning, you can find very few Men who stand it after
Forty.' They left 'Because their Constitution cannot stand it'.[253]

Dr Carbutt did not agree. 'You stated that you observed that those Persons
were the healthiest in the Factories who had worked there the longest? . . . Do
you not think it may be ascribed to the Circumstance, that so many have died
in the Seasoning, and that only the robust ones have held it out?' he was asked.
'I do not think that; for this Reason, that I have been informed, in a Manner
to induce me to give Credit to it, that the Deaths amounted to very few indeed,'
came the reply, but in the next breath: 'I presume that no Man continues to keep
a Servant after he is unable to do the Work which he has for him.'[254]

In an attempt to identify old and long-service workpeople the Lords committees had brought to their notice sixty-eight-year-old John Ward[255] at J. & R.
Simpson and David Kirk,[256] a seventy-seven-year-old 'Proving Sorter' who had
been employed for sixteen years in cotton mills and was now at B. & W.
Sandford. The Rev. John Jones of Holywell claimed to know 'One old Man
above Eighty who has been working there ever since the Factories have been
established; others Forty, Fifty, and Sixty'.[257] Fifty-three-year-old Joseph Piercy,

a spinner at A. & G. Murray, was said in 1818 to have entered the mill in 1791.[258] (And on his death in April 1829 the *Manchester Mercury* reported that 'except [for] part of the two winters previous to his decease, [he] was hardly ever known to be absent from his work on account of illness.'[259])

Dr Samuel Barton named as long-service workpeople Daniel Wood, aged fifty-two, who had been employed twenty-eight years, and Thomas Marsden and William Mitchel, both aged fifty, who had worked in mills for twenty-seven or twenty-eight years. Asked, 'What was the greatest Number of Years you found any Person to have been employed?' Barton recalled, 'A Person of the Name of John Prince, fifty-seven years, had been employed forty-six Years; first by Sir Richard Arkwright, in 1772.'[260]

In 1834 the Factory Commissioners were told of the career of sixty-nine-year-old James Potter, who had begun working for Arkwright in 1775 (was he the brother of the Charles who on 8 October 1782 agreed to work at Cromford for a wage of 8s a week, rising to 11s six years later?) and was to spend a total of fifty-eight years in cotton mills, for almost half this time with M'Connel & Kennedy. Dr C. Phillips reported that 'in the night, not long ago, he lost his left arm, in consequence of an accident amongst the machinery. He is now quite well, and lives in Derbyshire. His complete recovery from this accident, taken in conjunction with his advanced age, clearly indicates that his health had not suffered from factory labour.'[261] The *Derby Mercury* of 27 May 1835 recorded the death at seventy-three of George Cotterill, who 'had been employed in the Cotton Factory of Messrs. Arkwright, at Cromford for more than 50 years'. Of almost identical length of service were Joshua Tomison and James Brailsford, who in 1841, having been with the Arkwrights 'for near 50 years', were said to be among Cromford's oldest managers.[262]

But these workpeople, as the Manchester mill owners' own figures supplied to the Lords committees reveal, were the exception. Out of the 7,148 names listed only 298, or 4·2 per cent, were aged above forty.[263]

NOTES

1 P.P. 1816 (397) III, *Children in the Manufactories* (henceforth 1816 Comm.), p. 277.
2 J. Britton and E. W. Brayley, *England and Wales*, III, p. 517.
3 1816 Comm., p. 217.
4 P.P. 1818 (90) XCVI, *House of Lords, Evidence . . . of the Health and Morals of Apprentices, and others, employed in Cotton and other Mills, and Cotton and other Factories* (henceforth 1818 Comm.), p. 116.
5 1816 Comm., p. 20; see Fitton & Wadsworth, p. 193 n.
6 736 - 1816 Comm., p. 374.
7 P.P. 1819 (24) CX, *House of Lords, Evidence . . . of the State and Condition of the Children employed in the Cotton Manufactories of the United Kingdom* (henceforth 1819 Comm.), p. 449 (by 1819, 865 workpeople).
8 1819 Comm., App. p. 45.
9 1816 Comm., p. 240.

10 1816 Comm., p. 240.

11 1819 Comm., p. 104.

12 1819 Comm., pp. 348–349.

13 1819 Comm., p. 341.

14 1816 Comm., p. 197.

15 Full edition, III, p. 113.

16 1816 Comm., p. 117.

17 P.P. 1834 (167) XX, *Employment of Children*, C1, p. 209. By 1784 the partners had completed an offshoot, Langcliffe High Mill, on the Ribble near Settle. T. Brayshaw and R. M. Robinson, *A History of the ancient Parish of Giggleswick*, London, 1932, p. 209.

18 6 and 20 May 1783.

19 All figures from 1816 Comm., p. 374.

20 Farey for authorship.

21 See Fitton and Wadsworth, p. 195.

22 1819 Comm., pp. 280–1.

23 1818 Comm., p. 227.

24 1819 Comm., p. 442; see Fitton and Wadsworth, p. 193 n. 4. This mill was advertised for sale in the *Manchester Mercury* of 20 September 1785.

25 1816 Comm., p. 317.

26 Letter from William Grant's son, reproduced in W. Hume Elliot, *The Story of the 'Cheryble' Grants*, Manchester and London, 1906, pp. 197–9, and in F. Collier, *The Family Economy of the Working Classes in the Cotton Industry, 1784–1833*, Manchester, 1964, pp. 14–15.

27 *Ibid.*; the Garratt mill was advertised for sale in the *Manchester Mercury*, 20 September 1785.

28 See Mrs Elizabeth Raffald's *Manchester Directory* for Douglas (1781) and Thackeray (1772, 1773, 1781).

29 *Manchester Mercury*, 27 November, 4 and 11 December 1781.

30 Chaloner, 'Owen and Drinkwater', p. 86, writes, 'It lay just off London Road, between Auburn Street and Upton Street,' and n. 1, . . . across what is now Aytoun Street'. Drinkwater's mill later Peter Appleton & Co. (Appleton also had a partner, Ogden). Died 1 September 1815 (will at L. C. R. O.).

31 Chaloner, 'Owen and Drinkwater', p. 82; R. Owen, *The Life of Robert Owen, written by Himself*, London and Philadelphia, 1857, pp. 24, 25, 27, 28, 91 n.

32 *Manchester Directory*, 1788.

33 *Manchester Directory*, 1794.

34 John Kennedy, *My early Recollections*, 1827, pp. 9, 12–14.

35 L. G., 1795, p. 467.

36 *Early Recollections*, pp. 17–18.

37 *Manchester Mercury*, 1 March 1803.

38 P.P. 1834 (167) XX, *Employment of Children*, D1, p. 226.

39 *Early Recollections*, pp. 8–9.

40 1816 Comm., p. 374.

41 D. C. M. M'Connel, *Facts and Traditions collected for a Family Record*, Edinburgh, privately printed, 1861, p. 133.

42 *Ibid.*, p. 151 n.

43 P.P. 1833 (450) XX, *Employment of Children* D1, p. 56.

44 *Manchester Directory*, 1794.

45 P.P. 1834 (167) XX, *Employment of Children*, D1, p. 231.

46 M'Connel, *Facts and Traditions*, pp. 160, 155.

47 *Ibid.*, p. 155.

48 *Ibid.*, p. 141.

49 1816 Comm., p. 234.

50 *Manchester Directory*, 1797.
51 1816 Comm., p. 235.
52 *L.G.*, 1800, p. 428. Rocester Mill was advertised in the *Staffordshire Advertiser* of 23 July 1831 and bought by Thomas Houldsworth, who paid off the mortgage on 16 January 1833. Thomas Houldsworth died 1 September 1852, leaving Rocester to his family. His Manchester and Rocester mills were together valued at £110,616 16s 2d. For Houldsworth and new subsequent careers see D. C. M. M'Connel, *Facts and Traditons*, pp. 152–3, and J. O. Mitchell, *Old Glasgow Essays*, Glasgow, 1905, pp. 152–3.
53 *Glasgow Mercury*, 17–24 March 1785, p. 94. Gillespie's mill 'is now a-going; a specimen of the yarn which we have seen is unusually fine form first essay, will sell from 20 to 25 shillings a pound, and will make a cloth capable of bearing any ornament'. Two other Nottingham drapers were associated with him in the venture. *G.M.*, 1798. p. 815: 'Died at his house in Glasgow September 3 1798. Mr. Thomas Millegain (of James Trial) a native of Nottingham and late conductor of the cotton mill at Woodside belonging to Gillespie and [Robert] Almond . . . in which concern the deceased had a share.' Gillespie died 1807. (G. Stewart. *Curiosities of Glasgow Citizenship*, p. 215.) See also Reid, *Glasgow*, pp. 214–15.
54 O.S.A., XII, p. 116.
55 1816 Comm, p. 240.
56 1816 Comm., pp. 234, 235.
57 1819 Comm., p. 349.
58 1819 Comm., p. 309.
59 1818 Comm., p. 168.
60 1819 Comm., p. 423.
61 1819 Comm., p. 430.
62 1816 Comm., p. 350.
63 Atholl MSS.
64 1816 Comm., p. 139.
65 *Manchester Mercury*, 9 November 1784.
66 W. Bray, *Sketch of a Tour into Derbyshire and Yorkshire*, London, 1783 edition, p. 119.
67 1816 Comm., p. 280.
68 1816 Comm., p. 280.
69 Byng, II, pp. 195, 196.
70 B. Nicholson, *Joseph Wright of Derby*, London, 1968, p. 166.
71 Collier, *Family Economy*, p. 73; A.F. MSS.
72 1804, I, p. 495.
73 1819. Comm., p. 421.
74 1819 Comm., App., p. 45.
75 1816 Comm., p. 282.
76 A.F. MSS.
77 P.P. 1833 (450) XX, *Employment of Children*, D1, p. 56.
78 *Trans. Soc. of Arts*, 1783, p. 34.
79 Article, 'Manufacture of cotton'.
80 1816 Comm., p. 277.
81 Unwin, *Samuel Oldknow*, pp. 170–3.
82 June 1804, p. 494.
83 J. Simmons (ed.), *Letters From England*, London, 1951, pp. 207–8.
84 1816 Comm., p. 132.
85 K. Garlick and A. D. Macintyre (eds.), *The Diary of Joseph Farington*, V, New Haven, 1979, pp. 1593–4.
86 III, p. 517.
87 1816 Comm., p. 279.

88 1816 Comm., pp. 279–80.

89 1816 Comm., p. 277.

90 1816 Comm., p. 282.

91 P.P. 1819 (66) III, *House of Lords, An Account of the Cotton and Woollen Mills and Factories in the United Kingdom . . . also a return of the names of the several visitors 1803–1818* (henceforth 1819 III), pp. 6–9, 47–9 (appendices).

92 1816 Comm., p. 278.

93 1816 Comm., p. 280.

94 1816 Comm., p. 278.

95 1816 Comm., p. 282.

96 1818 Comm., p. 176.

97 1819 III, pp. 57–8.

98 P.P. 1834 (167) XX, *Employment of Children*, D1, pp. 96–7; see also pp. 578–9. See Fitton and Wadsworth, p. 193.

99 Pages 4 and 7 (M.C.R.L., P 3425).

100 *Life*, p. 226.

101 William Strutt to his son Edward (Lord Belper), April 1818. Fitton and Wadsworth, p. 189.

102 1819 Comm., pp. 352, 400.

103 1819 Comm., p. 135.

104 Evidence of Jos. Smith, p. 233. 'Gray bankrupt 2 or 3 times before going to Ireland. Gray was the first English manager of Col. Talbot's near Malahide, 8 miles from Dublin (Irish Papers).

105 1819 Comm., pp. 431–3.

106 1819 Comm., p. 440.

107 1819 Comm., p. 436.

108 1819 Comm., p. 194.

109 1819 Comm., p. 190.

110 1819 Comm., p. 188.

111 1819 Comm., pp. 192, 193.

112 1819 Comm., p. 198.

113 1819 Comm., p. 429. James Frost.

114 1819 Comm., p. 197.

115 1819 Comm., pp. 429, 430.

116 1818 Comm., p. 130.

117 1819 Comm., p. 200.

118 1819 Comm., p. 192.

119 1819 Comm., p. 165.

120 1819 Comm., p. 399.

121 1819 Comm., p. 206.

122 1819 Comm., p. 208.

123 1819 Comm., p. 209.

124 1819 Comm., p. 210.

125 1819 Comm., p. 362.

126 1816 Comm., p. 96–7.

127 1818 Comm., pp. 94–5.

128 1818 Comm., pp. 39, 50.

129 1818 Comm., pp. 45–50.

130 1816 Comm., p. 382.

131 1816 Comm., p. 354.

132 See also 1816 Comm., pp. 282–3.

133 1816 Comm., p. 217.

134 1816 Comm., p. 277.
135 1816 Comm., p. 281.
136 1816 Comm., p. 283.
137 1816 Comm., p. 283; A.F. MSS.
138 1816 Comm., p. 281.
139 1819 Comm., p. 124.
140 P 3425, pp. 22–3; 1816 Comm., p. 278, for Arkwright II's confirmation of this.
141 1816 Comm., p. 277.
142 1818 Comm., p. 168.
143 1818 Comm., p. 168, and 1819 Comm., p. 435.
144 1819 Comm., pp. 435, 436.
145 1818 Comm., p. 168.
146 1818 Comm., p. 169.
147 1818 Comm., p. 175.
148 1819 Comm., p. 397.
149 1819 Comm., p. 363.
150 1819 Comm., pp. 461, 462.
151 1819 Comm., p. 187.
152 1816 Comm., p. 283.
153 1816 Comm., p. 283.
154 1818 Comm., p. 190.
155 1819 Comm., p. 436.
156 1819 Comm., pp. 361, 362.
157 1819 Comm., p. 168.
158 And see L.C.R.O., Will, Hugh Batho, April 1829.
159 1819 Comm., p. 421.
160 1818 Comm., p. 187.
161 1818 Comm., pp. 138, 140.
162 1816 Comm., p. 288.
163 1816 Comm., pp. 278–9.
164 1816 Comm., p. 281.
165 1816 Comm., p. 281.
166 1816 Comm., p. 278.
167 1816 Comm., p. 88.
168 1816 Comm., Manchester, pp. 96, 144, 252; Bolton, p. 296. Horrocks's, p. 258.
169 1819 Comm., App., p. 45.
170 1819 Comm., p. 397.
171 1819 Comm., p. 349.
172 1819 Comm., p. 440.
173 1818 Comm., p. 99.
174 1818 Comm., p. 87.
175 1818 Comm., p. 143.
176 1816 Comm., p. 284. For mill schools see P.P. 1839 (42) XLII, *Reports from the Factory Inspectors on the Educational Provisions of the Factories Act*, p. 50.
177 1816 Comm., p. 188.
178 1816 Comm., p. 240.
179 1818 Comm., p. 194.
180 1818 Comm., p. 189.
181 1818 Comm., p. 186.
182 1818 Comm., p. 167.
183 1819 Comm., p. 436.
184 1818 Comm., p. 131.

185 1816 Comm., p. 100. Owen: 'to go under the machines, where bigger people cannot creep, and the smaller they are the more conveniently they can go under the machines' (1816 Comm., p. 88). View contested by Saunders ∕ see 1834 (167) XIX, *Employment of Children*, p. 119.

186 1819 Comm., pp. 280–1.

187 1816 Comm., p. 266, and 1818 Comm., p. 195.

188 1819 Comm., p. 137.

189 1816 Comm., p. 280.

190 1816 Comm., p. 283.

191 1818 Comm., p. 49.

192 1818 Comm., p. 166.

193 1819 Comm., p. 438.

194 1819 Comm., p. 437.

195 1819 Comm., p. 441.

196 1819 Comm., pp. 114, 115.

197 1819 Comm., p. 437.

198 1819 Comm., p. 123.

199 1819 Comm., p. 437.

200 1818 Comm., p. 48.

201 1818 Comm., p. 167.

202 1819 Comm., p. 437.

203 1818 Comm., p. 177.

204 1819 Comm., p. 126.

205 1819 Comm., p. 134.

206 1819 Comm., p. 363.

207 1818 Comm., p. 193.

208 1816 Comm., p. 280.

209 Collier, *Family Economy*, p. 119.

210 Fitton and Wadsworth, p. 296; *Manchester Literary and Philosophical Society*, second series, III (1819) p. 130.

211 1816 Comm., p. 306.

212 1816 Comm., p. 284.

213 1818 Comm., p. 174.

214 1819 Comm., p. 363.

215 1819 Comm., pp. 61, 125.

216 1819 Comm., p. 442.

217 1819 Comm., p. 444.

218 1816 Comm., p. 294.

219 1816 Comm., p. 298.

220 1816 Comm., p. 334.

221 P.P. 1834 (167) XIX, *Employment of Children*, D3, pp. 260–2.

222 The Arkwrights' doctor, who was paid £50 on Richard Arkwright II's death in 1842.

223 P.P. 1834 (596) XLIII, *Reports of Factory Inspectors*, pp. 68–9.

224 1818 Comm., pp. 5, 108, 113, 128.

225 1818 Comm., p. 112.

226 1818 Comm., p. 134.

227 1818 Comm., p. 196.

228 1818 Comm., p. 63.

229 1818 Comm., p. 84.

230 1818 Comm., p. 240.

231 1818 Comm., p. 39.

232 1818 Comm., p. 398.

233 1818 Comm., p. 193.
234 1818 Comm., p. 170.
235 A.F. MSS.
236 1816 Comm., p. 280.
237 1818 Comm., p. 153.
238 1819 Comm., p. 139.
239 1818 Comm., pp. 243–4.
240 1818 Comm., p. 165.
241 1816 Comm., p. 343.
242 1816 Comm., p. 279.
243 1818 Comm., pp. 210, 211.
244 1818 Comm., p. 202.
245 1818 Comm., pp. 167, 168.
246 1816 Comm., p. 281.
247 A.F. MSS.
248 1819 Comm., p. 438.
249 1819 Comm., p. 436.
250 1819 Comm., pp. 117, 119.
251 1819 Comm., p. 137.
252 1819 Comm., pp. 105, 110.
253 1819 Comm., pp. 234, 235.
254 1818 Comm., p. 133.
255 1818 Comm., App. 5, p. 43.
256 1818 Comm., App. 5, p. 46.
257 1819 Comm., App. 3, p. 22.
258 1819 Comm., App. 3, p. 22.
259 14 April 1829.
260 1818 Comm., p. 226.
261 P.P. 1834 (167) XIX, *Employment of Children*, D3, p. 294, D3, p. 230. C. Phillips, MD, Piccadilly, Manchester.
262 P.P. 1841 (311) X, *Report of Inspectors on the Practicability of legislative Interference to diminish Accidents . . .*, p. 90.
263 1818 Comm., App. 1–10, 16; 1819 Comm., App. 7, 8.

CHAPTER VII

The knight's last years

A LITTLE OVER A YEAR before the first of the great patent trials Arkwright's son and daughter both married. Richard's wife was Mary,[1] the only daughter of Adam and Elizabeth Simpson, of Bonsall, a family having interests in the Derbyshire lead mines[2] and in Lumbs (or Lums) cupola and slugg mill, near Matlock.[3] Eighteen-year-old Susanna Arkwright was hardly out of Mrs Latuffiere's school at Derby when, on 12 June 1780, she married by licence at Wirksworth Charles, second son of Francis and Mary Hurt, lead merchants and iron manufacturers, of Alderwasley. The *Derby Mercury*[4] described Susanna as 'an agreeable young Lady, with a large Fortune'. Her dowry was in fact £15,000, payable over four years, and was among the earliest signs of Arkwright's rapidly rising prosperity.

Matthew Boulton, writing to James Watt[5] soon after the Mordaunt trial, considered that had Arkwright 'been quiet he might have gone on & got £40,000 pr annum by all the works he has now erected even if there had been some interlopers', while, more conservatively, Bearcroft calculated that by the time the patent for the water frame had expired in 1783 Arkwright had 'raised a great fortune of above 100,000l'.[6] But whatever the accuracy of these estimates Arkwright was able by the 1780s to look from the Rock, his large red-brick residence built on a limestone outcrop overlooking the Derwent Vale, at the nucleus of an empire the income from which was sufficiently large for him to add to his role of overseer that of squire.

Since his lease of the land upon which he built the first of the Cromford mills Arkwright had added to his holding piece by piece until under the enclosure of Matlock Common in 1780 he was allotted fourteen titles amounting in all to some 299 acres the largest of which was a 183 acre stretch on High Moor Common.[7]

Two years later Arkwright bought the manor of Willersley from Thomas Hallet Hodges for £8,864, putting up by way of mortgage deeds of properties in Cromford, Willersley and Matlock valued at double that amount.[8] The purchase soon threatened to become the subject of litigation. Willersley was part of the manor of Matlock, and when this was enclosed in 1780 Hodges and Peter Nightingale had 'each applied to . . . the Comm[issione]rs for an Allotmt. of

Scarthin-Nick Common', which lay across the Derwent from Willersley. The commissioners, Arkwright advised Kenyon, '*Allotted it to P.N.* as being Contiguous to his Estate in Cromford', although no part of Nightingale's Matlock estate lay within half a mile, but 'had they Allotted Scarthin-Nick also to Wildersley it wod. have laid the old Estate and the new Allotmts together, save being separated by the river'. Accordingly in November 1783 Arkwright consulted Kenyon ('Expedition is requested') and the Attorney General as to the validity of the commissioners' decision and the possibility of remedy 'to the Sessions or the Court of Chancery or to Parliament'. Kenyon's reply was not encouraging:

> The Contiguity of Estates ought to operate on the *Discretion* of the Com-missioners . . . and they were not bound to allot Scarthin-Nick Common to P.N. or to any other Individual. They were as to the Allotmt final Judges constrained by nothing but, that which will constrain any honest man, an Intention to do right . . . How far Parlt may interfere I cannot say, supposing a strong Case shd be made; but neither Appeal or Chancery can aid P.N.

The following year Arkwright again sought Kenyon's opinion, this time as to the possibility of laying the case before the House of Lords. But Kenyon was apprehensive. 'I do not see any ground to alter my opinion,' came the reply, and there the matter rested.

Arkwright's wealth naturally created envy in the trade. Even before his acquisition of Willersley the 'poor cotton spinners' had in 1780 drawn a class-conscious contrast. One man:

> within the small space of ten years, from being a poor man not worth £5, now keeps his carriage and servants, is become a Lord of the Manor, and has purchased an estate of £20,000; while thousands of women, when they can get work, must make a long day to card, spin, and reel 5040 yards of cotton, and for this they have *four-pence or five-pence and not more.*[9]

The anonymous writer could well have had in mind the manor of Cromford, sold by William Milnes to Peter Nightingale in 1776. Arkwright's name appears together with six others in the deed of transfer, a transaction perhaps referred to in a letter of 7 July 1776 from Edward Saxelby in London to William Strutt:

> I am told Mr Arkwright has set up his Carriage & parted with the greatest part of his purchase, I suppose he had made a good Bargain as he wd not have sold as he seemed very much elevated upon the strength of his own Contract with Mr Milnes: when I come into the County I shall not know Cromford, I am informed it is so much improved, I always thought it a place very capable of great additions.[10]

Can it be that Arkwright had already bought the Cromford estate in 1776 but parted with it to Milnes, perhaps to raise money for the building of his new mill in the summer of that year? But whatever the position then, Arkwright purchased the manor of Cromford, together with a further seventy-three acres in Matlock and Bonsall, from Nightingale for £30,000 in April 1789.[11]

On 22 December 1786,[12] the eve of his fifty-fourth birthday, Arkwright was knighted on presenting a loyal address on George III's escape from assassination at the hand of Margaret Nicholson. 'Fees due to His Majesty's Household Servants &c. from all Persons who receive the Honor of Knighthood' put him back £98 8s 2d, though he doubtless paid up willingly.[13]

An account of the ceremony has come down from Wilhelmina Murray, who on 25 December wrote to her husband, Captain George Murray, RN,[14] uncle to the Duke of Atholl, of her visit the previous Saturday to the house of Sir Joseph Banks in Soho Square, where she:

> was much entertained at the scene they had had the Morning before, in the arrival of the *Great* M^r. Arkwright who came to Sir Josephs in a black wig, brown frock, woosted stockings & Boots to ask him to go with him to the levee when he was to present an adress on Margaret Nicholsons affair. Sir Jos. too good natured to refuse agreed but asked him about his dress. M^r. Ark—— proposed going as he was, for he was not afraid they were but Men — and so was He — however it was agreed he should take off his boots & return with good shoes at the proper hour *our* friends had a hint he would be worth seeing so took care to be in the way, but were not a little surprised to see little fatty apear a beau with a smart powderd *bag* wig so tight that coming over his ears it made him deaf; a handsome striped sattin Waist coat & proper coat with a sword, which he held in his hand, all provided it is suposed by M^r. Dempster, to crown the scene M^r. More introduced him telling Sir Joseph he did not know if he was prepared for the ceremony but M^r. Arkwright intended to accept *the Honor* his Majesty offer'd — this surprised all the company but proper dispatches having been sent to the E[querr]^y in Waiting, Sir Joseph carried off his Beau and Brought him back Sir Richard Arkwright. What a pity You happened not to be there then as the scene was excellent, the little great Man had no idea of kneeling but crimpt himself up in *a very odd* posture which I suppose His Majesty took for an *easy one* so never took the trouble to bid him rise.[15]

Some thirty years later a not entirely dissimilar story was to be recalled:

> During his stay in London, he was in company with some noblemen, one of whom possessing more pride than parts, asked him whether he had not once been a barber. 'Sir,' replied Arkwright, with a spirit truly noble, 'I was once a barber, and I am apt to conclude, had your lordship been a barber, you must have continued a barber still.'[16]

The tale may well be apocryphal. But not so Arkwright's response. In the cotton tree, the hank of cotton, the bee and the eagle of his armorial bearings he was careful to commemorate his toil and his achievement. And well he knew the meaning of his adopted motto, *Multa tuli fecique*.

In February 1787[17] Sir Richard was appointed High Sheriff of Derbyshire, an office he performed with great ostentation. True, others had attempted to cut a dash, not least Francis Hurt (Susanna's brother-in-law), who, nine years earlier, had given 'a Ball to the Ladies, at the New Assembly Rooms, at which the Company were very numerous and brilliant; every Thing was well conducted, and on so generous a Style that it Bordered on Profusion'.[18] But the county had witnessed nothing quite like the manner in which Arkwright performed one of the earliest of his duties, his arrival at the Assize:

> On Sunday last [reported the *Manchester Mercury*],[19] Sir Richard Arkwright, Knight, High Sheriff of the County, arrived at Derby, accompanied by a great Number of Gentlemen, &c. on Horseback: his Javelin Men, (thirty in Number, exclusive of Baliffs, &c. &c.) dressed in the richest Liveries ever seen there on such an occasion. Their Coats were dark blue elegantly trimmed with Gold Lance; scarlet Waistcoats laced with gold, and buff coloured Velvet Breeches; they had also blue great Coats, buckled behind after the manner of his Majesty's Regiment of Horse Guards; their Hats were smartly cocked, with Gold Button, Loop and Tassels; they all rode on black Horses, and had new Bridles given them by the Sheriff, also new Boots, &c. The Trumpeters were mounted on grey Horses, and elegantly dressed in Scarlet and Gold. The High Sheriff's Coach was very elegant and fashionable, with plated Furniture, lin'd with drab Cloth, and bound with Livery-lace; purple Festoons at the Windows, trimmed with Silver Fringe; the Body painted *Batwing Colour*, with a white Border; the Arms painted in Mantle; Carriage and Wheels painted red and pick'd in the same Colour as the body; the Coach-box ornamented with an elegant Hammer-cloth, and very elegant plated Harness. We must not forget to inform our Readers that Sir Richard during the whole of the Assize provided a plentiful Table, with the choicest Wines, &c. for such Gentlemen as pleased to partake of the noble Banquet (which was conducted by Mr. Mason of Matlock Bath.)

Greville, visiting Arkwright's grandson, Robert, at his residence, Stoke Hall, near Bakewell, in 1834 was told of an unexpected sequel to the assize ceremony which he recorded in his *Memoirs*:

> His Grandfather began life as a Barber, invented some machinery, got a patent, and made a fortune. His Son gave him offence by a marriage which he disapproved of, and he quarrelled with him, but gave him a mill. Arkwright, the Son, saw nothing of his Father for many years, but by industry and ability accumulated great wealth. When Sir Richard served as Sheriff, his Son thought it right to go out with the other gentlemen of the County to meet him, and the old gentleman was struck with his handsome equipage, and asked to whom it belonged. Upon being informed, he sought a reconciliation with him, and was astonished to find that his Son was as rich as himself. From that time they continued on good terms, and at his death he bequeathed to him the bulk of his property.[20]

Arkwright's nomination as High Sheriff,[21] the oldest secular dignitary under the Crown (officers called sheriffs first appear on the records in the reign of Ethelred the Unready, leading the levies of their shires against the wave of Danish invaders), must have given him special satisfaction. The appointment, an unusual one for a man in trade, was, like that of Lord Lieutenant, directly by the Crown. And above all Arkwright was a King's man. Cromford's celebrations on George III's recovery from serious illness in 1789 went beyond mere convention. The *Derby Mercury* of 26 March reported:

> On Saturday the 21st inst. Sir Richard Arkwright, at Cromford, celebrated his Majesty's recovery in a style of superior elegance to any thing ever exhibited in that part of the country. During the day a large bonfire blazed, and the populace had a great quantity of ale distributed amongst them. At night a transparency was exhibited, the whole length of the semicircular building, with this motto, in large characters — 'Rejoice all men for the King liveth;' which, with the brilliant display of lights, in the building on each side, had a very magnificent and striking appearance. About eight o'clock, two Club Societies, attended by several hundred people, preceded by torch-bearers, each with a broad ribbon on his hat; on which was inscribed the motto above quoted; a band of music, flags, &c. walked in procession to Sir Richard's house, where he, attended by several gentlemen, gave many loyal and constitutional toasts, which were drank, and accompanied by the hearty cheers of the whole company. Several songs were sung, applicable to the occasion, and the people then returned; having a transparency of a square form, borne aloft before them, on the side of which apt mottoes were inscribed. To crown the whole, Sir Richard, with a truly benevolent, and charitable spirit worthy of imitation, gave away near 2,000 loaves of bread, among the poor inhabitants of Cromford, and the vicinity.

And in June 1789 Arkwright received from the Rev. Dr Francis Willis, physician to George III, acknowledgement of a gift he had sent by Jefferys & Jones, goldsmiths and jewellers, of Cockspur Street, Charing Cross:

> Dear Sir,
> I take the earliest oportunity to return You my sincere thanks for the very noble present which You have been ples'd to honour me with by the hands of Jefferes & Jones; And I have only to lament that the business which has call'd me to Town will not allow me to return those thanks, as I most ardently which to do, in person: But be Assur'd Sir I shall anxiously seize the first opportunity of paying my respects to You, & be ever proud to cultivate the acquaintance of a Man for whose Publick Merits I have long had the highest veneration.
> I am realy at a loss in what manner to express my obligations to You for this singular mark of distinction, which has been confer'd too with a liberality that reflects equal honour on Yourself & me; And, while it testify's your own happiness on the recovery of our beloved Monarch, marks in the most flattering

term the opinon You have form'd of my poor exertions.

> I have the honour to be
> Dear sir with the greatest
> esteem Your most oblig'd &
> very humble Servant to Comd
> Francis Willis[22]

Han[r] Square No. 5
June 4 1789

A period of rapid development accompanied the building of Cromford's second mill in the summer of 1776, and among the houses Bray[23] then saw under construction must almost certainly have been those in North Street, two rows of three-storey gritstone houses each with its living room, bedroom and attic, clearly shown on the *Plan of Cromford Moor Longsough* surveyed for Anthony Tissington in 1777.[24]

Arkwright's houses are among the finest examples of the domestic architec-ture of the period. 'Much to Sir Richard's credit, these habitations are most comfortable', observed J. P. Malcolm,[25] a visitor to Cromford in 1792. Twenty-one years later John Farey[26] found them 'neat and confortable', their tenants 'much better provided . . . than they commonly are in the Southern Counties of England', while in 1836 Peter Gaskell, a critic of the factory system, listed the Arkwrights' cottages among those 'often exhibiting signs of comfort and cleanliness highly honourable to the proprietor and the occupants'.[27]

The houses in North Street cannot have been long occupied when in 1777[28] Need built at Masson a chapel to hold 300. Next to it was a small but neat brick house with a Tuscan porch and a canted bay. After Need's death the chapel was used as a storehouse until, together with the adjoining house, it was bought in 1784 by the evangelical chapel-owning Lady Glenorchy, who, staying in Matlock following a mishap to her carriage, had been told upon enquiry that 'the state of religion' was 'very low'.[29]

The same year a remarkable wave of enthusiasm for Sunday schools — widely regarded as cheap solvents for the twin problems of vice and ignorance — spread over the country. Arkwright responded in February 1785 by setting up a school at Cromford where, reported the *Manchester Mercury*,[30] it 'already consists of two hundred children. Pleasing it is to the friends of humanity, when power like his is so happily united with the will to do good.' Even so, there were limits to be observed. Asked 'whether he did not allow that a manufactory was a very bad school to form the Female character for domestic life, and . . . whether he could not contrive to give up *one half day* in the week to instruct the women in sewing, and in their Christian duties . . . [Sir Richard] assented to the importance of the objects, but said he could not possibly allow his neighbouring competitors such an advantage over him as the sacrifice of half a day would prove.'[31]

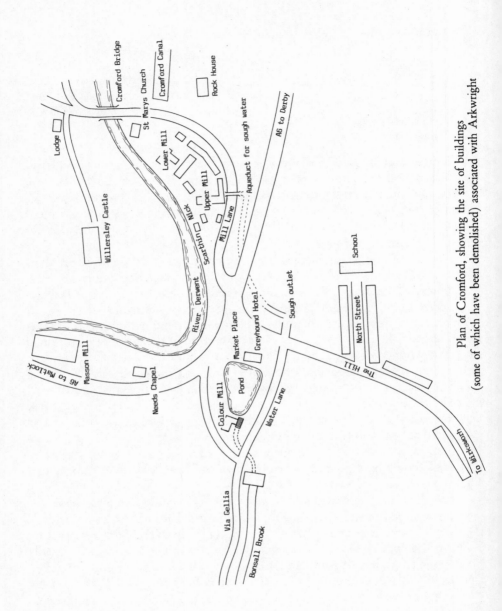

Plan of Cromford, showing the site of buildings (some of which have been demolished) associated with Arkwright

For a detailed plan of the mills and water courses, particularly from Bonsall brook and the pond, see the plan in *Arkwright and the Mills at Cromford* (Arkwright Society, 1971)

[188]

Bray meantime had visited Cromford again in 1780 and noted 'a large handsome inn' built two years before.[32] This was the Greyhound, known as the Black Greyhound and tenanted by Bernard Pearson when in August 1779 Arkwright insured the property with the Royal Exchange.[33] Four years later it went under the 'sign of the Hound'. A notice in the *Derby Mercury* of 27 September 1787 announcing the letting of the property described it as 'A Convenient and Well-accustomed INN, known by the Sign of the GREY-HOUND, with extensive stabling and Outhouses . . . Carriage might be secured to the Amount of between 5 or 600 Pounds per annum; and an Opportunity offers of purchasing a regular Stock of Waggons, &c. now at work.'

It was here that John Byng lodged during his first visit to Cromford, in June 1789. He was there again the following year, when on 18 June he wrote in his diary:

By two o'clock I was at the Black Dog at Cromford; around which is much levelling of ground, and increase of buildings for their new market, (for this place is now so populous as not to do without) which has already been once held, and will be again tomorrow. — This house, and village appear so clean, and so gay, as quite to revive me, after the dirt and dullness of Bakewell.[34]

Byng had seen the outcome of the activities of Saturday 12 June, when, reported the *Derby Mercury*,[35] there had been:

held at Cromford the first Meeting for the supply of that place with provisions &c. at which an immense concourse of people attended. Very large quantities of different articles were offered for sale. The festivities of the day were also numerous; eight clubs of the town, and neighbourhood were in procession, attended by several bands of music, to the place of meeting, where they were regaled with ale &c. — To the beneficence of Sir Richard Arkwright are the inhabitants of this populous village indebted for this beneficial institution, which we hope will meet with the encouragement it so greatly deserves.

Byng set out a further but consistent aspect of the scene:

The landlord has under his care a grand assortment of prizes, from Sr R. Arkwright, to be given, at the years end, to such bakers, butchers, &c, as shall have best furnish'd the market: how this will be peaceably settled I cannot tell!! They consist of beds, presses, clocks, chairs, &c, and bespeak Sr Rd's prudence and cunning; for without ready provisions, his colony cou'd not prosper: so the clocks will go very well.

The occasion, he noted, was celebrated in rhyme:

Upon the Inn door, a paper incribed with the following verses, was pasted at the last market day: they were written by an old woman.

[189]

1

Come let us all here join in one,
And thank him for all favours done;
Let's thank him for all favours still
Which he hath done besides the mill.

2

Modistly drink liquor about,
And see whose health you can find out;
This will I chuse before the rest
Sr Richard Arkwright is the best.

3

A few more words I have to say
Success to Cromford's market day.[36]

Byng was witnessing the great upheaval that followed Arkwright's decision in 1785 to separate the water flowing out of Cromford sough from that of Bonsall brook, into which it emptied. To do this, water was diverted down a new sough built from about 200 yards from the tail of the existing sough into a reservoir before being carried over the road in a wooden aqueduct to turn the wheel of the 1771 mill.[37] Bonsall brook was used to drive the 1776 mill. These alterations prevented the sough from being inspected or repaired, and when some of the Wirksworth lead mines became waterlogged Arkwright was forced to allow the dispute which arose with the owners of the sough to go to arbitration. All this was but a prelude to the 'very considerable additions' made to the Cromford mills in 1789.

To Byng the scene was of 'Rocks, mills and water "in confusion hurled"' and he was dismayed at what he saw:

I dare not, perhaps I shou'd not, repine at the increase of our trade, and (partial) population; yet speaking as a tourist, these vales have lost all their beauties; the rural cot has given place to the lofty red mill, and the grand houses of overseers; the stream perverted from its course by sluices, and acqueducts, will no longer ripple and cascade. — Every rural sound is sunk in the clamours of cotton works; and the simple peasant (for to be simple we must be sequester'd) is changed into the impudent mechanic: — the woods find their way into the canals: and the rocks are disfigured for lime stone.[38]

The next blow, he feared, would destroy the beauty of the Derwent:

An Act of Parliament is soon expected to pass to render the river navigable to Cromford, from which much benefit must accrue to these works, and much destruction to the beauty of the river, — for when was any river made navigable that its beauties were not[39] demolished?

The Act[40] was that authorising the building of the Cromford Canal, which received the royal assent six weeks after Byng's visit. Our earliest hint of the venture is a notice in the *Derby Mercury*[41] of a meeting to be held on 31 July 1788 at the Old Bath,[42] Matlock Bath, to consider 'the Expediency of making the River Derwent navigable from Derby to Cromford Bridge; and also the River Amber to the Collieries when the Noblemen, Gentlemen, and the others interested, are desired to attend'.

By the next meeting (18 August 1788) Arkwright was actively involved. 'Those Friends to this Measure, who have any Plan to propose, . . . are desired to send the same to Sir RICHARD ARKWRIGHT, at the Rock House, Cromford,' reads the notice in the *Derby Mercury*.[43] Twelve days later[44] it was unanimously decided 'that the Canal be made from Langley Mill to Cromford, and a Branch from the same at Codnor Park Mill to Pinxton Mill' and 'That Messrs [William] JESSOP and [Edward] FLETCHER[45] be appointed to make a Survey and Estimate of such Canal, and deliver the same to Sir RICHARD ARKWRIGHT, at Cromford who is empowered to call a Meeting in consequence thereof'.

Jessop's proposals were discussed at a meeting held at Alfreton on 15 December 1788. Arkwright, surprisingly, did not attend, although on 23 November he had told Philip Gell[46] that he intended to be there and was 'glad to here the monies to Comp.' this Canal will not [be] wanting but before any Petition to the House [of Commons] be presented it will be necessary to know how it is to be raised'. In the same letter he set out, but did not elaborate, what proved to be the first of a long series of objections to Jessop's plans: 'I am fear full the Proposd alteration in taking the water as soon as it leaves the [Cromford] Cotton mill Will be an Inconveaniance & a loss to me'.

The seventy-eight persons who petitioned Parliament for a Bill were mainly Derbyshire and Nottinghamshire gentry, together with a sprinkling of professional men. At their head was Philip Gell of Hopton, from whom a decade earlier Arkwright had leased land at Bakewell, and Wirksworth. The London end of the parliamentary negotiations was looked after by Philip's brother, Captain (later Admiral) John Gell of Crich, Derbyshire, and of Wimpole Street.

By 19 March 1789, believing that the proposed canal would prove detrimental to his interests, Arkwright had commisioned the London attorneys Winter and Kaye, petitioned Parliament against the Cromford Canal Bill and withdrawn the petition upon the company agreeing to make amendments to the Bill.[47]

Early on, tantalisingly brief hints as to the nature of the negotiations between Arkwright and others of the Cromford Canal proprietors began to emerge. Thus on 18 April 1789 Captain Gell confided to his brother that 'Sir Richd Arkwright has his whims'; he also remarked as to 'his coolness'.[48] Three days later he was to observe, 'The Knight is so kind & civil to me that he insists in my calling on him every day — but he will not acknowledge of any benefit to Cromford'.[49]

On 22 April Benjamin Outram told Philip Gell, 'Your brother the Capt[n]. looks very well after his journey and has been this morning along with M[r] Berrisford to Sir Rich[d] Arkwright who behaves rather strangely, I do not know what to make of him.'[50] The same day Captain Gell wrote to his brother that Arkwright had:

> said much of being neglected and was always against the Canal running so near the House . . . he will be satisfyed if we can carry it near the Bridge & as close the Derwent as possible he wants the Green — & will not be so closed hemmed in if he can help it — we certainly softened him favouribly to us — appeared to think that he had been deceived — and even angry at Nightingale's name being in the Plan and perhaps not his own — how frivolous I never knew before he liked a touch of flattery.[51]

And the next day (23 April 1789) Francis Beresford[52] told Philip Gell:

> Sir R[d]. Arkwright has declared his direct *opposition* to our Plans unless a certain alteration can be adopted which M[r]. Jessop declares is quite impracticable and which there is some reason to fear S[r]. Rich[d]. knows to be so — but this is between ourselves. He seems to have no regard to consistency of Character.[53]

Those parts of the remaining letters relating to Arkwright's negotiations with the Cromford Canal proprietors are worth printing in sequence. They reveal him as a man of rapidly changing moods whose actions puzzled, amazed and irritated his associates.

Philip Gell to Captain John Gell   25 April 1789

> I had Sir Richd here this morning very early — both Jessop & Berrisford think him unreasonable & that he has ideas prejudicial to the scheme that is to monopolize if he can he declars no Lime shall be sold to him . . . There is certainly some jealousy in the Knight — and he intends if he can a Lime monopoly which must be prevented — he tells of having an order for Peter [Nightingale] to come & give evidence from the [Commons] Committee — he will work hard against us & talks much of *my property* — and they say what he agreed to with me he will undo again tomorrow if assented to — so they look on it there is no end to him[54]

The previous day Arkwright had instructed Winter and Kaye to prepare a petition against those clauses in the Cromford Canal Bill relating to the passage of the canal through his lawn and grounds. Two counsel, Anstruther and Cullen,[55] were retained, and on 27 April Arkwright told Winter and Kaye to write asking George Goodwin to come up to London to help prepare the petition.

Captain Gell to Philip Gell   30 April 1789

This morning we have been with Sir Richd and M[r] Milnes[56] who resides
with him — now we are attending the Canal Office to consider of another
proposal from Sir Richard — which he has struck himself — which is to take
the Water by an Aqueduct from his Dam at Masson Mill which must be raised
some few feet — & he will submit to the Aqueduct coming on the Willersley
side under the new Mansion — this appears to M[r] M ——— & myself to be an
eligible business & in fact better for us — for he stops Cromford Sough every
Sunday himself to fill the Dam above the black Dog[57] & the Sough will at a
future time be drained by the Birchwood sough — Sir Richard has trusted his
plan to me shown in the sough — but before Jessop Beresford & Evans having
had words with Sir Richard and all Let there can be no agreement among them
. . . Jessop says Sir Richard's Scheme is practicable so I have recommended it
much — he intrusted me with his draft & would not any body else — both
Fletcher[58] & Jessop say it may be done — the first says 16 feet raising the dam
will do for he has all the Levels from Bakewell.[59]

Captain Gell to Philip Gell   Friday, 1 May 1789

Sir Richard is now setting of for Cromford & M[r] Goodwin is expected in
Town who is to be entrusted with his affairs. — I am his Friend in the channel
from the upper Dam — he even smiled to day which he has never done before
on the subject & talks of pleasure Boats & entertaining my Company in the
Water & talked of having inserted in the Act his Boat — an open Canal where
every Man an Englishman may have a Boat that pleases[60] — what do you think
of him now — I think more than I shall say . . . I am for treating Sir Richard
in his wishes & plead his Case with Jessop — Sir R meadows will become by
this Channel Water Meadows and I told him so — he does not like people
finding these things out.[61]

When, the following day, Arkwright and Winter and Kaye met Captain
Gell, Francis Beresford and other unnamed proprietors of the Cromford Canal
Company the latter agreed to make such changes to their Bill that Arkwright
felt no longer constrained to petition against it. Details were worked out over
the next few days, during which time Winter and Kaye were again in constant
touch with Arkwright as well as with Anstruther, Goodwin and Captain
Gell.

During the summer Philip Gell was to be made increasingly aware, mainly
by his brother, of the ever-changing complexities of negotiating with Arkwright:

Captain Gell to Philip Gell   8 May 1789

Sir Rich[d] Arkwright will move every thing for the Canal so far have we
satisfyed him — and he has begun to move among the Lords — particularly
the Scotch Lords — and we have promised & agreed about his clauses —[62]

Captain Gell to Philip Gell   11 May 1789

Yesterday the Knight was in good humour and the clauses were drawn out in fair and he had a letter ready to publish — expressing himself satisfyed with the clauses to be introduced in the Bill & that it would be of the greatest use to the Country and should have every support in his power — now you must know had we not satisfyed him he would have given such a strength to the Derby apponents that we could not have stood it — and he could have spent his money too — so I am sure we shall have the concurrence of all the Proprieters — he said something about his expences that he had been at this . . . complains of Outram talking disrespectfully of him, of which he hears in the Country — such as he ought to have his head off — I wish Outram would not say any such thing, nor is it proper he should . . . The knight says no Man in England would have given up what he has done and talks of his expenses & journies at the same [time] says he does not mind the money . . .[63]

Francis Beresford to Philip Gell   15 May 1789

I find that it is *insisted upon* by many of our subscribers that no person shall be intitled to more than *10 shares*, or £1,000, in the Cromford Canal and the ostensible reason is to prevent S[r] R A. from obtaining a monopoly, be that as it may, we have rec'd directions from Nott[m]. to insert a clause in the Bill for that purpose.[64]

Benjamin Outram to Philip Gell   London May 23rd 1789

. . . the alterations agreed upon to accommodate Sir R[d] Arkwright will be a little inconvenient but I think he will not wish to have them adopted when he sees more clearly the business on the whole every thing now stands as well as possible.[65]

Captain Gell to Philip Gell   11 June 1789

If Sir Richard Ark—— is such a child that he was to know when & how & he came to Town he must imagine some inspiration in all the party. The first time that it was known I was in Nocks[66] shop on Ludgate Hill saw him pass on Tuesday last in a Hack & yesterday was at his house——his servant said if they wanted him they knew he was in Town——& he was going to set of again into the Country——what pettish conduct & childish——& looks what he would be——yet he will talk of his expences at the first meeting of the Canal & his employing his 6 sollicitors when one would have done——I do not say but his name was usefull to us——but if we are to pay for it the matter is at an end——the D of New [castle] & Duchess might as well bear their expences ——for their names had the most influence——why Sir Richard could not announce himself I must leave to his own petulant temper. I do not want to quarrel with any body and shall not with him——but if opportunity offers shall explain myself to him——he might be the greatest use to us particularly among the Scotch Peers as they all know him & esteem him much.[67]

Rock House, Cromford, Richard Arkwright's residence

North Street, Cromford, with school building to the extreme right

overleaf
Three children of Richard Arkwright
(*left*) with a goat, (*right*) with a kite,
1791, by Joseph Wright

Sir Richard Arkwright's town house, 8 Adam Street, London

Captain Gell to Philip Gell   18 July 1789

. . . The clauses added to please Sir Richard — particularly raising his Weir & making a channel thro' his meadow — my opinion from the first was we should not have occasion for this but it pleased him so we made a friend of him but he held us all here as Enemies — now we are to take Water at any four places we please — and no doubt our way will be that which is the cheapest & most commode for our purpose — and I find Sir Richard has never paid any subscription Money — & perhaps has some intention of making a charge of his expenses — & employing Counsil & four Sollicitors which he had at one time — I do not intend myself to allow of this charge — and if he should make any such thing it will open such a door or doors that there will be no End to it — and those clauses of his gave us trouble in the Lords — . . . I have never been well pleased with him for putting that question to me that if ever we had 10 p^{Ct} for our Money & it was necessary to lower the Tonnage for the good of the country if I would Vote for it. I told him most assuredly I should — he said he never would. I found he was disappointed by my answer — and am convinced he has many designs which the world cannot know of and all forgetting he has not so much of the Milk of human kindness in him as the world would give him credit for. I know he will oppose M^r. Jessop where you will find a better Engineer or a more Able practical Man I do not know — & by the bye he is a Proprietor of the Canal though he has not appeared but his Brother has subscribed I see —[68]

Captain Gell to Philip Gell   Saturday 8th Augt 1789

. . . I am glad that Jessop is likely to be employed & B——— Outram they are certainly very proper Persons — it is a very serious business the carrying on our Works with judgements — and M^r. Jessop has seen much & observed much — and I do not see why if it is no use to us — that we are obliged to raise Sir Richards Weir for him — it is in the Act but we afterwards agreed to take the Water at four differ^t. places for the Derby people objected to his being the sole deliveror of Water — our clauses in addition must be reported at Mich^s quarter Sessions and advertised three times in the Paper —[69]

Meanwhile on 3 July Captain Gell had advised his brother that Arkwright and his lawyers 'now object to the clauses *wch* were made purpusely for him'.[70] Nevertheless difficulties were patched up — temporarily, as it turned out and the Cromford Canal Bill received the royal assent on 31 July 1789.

The following year the Act[71] was amended to give Arkwright rights to 'any Mine or Mines, Vein or Veins of Lead Ore' discovered on his lands during the construction of the canal. This was a prelude to further discussions with the Cromford Canal Company, and on 18 May 1790 Arkwright negotiated with the company's representative, William Fillingham, for 'upwards of two hours settling & arranging the terms of an agreement . . . for the Sale of part of . .

. [his] Garden & Lawn &c.'. Three days later Arkwright 'directed some additions and alterations', and by 25 May[72] everything had been settled, with his agreeing to sell to the company a dozen contiguous pieces of land stretching along the Derwent from Cromford Green to Carr Wood. The prices ranged from £330 an acre (for the Upper Garden and the Lawn) to £19 16s an acre, and the total cost to the company came to £1,535 3s. In addition Arkwright received £50 'as a Compensation for the injury to be done to his Garden' and a further £207 5s 10d for building 'new Garden Walls' and removing soil from the old to the new garden. Water rights (especially those at the Masson weir) were safeguarded and mineral rights preserved. In January 1791 it was further agreed that should the company build 'more than one Dwelling House for the Use and Occupation of a Wharfinger or Toll-gatherer' it would, within three weeks, pay to 'Sir Richard Arkwright the Sum of Twenty thousand pounds Sterling'.

In 1786,[73] the year he was knighted, Arkwright began building his mansion, Willersley Castle, on the estate he had acquired four years earlier. His architect was William Thomas, a native of Pembroke (said to have been descended from the Flemings sent there by Henry I in 1111) but now of 13 Charlotte Street, Portland Place. In 1800 he was described as 'architect to his Royal Highness the Duke of Clarence'.

Believing that 'Architecture, properly defined, is partly an Art and partly a Science', Thomas,[74] an occasional exhibitor at the Royal Academy of Arts, had published in 1783 *Original Designs in Architecture*, a slim volume of designs for villas, temples and grottoes, a work which included a garden temple designed for the Earl of Shelburne's park at Bowood, Wiltshire, together with details of works already executed at Brownslade House and Stackpole Court, both in Pembrokeshire, and the Surrey Chapel, Blackfriars Road, Southwark. In 1785 Thomas presented to the Society of Arts a copy of his book and two years later addressed the society.[75] It was probably here that he attracted the attention of Arkwright, who had been elected to the society in 1782[76] and was well known to its secretary, Samuel More.

The knight set about building his castle to face due south from the slopes of Wild Cat Tor, some 400 ft above sea level. Below stretched parkland falling towards a grand sweep of the river Derwent, immediately beyond which towered the massive perpendicular limestone crag of Scarthin Rock, fringed with trees and undergrowth and obscuring Willersley's view of the Cromford mills, though not of the higher parts of Cromford village, lining the road to Wirksworth. The recently built Masson Mill was visible from the grounds but not from the castle. The higher parts of Wild Cat Tor behind Willersley afforded fine panoramic views of Matlock Bath, the Heights of Abraham and Jacab, noted for their caverns and thermal springs, Masson Hill and the summit of High Tor.

Arkwright's mansion, an ambitious seven-bay gritstone building of two and a half storeys, entirely classical in conception but romanticised by semi-circular turrets at the angles of the side wings (those on the east wing were intended for use as strong rooms) ushered in the Gothic Revival in the domestic architecture of Derbyshire. The oval hall with galleries on both upper storeys and a skylight is in a modern judgement the finest of its rooms.

Willersley's foundations were built upon a huge rock reputed to have cost, £3,000 to level, a sum which presumably included the cost of three ale and five wine cellars built under the east and west wings respectively. A counting house, dairy, brewhouse, bakehouse, wash house and laundry were among the rooms to the rear of the ground floor and its wings.[77]

On 14 June 1789, a year after the mansion had been roofed, Byng looked over Willersley Castle and wrote scathingly about what he saw:

> We took a meand'ring walk around these little mills, bridges, and cascades; and went to where Sr R: A is building for himself a grand house (Wensley Castle) in the same castellated stile as one sees at Clapham; and *really* he had made a *happy* choice of ground, for by sticking it up on an unsafe bank, he contrives to overlook, not see, the beauties of the river, and the surrounding scenery. It is the house of an overseer surveying the works, not of a gentleman

Willersley Castle

wishing for retirement and quiet. But light come, light go, Sir R^d has honourably made his great fortune; and so let him still live in a great cotton mill!^78

Only when seen from the vantage of Cromford Hill did Byng go so far as to admit grudgingly that Willersley 'appear'd to an advantage, it does not deserve'. Twelve months later, 19 June 1790, his opinion remained unchanged:

> I took a short walk to look at the weather, and at Sr Rd A's new house . . . The inside is now finishing; and it is really, within, an effort of inconvenient ill taste; built so high as to overlook every beauty, and to catch every wind; the approach is dangerous; the ceilings are of gew-gaw fret work; the small circular stair-case, like some in the new built houses of Marybone, is so dark and narrow, that people cannot pass each other; I ask'd a workman if there was a library? — Yes, anser'd he, at the foot of the stairs. Its dimensions are 15 feet square; (a small counting house;) and having the perpendicular lime stone rock within 4 yards, it is too dark to read or write in without a candle! There is likewise a music room; this is upstairs, is 18 feet square, and will have a large organ in it: what a scheme! What confinement! At Clapham they can produce nothing equal to this, where ground is sold by the yard.^79

Sir Richard was destined never to enjoy his castle, for in the afternoon of Monday 8 August 1791 an 'alarming fire', said to have been started by an overheated stove, greatly damaged the interior, although, reported the *Derby Mercury*^80 'most of the elegant furniture was preservd'. Arkwright was in fact then only in the early stages of furnishing. For just over a year he had been ordering furniture and fittings from Edward Wilson's, 'Cabinet-Makers Uph-olsterers Appraisers & Undertakers', of 376 Strand, 'nearly opposite Beaufort Buildings', and by the time of the fire items to the value of £415 18s 9d had been delivered, some of them to Arkwright's recently acquired house in the Adelphi. By the end of July 1792 an additional 150 articles worth £906 12s 11½d, some of them not yet completed, had been ordered and were stored at Wilson's premises.

In this same period Arkwright also placed orders with Wilson for French plate glass to the value of £641. The demand for plate glass, a luxury product thicker than ordinary window panes and with an even, lustrous finish, was rapidly growing as it increasingly became the fashion of the well-to-do to specify large windows and silvered plate glass made into mirrors for their residences. Much of the plate glass was imported or smuggled in from France, but whether Willersley's was of Continental origin or manufactured by the newly formed company of British Plate Glass Manufactures is uncertain.^81

In all, expenditure during the year ending July 1792 came to £1547 13s 0¼d. Of this, £644 16s 5¾d went on the 30 ft by 20 ft drawing room (£240 of it on '2 Magnificent French Plate Glasses for Piers Repolished & Silvered Complete

90 by 50' and £102 10s on 'One very large & Magnificent French Plate 84 by 54½ for Chimney Glass') and a further £162 11s 6d on the dining parlour, of which just over half was for 'A large Magnificent French Glass Plate . . . 70 by 47 & 2 small 70 by 12 each'.

Willersley's library and music room, both so disparagingly commented upon by Byng, set Arkwright back £71 1s 6d (£42 of it on 'A Large Magnificent French Plate of Glass') and £152 12s respectively. Thomas's plan of the library (20 ft by 14 ft 10 in.) included a single window with curtains on one side, bookshelves and a door surrounded by bookshelves on two others, and a fireplace on the remaining side.[82] The furniture was to consist of 'A Large Mahog[any] Library table in 3 parts on a Particular Construction' and a bookcase ('Making a Drawing of a Bookcase' 10s 6d) The 20 ft 4 in. by 20 ft 2 in. music room was at the centre front of the first storey and had 'Grey Sattin Windsor Curtains that came from the Adelphi'.

Expenditure on the pink bedroom and dressing room amounted to £259 3s 2½d, the French bedroom £60 1s, the Chinese bedroom £94 4s 1d and its dressing room £61 1s 9d. The drawing room and dining parlour (both at the front of the ground floor) received special attention and were clearly intended as showpieces. 'Agreeable to Sir Richard's request', Wilson made 'a Ground Plan & Section of the [Drawing] Room to a Scale drawing the different furniture in D°' (£5 5s). And for the dining parlour he 'Paid the Carpet Manufacturers [£3 13s 6d] for Making a drawing in Miniture of a Carpet to Correspond with the ceiling & making a Pencil drawing of the 4 sides of the Room with all the furniture properly placed'.

When in 1790 Thomas submitted his account Arkwright, like a later man of property, disputed the total. Thomas resorted to legal action and on 29 April 1790 Arkwright, 'having been served with a special Original at the Suit of Mr. Willm Thomas', discussed with Winter and Kaye his objections to Thomas's demand. The same day Winter and Kaye called upon Thomas's attorney, Henry Foulkes of Covent Garden, 'to get him to stay proceedings' till you could get Thomas's account examined but which he refused'. Arkwright now gave his attorneys 'instructions to prepare an Affidavit to ground an Application to the Court to stay Thomas's proceedings' till . . . [he] could get his Bill Examined'. Erskine was engaged, whereupon 'Thomas's Attorney at length agreed to give time without applying to the Court' and 'proposed a reference to Arbitration'. Arkwright consented, but on 10 June, Winter and Kaye advised, 'The time appointed by the Bonds having expired without the Arbitrators having made an Award . . . Mr Foulkes . . . proposed to refer the business to one Arbitrator' agreed by Arkwright. By early August a decision had been reached. Thomas was awarded £90, a sum which included costs. Unfortunately we do not know how far it went in meeting his claim.

While Willersley was being built Arkwright bought from William Osborne a London residence, No. 8 Adam Street, Adelphi.[83] The property, up to then used as an hotel,[84] was, Sir John Summerson tells us, part of a 'gallant and imaginative enterprise' by the Adam brothers who 'bid to realise a big architectural idea with no more backing than a modest professional fortune and a sanguine anticipation that a living-quarter of such unique splendour could not want tenants'.

Edward Wilson, as the following entries from his account reveal, was kept busy maintaining the house for the family's visits:

1790		
15 May	Workmans time packing up Furniture prior to the family leaving Town	2s. od.
5 Aug.	12 Large Mahog[any] Hall Chairs with taper theme feet your Coat of Arms & Initials neatly Painted in an Oval Grey Ground	£25 4s. od.
28 Aug.	Taking down 2 Bedsteads brushing & cleaning them for Bugs & fixing the Bedsteads & furnitures up again	12s. od.
1791		
21 Mar.	Paid for Sweeping all the Chimneys in the House	5s. 6d.
	Paid for lacquering the Street door Knocker fixing it on again, Repairing the Bells in the different Parts of the House, us'd a New Pull to the Street door Bell, a Crank & 2 Check Springs	18s. od.
	Repairing doors Window frames & Sundry Cabinet Furniture prior to the Family coming to Town	18s. od.
7 May	Taking down Bed furnitures Window Curtains altering & Putting Sundry furniture to Right after the family left Town	9s. od.

It was for his London residence that in 1789 or 1790 Arkwright commissioned the American artist Mather Brown to paint his portrait. Brown, who in 1784 had taken a twenty-year lease of a pretentious house close to that of George Romney in fashionable Cavendish Square, had recently been appointed Portrait Painter to HRH Frederick Augustus, Duke of York, George III's second son, and was now at the height of his career. In March 1786 he had painted the earliest known likeness of Thomas Jefferson, who had recently succeeded Benjamin Franklin as American envoy to Paris. The following year Jefferson, through John Trumbull, commissioned from him a portrait of Thomas Paine, and in 1787 Brown executed, probably for Jefferson, the portrait of John Adams now at the Boston Athenaeum.[85]

The portrait of Sir Richard (now in the New Britain Museum of American Art), together with two others—those of Lord George Augustus Cavendish[86] (who had been of assistance in his parliamentary affairs in 1783) and Maynard Esquire[87]— was carried from Cavendish Square to the Adelphi on 26 June 1790. A month earlier Arkwright had bought from Brown *The Death of Cato*,[88] painted in 1788 from Thomas Macklin's *Gallery of Poets*. This depicted the death of a noble Roman surrounded by his family and friends and was taken from Addison's play *The Tragedy of Cato*, which caused a political sensation when first produced in London early in the eighteenth century. Another Arkwright purchase at the same time was Brown's *His Majesty* (1790), a large full-length portrait of George III at Windsor with the Horse Guards in the background.[89]

Mather Brown was not the first or only painter to attract Arkwright's attention. Already in 1783 he had shown interest in Joseph Wright, who on 29 May confided to Wedgwood, 'As soon as M[rs]. Wright is brought to bed, w[ch] she expects hourerly I shall set off to Cromford by appointment to paint M[r]. Arkwright and his daughter . . .'[90] But for whatever reason he did not paint Arkwright until 1789, a year after he had executed the portraits of his daughter, Mrs Charles Hurt, and her husband.

It was, however, earlier in the 1780s that Wright began a task undertaken by no other eighteenth-century English artist of equal calibre: he painted a series of views of the country around Cromford and of the mills which formed the core of Arkwright's empire. The starting point appears to have been a view of Cromford Bridge (*c.* 1780), followed (*c.* 1782–83) by Arkwright's *Cotton Mills, by night*. These were sold not, as one might imagine, to Arkwright — whose earliest interest in this type of art seems to have been in 1790, when he had Wilson send him from London 'Books of Landscapes for Drawings' (12s)[91] — but to Daniel Parker Coke, MP for Nottingham and Fellow of All Souls.[92]

The Cromford mills were the subjects of a second painting, *Arkwright's Cotton Mills, by day*, (*c.* 1790), a view which while concealing the 1776 mill and later additions to the site behind the seven-story first mill, resembles the present-day scene more accurately than the earlier painting.[93] Nevertheless a comparison of the day and night paintings brings out the great changes which had taken place between 1783 and 1790: the 1771 mill has been extended towards the barrier of Scarthin Rock and the waters of Cromford sough, now separated from those of Bonsall brook, are carried in a wooden aqueduct over a newly constructed road. Near to the road in front of the 1771 mill is Grace Cottage,[94] while a three-storey workshop building and red-brick cottages are concealed behind the trees.

About 1790 Wright painted a companion piece, *Willersley Castle*, depicting the country to the left of the mills, beyond Scarthin Rock. This picture shows Willersley overlooking the Derwent as it flows gently through the valley towards Cromford Bridge, to the right of which are to be seen Arkwright's church and a fisherman's rest. A much smaller picture showing the *Cut through the rock, Cromford* (*c*. 1790) — a scene barely recognisable since the building of the A6 road and subsequent alterations — completed Wright's landscapes of the area. During the first of his visits Bray had noted that the entrance to Matlock Dale through the 'passage cut through the rock . . . makes a very striking app-earance'.[95] Had Arkwright had his way the view would have been even more spectacular. He had, Pilkington records, 'intended to have left a rude arch, when this passage was made. The idea was a happy one, and had it been carried into execution would have had an excellent effect.'[96] All this goes to remind us that although by no stretch of the imagination can Arkwright be considered an avid patron of the arts (however defined) he scarcely fits into the philistine mould into which he has so often been cast.[97]

In the late 1780s Wright was commissioned to paint the portraits of Sir Richard and his family, and we learn from Wright's close friend John Holland of Ford Hall, Chapel en le Frith, that Arkwright's portrait had been completed by the end of 1789 and 'was intended for Bakewell'. Further, 'Not very long since,' he told the younger Arkwright on 4 December, 'I saw M^r. Wright who is exceedingly grateful for the kind offices done by you and M^{rs}. Arkwright for his benefit when at Cromford.' Holland considered the portrait 'Admirable' and hoped 'that the World might be favoured with a print of so conspicuous a personage'. Wright, it comes out, had by this time also completed the portrait of a second 'Gentleman' about which Holland commented, 'I think nobody can deny his success in the two portraits as he seems precisely to have hit the characters as far as I may judge who have only accidentally seen either of the two Gentlemen.'[98]

Sir Richard, as in the more relaxed portrait by Mather Brown, occupies a canvas to himself, but instead of holding in his hand a roll of parchment — a copy perhaps of his letters patent or the plan of a newly acquired estate — rests his left hand on a table upon which stands a set of rollers for spinning cotton, the fundamental part of the machine upon which his fortune was based and which contributed more than any other to the transformation of the industrial face of England. 'Sir Rich^d.,' Wright wrote to the younger Ark-wright on 21 January 1790, 'was much pleased wth. the execution of his picture' and gave a hint of more commissions: 'Sir Rich^d. has sent the persons card where he saw the Groupe of Charity he sometime expressed a wish for me to paint, wch. looks as if he continued his intention.'[99]

Carlyle, half a century later, saw in Wright's portrait 'not a beautiful man; no romantic-hero with haughty eyes, Apollo-lip, and gesture like the herald Mercury; a plain almost gross, bag-cheeked, potbellied Lancashire man, with the air of painful reflection, yet also of copious free digestion',[100] while to Espinasse the portrait 'with its air of rude health and beaver sagacity, and triumphant joviality' revealed 'a vulgar Lancashire man, successful over much'.[101] A recent view sees in it a 'monument to the triumph of ruthlessness'.[102]

But whatever, if anything, portraits reveal of the man, it had taken more than the water frame and carding machine (however acquired) to achieve all this. Throughout his career, as two near contemporaries put it:

> He was taking measures to secure to himself a fair proportion of the fruits of his industry and ingenuity; he was extending the business on a great scale; he was introducing into every department of the manufacture, a system of industry, œconomy, order, and cleanliness, till then unknown in any manufactory where great numbers were employed together; but which he so effectually accomplished, that his example may be regarded as the origin of almost all similar improvements.[103]

The complete entrepreneur — he more than any other may claim to be the creator of the modern factory system — Arkwright pioneered and perfected business organisation in all its many and varied aspects. From the beginning he showed himself to be no stranger to the arts of industrial incentive. 'Saturday last,' reported the *Nottingham Journal* of 12 September 1772, 'upwards of 300 young people, belonging to Mr. Arkwright's cotton manufactory in this town, paraded thro' the streets, with streamers flying and led by a principal workman, cloathed in white cotton; after which they paraded into Marshall hills to gather nuts, and in the evening returned, and partook of a plentiful supper, concluding the day with great harmony and decorum.' And every September Cromford celebrated the festival of 'candlelighting',[104] as in 1776, when about 500 workmen and children, led by a band and a boy working in a weaver's loom, paraded from the mills round the village, where they were watched by 'an amazing Concourse of People'. Upon returning to the mills they were given buns, ale, nuts and fruit, and the evening ended with music and dancing. The same day Arkwright feasted over 200 workmen who during the summer had erected Cromford's second mill, 120 ft long and seven storeys high. These builders were 'regaled with a large Quantity of Strong Beer &c. yet the Day was spent with the greatest Harmony imaginable'.[105]

Again in 1778 Arkwright entertained his workpeople 'according to annual Custom'. This time a song 'composed on the Occasion by one of the Workmen' was rendered 'in full Chorus, amongst Thousands of Spectators from Matlock Bath, and the neighbouring Towns, who testified their Satisfaction at so pleasing a Sight.——The Evening was concluded by a Ball, which Mr. Arkwright gave at his own House, to the neighbouring Ladies and Gentlemen, at which the Company was very numerous and brilliant.'

The song, almost a eulogy to Arkwright's creation, went:

TUNE, *Roast Beef of Old England.*

YE num'rous Assembly that make up this Throng,
Spare your Mirth for a Moment, and list' to my Song.

The Bounties let's sing, that our Master belong,
   At the Cotton-Mills now at Cromford,
   The famous renown'd Cotton-Mills.

You know he provides us a Feast once a Year,
With Fruit, Cakes, and Liquor, our Spirits to cheer,
He asks no Return, but we decent appear, &c.

Our Number we count seven Hundred or more,
All cloathed and fed from his bountiful Store,
Then Envy don't flout us, nor say any's poor, &c.

Ye know we all ranged in Order have been,
Such a Sight in all Europe sure never was seen,
While Thousands did view us to complete the Scene, &c.

Likewise for to make our Procession more grand,
We were led in the Front by a Musical Band,
Who were paid from the Fund of that bountiful Hand, &c.

Ye Hungry and Naked, all hither repair,
No longer in Want don't remain in Despair,
You'll meet with Employment, and each get a Share, &c.

Ye Crafts and Mechanics, if ye will draw nigh,
No longer ye need to lack an Employ,
And each duly paid, which is a great Joy, &c.

To our noble Master, a Bumper then fill,
The matchless Inventor of this Cotton-Mill,
Each toss off his Glass with a hearty Good-will,
   With Huzza for the Mills now at Cromford,
   All join with a jovial Huzza.[106]

In October 1781 Sylas Neville, who had presumably heard of the 'cand-lelighting' festivities of the previous month, noted in his diary that Arkwright:

who is very rich . . . by his conduct appears to be a man of great understanding & to know the way of making his people do their best. He not only distributes pecuniary rewards, but gives distinguishing dresses to the most deserving of both sexes, which excites great emulation. He also gives two Balls at the Greyhound to the workmen & their wives & families with a weeks jubilee at the time of each ball. This makes them industrious & sober all the rest of the year.[107]

Two years later the rewards took a different form. Arkwright, reported the *Derby Mercury*, 'has generously given to 27 of his principal Workmen, Twenty-Seven fine Milch Cows, worth from 8*l*. to 10*l*. each, for the Service of their respective Families'.[108]

Arkwright's methods were observed at first hand by Archibald Buchanan during the eighteen months he spent at the Rock. Returning to Scotland in 1787, he was put in charge at the age of eighteen, of the Buchanans' recently built Deanston mill, at which, 'an apt pupil of his great master', he lost no time in putting his newly acquired knowledge to account. The beginnings were described by James Smith:

> At this early period in the progress of cotton-spinning it was difficult to find a sufficient number of people with skill and experience for carrying on the work, and it was necessary that most of them should be taught personally by Mr. Archibald, who was himself an expert operator in all the processes. A few persons professing knowledge in the art were occasionally got from Glasgow, and some from England; but those were generally of loose and wandering habits, and seldom remained long in the establishment. The more respectable part of the surrounding inhabitants were at first averse to seek employment in the works, as they considered it disreputable to be employed in what they called 'a public work;' and, indeed, there might be some good ground for their caution, for the roving and dissolute characters who are always the first to seek employment in any new establishment brought no great credit to the manufacturing community by their loose conduct. From the excellent regulations, however, instituted by Mr. Archibald Buchanan, on the model of Arkwright, and rigidly persevered in, great order was in due time established; and, from the great wages which the people earned, the better part of the surrounding population were ultimately attracted to the works. The first supply was chiefly from the Highlands, where, from the introduction of sheep, the farmers and small cotters were forced away to seek employment in such establishments. Many of the offspring of the old stock still remain.
>
> It has been uniformly found that the people of the immediately surrounding neighbourhood have proved the best population, and these works have been an asylum for many a reduced farmer, with his family, and for the widows and orphans of the agricultural and village population.[109]

A more detailed account of Buchanan's methods is set out by an anonymous writer in the *Inverness Courier* of 6 February 1839:

> The general order of management of the Deanston Works is very much on the principle of Arkwright — a proof of the talents of that eminent person. There is a head or superintendent to each department — every one has his own allotted part — and in most cases they are paid by the piece — not in weekly wages. They receive the amount of their earnings every Thursday morning (that being the market day), and the youngest individual about the works is paid his or her wages into their own hand, which seems to give them an idea of personal consequence. They have all the privilege of leaving any moment they choose, without previous warning; and we were informed that this is found to insure a more steady, agreeable, and lengthened service than could be obtained by the firmest indenture. There is no fine or punishment, excepting for damage to the works through evident carelessness. The order of the establishment is preserved

by the dismissal of offending individuals or their banishment for a limited period. By 'stopping the supplies' every member of the family is interested in the good conduct of the whole, and a banished child, man, or friend, finds no rest at home. The morals of the people are in general very correct — no drunkard is permitted about the establishment.[110]

And when in 1801 Kirkman Finlay bought the Catrine mills, Buchanan, as he was to testify in 1839, almost at the end of his career, reorganised them on Arkwright principles:

a system of management was adopted, and is still acted upon, which has had a very salutary effect, both as regards the conducting of the establishment with regularity and satisfaction to all parties, and also as regards the comfort and respectability of those employed in it. In the works there are 21 different rooms or departments; in each of these the master or overlooker is at liberty to choose his own hands; and, in like manner, the workers have it in their power to change at the end of every week, and to go to any room within the establishment, where the master of that room can employ them, upon giving six days' previous notice to the master they leave. In this way each master soon gathers around him a set of workers to his mind; and in reality there is very little changing from one room to another. The master, as well as all the workers, with the exception of learners and extra hands, are paid by piece-work; of course it is his interest to have the best workers he can get, and, should a worker not be able to obtain employment from any master, it is pretty evident that the fault lies in the individual, who must choose some other employment. No corporal punishment has ever been permitted; and the above regulation is a check upon the severity on the part of the master, as his workers can leave him at any time, upon giving the proper notice.[111]

Although Arkwright's career confirms the superiority of instinct in business over rules, his was an instinct supported by unremitting toil and a meticulous attention to detail extending from the highest policy decisions to the personal supervision of the mill rooms. So much so that, according to Ure, 'when bad yarn made its appearance in any one of his mills, he swore a loud oath, according to the vile fashion of the time, and ordered his people to look after their drawings, convinced that if *they* were right, every thing else would go well'.[112]

To all agreements, and especially to those legally binding, Arkwright never put his signature without first understanding fully the terms and pondering all foreseeable consequences. 'Sir Richard Arkwright objecting to Execute the Agreement on Account of his not Acquainted with the Business writing a long letter to him explaining the Business and the Proceedings therein,' Winter and Kaye noted on 9 July 1789. And later: 'writing several times afterwards to Sir Richard on the subject, and attending Mr Laroche's Attorney several times on the difficulties which retarded the reference.'

Accounts were closely scrutinised, for, as the *Gentleman's Magazine*[113] was to put it, 'Sir Richard . . . with the qualities necessary for the accumulation of wealth, possessed, in an eminent degree, the art of keeping it.' Mindful perhaps of Arkwright's dispute with his architect, Edward Wilson hesitated more than a year before submitting his own expenses for work done up to July 1791:

> For my Travelling Expenses three times to & from Cromford and Various attendances respecting the Chimney Pieces, the Arbitration Respecting to Thomas the Surveyor & Various other Occurences out of the Common Course of Business for which Sir Richard always Proposed to Pay me (but to which I shall omit making any Specific Charge till I see you again.)[114]

Eventually Wilson put in for £26 5s and at the same time submitted his account for 'Coach, Hire, Board Carriage of Material, [and] loss of Tools at [the Willersley] Fire' (£7 10s).

Although Arkwright's wealth was notorious he had a reputation for parsimony, and certainly he could hold on to his money with the tenacity with which he had defended his patents. To this end there were occasional brushes with the Revenue over non-payment of taxes, as when in 1783 after a threatened action in the Court of Exchequer the 'Com[missione]ʳˢ agreed to accept a Fine with Costs [£7 19s] . . . For not entering Paper properly'. and in April 1791 he was listed as a defaulter in the payment of taxes: window tax (£3 9s 4d); commutation tax (£5 10s); horse duty (12s).

Nor did Sir Richard hurry to settle his accounts (though he always paid up). Anthony Lax's £20 3s 9d bill for his part in the conveyance of the Willersley estate early in 1782 was not settled until 27 November 1784 (by a draft on Gibson & Co.). In 1783 £1 15s of Goodwin's charges of £11 15s for his services in the paper case remained outstanding, although he had by this time 'Received of Mʳ. Arkwright on this Acc[oun]ᵗ when he was at Derby on his way to London a Bank Note value £10'. By April 1788 £90 2 s 9d of Goodwin's account dating from Arkwright's action of 1784 against Nightingale for 'seducing and employing a Manufacturer' from Cromford remained unpaid although on 9 November 1786 he had received £6 3s 5d 'By Paper & Muslin' in part settlement. And on 22 April 1788 Joseph Fletcher wrote to Josiah Wedgwood on Arkwright's behalf: 'Inclosed you have a Dft value Twelve Pounds Four Shillings which pays for a parcel of Pots received last September receipt please acknowledge in course — Sir R. A. gave orders for a Bill to be sent immediately after the Pots was delivered but by some means it has been overlooked.'[115]

But perhaps the most sensitive guide to Arkwright's reputation in money matters is to be found in a note at the end of the younger Adam Wolley's account of 25 October 1788: 'For my trouble in selling your Allotment to Mr

Simpson you promised me 5 Gns in case I could sell same for £10 p acre but having sold same for £12 p acre I leave the Sum to your Generosity.' The knight could be generous but he was not to be taken for granted.

Arkwright's boundless self-confidence — he did not stop short of trying to teach James Watt how to improve his steam engines[116] and is said to have made light of discussions on taxation with the boast that he would pay off the national debt — contrasted strangely with his sometimes apparent reluctance to come to a decision.[117] A letter of 8 February 1790 from Goodwin to the younger Arkwright shows this. The reason for Sir Richard's hesitation is tantilisingly concealed. 'Debts . . . larger than he expected and the whole property . . . worth £240,000' are referred to but not disclosed; but the property can hardly have been the estate about to be auctioned at Matlock Bath and advertised in the *Derby Mercury* of 4 February 1790. Goodwin's letter reads:

Winster Monday Evening, 8th Feb 1790

Dear Sir

I am just return'd from Cromford where I went this morning, and sorry to say that is is not in my power to give you full satisfaction on the subject we talk'd about on Saturday. A conversation relating [to] other things gave me as I tho'. a favourable opportunity of bringing on that subject; Sir Richard was relating the various disagreeable circumstances, difficulties & mistakes that he labour'd under, to which I replied that I was fully convinc'd of what he say'd, and mention'd how difficult it wo^d. be for him to get thro' them himself in any other way than being either assisted by you, or by concluding the contract enter'd into by him and you, and which I told him brought me to mention that you had call'd on me twice, to know whether he had come to a resolution on that head & if he had mention'd it to me and that you had requested me to speak to him about it, on which he rather quickly replied, you might call on him yourself, I then say^d. I was sure if you tho'. it wo^d. be agreeable to him you wo^d. do it immediately, as your sole wish was to do what wo^d. be most to his ease and satisfaction but that he must recollect what he say'd the last time we met all together, and after that conversation, how very disagreeable it must be for you to renew it with^t you knew it w^d. be agreeable to him he then was silent a short time, & so soon as I saw him in a disposition to talk, I ask'd him whether he had made up his mind whether the business sh^d. go forward or not, he replied he had not made up his mind about it — I ment^d. what a very disagreeable situation you was in from being under such an uncertainty that you co^d. not otherways dispose of your money to advantage that there was an Estate to be sold on Wednesday at Matlock Bath, which w^d. be eligible for you to buy, but that you did not wish to do it if the agreement was to go forward, he then say'd you might buy it if you chose, and desired I wo^d. not mention the subject any more at present, this being rather premptory, I gave it up, till just before I left him, when I mention'd to him, what he had say'd when we first began to talk about it, — 'that you might come & speak about it yourself,' and ask^d. him whether he wo^d. give me leave to say to you, that you might call on him and talk about it, he replied he wo^d. not send any message about it, & again repeated that nothing further sho^d. be say^d. about it at present — and in this way it ended — and you will judge what will be best to do, I confess myself, I wish you to go down, and mention it, at the same time I am afraid you must expect some little being say'd that wo^d. be disagreeable, but I hope & think not much — I yet think he intends to do it sometime, but perhaps not before he has more fully mention'd it — I find Accounts have been sent out to [ ] deals with, and he once mention'd that the Debts are larger than he expected and that the whole property wo^d. be worth £240,000.

He talk'd of going to Nottingham tomorrow, but I scarcely think he will, as he has got a very bad cold — he was in perfect good humour all day. I don't know whether you will be able to read this, but I am heartily tired (for I went & came on Horseback) that I can neither correct nor copy — but I am Dear Sir

Yours faithfully
G Goodwin

But, whatever Arkwright's uncertainties, work to him was a vocation, perhaps also his only relaxation. Nothing was allowed to stand in the way. Not even his wife, from whom he separated because of her opposition to his schemes. Two conflicting stories have come down as to the immediate cause. According to Guest, whose authority he claimed to be Arkwright's niece, the separation took place 'about 1779; Margaret Arkwright having refused to sell some jointly owned property valued around £400, so little was her faith in her husband's plan for employing it in his spinning concerns. 'The separation,' Guest tells us, 'was chiefly her own act. She never spoke ill of Mr Arkwright, and, never would allow any one else to do so in her presence, though, for some years afterwards, she lived entirely upon her own means. Even when Mr. Arkwright had accumulated a large fortune, he allowed her no more than thirty pounds a year. On that allowance she lived, as far as his support went, during his life time.'[118]

For whatever reason, Guest does not tell us that Lady Arkwright took up residence at Wirksworth shortly after Sir Richard's death, a move made possible, it seems, by the financial provision he made for her in his will. But the real difficulty with his account is that in 1779 Arkwright, already rich and famous, can hardly have been wanting for £400; a decade earlier, when struggling to perfect his machine at Nottingham, he would doubtless have been glad to have such a sum.

Baines's version, obtained from his 'private source', had it that Arkwright separated from his wife while still in Bolton 'because she, convinced that he would starve his family by scheming when he should have been shaving, broke some of his experimental models of machinery'.[119] True or not, this story has all the ring associated with heroic invention.

Although the new squire undertook some of the obligations expected of his class — his ten-guinea subscription to the fund raised in 1783 for the relief of the maimed and wounded of the Royal Manchester Volunteers and for the dependants of 'those soldiers as have Lost their Lives in the ever-glorious and memorable Defence of Gibraltar',[120] his ten guineas' annual donation to the Manchester Infirmary; his stewardship of the Festival General Hospital, near Nottingham;[121] his chairmanship of the Derbyshire Anniversary[122] and his part as a trustee of the Wirksworth General Provident Society[123] — none of these activities was unduly time-consuming. Perhaps because he considered field sports a waste of his valuable time or simply through lack of interest (probably both) his name never appeared in the lists of the holders of game certificates. Nor, unlike his near neighbours, the Hurts, Gells and Fitzherberts, did he seek to protect the sporting potential of his estates through membership of the Matlock Old Bath Association for the Protection of Fish and Game.[124]

Instead, Baines tells us, 'when considerably more than fifty years of age, — feeling that the defects of his education placed him under great difficulty and inconvenience in conducting his correspondence, and in the general manage-ment of his business — he encroached upon his sleep, in order to gain an hour each day to learn English grammar, and another hour to improve his writing and orthography!'[125] Certainly Arkwright delegated most of his letter writing to his nephews, William Melling and Joseph Fletcher, or to his clerks, William Gibson junior at Cromford and George Trueman at Nottingham. But although misspelt and ill or rather unpuctuated his own letters were otherwise clear and to the point. He was no waster of words, which to him, like time, were a valuable commodity.

Small wonder the knight's work day stretched from five in the morning until nine at night and that in order not to waste a moment he had his carriage drawn by four horses and at a rapid speed.[126] Even when he might have been resting at the Rock his mind continued to be absorbed with business. So much so that the young Archibald Buchanan found him 'so intent on his schemes and calculations' that they 'often sat for weeks together, on opposite sides of the fire without exchanging a syllable'.[127] And Wedgwood, writing to Watt from Matlock on 17 September 1785, related a similar story:

> I have visited Mr Arkwright several times and find him much more convers-ible than I expected, and he invites me to come and see as often as I can, tho he tells me he at present shuns all company as much as possible because it robs him of his time and breaks in upon his plans — And besides he says he is no company for them, for whilst they are talking to him upon one subject he is thinking upon another, and does not know what they say to him.[128]

'He is,' Wedgwood went on, 'much affected by the ill usage he received at the last trial, particularly from Mr Bearcroft who pointing to him said *There sits*

the theif. He had just now got the trial down translated out of short hand, &
I believe means to prosecute some of the evidences for perjury. I do not yet know
if he has any thoughts of a new trial.'

But, whatever Manchester's feeling about Arkwright in the heat of the great
patent trials, it recognised him as its leader. He fixed the price of cotton twist,[129]
and his lists, with their sometimes dramatic changes in prices and in rates of
discount were anxiously scanned by competitors, who responded as best they
could.[130] His name headed the trade movements, as in the dark days of 1788
when the bill holders of Livesey Hargreaves & Co., meeting at the London
Tavern to survey the wreck, voted him to the chair,[131] while the early months
of 1791 saw him among the leaders in the struggle to end the monopoly of the
East India Company.[132]

Yet, even with his patents lapsed or set aside, Arkwright's own propensity
to monopolise did not diminish and when, in 1784, Pitt proposed a new excise,
the so-called Fustian Tax, as a part of his plan to repair the financial ravages
of the American war Arkwright submitted his own scheme, which the
Manchester manufacturers, already hostile to Pitt's proposals, denounced as
monopolistic.

Arkwright's plan, with its estimates, the earliest we have, of the numbers of
mills, machines of various types and spindles then in use, was set out in some
detail:[133]

Propositions submitted to the Chancellor of the Exchequer

Spinning Mills

1st   The Mills erected for the purpose of Spinning Cotton
are Computed at 50, Each of which shall have an
Annual Licence, and pay for the same
£20.   1,000   0   0
The above Mills are computed to contain on the
Average 1,200 Spindles each making 60,000—each
Spindle to pay 20⁵/⁻pr Annum   60,000   0   0
                                                         £61,000   0   0

Spinning Jennies

2d   The number of Jennies with which Rollers are used
(mules) are computed at 60.—These are proposed to
have an Annual Licence of £3.   180   0   0
Each of the above Jennies is computed to contain on the 1,050   0   0
Average 70 Spindles. 4,200 Spindles at 5⁵/⁻pr Annum
3d   The number of common Jennies are Estimated at 8,000
of which it is supposed there are 2/3rds the property of
the lower class who possess not more than one Jenny
each, and who only spin the Cotton they receive for the

purpose of weaving it in their own families, these are
persons who are incapable of paying any Tax more than
is necessary, to ascertain them two thirds of 8,000 is
5,333 to pay for a Licence, permitting them to
work only one Machine not exceeding 30 Spindles 2^s/6. 666 0 0
The remaining 1/3rd of the 8,000 Jennies are those 1,333 0 0
which are the property of persons possessing more than
one, or which are work'd for hire—These amount to
2,667 and are on the Average computed to contain 74
Spindles each—for these it is proposed an Annual
Licence shall be taken out and charged at 10^s/
2,667 Jennies at 74 Spindles each, are 197,358 Spindles
each of which it is proposed shall pay pr
Annum 3^s/6. 34,537 0 0

Carding Machines for Jennies Spinning

The number of Carding Machines is Computed at
2,000 which are worked for hire either by hand, Horses,
or Water—these it is proposed shall
have an Annual Licence of £5. 10,000 0 0

Roving Jennies for Jennie Spinning

The number of Roving Jennies are Computed at 1,000.
These it is proposed shall have an Annual
Licence of 10^s/ 500 0 0
Each of the Roving Jennies are Computed on the
Average to contain 20 Spindles. 20,000 Spindles, each
of which it is proposed shall pay pr Annum
3^s/6. 3,500 0 0
 £51,766 0 0

Amount of Tax proposed upon the large
Spinning Mills £61,000
Amount of Taxes proposed upon the Spinning Jennies,
Carding Machines, and Roving
Machines 51,766
 £112,766

The Sums proposed will Amount to 3^{d}¼ p lb upon all
Spun and Manufactured Cotton, of which it is
computed about 1/7th part will be exported, and upon
which a Drawback will be
necessary which will amount to 16,109
 £96,657

Amount Nett of the various Taxes on Spinning
&c. 96,657

Amount proposed in Addition to the present   <u>22,000</u>
Taxes on Printed Goods   <u>£118,657</u>

Manchester's reaction to Arkwright's scheme is recorded in the early pages of James Whitaker's minute book[134] of the activities of the manufacturers' delegates to the Lords of the Treasury, who, although failing to prevent the passing into law of Pitt's proposals on 1 October 1784,[135] were successful in securing their repeal seven months later:

> As M'. Arkwright an ingenious Mechanic (who resides at Cromford in Derbyshire where he now has, and has had for some Years most extensive Cotton Spinning Works, and has lately erected in S[h]ude Hill within Manchester a very extensive Brick Cotton Spinning Work) in the Spring of 1784 laid before, the above mentined Minister [Pitt] a scheme of Taxing Cotton Works (which would have nearly operated as a prohibition on the other Cotton Works of the Country and for that reason have given him an almost entire command of the Cotton Spinning Trade) therefore on the 13th July 1784 the following memorial from the Manufacturers of Cotton Goods in the Town and neighbourhood of Manchester was also presented to the Lords of the Treasury to prevent such a destructive measure being executed —

This memorial ('unconnected with the Callicoe Printers') maintained that Arkwright's tax proposals 'would bear rather hard on the Callicoe Printers . . . [and] would be very injurious to the Cotton Manufacture in general, and more particularly to the lower sort of Articles called ffustians, which constitute the principal part of their Manufactures'. Further, exports would suffer, and as it would prove 'impossible to ascertain the drawbacks equivalent to these Taxes' Arkwright's plan 'would open a door to endless frauds equally injurious to the fair Trader and the revenue; it also alters the Nature of the Tax by converting it from a Tax on Consumption to a Tax on Commerce'.[136]

A further memorial, presented on 21 July 1784, observed that

> the Cotton Manufactures of Manchester have risen to such consequence, as to become the object of envy and imitation of every neighbouring Nation, . . . [and] that a Tax on them must prevent further inventions and improvements, and inevitably ruin the Trade of this Country, and cause great emigrations of Artists to France, Ireland, &c. who are at this time giving every encouragement to establish this species of Manufacture, and who are almost Daily sending over Emissaries at a great Expence for that purpose. Besides your Memorialists conceive, that the proposed substitution of Taxes has been recommended to your Lordships with a view to enable a few wealthy Individuals to monopolize the whole Spinning Trade to themselves.[137]

Another projected Arkwright monopoly, or so it was alleged, was his 'vast and daring' scheme to buy up all the world's cotton so as to make an enormous profit by cornering the market.[138] And certainly Arkwright had his dealings in cotton. As early as 1780 he was supplying India cotton to Nottingham hosiers,[139] and it was probably about 1783 (in which year an action brought against him in the Court of King's Bench by George Lomas, who had his 'Cotton Warehouse' at 19 Cloak Lane, London, set him back over £1,200)[140] that he became a partner with John Clegg in John Clegg & Co., cotton merchants, of Oxford Court, Cannon Street, London.[141] The Cleggs also carried on business in Manchester as cotton merchants of Cromford Court and fustian manufacturers of Crow Alley.[142] About the same time Arkwrights's son joined Robert Spear in the firm of Robert Spear & Co., also of Crow Alley.[143]

In the early 1780s 'Messrs Clegg's & Spear' owned joint property in Withy Grove, Manchester.[144] The families were linked by marriage, Robert Spear's father, John, a linen draper, of Hanging Ditch, having married Betty Clegg at the Collegiate Church in 1762, while Robert's aunt Martha also married a Clegg.[145] Spear, whose sister introduced Robert Owen to his future wife, Caroline, the daughter of David Dale, was later described by Owen as a broker 'who stood high in his line of business, as a man of integrity and knowlege' and figured in the legendary story of the introduction of Sea Island cotton into England when in 1790 or 1791 he sold to Owen the first two packages 'consigned to him by the Liverpool agent of the American planter, with a request that he would apply to a competent spinner to try its quality and to give an opinion of its value'.[146]

The Arkwrights' partnerships with John Clegg and with twenty-six-year-old Robert Spear were ended, both 'by mutual Consent', in 1788 and 1790 respectively.[147] The winding up of Sir Richard's association with Clegg was followed by friction owing to disagreement about the recovery of debts (Arkwright demanded to have 'the Partnership Books placed in his Hands' and, when Clegg refused, called in Winter & Kaye[148] to advise him upon 'the measures to be pursued in consequence of Mr. Clegg's refusal') and the disposal of cotton which under the 'Deed of Dissolution' had been deposited with Robert Spear & Co. and with Godwin & Coles, general brokers, of Scotch Yard, Bush Lane, Cannon Street.[149] By April 1790 Arkwright had determined to sell the cotton, only to meet with Clegg's refusal, whereupon, noted Winter & Kaye, 'Sir Richard having agreed to postpone the Sale on certain conditions' advised Clegg, who 'rejected the Terms'. The attorneys then passed on to Clegg 'Further proposals on the subject [but] without effect'.

The matter of the debts owing to the former partners proved equally time-consuming.[150] At almost every stage Winter & Kaye consulted Arkwright 'a great many times', as on 4 June 1790, when they called upon him 'this Evening in the Adelphi from 8 till 11 o'Clock advising on your concerns and differences with Mr Clegg and on other Affairs'.

The question of at least one of the debts was eventually resolved in the Court of King's Bench. John Evans, who had his 'cotton manufactory' in Bear Lane,

Southwark,[151] had, it came out, bought cotton from John Clegg & Co. through William Edensor,[152] a London cotton broker who had been declared bankrupt in 1788. Evans, Winter & Kaye told Arkwright, had 'refused to Pay alleging they Paid the Money to Edensor on your Account'. At length 'Sir Richard determined to commence an Action', whereupon Winter & Kaye discussed with George Greaves, a London broker from whom the Strutts obtained some of their supplies,[153] and 'a great many Cotton Brokers and Agents as to the usage in the Trade'. Also examined at the Castle inn, Wood Street, were 'the Books in which Cottons sent to the Defendants, were entered . . . [and] the Book keeper respecting the same'. The trial came on before a special jury on 17 December 1789, when, after the jury had withdrawn for three hours, 'upon the recommendations of the Counsel it was agreed to divide the loss that should result from Edensor's Bankruptcy and each party to Pay their own Costs'.

The rising demand for cotton in the 1780s both put up the price and called forth new supplies. The near seven fold increase in the amount imported from the British West Indies, the traditional source of supply, proved insufficient to meet the needs of the industry and in 1786 the manufacturers presented to the Board of Trade their case for increased supplies.[154] Africa was regarded as a likely source. A sample of cotton grown in Senegal proved 'very good and fine, . . . superior in quality to any of the Brazil cotton, and nearly equal to the East India'.[155] One of the attempts to establish cotton plantations in Africa about this time was the Sierra Leone Company, founded by Thomas Clarkson, the philanthropist who played a prominent part in laying the foundations of the anti-slavery movement. Subscribers to the company's £50 shares included Josiah Wedgwood and his family, with twenty-two, Richard Cardwell, a Blackburn merchant, with ten, William Wilberforce, with the same number, and Henry Thornton, his cousin, who headed the list with fifty-eight.[156]

Arkwright, who on 7 November 1782 had written to the Society of Arts[157] giving his opinion on a sample of Barbados 'Vegetable silk' and who five years later had advised the Board of Trade on cotton grown there from Persian seed,[158] took up three shares not, one suspects, because he was taken in by Clarkson's glowing but, as it turned out, inaccurate forecasts as to the certainty of financial gain but rather through the influence of his partners in his Manchester mill, William Brocklehurst and John Whittenbury. Brocklehurst, who in 1780 had been the main contributor to the fund set up to build the Oldham Street Methodist chapel,[159] and John Whittenbury, who died in 1805 worth 'above seventy and under eighty Thousand pounds',[160] were both members of the Manchester committee of the Society for the Purpose of effecting the Abolition of the Slave Trade.[161] The younger Arkwright's partner, Robert Spear,[162] an Independent (Congregationalist), also bought shares, as did others of the Arkwrights' friends and business acquaintances — David Dale, Erasmus Darwin, Walter Evans of the Darley Abbey mills,[163] William Salte, who with his brother, Samuel, was one of the leading London warehousemen, and John Toplis, the Wirksworth banker.

Arkwright's was by any reckoning a remarkable achievement, the more so when it is remembered that throughout his life he was 'afflicted with a grievous disorder (a violent asthma) which was always extremely oppressive, and sometimes threatened to immediately terminate his existence'.[164] Yet, this apart, he seems to have suffered only minor ailments, as when on 6 June 1786 his son advised Samuel Oldknow that Sir Richard had been 'extremely ill the night before the last' but was now 'pretty well again'.[165] On 3 November 1789 he felt 'not very well' and 'imagines he shall not venture to undertake the journey' to attend a meeting of the Cromford Canal Company at Nottingham the following day. And in February 1790 'a very bad cold' seems to have prevented his going there yet again.

But in the end something had to give. The younger Arkwright was on one of his frequent visits to Scarborough when he heard from William Melling:

Dʳ. Sir
Your Father's Health continued much the same I wrote you last till Saturday last since when he has been much worse but this Evening and most part of this Afternoon has been and still is much better again which I assure you am glad to inform you of, he is swell'd rather more and oblig'd to let out his Waistcoats &c. In hopes of his perfect Recovʸ remain

Dʳ. Sʳ. obᵗ Servᵗ
Will Melling

Cromford
Monday Evenᵍ 16ᵗʰ July 1792

Melling's letter was followed by the summons to the Rock of Sir Richard's physician, Dr Joseph Denman, of Bakewell, uncle to the future Lord Chief Justice. Dr Denman considered his patient's condition sufficiently grave to call in Dr Darwin, reputedly the finest physician in the country, and to inform the younger Arkwright about the 'highly alarming' state of his father's health:

Dear Sir,
Finding, on my second visit to Sir Richard Arkwright, that his complaints were but little abated, I judged it proper in every respect to have a consultation with Dr. Darwin, who had seen him in an earlier stage of the disorder. We met yesterday, and are both of us of opinion that his situation is a very dangerous one indeed; and though no present appearances indicate immediate danger, yet it is

impossible to say what sudden alterations may happen in such a case. We are by his desire to visit him again on Saturday.

The very measure which we thought indispensably necessary for the relief of the distress arising from bulk and pressure, will describe to you, better than any words, the serious state of our patient. A few small punctures on the Legs in order to discharge of a part of the burden, though in effect a trifling and not painful operation, yet as it is never performed except in complaints in other respects threatening, implies such general ideas as are highly alarming.

Mrs. Denman joins in best compliments to yourself and Mrs. Arkwright with, Dear Sir,

your obliged, and

most obedient Servant

Jos. Denman

Bakewell
Thursday morning
I will write to you again on Sunday.

The treatment prescribed for Arkwright, apparently suffering from a collection of fluid caused either by the failure of his kidneys or, more likely, his heart, would, we now know, have alleviated the symptom rather than the cause of his complaint. One wonders if Dr Darwin, a friend of William Withering, the discoverer of digitalis, also recommended a 'course of Foxglove for a dropsical habit' which he was to prescribe for Joseph Wright, suffering from severe fits of asthma and suspected dropsy, in 1796.[166]

Arkwright made his will,[167] a short, uncomplicated document, on Sunday 29 July. Five days later he died at the Rock. The only letter of condolence to survive is from James Robinson of the Papplewick mills, who on 10 August wrote to the younger Arkwright:

I beg to Condole with you on the Death of your Father S^r. R^d. Arkwright, whose short illness and sudden Death must have given you much concern.

The prompt & wonderful Inventive powers of S^r R^d mind and his Labourious and persevering spirit will hand his name down to the latest posterity & whose Country derives & will continue to receive the greatest benefits from his inventions that ever was experienced by any individual — or even body of men — and it would be ingratitude in the greatest degree in those who best know how to appreciate his merits to withold what is so justly due to him — and I cannot doubt but that every one will now unite in doing his memory that justice wch I have always considered has been witheld from him.

It was a sentiment now apparently shared even by Manchester, where the *Manchester Mercury* of 31 July had reported:

We hear that a Statue of Sir Richard Arkwright, Knt. is intended to be erected, in the centre of a spacious square lately laid out in Manchester, called Grosvenor square: and that a Subscription is already begun, to effect the tributary views a whole community are desirous of testifying to a character, who has been the means of bringing so much wealth to the nation.

And Lancashire would have agreed with the verdict of the *Derby Mercury*[168] that Arkwright's system of spinning 'by giving perpetual employment to many thousand families has increased the population, and been productive of greater commercial advantages to this country, and contributed more to the general benefit of mankind, in so short a period of time, than any other single effort of human ingenuity'.

Arkwright was buried at Matlock Church on 10 August. The procession was watched by more than 2,000 persons, among them J. P. Malcolm, a writer in the *Gentleman's Magazine*,[169] who set out his impressions of the cortege as it made its way past High Tor:

> The road was now nearly impassable from the crowds of people and carriages; for, Sir Richard Arkwright's funeral passed the Torr for Matlock church, where he is to lie till a chapel now erecting, and begun by him, shall be finished. I no longer wondered at people on the rocks; a better opportunity of judging of the population of this place could not have offered, and it is surprisingly great. The ceremony was conducted with much pomp, and, as nearly as I can remember, was thus: a coach and four with the clergy; another with the pall-bearers; the hearse covered with escutcheons, surrounded by mutes, followed; then the horse of the deceased, led by a servant; the relations, and about fifteen or twenty carriages, closed the procession, which was perhaps half a mile in length.
>
> The evening was gloomy, and the solemn stillness that reigned was only interrupted by the rumbling of the carriages, and the gentle murmurs of the river; and, as they passed, the echo of the Torr gently returned the sound. The whole was so rich and uncommon, that I continued to gaze till a turn in the road closed the whole. How greatly would the effect have been heightened by a choir chaunting a dirge!

Sir Richard's final resting place was to be beneath the altar of the small but neat chapel of hewn stone he had begun to build at Smelting Mill Green, close to Cromford Bridge, soon after he had bought the manor of Cromford. In his will he directed that his son should 'with all convenient speed after my decease . . . compleat and finish the Chappel I have lately built'. To its minister he bequeathed an 'Annual payment or sum of Fifty pounds'.

To his widow (who was to survive him by nineteen years) Arkwright left £500 a year; to his son and to William Strutt £10,000, with instructions to invest 'at Interest on Government or Real Securities' in trust for his daughter, Mrs Susanna Hurt, who was to enjoy the income during her lifetime and was free to dispose of the capital as she wished at her death. To each of his twenty grandchildren he left £5,000 on reaching the age of twenty-one or at marriage, if earlier; each of his five sisters was to have £100, and eight nephews and fourteen nieces £50 each. His remaining nephew, William Melling, received an annuity of £30. The residue of his estate went to his son, who, with William Strutt, was named as executor.

Sir Richard, as the *Gentleman's Magazine*[170] put it, 'died immensely rich, and has left manufactories the income of which is greater than that of most German principalities, though derived from very opposite circumstances, those that promote the prosperity of a country. His real and personal property is estimated at little short of half a million.'

NOTES

1 Richard married at Bonsall on 1 May 1780. F. A. Crisp, *Visitation of England and Wales*, Notes VII, privately printed London, 1917, p. 17.
2 *Derby Mercury*, 14 August 1783.
3 *Derby Mercury*, 30 October and 6 November 1783; 9 September 1784.
4 16 June 1783.
5 B. & W. MSS, 7 August 1781.
6 *S.F.*, p. 165.
7 D.C.R.O., Enclosure Award.
8 B.M. Add. MSS, 6668, p. 113 (Black), p. 225 (Red) and p. 115 (Black) and p. 229 (Red).
9 *Impartial Representation*, p. 5.
10 B.M. Add. MSS, 6689, p. 756 (Red) and p. 375 (Black); D.P.L., Strutt MSS.
11 Colonel Arkwright's London solicitors; and see n. 10, B.M. Add. MSS, above.
12 *L.G.*, 1786, pp. 609, 610.
13 A.F. MSS.
14 He became Vice-Admiral of the White, June 1795.
15 Atholl MSS, Box 65, Bundle 5, 171.
16 *Macclesfield Courier*, 13 June 1818.
17 *L.G.*, 1787, p. 69.
18 *Derby Mercury*, 14 August 1778.
19 27 March 1787; *Derby Mercury*, 22 March 1787.
20 III, p. 5.
21 See *Times*, 25 November 1790.
22 A.F. MSS.
23 1778 edition, p. 71.
24 Sheffield Central Library.
25 *G.M.*, 1793 p. 506.
26 Farey, *General View of Derbyshire*, II, p. 21.
27 *Artisans and Machinery*, London, 1836, p. 294.
28 W. Adam, *The Gem of the Peak*, London, 1851, p. 60.
29 T. S. Jones, *The Life of . . . Willielma, Viscountess Glenorchy*, Edinburgh, 1822, p. 501.
30 15 February 1785.
31 J. S. Harford, *Some Account of the Life, Death and Principles of Thomas Paine*, third edition Bristol, 1820, p. 94 n.
32 1783 edition, p. 119.
33 Guildhall Library, MS 7253 4/76106.
34 II, pp. 194–5.
35 17 June 1790. See also *G.M.*, October 1792, p. 931: 'and that it was argued against the late Sir Richard Arkwright that no attention was paid to the morals of the youth when so employed' (small part of long letter to Lord Bishop of Chester).
36 II, p. 197.

37 Arkwright Society, *Arkwright and the Mills at Cromford*, 1971.

38 II, p. 195.

39 II, p. 40.

40 29 George III, c. 74, 1789.

41 17–24 July 1788.

42 Old Bath, managed by Robert Mason. 'At Matlock are two baths, the old and the new [wrote William Bray in 1777]. The Company dine together in a large room at two, and sup at eight, after which there is music for those who choose dancing, or cards for those who prefer them. The charge for dinner is one shilling, and the same for supper; every one drinks what he likes' (pp. 125–6).

43 21 August 1788.

44 Repeated in *Derby Mercury*, 4 September 1788.

45 R. B. Schofield, 'The promotion of the Cromford Canal Act of 1789: a study in canal engineering', *B.J.R.L.*, 64, 2, 1981–82, p. 249.

46 D.C.R.O., Gell MSS, D258/41/32a (henceforth D258/).

47 A.F. MSS.

48 D258/50/41ha.

49 D258/50/14t.

50 D258/50/14sa.

51 D258/50/14b.

52 Of Ashbourne, solicitor (R. B. Schofield, 'Cromford Canal', p. 246).

53 D258/50/14ea.

54 D258/50/14d.

55 Probably Archibald Cullen of Boswell Court, Carey Street, described as 'Counsel' in *Universal British Directory*, I, 1790, p. 360.

56 Perhaps a member of the Milnes family of either Aldercar Park, from whom the land for the first Cromford Mill was leased, or the William Milnes of Ashover to whom George Goodwin in his will left 'my coloured drawing or view of the cotton mill at Bakewell'. A generation later a James Milne(s?) was a pall-bearer at the funeral of Richard Arkwright II.

57 Greyhound.

58 Edward Fletcher surveyed the route: he was Jessop's assistant (R. B. Schofield, 'Cromford Canal', p. 249).

59 D258/50/14e.

60 Young, *The Farmer's Tour*, I, p. 209 n., for pleasure boat on the river at Matlock.

61 D258/50/14f.

62 D258/50/14kb.

63 D258/50/14t.

64 D258/50/14m.

65 D258/50/14qa.

66 *G.M.*, 1804, p. 1173, 'November 26 1804 At Sutton, Co. Surrey, age 63, Mr. Henry Nock, late of Ludgate Street, gun maker to his Majesty'.

67 D258/41/32ma.

68 D258/50/14ab.

69 D258/41/32ha.

70 D258/50/14pb.

71 30 George III, c. 56, 1790.

72 A.F. MSS.

73 A.F. MSS.

74 For Thomas see H. M. Colvin, *A Biographical Dictionary of English Architects, 1660–1840*, London, 1954, pp. 608–9.

75 *G.M.*, 1788, pp. 577–9. He addressed the society on 29 May 1787.

76 Proposed for membership by John Pratt, of Lower Brook Street, a director of Westminster Fire Office. *Universal British Directory*, I, p. 353.
77 Gough maps, 41A, At Bodleian Library.
78 II, p. 48.
79 II, pp. 196–7.
80 II, August 1791.
81 For plate glass see T. C. Barker, *Pilkington Brothers*, London, 1960, pp. 41–5.
82 Gough maps.
83 London County Council, *Survey of London*, XVIII, London, 1937, pp. 119, 137.
84 *Times*, 6 June 1785, 10 December 1789.
85 For Brown see Dorinda Evans, 'Mather Brown (1761–1831): Critical Study', (phD, May 1972, Courtauld Institute of Art, University of London).
86 Now held by J. P. Spang III, Historic Deerfield Inc., Deerfield, Mass., USA.
87 A.F. MSS; perhaps Anthony Lax Maynard, attorney and agent to the Duke of Devonshire (*Bailey's Northern Directory*, 1781) and attorney, of Chesterfield, to Richard Arkwright, 1782–84 ⁄ Clerk of the Peace, County of Derby, upwards of fifty years, he died 3 July 1825, aged eighty three years.
88 A.F. MSS.
89 A.F. MSS.
90 Barlaston MSS cited Nicolson, *Joseph Wright*, p. 164.
91 A.F. MSS.
92 Nicolson, *Joseph Wright*, pp. 164–5.
93 The 1776 mill was destroyed by fire in 1890 (*Derby Mercury*, 12 November 1890; Arkwright Society, *Arkwright and the Mills at Cromford*). Two storeys fo the sevenstorey first mill were lost by fire in the 1920s (Nicolson, *Joseph Wright*, p. 167 n. 2).
94 Grace Cottage, redbrick cottage, 1771 and 1772.
95 Pages 74–5.
96 Pilkington, *Derbyshire*, I, 1789, pp. 11–12.
97 H. Coleridge, *The Worthies of Yorkshire and Lancashire*, London, 1836, p. 476. 'Arkwright had no pretensions to the philosophic mind of Watt, or the tasteful genius and magnificent soul of Wedgwood; he did not value his discovery for the scientific power it displayed, nor did he make it subservient to the revival of the forms of antique beauty. He saw its utility and that was enough!' Also, e.g., Espinasse, *Lancashire Worthies*, I, p. 451, *Cotton Manufacture*, p. 148.
98 A.F. MSS.
99 Nicolson, *Joseph Wright*, p. 168 n. 7, citing A.F. MSS, Wright to Richard Arkwright II, 12 December 1790.
100 'Chartism', in *Miscellaneous Essays*.
101 *Rescome Magazine*, I, 1849, p. 205.
102 Nicolson, *Joseph Wright*, pp. 168–9.
103 Britton and Brayley, *England and Wales*, III, 1802, p. 520; and see similar by Dugold Bannatyre, 'Cotton manufacture', in *Supplement* to fourth, fifth and sixth editions of *Encyclopaedia Britannica*, Edinburgh, 1824.
104 Arkwright's 'candlelighting' may owe something to rather similar festivities held at the Lombe's Derby Silk Mill (about these see Bray). A difference is that the Lombe festivities were paid for by money given by persons visiting the mill; Arkwright did not admit strangers and financed the festivities himself.
105 *Derby Mercury*, 19 September 1776.
106 *Derby Mercury*, 25 September 1778; Fitton and Wadsworth, p. 100.
107 Page 279.
108 24 July 1783.
109 1839 (159) XIX, *Factory Inspectors*, pp. 97, 98.
110 Reproduced with errors in *N.S.A.*, X, 1845, p. 1253.

111 1839 (159) XIX, *Factory Inspectors*, p. 96.
112 Ure, *Philosophy*, p. 118.
113 1792, p. 771.
114 Words in brackets crossed out.
115 Barlaston MSS, 18148–98.
116 B. & W. MSS, Watt to Boulton, 12 October 1780.
117 Baines, *Cotton Manufacture*, p. 196.
118 Guest, *Compendious History*, pp. 110, 111.
119 Baines, *Cotton Manufacture*, pp. 196, 196 n.
120 *Manchester Mercury*, 2 September 1783.
121 *Derby Mercury*, 11 November 1788.
122 *Derby Mercury*, 28 April 1791 and 17 April 1788.
123 *Derby Mercury*, 24 February 1791.
124 *Derby Mercury*, 27 July 1786.
125 Pages 195, 196.
126 *Ibid.*
127 *Inverness Courier*, 6 February 1839.
128 B & W. MSS.
129 Baines, *Cotton Manufacture*, p. 193.
130 P.R.O., E 112/1531/260. See also the letter cited in S. D. Chapman, 'James Longsdon (1745–1821), farmer and fustian manufacturer: the small firm in the early English cotton industry', *Textile History*, III, 1970, p. 276. 'We have news that Mr. Arkwright hath dropped his spinning 1s. 6d ib. in order to suppress the many mills erecting'. (Joseph Wilkes, of Measham, to Thomas Harrison, 2 February 1784, at Staffordshire C.R.O., Paget MSS, CE 286.)
131 *Manchester Mercury*, 13 May 1788.
132 *Manchester Mercury*, 25 January 1791.
133 P.R.O., T 1/610.
134 M.C.R.L., MF. 801, James Whitaker's Minute Book.
135 For a possible connection between the agitation concerning the fustian tax repeal and the efforts to block the proposed treaty with Ireland see C. D. Saggus, 'Social Identification, Attitudes and Relationships in the 1780s of those Cotton Manufacturers of Manchester listed in the Trades Directories of the Period' (PhD, Emory University, 1974), Ann Arbor, Michigan and London, 1977, pp. 95–6. . . . at one point in Thomas Walker Junior's appearance before the Privy Council during this period he thought he was being examined relative to the Fustian Tax but found his information was being used with regard to the Irish Proposition' (James Whitaker's Minute Book).
136 P.R.O., T 1/610, and James Whitaker's Minute Book.
137 James Whitaker's Minute Book.
138 E. Baines junior, *Cotton Manufacture*, p. 196.
139 *Derby Mercury*, 10 and 17 March 1780.
140 George Lomas was also in partnership with Thomas Beswick as a calico printer and dyer, of Strangeways, Manchester (*Manchester Directory*, 1788). The partnership was ended 'by mutual consent' in February 1790, a few months before he was declared bankrupt (*L.G.*, 1790, pp. 106, 163). G. Lomas, 'cotton manufacturer, formerly of Manchester, died in London on 20 June 1794' (*G.M.*, 1794 p. 672).
141 *London Directory*, 1783, 1785 (not 1782). John Clegg & Co. cotton merchant, 7 Oxford Court, Cannon Street, Thames Street, is from *L.G.*, 1788, p. 579.
142 *Manchester Directory*, 1788.
143 *Manchester Directory*, 1788; *L.G.*, 13–17 April 1790, p. 227.
144 L.C.R.O., Land Tax for 1780, 1781, 1782.
145 Will of John Spear, 1796.

146 Owen, *Life*, p. 33.

147 *L.G.*, p. 579; 1790, p. 227. It was probably about this time that Arkwright transferred his business to Nicholas Waterhouse, the largest of the Liverpool cotton brokers. Waterhouse's accounts show that in 1799 he bought for the younger Arkwright 1,300 bags of cotton valued at £36,000. (S. Dumbell, 'The cotton market in 1799', *Economic History*, I, 1926–29, p. 143).

148 Winter & Kaye, attorneys, of 29 St Smithins Lane.

149 The concern advertised 'Sales by Candle' at Garraway's Coffee House in Exchange Alley, Cornhill. *London Directory*, 1785; *L.G.*, 30 December 1783–4 January 1794; *Times*, 4 January 1785.

150 Among the debts owing were those of Arkwright's brother-in-law, Thomas Wood, then in partnership with Thomas Mason at Eton — see *L.G.*, 1790, p. 579. James Holford of Manchester, *L.G.*, 1788, p. 376, and Messrs Buchanan, *L.G.*, 1788, p. 381; *L.G.*, 1792, p. 322.

151 *London Directory*, 1792.

152 William Edensor, probably the author of *A Letter to the Spinners and Manufacturers of Cotton Wool upon the present Situation in the Market*, London, 1792 (cited Mantoux, p. 505), was also in business as a cotton merchant in Hunter's Lane, Manchester (*Manchester Directory*, 1788), and other Edensors in cotton are listed in the 1781 and 1788 directories.

153 Fitton and Wadsworth, pp. 270, 271, 342, 343.

154 M. M. Edwards, *The Growth of the British Cotton Trade, 1780–1815*, Manchester, 1967, pp. 75–80.

155 C. B. Wadstrom, *An Essay on Colonisation*, London, 1794, p. 155.

156 *Ibid*, Part II, pp. 341–3, for a complete list of subscribers.

157 Society of Arts, L.A., A 9/4.

158 P.R.O., BT 6/246.

159 J. Aston, *A Picture of Manchester*, Manchester, 1816, p. 99, according to whom he was the 'worthy and respectable architect of his own fortune'. He died 25 July 1792, worth £5,000 (will at L.C.R.O.). See also Smith, *Manchester Registers*, II, p. 132, and B. Nightingale, *The Story of the Lancashire Congregational Union, 1806–1906*, Manchester, 1906, pp. 147–9.

160 Will at L.C.R.O.

161 *L.G.*, 15–19 June 1789, p. 29. They also supported the London Hospital and Asylum, to which Whittenbury bequeathed £100, as he did also to the London Missionary Society.

162 His father, John, had been one of the trustees who bought the land upon which was built the Cannon Street Independent Chapel. (A. A. Mumford, *The Manchester Grammar School, 1515–1915*, London, 1919, p. 245 n.2; see p. 188 for John Byrom, from whom the land bought.)

163 For full account see Jean Lindsay, 'An early industrial community: the Evanses' cotton mill at Darley Abbey', *Business History Review*, XXXIV, 1960.

164 Britton and Brayley, *England and Wales*, p. 520; Baines, *Cotton Manufacture*, p. 194.

165 Marple Antiquarian Society.

166 Nicolson, *Joseph Wright*, p. 20.

167 Will at P.R.O.

168 9 August 1792.

169 1793, p. 506.

170 1792, pp. 770–1.

CHAPTER VIII

The second Arkwright:
a fortune made

UNDER SIR RICHARD'S WILL his only son, thirty-seven-year-old Richard, inherited the greater, though by no means overwhelming, part of his fortune. Included in this was his entire cotton-spinning empire. The younger Arkwright had been in cotton for the whole of his working life and was already one of the country's greatest spinners. He had learned his trade at Cromford and set up in business for himself in January 1783 with the purchase of his father's mill on the river Dove at Rocester in Staffordshire. Six months later he acquired his father's concern at Bakewell, and went on to add a second Derbyshire mill, at nearby Cressbrook. In 1784 he bought his father's recently built mill at Manchester, brought in as partners his brothers-in-law, John and Samuel Simpson, and sold out to them within three years. Also during the 1780s he was for a short time a partner in Robert Spear & Co., cotton dealers, of Crowe Alley, Manchester.

The younger Arkwright did not for long retain control of his now enlarged cotton-spinning empire. Within a year of Sir Richard's death he sold the mills at Nottingham and at Wirksworth, and all that now remained of his father's creations were the Cromford and Masson mills. About this time Arkwright sold most of his own mills. In October 1792 a half share of Bakewell went to Samuel Simpson, who, five months later, also acquired Cressbrook. Rocester remained in Arkwright's possession until 1803, when Richard Briddon, his partner there since 1786, became sole owner. Thus of the two former spinning empires only Cromford, Masson and part shares in Bakewell and Rocester remained in Arkwright hands.

Sir Richard's empire had reached its zenith with the coming into production of the Masson Mill in the mid-1780s — his partnerships at New Lanark and at Stanley in Scotland, entered into perhaps to spite Manchester, were short-lived — and when during the boom of 1786-87 Sir Richard took steps to increase his production of yarn he did not build or otherwise acquire a mill of his own. Instead, on 2 November 1786, he summoned attorney, Adam Wolley junior, to Cromford to meet Thomas Evans and himself for the purpose of 'taking Instructions to prepare [a] Lease of Mʳ Evans's Mills' at Darley Abbey, on the river Derwent, a mile to the north of Derby.[1]

Sir Richard's decision to lease the Evanses' mills was not due to any lack of capital for further expansion. Indeed, since the early 1780s his empire had been sufficiently under control to enable him to add to his role of mill owner that of squire, and shortly before the lease was negotiated he had begun to build his mansion, Willersley Castle, on the estate he had bought for £8,864 some four years earlier. In 1788 he acquired a fashionable London residence in the Adelphi and a year later added to his lands by the purchase of the manor of Cromford for the sum of £30,000. Sir Richard now ventured into the Funds, in which by the end of 1791 he had invested some £66,000; he also purchased £2,000 worth of Bank of England stock.

Meanwhile in 1787 the younger Arkwright made his first purchase of government stocks, of which by 1789 he held some £40,000 worth. And this was but a modest beginning. During the course of his long life he continually added to his holdings, ultimately becoming the largest holder of the Funds in England. Second only to Arkwright's investment in the Funds was the amount of capital he laid out in the acquisition of landed properties. This began in 1790 with the purchase of a small Derbyshire estate, and some six months before Sir Richard's death he bought land and properties in Yorkshire valued at £45,000. They were followed by large-scale investments in Derbyshire, Essex, Herefordshire, Leicestershire and Staffordshire.

These outlays placed him in the higher reaches of the landed gentry, and the rents they brought in, together with interest from the Funds, provided Arkwright with a steadily increasing income which enabled him to accumulate a new and huge fortune. To this we shall return. But first as to cotton, the original source of all Arkwright wealth.

Sir Richard had died towards the end of a period of boom greater than any previously recorded.[2] 'The three per cents are so high and the country is in such a damned state of prosperity under that fellow Pitt, that it goes against me to purchase at such low interest,' wrote Edward Gibbon from Lausanne to his friend Lord Sheffield on the last day of 1791,[3] but after the inflammatory decree issued by the convention of 19 November 1792 the ever-increasing likelihood of war with revolutionary France undermined confidence and gave rise to uncertainties that were to be aggravated by the declaration of war at the beginning of 1793.

When, on 24 January that year, the French ambassador was ordered to leave the country there was universal panic.[4] Cotton did not escape. Some of the Manchester mills stopped working, while at Cromford and Bakewell profits for the year ending 14 October 1793 came to only £6,000 — less than a quarter of the annual average of £26,355 for the remainder of the 1790s.[5]

The upward movement in the economy that began in the spring 1794 was brought to an end by politics and war when in February 1797 the Bank of

England suspended cash payments.⁶ Yet it was in that year that Arkwright's profits of £40,837 reached their highest of the decade.⁷ But by 24 February 1798 he was confiding to his friend Samuel Oldknow, muslin manufacturer and cotton spinner, of Marple, Mellor and Stockport:

> I dread the consequences that seem likely to follow the present situation of trade. Many Mills are giving over. In this neighbourhood, M.ʳ Strutts have shortened their time of working, and so has M.ʳ Nightingale — I have been so much undercut, that I have made but little sales, for this long time. Nobody adheres to their lists, and what steps to take, I do not know. . . . I have a list of spinners who sell at a great disc.ᵗ, and you are amongst them: indeed you cannot avoid doing so; [for] money you must have. It seems to me, that trade can not mend, till there is a peace, or till one half or two thirds, or perhaps three quarters of the Mills have given over working.⁸

Arkwright's profits for 1798 (£19,135) were less than half those of the previous year but rose slightly to £23,976 in 1799, increased to £38,293 in 1800 but fell back to £34,500 in 1801 and to £25,700 in 1802.⁹ With the resumption of hostilities following the short-lived Peace of Amiens profits fell dramatically to £9,600 in 1803 and £8,200 in 1804. There was some recovery, to £13,000 in 1805, followed by a further decline to slightly less than half that figure (£6,157) in 1806 (when Arkwright noted in his accounts that his third son, twenty-two-year-old Peter, had become a partner) and £6,924 a year later.¹⁰

For the remainder of the war against France — years which in addition to the Napoleonic decrees and British orders-in-council saw the interminable complications of America's non-importation, embargo, prohibitions and suspensions of prohibition, which were to baffle merchants on both sides of the Atlantic — profits showed a considerable although fluctuating improvement, £25,000 in 1808, £10,215 the following year and £14,214 in 1810 (when the export frenzy that had followed close upon the revolt of the Spanish colonies in South America ended).¹¹ Profits fell sharply to £2,592, the lowest up to that time, in 1811, February of which saw the passing of the Non-importation Act. In 1812 the entry of Russia to the conflict brought Napoleon's Continental System to an end and profits rose to £13,812; that year, incidentally, Arkwright closed the warehouse in Cromford Court, Manchester, built by his father almost thirty years earlier. Profits doubled to £28,653 in 1813 but fell back to £17,570 in 1814 and to £10,340 in 1815, the year Arkwright wrote against his accounts, 'Declined Business.'

The post-war years (1823 and 1824 excepted) saw profits at a low ebb; in 1816 they declined to as little as £2,125, and the following year, perhaps in an attempt to push sales, Arkwright opened a London warehouse at 6 Dyer's Court, Aldermanbury. Profits in that year and in 1818 reached £7,529 and £7,275 respectively.

Worse was to come. 'Though out of Trade I often go into the City and sorrow to find a want of money and a want of Trade,' Sir Robert Peel, father of the future Prime Minister, wrote to Arkwright from London on 13 February 1819, and on 17 April he again observed, this time from Tamworth:

I with you deplore the wretched state of the Cotton Trade and am fearful that calamity is not confined to the Cotton districts. Similar complaints exist in other Trading parts of the Country. Though removed from personal responsibility we neither of us with our attachments and habits can be removed from a painful sense of the general misfortune.

That year Arkwright recorded his first-ever loss (£1,456), to be followed in 1820 by a massive £28,968 deficit. Looked at in this light, the £629 profit in 1821 makes healthier reading. The position was well summed up by the *Manchester Guardian* on 15 December 1821:

there is . . . little question that it [the cotton trade] has not, upon the average, for years past afforded those engaged in it a due remuneration for their capital and exertions. . . . Ever since the peace, the prices of raw material, and of the manufactured goods, have been coming down; and it is, therefore, impossible that dealers in those articles should have been able to realize those regular profits, which, in a settled state of trade, they might fairly have looked to obtain.

A small loss (£3,848) in 1822 was followed by profits of £20,640 and £20,850 in 1823 and 1824 respectively and of £5,542 in 1825. The expansion which reached its peak at the end of 1825 was to cast its shadow on the spinning trade into the '30s and not least in Lancashire, where a mill constrution boom had been financed largely by the issue of great quantities of accommodation bills:

In the year 1824, and the early part of 1825 [testified John Benjamin Smith, a director of the Bank of Manchester, before the Bank Charter Committee in 1832], many of the Lancashire Banks offered the strongest inducements to people to borrow money of them, it was so plentiful; and this led to the building of mills, and the increasing of manufactures to an amazing extent. We are now labouring under the effects of that pernicious system; mills and manufactories have been established, which ought not to have been established; they were established, not because there was an increased demand for their produce, but because the parties were doing well, and having an opportunity of borrowing money, thought that they would do better by increasing their manufacture.[12]

'We hear of nothing but the distress in the manufacturing districts, and every one seems at a loss to conjecture what will be the end of these things,' Arkwright's eldest son, Richard, then MP for Rye, wrote to his father from 30 Old Bond Street in 1829 or 1830.[13] Cromford and Bakewell had not been immune to the general distress. Profits of £6,167 in 1826 were followed by continuous losses until the records end in 1831: £12,217 in 1827 ('Mr A has

an *enormous* stock & is determined to sell it. Many spinners must break or stop,'
Strutts wrote to James Peirce, their London agent, on 2 August, and on 1
November they told J. Terrett, a Tewkesbury customer, 'we found Mr A was
determined to sell at all events'),[14] £15,498 in 1828, £21,638 in 1829, £9,700
in 1830 (against which year is written, 'Peter Arkwright alone') and £3,500
in 1831.[15] A visitor to Cromford in 1828 contrasted the position then with that
in earlier, more prosperous times: 'His [Arkwright's] habits lead him to
continue in business, though the profits are now trifling. Those of his father and
his own, formerly, were 2 or 300 per cent. but competition has now rendered
them nearly (*sic*) nominal.'[16] The general accuracy of Sir Richard Phillips's
observation is not open to question.

Throughout these years, which had seen the widespread adoption of
improved versions of Crompton's mule in large steam-powered urban factories,[17] Cromford had remained faithful to the water frame, for which steam
was less economical than water power.[18] Further, it does not seem that the
throstle (a variant of the water frame developed in the 1790s and so called
because its long tin roller was said to sing like a throstle, or thrush) was installed,
at least on any scale.[19] The water frame, the Factories Inquiry Commission of
1834 was told, is:

> still in use in Mr. Arkwright's mill at Cromford, and a few others, but now
> generally superseded by the throstle, in which *all* the spindles are turned by one
> long and light roller, instead of by a series of drums, turning each six or eight
> spindles. Thus a saving of power is effected by the use of a less costly machine.
> The throstle consumes less power, and costs less than the water-frame . . . . Most
> water-twist is still spun in water-mills, on acount of the great power required to
> turn the frames, and the labour is cheaper in the country.[20]

Little more than a decade later most, if not all, of Cromford's water frames
(a few early versions of which, claimed Ure in 1836, were, 'by dint of superior
tact and attention', able to produce 'good hosiery and thread yarns of eighty
hanks to the pound')[21] were forced to cease working owing to a decrease in the
amount of water issuing from Cromford sough. This resulted when Meer
Brook[22] sough (the construction of which had begun in 1773)[23] began drawing
from the Wirksworth lead mines water which up to then had been drained by
the older Cromford sough. The problem became particularly acute when, in
May 1837, the proprietors of Meer Brook sough opened the cast iron floodgates
which they had built to prevent this. Arkwright resorted to legal action in order
to safeguard the future of the mills but was finally defeated when, in April 1839,
a judgement was given against him in the Court of Exchequer.[24]

At midday on Saturday 21 September 1844 the mills stopped working for
the first time, owing to a shortage of water.[25] The decline of spinning at
Cromford, now almost inevitable, was witnessed by Thomas Carlyle, who on

8 August 1847 wrote to his brother John Aitken Carlyle from Matlock Bath:

> I have had, this morning, a considerable walk before breakfast, down to
> Cromford, past Arkwright's place and his two Mills; one of them, the Cromford
> one if I mistake not, the *first* erected Mill in England, had consequently the
> Mother of all Mills. Near by it is Willerslay 'Castle' so-called; a solid sumptuous-
> looking free stone Castle built by Arkwright, and now tenanted by his grandson
> [Peter]. The Mother of all Mills, I was sorry to hear, had lost most of its water,
> by new mine-drainings in late years; and was very nearly fallen silent now, likely
> soon to go out altogether.[26]

The possibility that the water from Cromford sough 'should, by the bringing
up of any other sough, or by any unforeseen or unavoidable accident, be taken
away or lessened' had been envisaged by Sir Richard at the outset of his activities
at Cromford, and the agreement of 1 August 1771 contained the proviso that
in such circumstances it should be lawful for him to take the mills down and
rebuild them on another specified piece of land.

Masson Mill, powered by the Derwent, was not affected, and when in 1854
the son of Johann Gottfried Brügelmann, a former Arkwright workman who
in 1783 had installed his machinery in a water-powered mill at Kromford,[27]
near Ratingen, east of Düsseldorf, visited Derbyshire it was recorded with some
nostalgia:

> The great inventor's machinery, mahoganied by age, is still at work there after
> more than seventy years of toil, and turns out, as is owned by the intelligent
> person who plays the part of *cicerone*, a much better article than the new
> machinery, though not producing with the same speed. The rooms where the
> people work are low, yet, on the hot summer's day of our visit to it there was
> a perfect coolness, the windows being all open, and no attempt being ever made
> to keep up the temperature to an artificial heat in order to aid the process of
> manufacture. Wise and humane regulations are at work in the relations between
> the employers and the employed, and in few seats of the cotton manufacture is
> everything so wholesome and so cheerful as in this its natal place.[28]

Arkwright fortunes were, however, by this time no longer dependent on cotton.
From the closing years of Sir Richard's lifetime there had been changes in the
direction of the family's investment that had created large and increasing new
sources of income.

The 1780s had seen the beginnings of investment in the government stock
market. In 1787 the younger Arkwright bought £5,000 worth of 4 per cent
Consolidated Annuities 1780 and two years later added a further £15,000
worth, together with £20,000 worth of Reduced 3 per cent Annuities. Sir
Richard's investment began in 1790 with £33,450 Consolidated 3 per cent
Annuities and £13,000 4 per cent Annuities Consolidated 1780. The following year he purchased a further £20,000 worth of Consolidated 3 per cent

Annuities and invested £2,000 in Bank of England stock.

Arkwright inherited his father's holdings and continued to add to them. By 1814 their market value had passed the £500,000 mark and by 1822 he had become a government stock millionaire. His holdings at the beginning of 1843 stood at £1,380,000, in addition to which he held £100,000 worth of India bonds and £110,000 of Bank of England stock (worth almost double at the current market price).[29]

Arkwright had meantime become equally involved in the acquistion of landed estates, although hardly, one suspects, owing to the undue insistence of Sir Richard, whose Cromford and Willersley properties were together valued at £68,000 in 1792[30] and who, when questioned as to why he had not invested more heavily in land, is reputed to have replied, 'Because I should thereby be enriching a steward at my own expense.'[31]

Arkwright's first venture was modest enough. In February 1790 he bought for £3,500 Darley Hall[32] (a mansion built by John de Derlegh in 1321) together with some 106 acres at nearby Cowley, properties recently advertised[33] for auction at the New Bath, Matlock.[34] Then in March 1792 he agreed to purchase from the Rev. William Browne, of Campfield Place, Hertfordshire,[35] for £45,500 the manor of Skerne, near Driffield, Yorkshire, together with its house, Skerne Hall Garth, two paper mills, a 'New Built Flour Mill commonly called Bolting Mill', and a trout stream, Driffield beck.[36]

Four years later Arkwright bought for £33,000 the manor of Normanton Turville,[37] the ancient Leicestershire seat of the Turviles, a family who had come to England with the Conqueror and whose name is inscribed on the roll of Battle Abbey.[38] The property had been advertised for sale soon after the death of its owner, the attorney Holled Smith, as:

> a valuable freehold estate, consisting of the manors of Normanton Turvile and Basset House, mansion-house, excellent stabling, gardens with hot and green houses; extensive and ornamental water well stocked with fish; and sundry eligible farms, together near 1000 acres; let to most respectable tenants at will, under proper terms of occupancy. The whole compact within a ring-fence. A considerable part extra-parochial and tithe-free, and a small and antient payment made in lieu of tithes for the remainder. Situate about eight miles from the town of Leicester, on the turnpike-road from thence to Coventry.[39]

The estate was to become the residence of Arkwright's eldest son Richard, who on 22 May 1803 had married Martha Maria, daughter of the Rev. William Beresford of Ashbourne.

In 1802 Arkwright bought from Sir Robert Wilmot a small estate at Crich, Derbyshire, for £2,000, after which, apart perhaps from small acquisition in and about Cromford, he made no further purchases until it was brought to his notice that Lord Essex was putting up for sale his estate at Hampton Court,

Leominster, the seat of the Coningsbys from the time of Henry IV. The property, said by Leland to have been completed from the spoils of Agincourt,[40] was advertised in September 1808 as:

> All abounding with game, the right of Fishery in the river Lug, and the ancient and magnificent mansion house called Hampton Court, (replete with accomodation for a large family) with the offices, gardens, pleasure grounds, park, farm tithes, watermills, lake and fishponds, picturesque cottages, groves, woods & plantations, highly ornamented with timber, chiefly oak. The perpetual advowson and right of presentation to the valuable rectory of Pencombe, the vicarage of Bodenham, with the chapelries of the Ford, and Hope, and the patronage of Coningesby's Hospital at Hereford. Together with . . . the surrounding and for the most part contiguous estate Freehold and principally tithe free, . . . [amounting to] nearly six thousand two hundred and twenty statute acres of very rich, arable, meadow, pasture, orchard, hop ground and wood land, delightfully situate in a beautiful country, five miles distant from the Borough of Leominster, nine from the city of Hereford, and 135 miles from London. . . . The ancient and magnificent mansion house called Hampton Court built with stone, and covered partly with lead and partly with slate, being upwards of 150 feet front north and south and 210 feet east and west with an open court or quadrangle in the centre.[41]

Lord Essex, who preferred his own seat at Little Cassiobury, Herefordshire, seldom visited Hampton Court. The Coningsbys had encumbered some of their estates with debt charges, and he was apparently anxious to get rid of a property which he seems to have made up his mind to sell two or three years earlier and to take as much out of it as possible in the meantime.[42]

On 5 December 1808 Arkwright acted. He wrote to John Smith, a partner in Pole, Thornton & Co., one of his London Bankers, asking him to act as his agent in negotiations to buy the estate. The agent's very name had the anonymity Arkwright intended of the forthcoming discussions. 'Of course, you will not mention my name,' he instructed Smith while asking him to seek Lord Essex's assurance that Hampton Court would not be sold until he had viewed it anonymously. Smith early suspected that another Derbyshire man, Sacheverell Chandos-Pole of Radbourne Hall, was already carrying on negotiations but after an interview with Lord Essex he was able to advise Arkwright:

> Mr. Pole would be obliged to sell all his Derbyshire property which would delay the payment of the purchase money. I remarked in answer that my friend was quite able to pay for any estate he might contract for, and though I was not authorized to say so I felt confident he would not require many months to pay the purchase of this large property perhaps not many days. Ld E—— was very much struck with this remark and said that would be very convenient indeed. His Lordship said that . . . £235,000 included the Timber, and every thing without exception. Wine Books Plate &c &c &c. In short that a purchaser

might go down, and commence Housekeeping the day he arrived.[43]

Arkwright now went to view the estate and, although taking an unfavourable view of the household effects, commissioned a surveyor to give an accurate valuation of the property. Another valuation was obtained as an unusual favour from Pole's surveyor, two more from one-time potential buyers who had dropped out, and a fifth from Smith, who quite by chance had a hold over another surveyor. Arkwright considered the valuations, which ranged from £235,000 to £301,844 unsatisfactory in detail. The one he had himself commissioned suggested £261,749, but after checking the property parcel by parcel he believed £264,444 to be a truer figure.

Arkwright put in his bid of £220,000 on the last day of 1808, so confident his draft of a complete proposal of terms of purchase he wrote, 'I do not like dodging . . . I hope the offer will be accepted or rejected in *one* week.' In this he was to be disappointed, for before there was time for a reply he heard from Smith that Pole had disclosed to Lord Essex that he was the anonymous bidder. This, Arkwright believed, was Pole's method of escaping from his own obligation to negotiate, but when Lord Essex turned his offer down Smith felt constrained to warn him that the estate could well go for £230,000 or £240,000 if sold off in small lots.

Arkwright refused to advance. On 14 January 1809 he wrote valedictorily to Smith in appreciation of his services and nine days later instructed him to invest £40,000 at 3 or 4 per cent, part of a considerable sum of money, for which I shall have no occasion'. But , despite outward appearances, Arkwright had not lost all interest. He repeated his offer of £220,000 and agreed with Smith if it were refused he would again visit the estate. Lord Essex hinted that he was prepared to accept £230,000. In February Arkwright settled, and was in secure possession by Lady Day.[44]

On 4 July 1809 Joseph Farington summed up the history of the transaction with some truth:

> Edridge[45] sd. Lord Essex sold His House and estate Hampton Court in Herefordshire the last Spring to Mr. Arkwright Son of the late Sir Richd. Arkwright for £230,000, the furniture of the House included, excepting the pictures & some articles. It was the ancient Seat of the *Coningsby's* who had posessed it from the time of Henry 4th. — It came to Lord Essex by his mother. — In making the agreement for the sale Arkwright noticed some things which Lord Essex called trifles. It is sd. Arkwright, by attending to small things that I am enabled to purchase Hampton Court. This noble estate yielded Lord Essex a very small income compared with its value, owing to the mismanagement of Agents.[46]

Arkwright had no intention of allowing the estate to become a millstone. Replacing Lord Essex's agent by a man of his own choice, George Nuttall of

Matlock, he sought to let the property.[47] An early enquiry came through a close friend, the Rev. Nicholas Waite Robinson, vicar of Bodenham, Hereford-shire,[48] on behalf of Lieutenant Colonel Francis Knyvett Leighton [49] of the Shrewsbury Volunteers, then responsible fo the surveillance of Lucien Bon-aparte, Napoleon's brother. Lucien's already strained relations with his brother had come to a head when Napoleon wished to make him a French prince on condition that he annul his marriage, contracted secretly despite Napoleon's express prohibition, to Alexandrine de Bleschamps. Lucien refused, left for America, was captured by a British ship and brought to England. The Rev. Robinson's letter reads:

Ludlow 24th April 1811

Dear Sir

As we are here upon a visit to Col: Eyton,[50] I have had the pleasure of meeting with a Friend of the name of Col. Leighton who has the Care of Buonaparte & knowing that we are living so near Hampton Court he appears anxious that I shou'd write to you on the subject of letting Buonaparte that place, which I hope will be a sufficient apology for my troubling you with this Letter. Buonaparte & his family wish to live in a retird a way a possible, he is now in Treaty for Morley[51] Sir Walter Blunt's House, and has the refusal of it & it is certainly a delightful House but entirely without Furniture. M[r] Lechmere Charlton has made him an offer of Ludford which joins upon Ludlow, the Rent was to have been £500 a year for a completely furnishd House a Park with 40 head of Deer 15 Acres of Land, a Gardener & Gamekeeper paid for by a M.[r]Charlton this they have declined as Buonaparte can't bear living in or near a Town. M.[r] Nuttall I understand has written to you, & I shall be much oblig'd to you to write a Line address'd to Lieut Col: Leighton Ludlow as soon as it is convenient, as all negotiations between Col. Leighton &c for a House will be suspended till your determination respecting Hampton Court is known — shou'd you Have any fears about you furniture they wou'd either purchase any part of it that is there, or buy the furniture they may want. Col Leighton thinks well of the Conduct of Buonaparte since he has been under his Care, & who I was told was hurt at your former refusal of Hampton Court to him, when your advertisem[t] for letting is appeard in the very first Hereford Papers. Please excuse the haste in which I have written this Letter as Col. Eyton is waiting for me to go into the fields with his local Militia, which are by far the best disciplind of any I have seen, we have Concerts & Balls every Night & I shall enjoy our vicarage the more afterwards. M[rs]. Robinson desires her Respects to M[rs]. Ark-wright &c

& believe me
dear sir
yours most sincerely
N. W. Robinson

But until his return to Rome in 1814 Lucien lived under light surveillance at Thorngrove,[52] Worcestershire, and in June 1812 Arkwright was receiving enquiries from Thomas Armstrong, agent to Lord Moira, on behalf of his brother-in-law the Earl of Granard, then resident in Ireland. A tentative offer of a rent 'including the Window Tax' not exceeding £300 a year was made, but for whatever reason Hampton Court remained unoccupied until 1819, when Arkwright's son John took up residence.

Arkwright's acquisition for £100,000 of the manors of Mark Hall, Latton Hall, Burnt Hall, New Hall and Kitchen Hall, near Harlow, Essex, put up for auction by Colonel Montagu Burgoyne at Garraway's Coffee House on 1 June 1819, was almost certainly influenced by the marriage seven months earlier of his youngest son, the Rev. Joseph, to Anne, daughter of Sir Robert Wigram, Bart, of Walthamstow.

> The Estate [reads the notice of auction] is perfectly compact; the Timber, which probably will not exceed in value 10,000l, is tastefully distributed, so as to prove most ornamental to the property. . . . As a Gentleman's Residence it unites one of the most perfect houses in England, 23 miles from the Metropolis, at the end of the Royal Forests of Epping and Hainhault . . . with Fox-hounds, belonging to Mr. Conyers or Mr. Hanbury on either side of it; a Neighbourhood abounding with Gentleman's Seats; the place itself celebrated for the tasteful and elegant way in which it has been laid out, replete with every possible convenience of the best Kitchen-garden, with Pleasure-grounds, Green-houses, Hot-houses, Ice-house, &c., the Lawn surrounding the House forming the appearance of a Park, with elegant Lodges, &c., rides through the whole Grounds of many miles, that it may be truly said, that this Property unites Consequence, Convenience, Pleasure, and Profit, to an eminent degree.[53]

In 1824 Arkwright bought from the Marquess of Ormonde Sutton Hall,[54] a two-storeyed stone mansion built by Francis Smith of Warwick in 1724 and considered the grandest of its date in Derbyshire. Speculation at the time was that the estate cost Arkwright £216,000, £1,000 more than the agent of the Duke of Devonshire had bid. It was a story discounted by the *Gentleman's Magazine* but not by Samuel Oldknow, who wrote to Arkwright from Mellor on 20 November 1824:

> I do most sincerely rejoice that you have bought Sutton Hall & Estates. I received the News here last night from W. B Thomas Esq' who adds — for 216,000£, which I have no difficulty in saying is *cheap*.[55]
>
> Why I should think that this event is favourable to the Making of the Grand Commercial Canal you will say is odd — but I think so — as I am told the Estate abounds with *untap[p]ed* minerals.

The Sutton estate was managed by Arkwright's son Richard (who seems to have been most interested in its sporting qualities) until his death in 1832. Four years later is became the residence of Robert Arkwright who, up till then, had lived at Stoke Hall, not far from the Bakewell mill in which he was a partner. Robert, an ardent agricultural improver, was elected president of the North Derbyshire Agricultural Society in 1837 and a govenor of the Royal Agricultural Society of England in 1843.[56]

Two years after his purchase of the Sutton estate Arkwright bought from Henry Horden for £42,000 Dunstall Hall,[57] with its genuine Roman floor mosiac said to have come from Tivoli, together with the manor of Dunstall, close to Needword Forest, in the parish of Tatenhill, Staffordshire. The manor, held by William de Ferrers, Earl of Derby, in the reign of Henry III, had been greatly improved by a recent owner. It was to be the residence of Arkwright's son Charles, who in 1811 had married Mary Wilmot Sitwell, daughter of Edward Sacheverell Wilmot Sitwell of Stainsby, Derbyshire.[58] Charles, an enthusiastic farmer specialising in animal husbandry, made Dunstall well known throughout the Midlands by his spring and summer sales of cattle and sheep.

The last of the Arkwright estates, Mellor and Marple on the Derbyshire–Cheshire border, came in 1828 in settlement of loans made to Samuel Oldknow over a period of more than forty years. The earliest was in 1784, when, after lengthy discussions at Cromford, Derby and Nottingham, the elder Arkwright, a supplier of one of Oldknow's chief materials, agreed to lend him £3,000 at 5 per cent. This was to enable Oldknow, then a maker of cotton goods, fustians and muslins at Anderton, near Bolton, to realise his ambition to develop his manufactures on a larger scale at Stockport.[59]

Two years later, in the autumn of 1786, Oldknow, anxious to obtain additional capital as well as a more regular flow of twist, and the younger Arkwright, wishing to retain and extend the market for his yarn in the face of the new machines then coming into use, came to the verge of becoming partners and of building a new spinning mill. Oldknow also received overtures from the Peels. The story is told in letters to Oldknow from Samuel and William Salte, wholesale linen drapers, of Poultry in the City of London.[60] The Saltes were among the largest buyers of Oldknow's goods, particularly muslins, and were his confidants on many matters:

> You Solicit my advice upon a very nice & difficult Subject [the Saltes wrote to Oldknow on 23 October 1786]. With respect to the proposals that the Two houses of the Peels made you, it required no hesitation on your Part. I considered them as selfish in the Extreme without the weight of a Feather to preponderate in your scale. M.ʳ Arkwrights proposals come in a less questionable Shape, & his Character determines much in his favour . . . there are many previous considerations which you judgment will weigh before you jump to the Conclusion. Are there not more Cotton Mills allready then can find employment?

What will be the probable amount of a new Mill, complete & ready to work? Will it not involve you in expence without paying you such Interest as you have some right to expect? Will it not interfere with your personall attention to a Manufacture that requires all your time & all your Skill? These & a variety of other considerations will suggest themselves to your Mind before you enter into the Engagement you speak of. If M.ʳ A. Jun.ʳ would give you a Share in the Bakewell Mill, & if you was to give him a Share of your Manufacture, might it not be for the mutual advantage of each? . . . This letter I hope you will receive before your Interview with M.ʳ A. If upon an impartial review of my Letter you think any observations not weighty enough to determine you opinion finally as to the Erecting a Cotton Mill you will let me know. My present Sentiments are against it.[61]

Samuel Salte's letter of 31 October reveals that Oldknow believed that his negotiations with Arkwright had 'brought matters to, or near it, an equitable conclusion'. 'Pray present my best Complᵗˢ to both the M.ʳ Arkwrights,' Salte wrote, '& tell them how much I approve of this new conexion. You will let me hear from you after you Visit to Bakewell & Cromford that I may rejoyce in learning your terms of partnership are compleated.'[62]

In a further letter of 18 November Samuel Salte referred to Oldknow's 'treaty with M.ʳ Arkwright', who, it seems, had offered to bring £15,000 into his trade. He knew of 'no person so Eligible in all respects as M.ʳ A. Jun.ʳ', the result we hope will be happy & fortunate for you both'. And three days later S. & W. Salte's letter reveals that Oldknow had given them 'part particulars' of his 'agreement with M.ʳ A., we cannot' (they wrote) 'foresee any cause that you will have for repentance. . . . When you have *done the deed* you will state further particulars.'[63]

But Samuel Salte's letter of 23 November noted a drastic change:

> From whence, or what cause, arises this sudden revolution, in your Mind, respecting the treaty with Mʳ A. Jun.ʳ I will not be inquisitive. You are a Perfect Judge of your own Concerns & certainly have weighed every Circumstance in a exact ballance & *better not to do the deed, then repent it done.* Doubts I have entertained myself respecting the Event, whether it might be so fortunate as your imagination had painted it. my Maxim was allways for a Man to have to Control & Management of his own Concerns, without admitting a Colleague unless Upon a principle of necessity. I think you was never reduced to this, & your Industry & ever Active Mind to make improvements in the Muslin manufacture, will in a short time make you perfectly easy & independent. Why give the Advantages of a Harvest to another, which your Labour & Skill hath been employed in raising.[64]

We have no further information as to the reasons for the breakdown of negotiations, although possibly the elder Arkwright's agreement of 2 November 1786 to lease Thomas Evans's Darley Abbey mills played some part.

Oldknow's personal misfortune was to stem from his failure to accept Samuel Salte's plea of 1 December 1786 that he should not involve himself 'in too many schemes, & too much business' but should 'Keep & confine . . . [his activities] to the improvement of Muslins particularly'.[65] The following spring he bought land at Mellor upon which to build the spinning mill Arkwright had urged him to begin three years before. But when boom gave way to crisis in the autumn of 1787 he abandoned his plan until exceptional profits in 1787-90 (according to Owen he made £17,000 in each of two successive years) gave him both the incentive and the means to pursue his ambition to become a leading spinner as well as the greatest muslin manufacturer.[66]

Accordingly in 1790 Oldknow, now at the turning point of his career, built a factory for spinning by steam power at Stockport and laid the foundations of what Owen was to describe as 'a large, handsome and very imposing cotton mill' at Mellor. Further, during the first half of 1791 he was becoming by exchange and by purchase a large landowner in Mellor and Marple.[67]

Before September 1791 the Stockport mill was producing yarn as fine as 140 and 150 hanks to the pound but Mellor, which was to make low counts, was not completed until 1793 before which time Oldknow's great venture in factory building, based largely on credit, had run into severe financial difficulties. An early hint of the problems that were to overtake him and were to be worsened (although not caused) by the crisis at the outbreak of the French wars is given in S. & W. Salte's letter to him of 17 December 1790. To Oldknow's request for advice about his estates and mortgages came the reply, 'you are the best Judge of what you have been doing at Mellor or elsewhere & . . . [we] hope you have not made a bad bargain'. And to his appeal for a mortgage of £5,000 on his premises at Stockport he was told that their other commitments prevented their granting him this 'till near Feby next . . . but you have resources in plenty at Manchester without foreign aid, at least for a short time'. And when on 13 September 1791 Arkwright acknowledged receipt of £700 towards the settle-ment of his account for the large quantities of yarn he had supplied to Oldknow four years earlier he remained him, 'It is true I did not expect a regular sum to be remitted me every week, but I understood the defalcations of one week were to be made up on others, which you have not done.'[68]

Yet in December Arkwright, to whom Oldknow was to turn increasingly for assistance, lent him an additional £12,000 at 5 per cent on security of his newly acquired estates at Mellor and Marple.[69] Oldknow failed to meet his repayments and on 1 September 1792 borrowed a further £11,000.[70] It was during this year that Peter Ewart, an apprentice of Rennie's and then with Boulton & Watt, 'induced by the liberal proposals of Mr. Oldknow', joined him in a partnership that lasted until the following year.[71]

In January 1793 Oldknow turned to Smith Payne & Smiths, 'of the City of London, Bankers', for a loan of £10,000 at 5 per cent on the security of various properties.[72] News of this raised Arkwright's expectations that his own loans were now to be repaid, but in this he was to be disappointed. 'You have repeatedly told me that you would lessen it and I thought in a considerable degree,' he wrote to Oldknow on 13 May 1794. And, he went on, 'You now propose to pay neither principal nor interest but that I should sit still and let Smiths receive 250£ or 500£ monthly, whilst I who ought to receive three times that sum am to have nothing, but we are to consolidate . . . . To be conclusive I neither can nor will suffer Messrs S to receive this money whilst my debt is to remain and even the interest unpaid.'[73]

Arkwright nevertheless lent Oldknow a further £11,500 in April 1795 and in August the following year he made possible the repayment of the loan from Smith Payne & Smiths, now standing at £6,500, by agreeing to pay £1,500 of that sum and to join Oldknow in repaying the outstanding amount eight months later. In return for this assistance Oldknow mortgaged properties to the value of £36,000.[74]

Some time before February 1799 Oldknow borrowed £8,730 from Robert Spear[75] (the Manchester cotton broker with whom Arkwright had briefly entered into partnership a decade or so earlier) and, meanwhile, continued to make extensive improvements to his Mellor estate as well as to add to his shares in the Peak Forest Canal, of which he was a leading promoter.[76] It is, therefore, hardly surprising that although the loan from Spear had been repaid[77] Oldknow's debts amounted by September 1800 to £97,400 18s 5d (of which £36,000 plus interest was owing to Arkwright) while the value of his estate came only to £83,794 10s 8d.[78]

From this predicament Oldknow was yet again rescued by Arkwright, who in September 1800[79] became his partner under terms which while leaving him in nominal possession of his estates and mills laid down restrictions as to his management of both. In return for a loan of £40,000 at 5 per cent Oldknow, who was to live rent-free at Mellor and was to give his entire time to the business, agreed that Arkwright should receive half the profits and have the right to intervene in the management if and when he considered it necessary. Further, Oldknow was to keep accounts in such a way that they could be easily and regularly inspected; he was not to take more than £400, or one tenth of the clear gain, for his yearly expenses but was to put any additional amount into the capital account.

But Arkwright failed in his attempt to ensure that Oldknow (whose success as a muslin manufacturer owed more to his creative[80] aesthetic gifts than to business shrewdness)[81] conducted his affairs efficiently, for by the time the partnership was ended on 2 January 1805[82] Oldknow's indebtedness to him had increased to £109,836 9s 7½d.[83] This sum had been secured by mortgaging to Arkwright various lands and properties, among them Mellor mill and its equipment, the Bottoms Hall estate, bought by Oldknow in 1787 as his first step in establishing a new community at Mellor, a further 715 acres of land at Mellor and Marple, upwards of an acre near Piccadilly, Manchester, with 'three Messuages and a large warehouse erected thereon', and forty-six shares in the Peak Forest Canal.[84]

After the end of the partnership Oldknow's indebtedness to Arkwright continued to mount. By 1823 he owed £185,426 5s 3d, and when he died on 18 September 1828 the figure stood at £205,979 14s 3d. In settlement the Mellor and Marple estates passed to Arkwright, the mills being managed by John Clayton, Oldknow's half-brother, on behalf of his former partner. Arkwright valued the estates at £160,000, a figure that did not include the mills.[85]

It was probably in 1787 — three years after the beginning of the Arkwrights' financial involvement with Oldknow — that the younger Arkwright made a personal loan of £5,000 at 5 per cent to Georgiana, Duchess of Devonshire, whose considerable gambling debts had been contracted without the knowledge of her husband. (The same year she had taken advantage of a £16,000 offer by Thomas Coutts, the banker to the royal family, who about then had offered his financial support to Charles James Fox, on whose behalf Georgiana had traded kisses for votes at the famous Westminster election of 1781.)[86] Arkwright wrote to her early in 1788:[87]

My Lady Dutchess

Not having received from your Grace as soon as I had reason, from the letter which I had the honour to receive on the 29.th of last month, to expect I should, I flattered myself with the hope that everything had turned out as you wished, I am sincerely sorry to find I was mistaken. Before I can possibly have the money paid into Drummonds'[88] hands, I must beg to be informed, whether to two Df[s] you allude to of the Duke's acceptance are at a longer date than the one you have already sent; for if they are not payable in three months, at the latest, it will not be in my power to advance the money. I must also request your Grace will say, whether I *may rely* upon the other notes being all regularly paid,l as they become due respectively. From the statement annexed, you will observe that some of them will fall due very soon. M.[r] Bennet will return on Tuesday or Wednesday, but as he may probably be too late for the post that evening, and as I do not, for reasons I have before mentioned, wish him to call here, you will be pleased to desire you answer my be left at the Greyhound public room in Cromford; I will send for it from thence, and by that means I shall be enabled to write to london by that night's post, if I find it necessary, and it will prevent, what I have continuously guarded against — suspicion.

Nothing has dropt from me to any person living that could lead to suspect what your Grace wishes to remain a secret. I must beg you will at all times be assured of my best wishes.

> I am with great respect
> Your faithful servant
> Rich.[d] Arkwright

Willersley 21ˢᵗ Jan: 1788

> 200£ due 20 February
> 406.3 „ 1 March
> 1021 „ 25 March
> 1033 „ 22 June
> 1579 „ 25 September

Georgiana failed to meet her commitments, and on 9 October 1789 James Hare counselled her;

> If you are in any scrape about money it will be impossible for you to conceal it from the Duke, and therefore the sooner he knows it the better, but, for God's sake, if you tell him anything tell him all, or Let Lʸ Elizabeth or let me tell him. There is no situation so desperate where there is not somehing to be done, and if you were in debt more han his whole estate would sell for, it would be equally advisable to acquaint him with it, as if you owed him but £5,000.[89]

Nevertheless the following year Georgiana made only a partial disclosure of her debts to her husband, whose concern turned to extreme anger with the almost simultaneous discovery that she was pregnant by the second Earl Grey. The duke exiled her to the Continent for twelve months.[90]

On Christmas Day 1790 in a letter to Thomas Coutts Georgiana listed debts totalling £61,697, adding,[91] 'I don't know that this is exact, near, I think; there are a few more little things of 100, 50 &cc.' Arkwright's loan had not been included but Georgiana told Coutts of it on 15 September 1801:

> to you *alone* I trust the names.[92] The 5000 is to one of the most interesting as well as respectable characters in the county, a man who unites to great talents uncommon simplicity, and with a heart replete with benevolence and a fortune almost princely, he is the most unassuming of characters. You already guess I must mean Mˑʳ Arkwright.

It was probably in November 1801 that Georgiana wrote to Arkwright:

> Dear Sir
> I should not think of troubling you with the inclos'd triffle were it not to obtain the right of writing to you. I have been at Messʳˢ Smith & Paynes where I have agreed to pay 50 more in the course of the next 10 days & afterwards £100 monthly.
> This is entirely independent of the arrangement which my friends are making for me & which my Mother & Sister expected to take place on the 15 of October. The delays are owing to several causes but chiefly now to Mʳ Parker[93] being fit of the gout which I fear may last him many weeks — & as I should be extremely sorry to be the least in the way of his recovery I have begun this payment which it is my intention to continue til such time as you are perfectly satisfied & that

Messrs Farrer & Atkinson[94] can lay their future plan before you. The present 50 & the one payable in 10 days are for the Month of Nov.^r — before the month of Decr is elaps'd another shall be paid, & so on.

I am not able to write fully to day as I must return to Chiswick & my own health is but just reestablishing. The debt to you is a constant source of anxiety to me tho' I have taken every precaution in my power, by writing in case of my death[95] to the Duke & my Son & also having informed Atkinson of the debt but I am from peculiar circumstances it is one I wish I could entirely discharge myself — & happy would be the day, as much as I trust to your honour, when I could either give you security or the whole of the money & receiving from you the letters occasioned by my rashness in very peculiar circumstances.

I can add no more to day, the payments will go on regularly & I should think that in the course of two more months every thing will be ready according to the plan prepar'd by my friends to the Duke & which he has intimated his intention to comply with, but had beg'd not to be named

Excuse this & believe me
you oblg'd & grateful L^y
G Devonshire[96]

'I am disappointed,' Arkwright wrote to Georgiana on 7 December 1801, 'in observing that the money is not to be repaid me at Interest tho I am glad to find that a plan is found for the purpose; and till that is executed, the interest is to be regularly paid monthly. . . . I have to beg the favour of a note for the *exact* balance dated the 10 Oct.^r *with interest.*'[97] (The debt on 10 October, the enclosed statement revealed, stood at £5,741 8s 8d a sum that had been reduced that very day when Georgiana's mother, Lady Spencer, had paid into Smith Payne & Smiths £300 together with '5 day's interest 4s 2d'). Eleven days later Arkwright asked Georgiana to send him a promissory note for £5,441 6s 6d 'with interest for the same' and enclosed in his letter a draft copy of the required document.[98]

Georgiana died at Devonshire House, Piccadilly, of an abcess on the liver on 30 March 1806, aged forty-eight, and was buried with great pomp in the family vault at St Stephen's Church, Derby.[99] And it was from Devonshire House on 27 May 1806 the Elizabeth Foster, widow of John Thomas Foster, whom the duke was to marry in 1809, wrote to Arkwright about Georgiana's debt:[100]

Sir,
The Duke desires that I will write to you, to say that he receiv'd your letter, & that he hopes soon to have it in his power to settle every thing with you; I found your letters, & the statement of your debt among the Dss's papers which she left me the care of, & I have by the Dukes direction put them into Mr Adam's[101]

hands — I hope that Mr Arkwright & all your family are well, & am Sir your very hum^{be} Servt

Elizth Foster

On 21 October 1806 Charles H. Ware of Gray's Inn, 'Solicitor to [the] four Gentlemen to whom [the] Duke of Devonshire has committed the investigation of the late Duchess Debts', acknowledged that interest formed an important part of the money owing to Arkwright, the 'probable amount' of which now came to £5,441 8s 8d. Arkwright, he calculated, had advanced from time to time £7,300, of which £4,385 14s 11 d remained unpaid.[102]

At 'the Meeting holden at Lord G. H. Cavendish's' on 20 January 1807 it was minuted that 'Mr Arkwright claims Interest but submits to the Trustees'.[103] Eight days later he was paid £4,396. In all, Georgiana'a debts had been found to total £109,135 17s 5d.[104]

The loan to Georgiana was but one of a series of Arkwright advances, some spectacular, to those who made their living in industry, to country landowners and, not least, to the nobility. Among the earliest was one in 1797 of £4,000 to five of the sons of John Twigg, grocer, of Ashover, Derbyshire, who, with Richard Burton, had founded in 1792 the Sneddon Mill, a cotton-spinning concern at Paisley.[105] Three of the Twigg brothers had from the late 1770s been in business as gauze weavers, of Gutter Lane, Cheapside, and as silk manufac-turers, of Paisley.[106] Some time before 1809 Arkwright loaned £3,000 to Mrs Helen Morewood of Alfreton Hall, Derbyshire, the owner with her husband, the Rev. Henry Case Morewood, of the Hermitage Colliery, while in 1814 the Butterley Company, a coal and iron concern founded in 1792, borrowed some £13,000.[107]

Among Derbyshire landowners who borrowed on mortgage about this time were Sir Thomas Hunloke, Bart,[108] of Wingerworth Hall, near Chesterfield, at whose death in Paris in 1816 some £30,000 remained outstanding, and members of two branches of the Mundy family. Francis Noel Clarke Mundy of Markeaton Hall, High Sheriff of Derbyshire in 1772 and author of *Needwood Forest*, a volume of poems published anonymously in 1776, borrowed £6,000 in 1813, while thirteen years later Edward Miller Mundy, of Shipley Hall, near Ilkeston, was granted a loan of £4,000. Member of Parliament for the Southern Division of Derbyshire from 1814 until his death at Barbados eight years later, his eighteen-year-old daughter Georgiana Elizabeth, 'one of the greatest Heiress-es then in England', with a fortune estimated at £190,000 in addition to an estate worth £12,000 a year, had married at Lambeth Palace on 18 July a future Arkwright mortgagee, the fourth Duke of Newcastle.[109]

The autumn of 1822 found Arkwright in the process of negotiating a mortgage to Henry Manners Cavendish, third Baron Waterpark. Arkwright's son, Charles, wrote to him on 9 October 1822 advising of complications that

Hampton Court, Herefordshire

Sutton Scarsdale, Derbyshire

Mark Hall, Essex

had arisen:

> I have seen Cavendish this morning, and from what he says, it seems probable that the business may be delayed some time. I understand from him, that it has been proposed, that Lady Waterpark should give you a prior claim, (on the Doveridge estate) to her jointure, and that, in that case, it would not be necessary to have anything to do, with the Irish property. Lady W. having refused to do this, makes it necessary to have recourse to the Irish property, and, as there is the difficulty, or irregularity about the abstract of that title, Mr Vizard[110] tells Cavendish, that the best way of getting on with the business, will be to send some one (his partner) to Ireland, Cavendish thinks this will be an expensive proceeding, but, as he is to make good any loss, which may be occasioned by delay, he wishes to know how far any arrangements, you may have made, about the money may subject him to loss; provided there is much delay, that he may choose between to two evils. I told him, that I did not know how the money was situated, but that I had no doubt you would be willing to save him unnecessary expence. He is going to London, leaving Derby either Friday or Saturday, when he will see Mr Vizard (not before Monday) and settle with him some plan. I told him I hoped to get your answer on Friday morning, which I trust I shall do, if it is not inconvenient to you to write.

In December 1822 agreement was reached for a loan of £70,000 at 4 per cent, the principal of which was to remain outstanding twenty years later.

Before 1830 there were loans of £20,000 (later increased to £43,000) to Sir Thomas Constable, Bart, of Tixall House, Staffordshire, and Burton Constable, Yorkshire;[111] £14,000 to William Drury Lowe of Locko Park, Derbyshire, a sum still owing by his executors in 1843; £6,000 to John Wood Duppa of Puddlestone Court, Herefordshire; £15,000 to Richard Price, MP for New Randor from 1799 to 1847 and £700 (repaid in 1831) to the steward of Hampton Court, Edward Wakefield, land agent of Pall Mall and father of Edward Gibbon Wakefield.

Arkwright's largest loan up to this time, however, was one of £80,000 at 4 per cent to the sixth Earl of Chesterfield, who, having succeeded to a large rental and accumulations at the age of ten, had become in his youth one of the most brilliant men of fashion.

> It makes me sad to see Bretby [Hall] and the mode of life there [Greville wrote of him in 1846][112] idleness, folly, waste, and a constant progress to ruin; a princely fortune dilapidated by sheer indolence, because the obstinate spoiled owner will neither look into his affairs nor let anybody else look into them. He lies in bed half the day, and rises to run after pleasure in whatever shape he can pursue it; abhors business and has no sense of duty.

Small wonder that interest at some £3,200 a year was still being paid in the early 1840s.

In 1833 Arkwright lent £10,000 to John Ryle, MP for Macclesfield, the husband of his niece, Susanna Hurt. The sum was increased to £24,480 in 1836 and so remained until its repayment five years later. Also in 1833 Constantine Henry Phipps, first Marquess of Normanby, who was sent to Ireland as Lord Lieutenant in 1835 and became ambassador at Paris 1846-62, borrowed £40,000 at 4 per cent.[114] The following year, 1834, there were loans of £10,000 (repaid four years later) to John Spencer Stone, of Callingwood, Burton upon Trent,[115] and of £100,000 (also repaid four years later), to George Osbaldeston, MP for East Retford 1812-18.[116] (The 'Squire of England', as he was known, began his thirty-five-year career as a master of hounds while still an undergraduate at Oxford. He hunted six days a week, sometimes taking out two different packs in one day, and rode 200 miles in eight hours forty-two minutes for a wager of 1,000 guineas in 1831 — the year he fought his famous duel with Lord George Bentinck on Wormwood Scrubbs. A daring steeplech-ase rider, in which he had no superior and is said never to have been beaten, and well known on the turf, he enjoyed a world-wide reputation in every branch of field sports.)

In 1839 Arkwright negotiated his largest loan, a mortgage of £125,000 to the fourth Duke of Newcastle, who, a year earlier, had strained his resources by the purchase for £400,000 of the Duke of Norfolk's Worksop estate,[117] regarded as one of the finest in England. Arkwright informed Smith Payne & Smiths of the transaction on 18 May 1839:

> I beg to apprize you, that Wednesday next the 22nd, is the day last appointed for the settlement of the contract between the Duke of Norfolk and the Duke of Newcastle. I beg you will place the 125,000£ which I am going to lend to the latter nobleman, at the disposal of my son, Mr. Charles Arkwright. As this is the largest portion of the money required upon this occasion, I conclude it will be desirable, with your permission, for all the necessary parties to meet at your Bank; and I have to request the favour of your advice and assistance to my son, upon this occasion, as to the most proper and convenient mode of making out and adjusting the accounts.[118]

Less than three weeks later (8 June 1839) Arkwright was again writing to Smith Payne & Smiths, 'I beg to apologise for not having given you more timely notice that I had agreed to advance an addtional £10,000 to his Grace and Lord Lincoln,'[119] and at the same time advising them:

> I am negotiating for a loan of £40,000 on mortgage to the Duke of Buckingham, upon an Estate which his Grace has just purchased from the Earl of Chesterfield. If that be so concluded, the money will be wanted very soon, probably in the course of a week. I shall be short about £15,000 in addition to the whole balance of my account with you. I beg to say, that if it be agreeable to you I should wish to borrow, on loan, for a month or two but if the scarcity of money at this time, of which I see so much in the papers, inclines you to prefer

selling the Indian Bonds I have in your hands, I beg, to add it is a matter of perfect indifference to me. When I know the result of this negotiation with the Duke's solicitor, I will write again.

The Duke of Buckingham (he is the 'Duke of Agincourt' and his wife 'the Duchess' in Disraeli's *Coningsby*) had succeeded to the title in January 1839; within eight years, by accumulating estates purchased with borrowed money and by excessive expenditure, he had become a ruined man. When he died at the Great Western Hotel, Paddington, in 1861 he was worth less than £200.[120]

Arkwright had other sources of income, modest by his standards, arising from his share in Richard Arkwright & Co., bankers, of Wirksworth and Ashbourne, and from his investments in Derbyshire turnpikes and canals, and in railways.

In 1804 Arkwright had become a partner in the bank founded at Wirksworth in 1780 by John Toplis, the only son of John Toplis, a linen draper there, and nephew of William Toplis of Mansfield, who with his son had established a small cotton-spinning mill on the Arkwright principle at Cuckney, Nottinghamshire, about 1785.

Although by no means a large concern, Arkwright Toplis & Co. carried on an extremely wide range of business. Serving, as it did, a many-sided economy, the bank drew its customers from local industry and from the local gentry and their families; it held the accounts of seven bodies of enclosure commissioners, lending money, mostly in 'Cash' — presumably local notes — to five of them and also made loans to three turnpikes, to two of which it probably acted as treasurer. John Toplis died aged seventy-nine in March 1826 worth £30,000 (some six times the amount left by his father) and three years later the bank became Richard Arkwright & Co. The partners were Arkwright and two of his sons, Peter and Charles, each of whom held a one-third share in the total capital, which by 1843 amounted to £51,157 3s 6d.

Arkwright held shares and sometimes loan stock in the turnpikes from Cromford to Bakewell, Belper and Newhaven, and in those from Wirksworth to Derby, from Enterclough to Chapel en le Frith and from Stockport to Marple. Some of the shares had been acquired from Samuel Oldknow, as had half his share in the Peak Forest and in the Macclesfield canals. Arkwright had ten shares (and his son Peter five) in the Cromford Canal Company. One-third of his shares in the Cromford & High Peak Railway had previously been held by Oldknow, and he also had a small investment in the Mansfield & Pinxton Railway. In 1843 the market value of his turnpike, canal and other shares amounted to £19,045 13s.

Since inheriting the lion's share of Sir Richard's fortune Arkwright's capital, and with it his income, had steadily increased. Early evidence of this is afforded by his tax payments. In 1798 he subscribed £500 to cover his assessed taxes,[121] a series of direct imposts on carriages, servants and horses increased and extended during the French wars so as to include taxes on hair powder, dogs, watches and clocks. The following year, when these amounted to £407 17s 7d,[122] he paid into the Bank of England, to the credit of the Commissioners of the treasury, a further £500, a sum he had promised to contribute annually.[123]

In 1798 Pitt introduced, for the first time, what was virtually an income tax. His Bill became law in January 1799 and came into operation on 5 April of the same year. The tax, instead of being calculated according to expenditure, was now imposed directly upon the entire income of the individual, and on 7 November 1800 Arkwright paid £3,900 into the Bank of England to meet any demand. The following year this was increased to £4,600.[124]

Arkwright's holdings of the Funds, his estates and his personal loans were by 1825 (the earliest date for which we have figures) bringing him in an income of £74,000. By 1833 it had increased to £85,400, by 1836 to £90,500, by 1839 to £100,640 and by 1842 to £105,460. Between 1833 (the first year for which detailed information as to the main sources of his income is available) and 1842 the interest he received from personal loans had almost doubled (from £12,300 to £23,740), while income from the Funds had risen from £42,800 to £51,120; income from rents, however, had increased by a mere £300, from £30,300 to £30,600.[125]

Arkwright's income — even in the 1790s — made it easy for him to carry out Sir Richard's 'express Will and direction' that he should 'with all convenient speed . . . complete in a proper manner the Mansion house I have lately erected'. Accordingly, in autumn 1792 Arkwright, already moved from Bakewell to the Rock, set about the more urgent tasks needed to prepare Willersley Castle for occupation.

By the end of the year everything was ready to receive the furniture and fittings ordered from Edward Wilson, whose account of 28 December reads:

Paid for a Man with a Waggon & 4 Horses to carry your large Glasses & Sundry other furniture to Cromford 141 Miles, about 3 Ton Weight	£45 0s. 0d.
Paid Workmans Travelling Expenses & Turnpikes for Waggon to and from Cromford 282 Miles	£12 18s. 6d.

But although much of Sir Richard's drawing-room furniture and the mirrors were eventually carried to Willersley, £776 6s 8½d worth, almost half, of the furnishings he had ordered remained in London as late as the summer of 1794.

Three years later Arkwright was enquiring as to those items of the furnishings ordered by Sir Richard that remained unsold. He heard from Wilson on 22 August 1797:

I am sorry to say that the present times does not promote their being used. I have the misfortune to add I have every article by me yet unsold — every person who furnishes wishes to have a choice of their own but it is very uncertain when I may make use of them — the total loss appears to be about Eighty pounds which considering the whole circumstances of the case cannot be conceived a very great sum.

By May 1797 Arkwright had placed orders with Wilson to the value of £4,413 9s 9½d. Included in these were items, mainly furnishings, for the following rooms:

	£	s.	d
Mʳ. & Mʳˢ. Arkwrights Bed & Dressing Room	103	16	3
M.ʳ Arkwrights Dressing Room	175	18	0
Chintz Bed & Dressing Room	338	0	2½
Middle North Bed & Dressing Rooms	263	10	1
French Bed Room	200	3	9
Best Bed and Dressing Room	675	3	8
Music Room	232	4	8½
Library	210	18	10½
Drawing Room	1246	9	2
Dining Room	269	6	4

It was in the 30 ft by 20 ft dining room that Arkwright hung Wright's portrait of Sir Richard, as well as those of his own family,[126] adding the *Picture of a Girl Looking thro' a Bladder* (bought from Wright's executors in April 1798 for thirty guineas)[127] and the large *View of the Head of Ullswater Lake from Lyulph's Tower*, bought from the sale of the contents of Wright's studio at Christie's on 6 May 1801 for 300 guineas and held by John Leigh Philips to be 'the finest of all his landscapes, and a work which alone would place his reputation along with that of the most eminent masters'.[128]

Meanwhile on 12 April 1794 (the date given in the accounts for 'Carriage of Tools to Cromford', 14s, and 'Books & paper to keep the Accts', 16s 3d) Thomas Gardner, of Uttoxeter, a former assistant of Joseph Pickford, designer of Etruria Hall and an intimate friend of Wright, began the task of completing the interior of Willersley Castle.[129] At the outset the work was supervised by John Hewitt (who received 3s 6d a day in addition to an allowance of 5s a week for board) and nine workmen whose earning ranged from 2s to 2s 10d a day, with no allowance for board.

Hewitt's name, together with those of a dozen other workmen, last appears in the accounts on 28 November 1795, from which time until Christmas Eve, when the work was completed, only three or four men were engaged. Throughout this time Hewitt put in six or seven days each week, but many of the workmen often appeared for only two or three days in any particular week. In October 1794 and again a year later Gardner's account notes sums of £1 5s and £1 2s 6d that he 'Gave the Men at time of Lighting Candles', references to the annual festivity at the Cromford mills. (From the beginning of November 1794 until mid-April 1795 about 2s a week had been spent on candles for normal lighting purposes.)

Altogether between March 1794 and the end of 1795 Gardner made '15 Journeys to Cromford, myself 53 days attending the finishing of Willersley Castle, & the additional Buildings to it: Measuring, & making a Bill of the Work done by Mr Dugdale the Plasterer, and in all the other Branches; Measuring & valuing the Lodge for the Mason, & the Peers to the Lodge Gates &c including incidental expences'. All this cost Arkwright £65 8s 6d. In addition Gardner charged £14 14s for 'Making the Design for the Plasterer, & all other Designs necessary for the finishing Business in the Different Branches; Making a Design for the Lodge & Gateway to d.°, & a set of Clear Drawings for the New Stables; & Plans, Elevations, & Sections of the Stables for the Workmen, calculated & figur'd'. In all, Gardner's expenses came to £1,930 13s 4½d, exclusive, he noted, of 'The time given for Work at the Chapel from Aug. 29th to Oct. 3^d [which] is not charged to the above Account'.

Sir Richard's chapel was completed by 1797 and dedicated to St Mary, after, it is supposed, a chapel that long before had stood on the site.[130] Built of red sandstone, it contained a marble font, an organ and two small galleries for the use of the children attending the mill Sunday schools.[131] Arkwright endowed the chapel with a further £200, and about 1825 commissioned the white marble monument by Chantrey which stands to the south side of the communion table.[132]

In his will Sir Richard made no stipulation as to the house in the Adelphi he had acquired from William Osborne in 1788. Arkwright, a much less frequent visitor to London than his father, decided to sell the property and again called upon the services of Edward Wilson. On 15 October 1792 Wilson 'paid for 4 Advertisements of the House in the Adelphi' (£1 8s) and began to prepare the premises for sale, as when on 6 December his workpeople were busy 'taking up all the Carpets & Green Baize covers' (12s) and again, five days later, when he engaged a 'Cheer [sic] Woman & Man to assist to scower & clean the House from top to the Bottom' (no price stated).

By the end of 1793, despite further newspaper advertisements in October, the property remained unsold. 'Appraising Sundry fixtures at N° 8 Adam Street, Adelphi' (£1 1s), Wilson noted in his account of 31 December 1793, and on the same day he 'Paid the Glaziers Bill for work done' (18s 6d); February 1794 brought in a bill for 'Repairing door keys' (7s 6 d), but later that year the house was sold to William Osborne's son.

[248]

NOTES

1 A.F. MSS.
2 Ashton, *Economic Fluctuations*, p. 63.
3 J. E. Norton (ed.), *The Letters of Edward Gibbon*, III, London, 1956, p. 242.
4 Ashton, *Economic Fluctuations*, p. 168.
5 1819 Comm., evidence of Robert Hyde.
6 Ashton, *Economic Fluctuations*, pp. 134/5, 170.
7 Profits were: 1794, £14,457; 1795, £30,432; 1796 £29,294.
8 Samuel Oldknow's papers, Columbia University.
9 Covenant period 15 October 1798 to 31 December 1799; from 1800 profits were calculated over the calendar year.
10 Arkwright's experience was similar to that of Kirkman Finlay, who 'first entered business
. extensively . . . in 1792 . . . . The best time that I ever knew the spinning was about 1802; it was however even better before that . . .'. The trade, he agreed, had 'materially altered since the war . .' (P.P. 1833 (690) VI, *Select Committee on Manufactures, Commerce and Shipping*). For a discussion of the controversy regarding profit levels in cotton spinning see C. H. Lee, *A Cotton Enterprise, 1795/1840: a History of M'Connel and Kennedy, fine cotton spinners*, Manchester, 1972, pp. 138/41. The Arkwright profits confirm Lee's contention (p. 140) that 'cotton spinning realised higher profits at the turn of the century, and indeed during the war period as a whole, than it did in the quarter century after 1815'.
11 For the various places see H. Heaton, 'Non/importation, 1806/1812', *Journal of Economic History*, I, 1941.
12 P.P., 1831/32 (722) VI, *Committee of Secrecy on the Bank of England Charter*, pp. 334/5, q. 4368.
13 See M. Stenton, *Who's Who of British Members of Parliament*, Hassocks, Sussex, 1976; also for John Ryle.
14 For material in text within brackets see Fitton and Wadsworth, p. 305.
15 A.F. MSS.
16 Phillips, *Personal Tour*, II, p. 127.
17 Of special importance was M'Connel and Kennedy's successful application of steam power to two of its movements in 1796/97. See Miss J. de L. Mann's review of G. J. French, *Life and Times of Samuel Crompton*, ed. S. D. Chapman, Bath, 1970, in *Textile History*, III, 1970.
18 'If there be a difficulty about water/power, why not use steam? Yes, but if one is the son of the richest commoner in England, why trouble himself about the matter at all, unless, indeed, for the sake of the poor people in the district?' *Manchester Weekly Advertiser*, 1855. Also F. Espinasse, *Lancashire Worthies*, I, p. 461.
18 D. J. Jeremy, *Transatlantic Industrial Revolution*, Oxford, 1981, p. 293.
20 P.P. 1834 (167) XIX, *Employment of Children*, D2, p. 191, information by Samuel Greg.
21 A. Ure, *The Cotton Manufacture of Great Britain*, I, London, 1836, pp. 328/9.
22 Now Meerbrook.
23 Farey, *General View of Derbyshire*, I, p. 330. In 1835 Richard Arkwright II recorded in his Memoranda Commencing 1815 notebook, 'Meresbrook Sough Commenced 1773,' and gave a detailed list of its ownership. It was owned almost exclusivley by F. Hurt, C. Hurt and P. Gell.
24 Roger Meeson and William Newland Welsby, *Reports of Cases . . . in the Courts of Exchequer and Exchequer Chamber. from Hilary Term 6 W. 11. IV to Easter Term 10 Vict. XVII*, V London, 1837/49, pp. 203, 234.
25 B. Bryan, *Matlock Manor and Parish*, London, 1903, p. 261 n.; p. 266 states that Cromford mills finally closed September 1846: this is not correct.
26 E. W. Marrs junior, *The Letters of Thomas Carlyle to his Brother Alexander, with related Family Letters*, Cambridge, 1968, p. 653.

27 About the German Kromford and its founder see W. O. Henderson, *British and Industrial Europe, 1750-1830: Studies in British Influence on the Industrial Revolution in Western Europe,* Liverpool, 1954, p. 142, p. 142 n. Henderson adds that R. M. R. Dehn, *The German Cotton Industry,* Manchester, 1913, p. 3, gives 1783 as the date of the establishment of Kromford.

28 *Manchester Weekly Advertiser,* 4 August 1855, cited by Espinasse, *Lancashire Worthies,* I, p. 461.

29 A.F. MSS.

30 A.F. MSS. ⁄ no separate valuation until 1817.

31 *Macclesfield Courier,* 13 June 1818.

32 Price from A.F. MSS.

33 *Derby Mercury,* 4 February 1790; *Manchester Mercury,* 9 February 1790.

34 D. and S. Lysons, *Magna Britannia,* V, London, 1817, p. 98; Glover, *County of Derby,* II, p. 359.

35 He (Browne) inherited Campfield Place from his father, Thomas, Garter King-at-Arms and an eminent land surveyor. The property was sold to the Earl of Rosebery in 1818 (J. and J. A. Venn, *Alumni Cantabrigienses,* Part II, I, Cambridge, 1940, p. 418).

36 Humberside Record Office at Beverley, B.R., pp. 34-8.

37 A.F. MSS.

38 Burke's *Landed Gentry,* 1849.

39 J. Nichols, *The History and Antiquities of the County of Leicester,* IV, Part II, London, 1811, p. 1002.

40 L. T. Smith (ed.), *The Itinerary of John Leland,* II, London, 1946, p. 72.

41 Hereford Record Office, C69/315, 'A descriptive particular of Hampton Court Estate'.

42 E. L. Jones, 'Industrial capital and landed investment: the Arkwrights in Herefordshire, 1809-43', p. 54 in E. L. Jones and G. E. Mingay (eds.), *Land, Labour, and Population in the Industrial Revolution: Essays presented to J. D. Chambers,* London, 1967.

43 A.F. MSS.

44 Jones, 'Arkwrights in Herefordshire', pp. 55-6.

45 Mr Edridge, father of Henry Edridge, ARA, a successful miniature and landscape painter, born at Paddington in 1768, the son of a tradesman.

46 Garlick and Macintyre, *Diary of Farington,* V, p. 202.

47 Farey, *General View of Derbyshire,* III, p. xviii.

48 G.M., 1843, p. 215; W. W. Rouse Ball and J. A. Venn, *Admissions to Trinity College, Cambridge,* III, London, 1911, p. 234; Venn, *Alumni Cantabrigienses,* Part II, V, 1953, p. 333.

49 G.M., 1835, pp. 94-6.

50 Thomas Eyton of Eyton (died 1816), High Sheriff of Shropshire in 1779 (Burke's *Landed Gentry,* 1849).

51 Morley in Manley Hull, Shropshire, an eighteenth-century mansion possibly designed by Francis Smith of Warwick.

52 *Memoirs of Lucien Bonaparte,* by himself, translated from French, I, London, 1818, p. 62. Thorngrove, which he bought after saying, 'obliged to quit Ludlow'.

53 Arkwright MSS at Essex County Record Office, CD/DAr T33.

54 Robert Arkwright took up residence at Sutton Scarsdale *Derby Mercury,* 18 February 1835; *Derby Mercury,* 18 January 1837.

55 Whatever the accuracy of Oldknow's estimate (Arkwright's own valuation was £237,000), the estate did have its mineral reserves, which were retained when, in 1920, the last of the Arkwrights to occupy Sutton Hall sold the mansion and the greater part of the estate. It was here in the years following World Warr II that coal was mined open-cast methods. But by that time Sutton Hall was a mere shell.

56 *Derby Mercury,* 6 September, 4 October 1837; *Derbyshire Courier,* 15 July 1843.

57 Henry Lord inherited the estate on the death of his father, (James, of Wolverhampton) in 1825 (will at P.R.O.). Arkwright seems to have had an earlier interest in the property. Samuel Simpson was living at Dunstall Lodge in 1810, and Charles Arkwright was writing to his brother Joseph from Dunstall in 1823 and 24; D.C.R.O., Cressbrook Papers, lease of 1800, Simpson to John Leigh Philips and Francis Philips; Strutt MSS at Essex Record Office. Letters, Charles Arkwright to Joseph Arkwright, 6 March 1823, 4 February 1824.

58 Dunstall: Charles Arkwright, 'Founder of this Church and of Schools connected with it'. 'The Church, Schools and Parsonage House were erected after the death of the Founder, from Funds which he had provided for the purpose and instrusted to his brother Peter Arkwright. . . .' The church was consercrated 5 October 1853.

59 Unwin, *Samuel Oldknow*, pp. 16-17.

60 For the Saltes see R. S. Fitton, 'Samuel and William Salte: an eighteenth-century linen house', *Explorations in Entrepreneurial History*, VI, 1969, pp. 286-96.

61 Samuel Oldknow's papers, Columbia, University.

62 Unwin, *Samuel Oldknow*, pp. 78-9.

63 *Ibid.*, pp. 81-2.

64 Samuel Oldknow's papers, Columbia University.

65 Unwin, *Samuel Oldknow*, pp. 83-4.

66 *Ibid.*, p. 124.

67 *Ibid.*, p. 149.

68 *Ibid.*, pp. 127, 143, 148, 149.

69 A.F. MSS.

70 A.F. MSS.; Unwin, *Samuel Oldknow*, p. 156.

71 W. C. Henry, 'A biographical notice of the late Peter Ewart Esq.', *Memoirs of the Manchester Literary and Philosophical Society*, VII, new series, 1844, pp. 120-1 124-5.

72 A.F. MSS.

73 Unwin, *Samuel Oldknow*, pp. 157-8.

74 All amounts from A.F. MSS. Oldknow had paid off the interest but not the principal of the loans of December 1791 (£12,000), September 1792 (£11,000) and April 1795 (£11,500).

75 A.F. MSS.

76 Unwin, *Samuel Oldknow*, pp. 194, 200.

77 A.F. MSS.

78 Unwin, *Samuel Oldknow*, p. 200.

79 A.F. MSS.

80 For the terms of the partnership see Unwin, *Samuel Oldknow*, pp. 200-1.

81 *Ibid*, p. 236, for views of Unwin.

82 *L.G.*, 1805, p. 961.

83 A.F. MSS; Unwin, *Samuel Oldknow*, p. 202, says £143,000.

84 A.F. MSS.

85 A.F. MSS.

86 Byng, *The Torrington Diaries*, p. 225 n. 60.

87 Chatsworth MSS, L/24 (henceforth L/24) /105.

88 L/24/105 Robert, Andrew B., John and Chas. Drummond & Co.

89 Earl of Bessborough (ed.), *Georgiana: Extracts from the Correspondence of Georgiana, Duchess of Devonshire*, London, 1955, p. 163; see also Judd, *G.M.*, 1804, p. 552.

90 *Ibid.*, p. 183.

91 *Ibid.*, p. 178 (see letter, pp. 177-8).

92 *Ibid.*, p. 244.

93 Is this Parker of Princess Street Soho, Gold and Silversmiths, who seems to have loaned Georgiana trinkets and rings?

94 *Universal British Directory*, I, 1790, p. 376, 'Farrer James, Farrer Oliver and Atkinson, Thomas, attorneys, Chancery Lane'.

95 L/24/105. In a letter to be given in the event of her death to Lady Foster, Georgiana gave her debt as £3,000, not £5,000.

96 A.F. MSS.

97 L/24/106.

98 *Ibid.*; should have been for £5,441 4s 6d.

99 G.M., 1806, pp. 386-7.

100 In a statement to the duke in December 1804 Georgiana's debt had been estimated at £36,000 (L/24/105).

101 William Adam, successively Attorney General and Solicitor General to the Prince of Wales and later Lord Chief Commissioner of the Scottish Jury Court. Dorothy M. Stuart *Dearest Bess: the Life and Times of Lady Elizabeth Foster, afterwards Duchess of Devonshire*, London, 1955, p. 106.

102 L/24/106.

103 L/24/105.

104 L/24/106; by January 1811 the trustees had repaid £67,411 19s 5d.

105 At Lichfield, the will of John Twigg of Bonsall, proved in 1797, mentions sons John, Joseph, Thomas, William, Samuel, James, Isaac. The five Twigg sons were Joseph, William, Samuel, Thomas, James. For Sneddon Mill see Signet Library, 321/13; Scottish Record Office, U/P ISH/A/7/49.

106 P.P. 1834 (167) XX, *Employment of Children*, A1, P. 197.

107 See Jean Lindsay, 'The Butterley Coal and Iron Works, 1792-1896', *D.A.J.*, LXXXV, 1965.

108 For Hunloake see *G.M.*, 1816, p. 186.

109 For E. M. Mundy see *G.M.*, 1849, p. 96. See *G.M.*, 1851, p. 309, for daughter's marriage.

110 Vizard & Blower, solicitors, 50 Lincolns Inn Fields: *Robson's Improved London Directory, Street Guide and Carriers' List for* 1820; letter in A.F. MSS.

111 *G.M.*, 1823, p. 470.

112 C. C. F. Greville, *The Greville Memoirs, 1814-60*, V, London, 1938, pp. 242, 346-7; see also Burke's *Peerage and Baronetage*, 1859.

113 John Ryle, MP, of the Macclesfield silk manufacturing and banking firm. In 1841 their Manchester bank fell, and the parent bank at Macclesfield also. 'He retired to the neighbourhood of Gosport, where he died in or about 1861, comfortable, happy, through his excellent wife being possessed of a moderate fortune of her own.' (L. H. Grindon, *Manchester Banks and Bankers: Historical, Biographical, and Anecdotal*, second edition, Manchester, 1878). His eldest son, the Rev. John Charles Ryle, was to become Lord Bishop of Liverpool (M. L. Loane, *John Charles Ryle, 1816-1900*, London, 1953).

114 *G.M.*, 1863, pp. 374-5.

115 Eton 1826 and 1829 Christchurch.

116 H. E. C. Stapylton, *The Eton School Lists from 1791 to 1850*, London, 1864; J. Foster, *Alumni Oxonienses, 1715-1886*, III, London and Oxford, 1888, p. 1045; *D.N.B.*; *G.M.*, 1866, pp. 419-20: R. Longrigg, *The History of Foxhunting*, London, 1975.

117 For Worksop estate see *The Times*, 11 and 16 April 1838, on both occasions citing the *Doncaster Gazette*.

118 National Westminster Bank Archives.

119 It was probably about this that Arkwright wrote to his son, Charles, on 9 July 1840: 'I thank you for giving me an opportunity of your occassional useful services, but I hope I shall [not] receive them upon so large a scale as those of last year. The Duke has just paid the interest, but I have not heard a word of the 10,000£ which I dont care much about, but I do not like borrowing to *accomodate*, at 5 p^r c^t and receiving but 4'.

120 Burke's *Peerage and Baronetage*.

121 *Derby Mercury*, 22 March 1798.
122 P.R.O., E/128/167 Year 1798.
123 *Derby Mercury*, 22 March 1798.
124 P.R.O., E/182/168 Year 1800, E/182/168 Year 1801.
125 A.F. MSS.
126 S. Glover, *The Peak Guide*, Derby, 1830, p. 119.
127 The 'elegant gilt frame' cost £2 17s and the 'Case, Package & Car. from London' 13s (A.F. MSS).
128 *The Monthly Magazine and British Register*, 1797, p. 292; *G.M.*, 1797, p. 804; Britton and Brayley, *England and Wales*, III, p. 518; Nicolson, *Joseph Wright*, p. 267.
129 For Thomas Gardner (pp. 331-2) and Joseph Pickford (pp. 634-5) see Colvin, *British Architects*. Also for Pickford see Edward Saunders, 'An eighteenth-century provincial architect, Joseph Pickford of Derby', *Country Life*, November 1972.
130 H. Moore, *Picturesque Excursions from Derby to Matlock Bath, annd its Vicinity: being a Descriptive Guide*, Derby, 1818, p. 24. 'It is of red sandstone neat and commodious; although the design and proportions are inelegant. The tower is too small for the body of the church, and the whole is a futile attempt at the Gothic style of Architecture.' See also the Rev. J. C. Cox, *Notes on the Churches of Derbyshire*, II, Chesterfield and London, 1877, p. 574, who gives details of Peter Arkwright's alterations in 1858-59, costing £3,000.
131 Britton and Brayley, *England and Wales*, III, p. 253.
132 Glover, *Peak Guide*, p. 126, and A.F. MSS.

CHAPTER IX

The second Arkwright: a family founded

IN 1796, as Arkwright moved into Willersley, three of his sons — Richard, the eldest, aged fifteen, Robert, two years younger, and Peter, born in 1784 — were sent to Eton. The family's long connection with the school had begun.

Letters home — mainly from Richard — give a view of Eton under Dr George Heath, Head Master at a time when academic standards were at their lowest. There is mention of Tutors, Masters and Dames, of food (or rather the lack of it), of boating (technically forbidden but freely practised), floggings, horses and (never to be lost sight of) the dates of forthcoming 'holydays'. Word is sent home of Derbyshire Etonians: John Bell Crompton[1] of Duffield Hall, a future sheriff of the county and several times Mayor of Derby; William Cavendish[2] (1783-1812), eldest son of the first Earl of Burlington, and his brother, George Henry Compton[3] (1784-1809), both of whom were to meet a tragic end: Major George Cavendish, MP for Aylesbury, perished in the transport *Dispatch*, homeward bound from Corunna when wrecked upon the Manacle rocks, near Helston, Cornwall, in January 1809, while three years later William, MP for Derby, was killed when thrown from his curricle in Holker Park, the Cavendishes' seat on the southern fringe of the Lake District. The John Carr referred to is probably a member of the family who ran the Derby porcelain works previously owned by the Duesburys, while Robert John Wilmot of Ormaston[4] was to become an MP, a Privy Councillor and a Governor of Ceylon.

The earliest letter, of 26 February 1797, was perhaps the first sent back to Derbyshire after the Christmas holiday, during which the Arkwrights were visited by Bache Thornhill of Stanton Hall, accompanied by his two sons, both at Westminster School. (One wonders if conversation went back to that summer when Westminster had challenged and easily defeated Eton in a cricket match on Hounslow Heath, and to Dr Heath having laid up with aches and pains for more than a week after flogging the Eton eleven and its seventy followers, not for their performance but for disobeying his order not to accept Westminster's challenge.[5])

The episode of the mine relates to Job Boden, one of the two men trapped by a fall of earth at Godbehere's Founder Mine, near the Cromford to Wirksworth road, who was rescued eight days later and was back at work fourteen weeks after that.[6] The letters read:

Richard Arkwright to his father   Eton Sunday Evening Feb.y 26 1797

    Dear Father

    I should have written to you before but have not had an opportunity of seeing my Tutor since I received your letter. I am very sorry to hear of the accident which has happened to my filly I should not like to part with her unless you think it would be better. I spoke to my Dame about a single room which she has promised me, after Easter, if not before. Crompton has had a very bad cold for these last three weeks but is well again he is very subject to catch cold. We have two whole holy days this week and one Half And we are only to do one exercise this week and any regular week we have three. We heard that the French had landed 12 hundred men in Wales[7] and they were all taken prisoners which is very good new. I suppose you will receive the intelligence as soon as you receive my letter. We saw the man who was got out of the mine and I am very glad to hear he is likely way to recover. I forgot to say before that we break up on Thursday the sixth of April 1797 and the lower boys go on that day but the fifth form go on Tuesday or Wednesday. I am glad to hear John & Charles are not to come till after Midsummer for then I can have them for the fagg's for I shall be in the fifth by that time. We expect Mr & Mrs Strutt here some time this week as you say they will come soon. I have no more to day at present. My Brothers join in love to yourself my mother and Miss Oldham

                        I remain your Dutiful son
                           Richard Arkwright ma

I put ma: because I am used to do so to my
exercises and I did not think of it. It is
short for Major.

Richard Arkwright to his father   Eton 29 June 1797

    Dear Father

    I have not received a letter from your for this long time and therefore I suppose you have not time. I was put into the 5 Form on last Sunday but one and I like it very well; my Brothers are in the upper school in the same place I was when I first came here. We all begin to grow short of Money, and therefore we hope you will send us an order in a letter to my Dame for as much as you may think proper. I dare say you have seen the nest which I put into the water to petrefie,[8] when you write tell me how it goes on. I hope you will get a good pair of oars made against we come home. Robert was to have had a water dress made by my dame will not let him unless you have said so. I dare say John and Charles will be tired of home if they are to return with us. I suppose we are to come home with my Sister. We break up on Monday the 31 of July and none of the boys will go sooner unless there is some particular reason assigned, and so if we are to come before you must have some reason. Is Charles Hurt come home yet, he was to come before us. Be so good as to write soon; My Brothers join with me in love to all at Willersley and I remain your dutiful Son

Richard Arkwright

Richard Arkwright to his father   Eton July 21 1797

Dear Father

I was made very happy at the receipt of your letter, and I should have answered before now, if I could have got leave sooner. We have now got leave to come on the Friday, we shall set off very early in the morning and mean to reach Leicester the same night, and if we do not find you there we shall set off before breakfast, because as it is uncertain weather you come to Leicester or not, we should perhaps wait in vain for your arrival. Crompton has had a letter from home to say that he is to come with use; and I dare say we shall have a vary pleasant journey. Mrs Devis was at Windsor on last Sunday but one, and was so good as to ask us to dinner. I thought John would have written me another latin letter, as he had once began, I think you ought to have bought me a horse as well as Bessy and Robert for you sold mine, and therefore I ought to have another

I am your dutiful Son
Richard Arkwright 1797.

Peter received a letter from you and Charles this morning which he has just now shew'd me, and I am glad to find you have got a horse for me.

Richard Arkwright to his father   Eton 17 Jany 1798

Dear Father

We arrived here safe last night about seven tho we were detained at Rickmans⁄worth about an hour because they had no post boy. We found only three boys here who came yesterday. There are but very few boys come in the whole school; Therefore I hope you will let us come later the next holydays; for, the last time, we came a fortnight after the proper time and then we found but a very few boys come; pray remember this til next holydays and then you will let us not come so soon. We hear that Bayley will not return to Eton but he is going to the East Indies. I drank with my dame last night and she told me that her niece Miss Hammersley had seen my mother at Scarborough and should be glad to know when she came to Town. I left my night cap at Leicester which I suppose you took home with you. Desire Anthony to keep my horses mane platted til it will lie flat. Give my love to all at home and receive the same from your dutiful

Son Richard Arkwright

Richard Arkwright to his father   Eton 27ᵗʰ Feby 1798

Dear Father

I should have answered you letter sooner, but I could not tell you what you wanted to know, which was when we came home nor am I now able to tell you the exact time but it is either the 26 or 27 of March. We intend to come home in post chaises, and you will have no occasion to send to Derby to meet us as it will be uncertain what day we come home till a day or two before. My flute master is paid by the month and therefore if you have not pray send an order. The thorn is got out of Peter's leg at last and he will soon be able to go into school. I hope you will defer your journey to town till after Easter, for we shall think a visit more agreeable in the middle of the school time, than so near the holy days. My Dame has not given me my backgammon board again yet, nor will she give me the money I gave for it, tho' I have asked her. I suppose she means to keep it for her own use, til' you come up, and only to sport it on particular occasions as her own is not so good. As I was one day rowing my Dame she said she would tell my tutor of me, and was very angry with me, presently after I shewed her your letter she then said that I was a very good boy, only a little too childish. Give our love to all at Willersley, and believe

your dutiful son
Richd Arkwright

Richard Arkwright to his father   Eton March 5th [1798]

Dear Father

My Brothers and my self think of pulling in a six oared boat after Easter, and if you will give us leave and money we shall be very happy. The Boys have man'ed 7 boats and they want an eight and have manned that all but three pullers. The expence attending it will be but trifling to you it will not exceed 7 Guineas each. The parents of all the other boys pay the expence; All the boys are very desirous to get us to pull as we are good pullers and we all impatiently wait for an answer, & flatter ourselves you will pay for us, as you have often told us you do not mind expence when it is not improperly applied. We shall be flogged about twice a week but that is quite a trifle. Pray write soon on account of ordering a boat from London. I am in haste

your dutiful son
Richard Arkwright

Richard Arkwright to his father

Dear Father

I am afraid you do not rightly understand about the boat. It is a custom for the boys between Easter and Midsummer to pull in boats and they wish to have a good many to go up this year as the queen came to see it last year and intends to come this. We shall not be flogged for pulling, but for not being at absence [roll call] every saturday night; I shall be out of eight oclock absence soon after the holy days. I assure you there is no harm in it. One of the masters asked a boy if he was not to steer in one of the boats; the boy said, yes, then he asked him if his father had given him leave, to which he also answered yes; then it is all very well said the master. Whilst the boats are going under Windsor bridge the masters sometimes walk over (as if by chance) to get a sight at them but never have them flogged. One of the Cavendishes steers in one of the boats. Peter does not wish to pull now, The masters do not think it a disgrace to be flogged for that, but they would never consent to it. One of Dr Heath's own sons steers which he could not do without his fathers knowledge so pray give Robert & myself leave.

Give my Love to all at Willersley that I know I remain you dutiful son

Richard Arkwright

PS. Crompton is going home with a boy of the name of Brandreth[9] Eton Sunday 11 March 1798.

Richard Arkwright to his father   Eton Coll 1ˢᵗ July 1798

Dear Father

I make no doubt but that you have heard of the Eton Boys going to Maidenhead on Tuesday last, But I do not suppose you heard a true account. The Boys who pull in the Boats have made it a custom for a many years to go to Maidenhead once or twice during the season, & Doctor Heath hearing it was to be on tuesday forbid them going, as they must necessarily miss 6 oclock absence, & said in a most serious manner that whoever should go should be sent away from school, but notwithstanding his threats they went up & some had tea & others dinner, some who did not shirk absence rode up directly after absence & said that Dr Heath had scratched their names out of the List, they then all agreed to make a row if they were expelled and went down with that intent, they entered colledge all in a body & were met by some of the masters who asked two or three why they did not pull off their hats, who answered they were expelled; then Dr Heath said that if they would give themselves up to be flogged & promise not to go again he would over look it, to which they all agreed & underwent the punishment; the next day one of the biggest boys, struck a sixth form boy, & went to a private tutor with some others to make him an apology for calling the boys a parcel of blackguards; at eleven oclock on Wednesday night the masters and all the sixth form were sent for to Dr Heaths & the boy who struck one of the sixth and they told him that unless he went away before six in the morning he would be publikly expelled; the boys soon discovered the trick and in school the next day all together hollow'd out the boy's name and asked where he was and why he was sent away. Dr Heath told the fifth form that he was sent away on account of the sixth form boy, and the sixth on account of the private tutor, in church on thursday dr Heath overheard them say that they would have it cleared up & was taken ill and went out of the church, the boys then sent to him saying that they had no ill will against him for that they had found out that it was all through my tutor who has been at Cambridge and is there now; so that we dont know what will be done to him when he comes home.

Give my love to all at Willersley & receive from all your sons who join with me in love to you.

Richard Arkwright.

Richard Arkwright to his father   Eton 28th October 1798

Dear Father

I had indeed begun to think it long before I heard from you, but I think the more your answer was defered the more pleasure I should enjoy it the perusal of it. We flatter ourselves we have not yet done anything since the holydays (tho' we rather did before in an expedition to Maidenhead) which deserves your displeasure, and hope to continue in the same way; we attend Mr Hexter[10] very regularly and stay about two hours at a time, he is very desirous for us to improve, and we do all that is in our power, therefore I hope you will have no reason to find fault with our accompting this time. We did not receive our newspapers regularly after our return, but they now come weekly; We have not keep any of them yet but we will begin from this time; it is Bell's[11] weekly messenger which we receive now and we like it very well. I am very sorry to hear of my loss in Viper but it is not *quite* so great as yours, of Pero & Dash. My sister Bessy gave me the history of a journey my Brothers had made from Ashbourne during your absence and said that you was very much displeased at them for it. When you write again tell me whether they are to return with us after the next holydays, or not, for if you defer their coming to Eton much longer they will not come much before they are old enough to leave school. My Brother Robert & myself have bought nine pound of Cheshire Cheese on which we sup every night, with some porter as the supper my dame gives us is not eatable except to those who cant afford to buy other things. Have you heard lately of my horse and how my uncle likes him. There have been a great many robberies committed near this place since the holydays. The two Pelham's[12] and their servant were stopped & robbed about a week ago as they were returning from town from seeing one of their sisters. The other day my dames boys played the school at foot ball and beat them, eleven of my Dames, and the eleven best in the school, we all three played. I believe the match is going to be play'd again when the weather is a little more suitable than at present, for we have had continual bad weather for some time. I hope Mr Hurt has been able to discover the gang of poachers of whom Bessy gave me an account, or at least some of them, for they deserve to be punished richly for such outrageous behaviour. I received a letter from Frank Goodwin on thursday who is at Cambridge [   ]. There is a boy here who has been at Mr Herrok's at Leicester & at Rugby and in acquainted with all the Hurts. There was a fair at Windsor last week and I went up to row and see the sights &c. I saw my tutor up town on Friday which is a thing which occurs so that I did not know him directly having a round hat on, and not being used to see him without his gown, so that I had scarcely time to shirk him, but as he is near sighted he could not see me.

Give our love to all at home and believe me your dutiful son

Richard Arkwright

P.S: I have just delivered your message to Miss Roberts who is much obliged to you, as it is the greatest kindness you could have done her.

Peter Arkwright to his father   Eton Nov[r] 25th 1799 Friday Morning

Dear Father

I should have written to you some since but I could not hear from Dr Goodall till this Morning when the Holydays began, when I took the first opportunity of letting you know, they begin on Tuesday the 10th of December. I think I told my Mother in my last letter, we intended going down in the Mail, and as I have not heard any thing contrary, have written to John Carr[13] to ask him to take the Mail for us with Crompton, and Wilmot. If we go down in the mail we shall be in Derby about 2 Oclock, and if we cannot get places we shall go down with Crompton in post chaises. I hope you will get me a horse to ride these Holydays, as John is to have Nimble, but I suppose we shall not have much time to ride, as John told me in his last letter that M[r] Ward[14] was to be with us every other day. We have not heard from Richard lately; when we heard from him last he said he liked Sudbury very well, and that he had dined with M[r] Hall two Sunday's since he had been there. Crompton says he is to go to Mr. Haggits in about a year, and I hope (if I am to go at all) to go at the same time. John told me they did not go home from Ashbourne till the Middle of December. We have had a hard frost for the two or three last night's, and I hope we shall have a little skating soon. Robert intends to send the trunk home some time before we set off ourselves, that it may be at home the same time we are. Give our love to all at home, and believe me your's

affectionately

P. Arkwright.

P.S. When you answer this letter tell me wether we are to get the money from M[rs] Harrington's or wether John Carr is to pay for the coach, and Robert wants to know if he must direct the trunk to the care of M[r] Greaves. Broadhurst is going to town on Tuesday, and as we cannot all go in a chaise Robert intends going with him in Tandem.

Peter Arkwright to his father   Eton July 18th 1800

Dear Father,

As I have not received an answer to the letter I wrote some time since, I suppose you do not intend to write till you know when our holydays begin. They begin on Monday the 28th of this Month, and if I do not hear any thing to the contrary, we intend to go down in a Chaise, as it is now too late to take the Mail, three of the places being taken. Crompton saw Ld. G. Cavendish, and is going to Derby with him. Wilmot has taken one of the places on the Mail. There was a very grand review here yesterday of all the troops on camp, and those quartered about here. Charles has not been well for two of three days, but is better than he has been. I cannot say what time we shall be in Derby, as it is uncertain when we can set off from here. Doctor Heath is very strickt about giving leave before speeches. John and myself are very well, and join in love to all at Willersley, I am

your affectionate son

Peter Arkwright

Richard had left Eton in 1799, as probably had Robert. Letters home were now written by Peter, who the following year was joined by his brothers, John, aged fifteen, and Charles, a year younger.

Arkwright had considered sending John and Charles to Eton as early as 1797 and in January that year was in touch with Dr Joseph Goodall, an assistant master, about this as well as the desirablity of engaging a private tutor for his sons:

Dr Joseph Goodall to Richard Arkwright   [Postmark: Windsor Jan. 25, 1797]

 Dear Sir

 I am most fully of opinion that it should be in the highest Degree eligible, that your sons should be under the Care of a private Tutor, who would devote his whole Time to their Instruction and the Intimation of your Intention of enrolling two new Etonians among us appears to me to be more likely to hasten than defer the Plan. I shall however without further preface take upon me to suggest at large whatever may occur to me on the Subject, pleading only my earnest Desire that your Sons may reap every Advantage which the Plan may be likely to produce. In the first Place the Experience of nearly a Quarter of a Century points out to me in the strongest Degree the Expediency of the Tutor having been bred at Eton himself. In the 2nd I can pretty nearly ascertain as having been the Go-between (I confess the *Shockingness* of the Metaphor) on two or three former Occasions what will be the Expectations of any young Man of Character and Abilities who might undertake a Charge of this Nature. His first Object, generally speaking, would be Preferment at the Expiration of his Engagement; his secondary one either an Annuity at the same Term, or a larger Income during the whole of his Engagement. Considering the Number of his future Pupils I should imagine that he would hardly undertake the Charge (I suppose him to be unexceptionable in Point of Scholarship, Morals, and of Good Connections) under the yearly Salary of 200£, His Board &c of course to be paid for by you. There will be some little Difficulty in procuring Lodgings, and for some Time at least Accomodation in the College will be out of the Question, but the Inconveniences will be only ideal; a Man & a Maid Servant will be almost necessary though the former may possibly be dispensed with. One Point, though I am aware it is a delicate one, I feel it my absolute Duty to mention. As Mrs Harrington keeps no second Table, where a Tutor can dine, he must provide for himself elsewhere, and it will put him in a very uncomfortable Predicament, if some of his Pupils at least do not board where he does, as the Profit arising from the Tutors Board must be very trifling, if anything. This Objection might be obviated by your two younger Sons eating where the Tutor does. Mrs Harrington could not reasonably be offended by an Arrangement of this Nature, of which she must immediately see the Justice. There might be many Modifications of the Manner of their boarding, but when the essential Point is settled, the others will soon find their Levels. In Regard to the Time *when*, I am persuaded the sooner the better, and shall be very happy to be able to contribute in any Manner in my Power to an

Arrangement, in my opinion, so devoutly to be wished. You will I am sure have the Goodness to impute my Explicitness to no other Motive by that which I feel myself actuated by a Desire of shewing me Sense of your Kindness, and good Opinion by throwing out such Hints, as may awaken your Discussion. My elder Pupil will work with Pleasure, assisted by one, who can bestow sufficient Portion of his Time, to illustrate the occasional Difficulties which may arise in the Books, which he will have to construe, and will I am convinced do himself Credit by his Compositions, when a few preparatory Hints shall have been well digested by mature Reflection. My two younger Charges will require an occa⁄ sional Spur, and will I trust profit more under the closer Inspection of a private Tutor than under the very fractional Care of their present Instructor. They neither of them want of application but certainly have no Aversion to Play, if they can contrive it, without Hazard of certain Punishments, which I fear Experience taught them is not to be very pleasant in their Operations. I am fully sensible that private Tutors might be found, who would most gladly undertake an Employment of this Nature for a more moderate Salary, but I doubt much, whether you or I should approve of them, and I should not think that I was doing Justice to your general Character did I supose that the Difference of a certain Number of Pounds for a few Years would influence you on so important an Occasion. I again add that I am convinced that your Sons will reap more Advantage from the Scheme you have done me the Honor to consult me upon, than from their continuance under my Care, and that I should consider myself as utterly unworthy of the Confidence of any Parent, did I endeavour to throw any unnecessary Obstacles in the Way of what I conceive so likely to ensure the future Well doing of great part of Family, for whom, I can not but feel interested. You will not I trust scruple to make any Enquiries of or lay Commands upon me, which it is possibly in my Power to satisfy or to execute. With best Comp^ts to Mrs Arkwright I have the Honor to be, Dear Sir,

y^r truly obliged & obed^t humble Servt

J Goodall

But, for the time being, John and Charles were sent to the Free Grammar School at Ashbourne, the recently appointed headmaster of which the Rev. Paul Belcher, provided instruction 'in the Eaton way'. Arkwright had been introduced to the school by Francis Beresford, a founder of the Butterley Company, whose neice was to marry his eldest son, Richard, in 1803:

Francis Beresford to Richard Arkwright   Ashbourne 23^d July 1797

Dear Sir

I have seen Mr Belcher who informs me that he teaches the Eaton Grammar, and that all the Boys in his School are intructed in the Eaton way, in which he was himself educated. Mr Belcher further adds that he shall be happy to receive your two young Gentlemen as soon as may be, and the sooner the better, since his School opens again to morrow after the midsummer Holydays. I told him of your intention to send them to the upper school at Eaton next Easter, and also of your design to send another Son to Ashbourne at Christmas.

I hope when you bring the young Gentlemen to Ashbourne you will introduce them to my Family and be assured that we shall be happy to shew them any civility in our Power. With the best regards of all this House to M.ʳˢ Arkwright yourself & Family I am

dear Sir Yours very Sincerely

Fran.ˢ Beresford

My Gardener will take this to Cromford.

Our only glimpse of Ashbourne is given in two letters to Arkwright, one of them from John and the other from the Rev. Belcher:

Ashbourne 28ᵗʰ 1797

Dear Father

As most of the boys want to subscribe fifteen shillings a piece and as all of them have given three parts of the money they have or at least most of the boys I should be glad if you will send me and Charles half a guinea a piece and we will make up the rest for Mʳ Belcher wants us all to give the same I told the boys this morning I thought it very unreasonable and they called me a Jacobin Mʳ Moore¹ˢ of Appleby subscribed five hundred pound and Mʳ Berresford only subscribed ten pound only. M.ʳ William Walker was so good as to give us a football on shrove tuesday and as we were playing the town boys came to take it from us they said they would only we were too many for them so we said we would let no more or our boys hinder them from taking it than they had on their side nor no bigger so we put the football before their feet and no one dare touch it

I am Dear Father

your ever dutiful son John Arkwright

Ashbourn Dec.ʳ 7ᵗʰ 1799.

Dear Sir,

We break up here, on Saturday, the 21ˢᵗ instant & I believe you know, that I wish none of my Pupils to leave me, before the day, on which the vacation commences. Your sons have all behav'd very well, and John & Charles are exceedingly improv'd in their knowledge of the Greek language & are quite masters of the Grammar. I am sorry, they should give Mʳˢ Arkwright the trouble of coming over, without first mentioning to me their want of clothes. Upon examination, I found, that they were perfectly whole, though the worse for wear & might have serv'd till the vacation. However, as Mrs. Arkwright seem'd to wish it, I have procur'd them each a new suit. Mrs. Belcher joins me in best compliments to Mrs. Arkwright. I am Dear Sir

Your most obed.ᵗ Servant,

P. Belcher

P.S. If John & Charles leave me at Midsummer, you will oblige me by

[263]

information, as I have several applications for vacancies.

In 1802 Dr Goodall succeeded Dr Heath as Head Master of Eton. He displayed, according to Thackeray, 'a peculiar talent of finding out and stirring up latent powers'[16] and, unlike his predecessor and Dr John Keate, who was to succeed him, was a mild disciplinarian — an attribute soon to prove of more than mere academic interest to John and Charles Arkwright (Peter had left by this time), as the following letters reveal.

Dr Joseph Goodall to Richard Arkwright   52 St James's Decr 22nd 1801

Dear Sir

The College having done me the Honor to appoint me Head master, I am no longer at Liberty to retain my Pupils. It would be a great Satisfaction to me, on this Occasion, to be able to say, that I thought my young Friend's Progress had been as great, as I could reasonably have expected; but I should violate Truth, were I to boast of the Elegance or Accuracy of their Compositions. I must therefore content myself with saying, that if they do not deserve Paneygric, they have at least so conducted themselves, as not to merit my Censure. In some subordinate Points there is perhaps somewhat to amend; but I shall hope still to continue a watchful Eye over them, and by frequent Visits at their House prevent the Growth of any Misconduct. To me personally they always have behaved with the utmost Propriety, and as I am induced to hope that they will not by any Irregularity offend me as their Master, when they have never offended as their Tutor. Our discipline must be tightened, and exemplary Punishment must await any one, who may wantonly provoke it. My only Reason for throwing out these Hints is, that parental Admonition may be added to any public Lecture which I may eventually be compelled to deliver. If they should become Parties in the Boats, and should presume to protract their Absence from their Houses, beyond the proper Period, or wilfully neglect their Attendance at the regular School Absence in the Evening, I shall consider such Neglect as a very flagrant offence. But I still hope, that they will have the good Sence so to behave themselves, that they may deserve the Approbation of their Tutor, Master, and Parents.

Mrs Goodall unites in best Comp^{ts} to yourself and Mrs Arkwright, and in Kindest Remembrances to the Etonians of past and present Times, with, Dear Sir,

Y^r most obliged and obedient humble Servt

J Goodall

Mrs S. Harrington to Richard Arkwright   Eton Thursday the 21.st Jan^{ry} 1802

Dear Sir,

I am truly hurt at the contents of your letter this morning, I have made every enquiry, & write the debts on the other side — the drinking of Porter in my House, I had hoped coud not be without discovery — I had had my suspicions that some of my family were in the habit of going to the Inn for it, but I flatter'd myself that it had ended after the Election holidays.

Previous to that time, I had found out that there had been some brought into the house, & with one of my family. I prevented it, & hoped it was an evil that woud not happen again. The servant who waits upon your Gentlemen declares it was unknown to her — I grieve at your having such just cause for uneasiness & dissatisfaction — I can only say, so relaxed has the discipline been of late, that all errors have encreased most generally, & that the present change of master will give an opportunity for many alterations, & I trust most essential benefit will ensue. Let me hope that you will venture to make another trial of this school, & my endeavours shall be exerted to make the Gentlemens future conduct to your comfort — truly

I am dear Sir your ever Oblig'd & Obedent

S. Harrington

John's debts, Mrs Harrington revealed, amounted to £15 1s, and those of Charles to £8 14s 2d.

Dr Joseph Goodall to Richard Arkwright   Eton Jany 22 1802

Dear Sir

I am mortified beyond Measure at the Subject of your to Mrs Harrington, but hope, that you will not, on my Account, pay such Debts, contracted not more to the Disgrace of the Individual, than to the Prejudice of the School. So new am I in my Authority, that I know not with what Powers I am legally armed, but I shall certainly use every Means in my power to prevent a Renewal of the Licence of the Tapster (for I beg to observe, that the Master of the Inn is, in this Point at least, innocent, as the Tap is entirely a separate Concern) and at all Events shall shew my marked Disapprobation of such Proceedings. In Regard to the Guns &c, I am shocked to find that such Irregularity has been systematically practised. Against Offences of this Nature I am determined to shew the full Weight of my Displeasure nor will I suffer any Boy to continue at Eton, who shall a second Time be convicted of practising so unwarrantable & dangerous an Amusement. I am no longer surprized at the little Progress made in my late Pupils' Studies. Unless they return, fully determined to alter their Conduct, I much fear, that they will find themselves in the most unpleasant Predicament, that can await Boys, who have any Regard to their Character. Without knowing any thing of their Water Expences, I have already expressed my Apprehensions in the Letter, which I did myself the Honor to write from Town.

I beg Leave to observe, that a Refusal to pay their Debts at least for the present, is likely to be productive of general Good, and the personal Inconveniencies they may suffer from being debtors they have richly deserved. If parents would be firm in resisting such Demands, I think the Evil would ultimately be crushed; but perhaps it is expecting too much to desire them to do a Violence to their own

Feelings on the Occasions and to expose their sons to the possible Obloquy, that may arise from the very People who have ministered to their Irregularities.

It would be very unjust in me to take Advantage of your Son's voluntary Confession, and do any thing harsh in the present Instance, but I must avail myself of my Knowledge of these unpleasant Facts to admonish them through you, and to express my Hopes, that no fresh Circumstances of the same Nature will ever bring to my Memory the Cause of my present Letter. Idleness & Sottishness are bad Guides in any Situation and can certainly never be considered as good Handmaids of Education. If a Boy's Time is dedicated to his Improvement, he will find little Leisure for improper Pursuits. Innocent Relaxations may always be found at a public School, and that Boy chooses very unwisely, who prefers Anxiety to Tranquility, and Disgrace to a fair Reputation.

In Regard to myself I should be very sorry that any of your Sons should leave Eton in a discreditable Manner, but I must avow my Determination to bolt to the very Bran any Improprieties which may come under my Notice, and I shall feel it to be my Duty to separate the Wheat from the Tares, whenever Circumstances may call on me to do so. With a grateful Lease of your Kindnesses & a Hope that a radical Reformation may be effected, where it is confessedly wanted believe me to be with best Comp^{ts} to Mrs Arkwright Dear Sir, yr most obliged

& obed humble Servt

J Goodall

By the time Arkwright's youngest son, Joseph, had gone to Eton in 1805 or 1806 Richard, who had been admitted as a Fellow-Commoner to Trinity College, Cambridge, in 1801 and had married two years later, decided to make his career in politics. He wrote to his father from Normanton Turville on 3 February 1806:

I have never before mentioned the subject to you tho I have long had a wish to be in Parliament and [as] I know you have not any intention of taking a seat yourself I write to say how happy you would make me by purchasing for me a Borough. I mention a Borough as the standing a contested Election is what I should by no means like more especially as the popularity & the consequence attached to such a situation is not my object. Not having any particular profession I feel that by going in to Parliament I should have an incitement to improve myself in the knowledge of the Laws and Constitution of the Country and Associating with some of the most clever men in the Kingdom.

Tho I despair of ever being *distinguished* as an *orator* yet I can safely say should you concede to my request you should not have cause to regret it by seeing me vote in support of any measure apparently contrary to true principle or spirit of Independence.

But it was not until 1812 that, with his father's backing, Richard contested Nottingham borough, Daniel Parker Coke, its Member since 1780, having declined to stand, at the same time offering him his support.[17] In an election, said to have cost Arkwright £20,000,[18] he was defeated by John Smith and Lord Rancliffe 'after a singular contest, in which the beauty and wit of Lady Rancliffe were most efficiently exerted'.[19] 'My Lady Rancliffe,' John Ark-wright, who was assisting Richard, wrote to his father on 13 October, 'canvesses in Person & Kisses the greasy chops of any person who will give her a vote. George Holcombe rides in the dicky of her barouche, and in that style they parade the streets with the mob. Whenever a vote appears coming into the town he is seized on by both parties, and unless very staunch, he is taken to a public house, made drunk and polled accordingly.' (And it was at this election that John obtained 'an idea of the pride of the Lowest orders. The omitting to call on them soliciting their vote is enough to make them vote for the first man, of whatever party he may be, who asks.') The following year, however, Richard was returned on a vacancy for the Treasury borough of Rye, and his name was added to the list of Members expected to support the government. Arkwright did not seek re-election in 1818 but was returned again as Member for Rye in 1826.

John Arkwright admitted to having no interest in politics. While yet up at Cambridge he had written to his father, 'We; (I mean most of the under-graduates (myself excepted)) are mad on politics. There is actually a Whig club, who meet dine and drink for the good of the nation. L^{ds} Harrington & Tavistock, at their Head, I suppose L^d H will be down in Derbyshire during the vacation.'

And in 1814, five years after graduating and having declined his brother Richard's offer of Normanton ('the Expense of Rent, furnishing and keeping such a house would prevent my being able to clothe myself like a Gentleman, besides as there would be no other *rational* amusement or employment than that of Foxhunting which lasts so short a time in the year, I should be obliged in order to keep off the blue devils to quit for some months, so that such a speculation would not pay'), he again confided to his father:

> I believe I have mentioned my wish of housekeeping to almost every one but you And indeed have pritty well considered the subject I feel that I could not with pleasure enter into any profession or business. I have no ambition of being employed in affairs of Church or state. I wish neither to be the Revd J. A nor J. A Esqre MP. but being tired of the life I now lead, without any desire of entering into the marriage state, I should like to have a home where I shall not be in the way of any one. Of all the situations I know; there is none which suits my tastes so well as Hampton Court. I do not mean that I wish to take a Lease of the Court, and the Furniture or a valuation, but should like to persuade Mr Nuttall, that he does not like the house in the Park, and that it would exactly suit me. I should like a small farm, grazing or breeding, with liberty to preserve, Shoot and Fish.
>
> I feel from your constant attention to the wishes of your Family that I need say nothing more on the Subject & that if you see no objection to my request it will be granted.

But another five years were to elapse before John took up residence at Hampton Court. For the previous decade his father, having failed to let, had shown a moderate degree of interest in the improvement of the property, but in the agricultural depression that followed the Napoleonic Wars he drastically cut even expenditure on estate maintenance.[20]

John persuaded his father to invest much more than Arkwright himself would have contemplated, and between 1819 and 1822 some £40,000 was spent on apparently rather trivial alterations. Work on the fabric of the house did not begin until 1834, six years after a neighbouring diarist had observed that Hampton Court 'would require a fortune to put into repair, and then would only be fit for a Prince to life in'.[21]

If John and Charles when at Eton had occasionally given their father cause for concern, so too did Joseph while yet an undergraduate at Trinity College, Cambridge. Arkwright viewed with distaste his son's undoubted extravagences and took an even more serious view of what he suspected to be his excessive taste for alcohol. Joseph well summed up the position after a conversation he had with his father during a visit to Hampton Court:

> I daresay you recollect that at the time I speak of you accused me of drunkenness and extravagance.
>
> There can be no stronger instance of my inability to justify myself when tax'd with a fault, than in the case where I was unable to convince you that I was not a drunkard.
>
> The one which I shall now mention, you will probably consider as an argument in my favour. When I first came to Cambridge, M.ʳ Tavel, the Tutor of my College said that as I came at a term when it was very common for fresh comers to be idle & disorderly (not having much College duty to attend to) he should watch my conduct very strictly: when I went to take my leave of him for the vacation, he said that he was very well pleas'd with my behaviour, & that he anticipated attention and steadiness during my stay at Cambridge.
>
> I have also naturally a great aversion to being drunk, and although I do not mean to say that I have never upon any occasion overcome that aversion, yet it is not a common practise with me: and I assure you I have gain'd a certain degree of odium among some sets at Cambridge, by leaving parties when I have perceiv'd that my stay must inevitably have attended with drunkenness.
>
> As to my extravagance; your charge in that respect was neither so unexpected or so unjust; I am well aware that I am not an œconomist; I am aware that I am extravagant; your allowance to me has always been liberal, and in the hands of some would have been more than sufficient; yet I must confess that I have during my life experienc'd more uneasiness on the subject of money than on any other.
>
> Although I may in a great measure throw away the money which you allow me, still I flatter myself that my expences are not less innocent than those of the generality of young men; perhaps the expences of the generality are less innocent than mine.

Believe me this subject has been a matter of considerable uneasiness to me ever since I saw you & I do not know that I could had had a better opportunity of importing my sentiments to you than the present. I wrote to John a short time since about some Venison which I believe I was promised; if you can spare it now it will be very acceptable.[22]

Joseph's next letter to his father returned to the same themes:

Before I receiv'd your letter this morning I had intended writing to thank you for the Venison, which arriv'd a few days ago safe and perfectly good. I have now also to return my thanks for your letter.

Notwithstanding the full discussion of the subjects which have for the most part occupied the sheets of our late letters; and your declar'd wish as well as my own hearty desire that these subjects should not again be renew'd; I must confess that I can't refrain from expressing my sentiments upon an opinion which you have form'd from my first letter to you. I am glad to find that you did not formerly suspect me of drunkenness; but I am at the same time sorry in much greater degree to find that you *now* do.

You say that you do not recollect any hint that you gave me of your suspicions of my being a Drinker. The whole of the conversation to which I allude, made so great an impression upon me, that I believe I could nearly repeat the words which you spoke. You will remember no doubt that you desir'd me to mention some of my chief expences at Cambridge, among which I spoke of 9 doz^n Wine; you seem'd much surprised that *I* should have drank so great a quantity in so short a time; I argued that it was not I but my friends who had drank it: your argument (which I daresay you also recollect) that *I* had drank the above said quantity although not out of my own cellar, was strong, but not sufficiently so to convince me; for if I had drank this quantity I should (upon a minute calculation) have been drunk every day during the last term, and knowing that I never was the least so but once, you will not consider me obstinate if my ideas do not coincide with yours.

'In regard to my Extravagance; as I have not so good grounds to work upon, that subject will not again be renew'd by me,' Joseph's letter concluded. And small wonder, for he was to continue to make repeated requests for additions to his already generous allowance. 'Knowing that when I came of age I should be entitled to the same sum of money which my Brothers all were, and which all of them have receiv'd, I have deferred the payment of several bills untill this time,' he told his father just thirteen days after his twenty-first birthday, adding that he congratulated himself 'upon the prospect of returning to Cambridge free from all debt. The part of my capital which I propose to dispose of in the above mention'd manner is five hundred pounds, and which I shall be very much obliged to you if you will place in the hands of Mr Mortlock, Banker, Cambridge.' Although now, as earlier, Arkwright complied with his son's wishes, Joseph had to wait another three years before receiving his £20,000 coming-of-age gift.[23]

When on another occasion Joseph wrote to acknowledge the receipt of £300 he professed to accept his father's maxim 'That no person is so dependent, or so little capable of enjoying what he has, as he whose expenditure exceeds his income.' But on 22 May 1814, the day after this ordination, came Joseph's plea for £800: 'This very large demand will not I am sure induce you to recant the opinion which I have so often heard you give respecting my inevitable ruin.'

A week later in a letter thanking his father for the money ('I can assure you I feel far greater than common sentiments of gratitude; and I trust that my future conduct will convince you that you have not conferred this, and many other favours upon me unworthily') Joseph went on to give an account of the rather inauspicious start he had made to his chosen vocation:

> I yesterday commenced my preaching career; I did not escape without having made sundry blunders during the service; for instance, preaching from the desk instead of the Pulpit; reading a morning Psalm instead of an evening one; kneeling down, when I ought to have been standing up.
>
> On my entering the Church, which was the smallest and worst in every sense that I have ever seen, I made the remark that there was no Pulpit, and I don't know at this time where it could have been; there was one however some where or other, for the Clerk asked Jim after the service, whether I had been much used to preaching, for I had neglected to go *'into the other place.'* I fear such proceedings as these would have astonished and shocked an enlightened Cromford congregation.

But Joseph, who in 1820 became vicar of Latton, a living that went with his father's Mark Hall estate, was a parson in little more than name. A curate had charge of the parish, and Joseph could be depended upon to appear in the pulpit only on Christmas Day. It is as a well known huntsman, Master of the Essex Foxhounds at a time when Anthony Trollope, then living at Waltham Cross, was gaining his knowledge of the field, that the Rev. Joseph Arkwright is best remembered.[24] It was a passion that has its beginnings during his Cambridge years. 'I am quite certain that my extravagancies will for the future be much diminished in magnitude and number, particularly the article of horse-flesh; the superabundance of which hitherto in my possession, you, no less than myself, are undoubtedly convinced of,' Joseph had written to his father on 22 June 1814. But five months later Arkwright was asked: 'Will you be so good as to let £300 be paid into Mortlock's for me. . . . I fear you and others must think me rather hunting-mad, having four horses. It will however I trust be some palliation for me, that you and all my acquaintance know that this line of conduct will be persued by me but for a very short period.'[25]

Arkwright made generous financial provision for his children. Thus Richard was given £30,000 in 1803, the year of his marriage, £500 a year from 1805 to 1821 and, from 1810, the rents of the Normanton Turville estate, worth some £1,500 a year. Peter received £500 in 1805 when he married his cousin

Mary Anne, daughter of Charles and Susanna Hurt, and £3,000 for furniture two years later. Robert was given £500 when he married in 1805; he also received £3,000 for furniture in 1812, as did Charles, who had married the previous year. Arkwright's daughter Elizabeth was given £15,000 on her marriage in 1802 to Francis Edward Hurt, of Alderwasley, as was Anne sixteen years later when she married James Wigram,[26] of Walthamstow. In addition Elizabeth was allowed £500 a year from 1805 and Anne the same sum from 1820 to 1828 from which time she had double the amount. Special provision was made for Arkwright's invalid daughter, Frances.

In 1833 each of Arkwright's five sons (Richard had died the previous year) was given £3,000, and from 1834 each received £2,000 a year. There were, in addition, spectacular gifts of £20,000 each to Robert, Peter, John and Charles in 1811, to Joseph in 1815 and to each of his sons in 1822 and again in 1828 and in 1840. It was probably these gifts that came to the notice of William Gardiner, who recounts in his *Music and Friends*, published in 1838:

> The private wealth of he present Mr. Arkwright has grown to such an enormous sum, by his unostentatious mode of living, that, excepting Prince Esterhazy, he is the richest man in Europe. A few years back I met his daughter. Mrs. Hurt,[27] of Derbyshire, on a Christmas visit at Dr. Holcomb[e]'s,[28] and she told me that a few mornings before, the whole of her brothers and sisters, amounting to ten, assembled at breakfast at Will[er]sley Castle, her father's mansion. They found, wrapt up in each napkin, a ten thousand pound bank-note, which he had presented them with as a Christmas-box. Since that time I have been informed that he has repeated the gift, by presenting them with another hundred thousand pounds.[29]

In all, from 1802 to 1841, Arkwright made gifts to his children of sums totalling £741,731; or, if we follow the practice adopted in his accounts of adding compound interest at 5 per cent a year to each gift from the time it was made, £1,949,226.

Although Johann Georg May, a Prussian civil servant sent to England in 1814 to report on the manufacturing districts, noted that Arkwright lived 'in the style of a lord',[30] his expenditure was in fact modest enough. And even when, a quarter of a century later, his income exceeded £100,000 a year he continued to live without ostentation, his 'House expences' amounting to some £2,800 a year. (It was a sum which, presumably, did not include the £1,000 he set aside for 'Sundries, Christ⁵ Bills &cr' — as, for example, £2 to his 'Keeper' at Cromford, as to those on his other estates, 10s to each of his '6 Maid Servants' — or his gifts to relatives and friends).

Of these latter we have information for the late 1830s and early 1840s. Mary, daughter of Arkwright's nephew Richard Simpson, received £100 on the occasion of her marriage in July 1841[31] to Captain Alexander Taubman Goldie, RN, son of Lieutenant General Goldie, as two months[32] later did

Caroline, daughter of John Ryle, on her marriage at Marylebone to the Rev. William Courthope, second son of George Courthope, of Bedford Square, London, and of Whiligh, Sussex. Caroline's mother, Susanna, daughter of Charles and Susanna Hurt, was given £150 in March 1842, her sons John Charles and Fredrick William £50 each and two of her daughters £25 each. A year later 'John & Fred & 2 Sisters Ryle' shared £140.

In the five years beginning February 1838 a total of £640 went to Francis Hurt and to five of his sisters, the children of Arkwright's daughter Elizabeth, the wife of Francis Edward Hurt. Another of the Hurt sisters, Mary, who in 1825 had married the Hon. Robert Eden, rector of Eyam, Derbyshire, received 'a present' of £100 in 1838 and again in 1839 and 1841 (when 'Eliz Eden, her daughter' had £3). Robert, who was chaplain to King William IV and to Queen Victoria, became third Baron Auckland on the death of his brother in 1849 and five years later was appointed Bishop of Bath and Wells.[33] A further £400 was given to Cecelia[34] (daughter of Robert Norman by his wife, Lady Elizabeth Manners, daughter of the fourth Duke of Rutland), wife of Arkwright's grandson, Francis Hurt. And on 29 May 1840 Francis had £100 'on going to London'.

John Wolley, grandson of Charles and Susanna Hurt (John's father, the Rev. John Francis Thomas Hurt, vicar of Beeston, Nottinghamshire, had changed his name to Wolley on the death of his father-in-law in 1827), received £824 10s between January 1838 and March 1842. All but £24 10s was, it seems, to provide for 'schooling expences' at Eton. John's younger brothers Charles (Newcastle Medallist, President of 'Pop' and later Assistant Master at Eton) and Edward, both of whom followed him to Cambridge, received £13 10s and 7s 6d respectively. Another brother, George, had £18. Philip Anthony Hurt of Wirksworth, grandson of Charles and Susanna, received £1 on each of five separate occasions (£3 of this 'for translating') between December 1838 and July 1840. And on 1 February 1842, when now a student at St John's College, Cambridge, Arkwright gave him £10.

Mrs Mary Gilbert, a daughter of John Simpson Arkwright's brother-in-law and wife of Captain Edmund Gilbert, RN, a lineal descendant of the Elizabethan navigator, received 'a present' of £100 in 1839 and the same amount on her visit to Ireland in the summer of the following year.

There were also specific gifts, as when, within a space of just under three years, eight of Arkwright's grandsons each received £50 with which to buy a horse and £20 was given to his granddaughters Emma Wigram in June 1842 to buy a watch.

The *Derby Mercury* and Arkwright's accounts and notebooks reveal something of his wider interests. There were in addition to his annual donation of ten guineas to the Derby General Infirmary gifts of £1,000 in 1805 [35] and again in 1807. To the Nottingham General Hospital he contributed £200 in 1802[36] and 100 guineas in 1816.[37]

Religious organisations benefited from his support. To the Derby Bible Society (an offshoot of the British and Foreign Bible Society) he donated ten guineas in 1812,[38] the year after its foundation. There were his annual two-guineas suscriptions to the Society for Promoting Christian Knowledge and to the Society for the Relief of the Families of Distressed Clergymen (founded at Derby in 1812).[39] In 1836 he contributed £100 to the relief of Irish clergy.[40]

Schools at Heage and Darley, Bonsall and Wirksworth Churches and Sunday schools, and Marple Church received his support. Cromford Chapel had its special place, as had Cromford's schools, as is shown by an account in the *Derby Mercury* of 24 September 1834 of the work of the school in North Street:

> On Thursday last the boys belonging to the School lately established by Mr. Arkwright, underwent a public examination. There were present several ladies and gentlemen, together with many of the children's parents, who expressed themselves highly satisfied with the result. The excellent order in which the boys are kept, together with their manifest improvement do Mr. Shaw, the conductor, great credit. A school so liberally supported and judiciously managed, must confer great benefit upon the town and neighbourhood. The system of education adopted is that of the late Dr. Bell, as used in the National Schools. The number of scholars in the Sunday school is 170, of which 130 belong to the day school. After the examination, the children were all treated with buns and wine. On Saturday the girls belonging to the same school, assembled at their room in the school, and proceeded to Rock House, the residence of Peter Arkwright, Esq. where 122 sat down to tea upon the lawn in front of the house. Every attention that hospitality could dictate, was paid to them by Mrs. and the Miss Ark-wrights.[41]

Arkwright contributed to collections to provide clothing for the poor of Matlock, Wirksworth, Bonsall and Derby as well as for coal at Bonsall and Middleton. The Matlock Labourers' Fund received £20 (February 1831). an 'Old Soldier' was given £1, as was a 'Distressed Seaman' on Christmas Eve 1839.

To the Derby Assembly Rooms he gave £50 in 1818, 1827 and 1828 and perhaps also on other occasions. He made one-guinea subscriptions to 'Concerts' (where is not stated), to the Harmonic Society at Wirksworth and to the Cromford Singers. On two occasions he subscribed one guinea to the Derby Races. Collections at Cromford and at Matlock to celebrate the corona-tion of Queen Victoria were each given £10.

A considerable part of Arkwright's expenditure, especially in the years following the death of his father, must have gone on his absorbing interest, the gardens of Willersley. John Webb,[42] architect and landscape gardener, of Lee Hall, Armitage, near Lichfield, a former pupil of William Eames, was commissioned to lay out the grounds, and by 1802 some 350,000 trees had been planted.

From the beginning Willersley was opened to the public from sunrise to sunset on Mondays and Thursdays, when George Stafford, Arkwright's long-service gardener, conducted a stream of visitors over the extensive walks and through the hothouses, noted for their pineapples, melons and peaches but above all for their winter grapes, cultivated since 1806 by a method which earned for Arkwright the gold medal of the Horticultural Society of London.[43] Among royalty to visit the grounds were Archdukes John and Louis of Austria in 1815, and Queen Adelaide and the Duchess of Saxe-Weimar in 1840, upon which occasion, reported the *Derby Mercury*:

> On arriving at Willersley grounds the carriages containing her Majesty and suite were ordered to drive down the chapel walk;[44] on perceiving which the venerable Richard Arkwright, Esq., came on to the terrace in front of Willersley and waved his handkerchief to her Majesty who condescendingly returned his kind attention. We regret her Majesty did not go over the whole of the beautiful grounds of Willersley, for of that kind, a wild and lovely scenary there is scarcely anything *like them*.[45]

Another royal visitor, the Duke of Sussex, viewed the grounds in September 1842.

Arkwright's Memoranda Commencing 1818 notebook, a leather-bound volume with entries down to 1842, shows that in 1819 he was paying assessed taxes of six male servants (the same number as in 1810) and that he then 'Gave the assessor notice of a reduction of one Servant one Horse & one 4 wheeled Carriage'. The servant referred to was probably Richard Redfern, who had been at Willersley for at least sixteen years, was now earning eighteen guineas a year, and of whom Arkwright noted on 5 April 1819 was 'To discontinue being a Servant'.

Of Arkwright's nine house servants (four male and five female) in 1843 several had been with him for many years. Jeremiah Ashmole, his coachman, had come in 1828 (though not in that capacity) at £18 a year. By 1836 his wages had increased to £22, in addition to which he received clothes to the value of £17 6s 11d. A note against his name reads, 'To be 40£ next year,' apparently an indication that he was now to receive money in place of an allowance for clothing. The previous coachman was William Gilbert, an entry for whom records:

came here from P. Arkwright's			
Tuesday 16 August 1822			
To have wages 20 Gs	21	0	0
Boots & Breeches 1 Gs ea	2	2	0
Aged 30	23	2	0

Another servant, John Whitehead, came to Willersley in 1825, becoming footman at £21 a year in 1832 and butler the following year at £50 in succession to Joseph Hunt, whose wife Fanny had been Arkwright's house keeper. Whitehead was succeeded as footman by twenty-two-year-old Thomas Gretton, who in turn was followed on 5 January 1837 by twenty-five-year-old Thomas Murfin, who was 'To have 19£ a year Clothes as usual'. (He received clothes to the value of £29 8s 9d in the four years 1839-42.) On 8 October 1838 the Memoranda records, 'Gave Tho⁵ Murfin notice to leave cancelled Decem.ʳ 1838.' On 5 January 1839 Arkwright noted, 'No advance next year,' but the following year he increased Murfin's wages by £1 to £21. By 1843 Murfin was earning £40, a sum which presumably included a previous allowance for clothing.

From time to time there were difficulties with servants. Shortly before moving into Willersley Arkwright received an inquiry from Richard Ramsbottom,⁴⁶ distiller, of Aldersgate Street, one-time acquaintance of Sir Richard, 'an old and much esteemed friend' for whom he retained a 'very respectful remembran ce . . . for his accumulated civilities'. Ramsbottom was seeking Arkwright's 'opinion and character' of John Bark, until recently his butler. 'Honesty, sobriety, civility and a long string of good qualities,' Ramsbottom stressed, 'are desirable acquisitions in Servants; but as they are generally mixt with faults, I shall be much oblig'd to you to communicate such, as, you may think it necessary and proper, he should be apprized of, and cautioned against.'⁴⁷

Arkwright had then recently received complaints about James Staggalls, his Cromford gamekeeper, about whom his neighbours wrote on 22 January 1795:

> M.ʳˢ Gell presents her compliments to Mr. Arkwright. She is very sorry to give him any trouble; but must request he will be so good to restrain his Gamekeeper from shooting the Woodcocks, & Wild Ducks, in the Via Gellia, not only as M.ʳ & Mrs. Gell have many Friends who like the diversion, but as the firing Guns there disturbs their Pheasants, which are with great pains, & care, foddered there, & become very tame. She also desires M.ʳ Arkwright's dogs may not be hunted there, as not only game, but trees are destroyed by that means and as the whole extent of the Via Gellia is the peculiar plaything of Mr. & Mrs Gell, & the ornamenting of it, & rendering the Game happy there, their most agreeable amusement, it is hoped M.ʳ Arkwright cannot think them blameably tenacious if they feel much dissatisfied to hear of the Cromford Gamekeeper making it the scene of his destruction diversion.

Staggalls replied two days later, but if the gamekeeper's future letters are any guide his note can hardly have been his own unaided work:

> Sir
> I am very sorry and humbly ask you pardon for taking the Liberty of coming a little way upon you manor upon the Turnpike Road, and never was ten yards out of it, I happened upon some Snipes and Shot four of them, and one Mallard,

which you may have if you will exept of them, Woodcocks I never shot one, neither was it my intention to seek after any, though we keepers in general take Liberty one with another with such things that are not Game, for of such we have plenty at home, I once more humbly beg you Pardon, but desire that Mr Ishman will be very cautious how he shoots without Licence.

> I am your Very Humble Servt
> Jas Staggalls

Cromford Jany 24.th 1795

A successor of Staggalls, Samuel Smith (one wonders if he was a relative of John Smith,[48] who began his working life with Sir Richard and remained at Willersley for upwards of half a century) must have given Arkwright some cause for concern. In November 1833 he was sentenced to three months' imprisonment in Derby gaol for poaching and was fined £20 for carrying a gun without having a certificate. Smith's wages at the time were £46 a year exclusive of extras.

But it was twenty-three-year-old James Taylor, previously employed by James Stansfield, of Stockport, who, Arkwright noted on 24 September 1834, 'Came to Willersley this day. To have 28£ wages no parquisites whatever, a smock frock in the year', who drew from him his sharpest comment. 'This man turned out a Scoundrel,' he recorded in his Memoranda on 6 April 1835, the date of Taylor's departure from Willersley. He had by that time earned £11 12s 9d (including £1 7s 6d for catching 110 rats). Arkwright gave him £12.

Like earlier generations of his family a Tory, 'the mainstay of Conservatism' in Derbyshire, Arkwright was nevertheless reluctant to enter public life and in July 1795 declined the invitation of Henry Walshman,[49] Mayor of Preston and son of one of his father's oldest acquaintaces, to contest the borough on the death of Sir Henry Hoghton, Bart, one of its Members of Parliament since 1768.

An admirer of Sir Robert Peel, the son of his friend, the first baronet, Arkwright supported the policies of William Huskisson and would have agreed with Greville that 'It is probably true that there is no man in Parliament, or perhaps out of it, so well versed in Finance, commerce, trade, and Colonial matters.'[50] Of Wellington Arkwright's view corresponded with that of his son, Richard, who wrote to him of the Prime Minister, 'The Duke of Wellington works himself so by his close attention to business that he cannot obtain sufficient sleep; they say he enquires into, and examines every thing of any importance, more than was ever done by any one in his situation.' And when at a meeting held at the Mansion House in may 1837 it was decided to open a public subscription for a bronze equestrian statue of the duke by Sir Francis Chantrey, Arkwright contributed fifty guineas.[51]

It was at a Conservative dinner at the Red Lion inn, Wirksworth, to celebrate the birthday of the Duke of Wellington that Peter Arkwright, in reply to E. M. Mundy's toast to his father as one 'whose influence has always been exerted in defence of Conservative principles . . . [and] the father of children . . . educated in the same principles', maintained that although there was not 'a more staunch or a better Conservative in his Majesty's dominions . . . [Arkwright] troubled himself little about politics'.[52]

There is truth in this view, for, as was later to be said of him, Arkwright was never 'the indiscriminating advocate of any ultra or party question'.[53] And it was an attitude shared by his son, Joseph, who, having voted for William Cavendish at the Cambridge University election of 1829, had applied for membership of the Pitt Club. 'I went to Cambridge yesterday to vote for M.ʳ Cavendish,' he wrote to his father. 'I believe I am considered rather heterodox by some of my friends for so doing; but besides Whig & Tory considerations there are others which make me take an interest in the success of that Gent.'' Called upon to justify his application, Joseph's letter read:

> I am now anxious to state more fully that I do not, and why I do not, feel guilty of any inconsistency in wishing to become a member of the Pitt Club, and at the same time giving my vote to Mr. Cavendish at Cambridge. I am a Tory, bred & born; my family, my connexions, and I may almost say my acquaintances are Tories. From habit, therefore, and from principle too (if a person so little versed in politics as I must confess myself to be may be allowed to say so) I am and always have been a decided Tory, and a disciple of the great Pitt. These are sufficient reasons, I think, for my wishing to be a member of the Pitt Club, more particularly when I see that the great statesmen of the present day whose characters I have always admired and still continue to admire are among the members of that Club. I allude more particularly to Lord Eldon, the Duke of Wellington & Mr. Peel.
>
> I will now give you my reasons for voting for Mr. Cavendish. I admit Mr. Cavendish to be a Whig, but his pretensions to represent the University are founded on other grounds, — those who brought him forward are of all parties, and it appears to me that no one, be he of what political party he may, need have any scruples on that score about giving him his vote. Mr. Cavendish has certainly distinguished himself in a most remarkable manner at Cambridge & I do not think that to represent the University in Parliament is a greater reward than he deserves nor do I think that the University could easily find a more fit person for that purpose. There is another consideration which weighs with me though perhaps it may be properly called a weakness. Mr. C. is a Derbyshire man and on that account I take an interest in his success.
>
> I have now given you an explanation which, whether it may be satisfactory or not to you, you certainly had a right, under the circumstances, to demand if you thought fit to do so. If, after the explanation I have given there is any thing in the principles of the Pitt Club which ought to preclude me from being a member, I have only to add that to the Pitt Club I have no wish to belong.[54]

Always guarded in his opinions, Arkwright never reached conclusions without deep thought and reflection. Whether, like the Strutts, he avowed sympathy with the Americans during the War of Independence or rejoiced with them at the news of the outbreak of the French Revolution is not known.[55] But there can be no doubt that, like them, he was later deeply moved by its excesses and on 21 May 1794 was present at a general meeting at the County Hall, Derby, 'one of the most respectable, from the number of gentlemen of weight and property, and of substantial freeholders, who attended it, . . . for the consideration of the Security of the County, and the Plans recommended by government for that purpose'. Among the resolutions passed was one 'that the Gentlemen and Yeomen of the County, present at this meeting, do pledge themselves to be in immediate readiness (the former with their chosen tenants and trusty servants) in SUPPORT OF THE CIVIL POWER, at the call of the Lord Lieutenant, the Sheriff, or the acting Magistrates; for the Suppression of Riots and Tumults of all description, and in any case of Real Danger with the County'.[56] Arkwright contributed £200 to a subscription raised at the meeting, a sum exceeded only by the Duke of Devonshire (£500) and Sir Henry Harpur, Bart (£300) and equalled only by Lord John Cavendish and Lord Vernon.[57]

In March 1798 Arkwright subscribed £2,000 towards the defence of the country[58] and a month later there were further 'Voluntary Contributions for Nation Defence' from Lady Arkwright (ten guineas) and by her servants (5s); Arkwright's own day labourers contributed £3 17s 6d, his house servants £4 11s and workpeople at the Cromford mills £45 10s 1d.[59]

On 30 April 1798 Arkwright was among the forty-two present at 'A general meeting of the Lieutenancy of the county of Derby' held at the County Hall at which it was unanimously resolved:

> THAT every endeavour should be made to call forth, that zeal and energy — that firm and manly courage, which, ever has, in trying conflicts, distinguished Britons, and which, at the present moment of danger, when we are menaced with destruction by a formidable and haughty enemy, is so essential to the protection of the many blessings we enjoy, and of the honour and Independency of our Country.[60]

The outcome of the meeting was the raising of Volunteer corps of Infantry in Derbyshire. Threatened with invasion by Revolutionary France, Pitt in 1794 had brought in his first Bill to facilitate the raising of a Volunteer and Yeomanry force by voluntary contributions. Derbyshire, less threatened than many counties, had so far not acted but by the end of 1798 infantry corps had been raised at Derby, Wirksworth and Ashbourne. In 1803 Robert (admitted the previous year as a FellowCommoner to Trinity College, Cambridge) and Peter Arkwright both received commissions as captain in the Supplementary Militia[61] and within four months Robert was in camp at Tynemouth, from which place he wrote to his father of conditions there and of his Cambridge and present allowances:

Tynemouth Novr 20th 1803.

My dear Father

I received a letter about a week since inclosed in one from Peter who does not seem to have a great deal of spare time from the shortness of his letters which I received since I came here, but hope soon to hear from him, when he will perhaps let me know what is going forward in your part of the world. We have very little to do now in the military line, as the days are so very cold, it is almost impossible to stand at their arms for two or three hours together, so that we have nothing to do now but to attend Parade twice a day, except guards. If the Weather is mild we shall be able to have a little hunting now if my horses are good enough, but I am afraid that they will not, as they are not made for hunting, being very heavy they will soon be tired, so that I am afraid that I must give up that plan. As for reading that is impossible, as we are interrupted every five minutes by calling upon us. We do not expect Gell for some time, altho' he fixed upon the 29th for the beginning of his journey, as we have so often heard of his setting off in a few days. When I left home you mentioned that my allowance was to be £200, which I am afraid I shall find very insufficient, as I find there are many small expences which the Captains are obliged to be at. My whole income will be a little more than £350 out of which I have to keep the whole of the Arms of my Company in repair, and bury all the men in my Comp^y who happen to die. When I was at Cambridge I think you allowed me more than that, when I was at home six Months in the Year, had only one horse to keep and dined at the College for about one third of the Expence I do now, altho we live very economically; you will perhaps have the goodness to take these into consideration at your leisure I now wish I had asked you to have let Redfern have come with me instead of Ralph, altho I am afraid he would not have been able to run about as Ralph does, at the same time, he would have taken much better care of my horses. Indeed I did mention it to my Mother but thinking that Redfern's leg might become weak it would be a very unpleasant thing at this distance from home. We have this day received an invitation from the Mayoress of Newcastle to a dance on the 1st of Decr We are now entirely free from all anxiety on account of the arrival of the French. Give my love to all at home and believe me your
dutiful Son
Robert Arkwright.

It must have been about this time that Robert met Frances Crawford, daughter of George Stephen Kemble, of the Theatre Royal, Newcastle upon Tyne, and niece of Mrs Siddons. Their marriage,[62] as the following letter from Richard reveals, was the cause of alarm and misgiving at Willersley:

Durham 1 July [1805] — Monday —

Dear Father,

On our arrival at Newcastle this afternoon we learnt that Robert was married to Miss Kemble on Thursday last —

We inspected the register & found that the licence had been granted by an old clergyman of 84, whose hand writing we saw, and which appeared to have been written upon pencil as if he was very infirm; We have no doubt he was given to believe that Miss Kemble had never quitted Newcastle, as we learnt at the Inn Kemble had given that out in the town — The marriage of course cannot be legal.

I called upon Kemble to enquire if he knew where my Brother was gone, he said he *believed* to Scarbro', not seeming to wish me to understand his daughter was with him. I told him he had behaved very ill in consenting to the marriage when he knew it was against the approbation of all my Brothers Friends; He said he had had very little to do with it having been at Coventry for the last month, wishing to suppose she had not been there but living at Newcastle. They certainly are gone to Scarbro —

I called at the Kembles after their dinner, saw M⁣ʳˢ K. & two of her sons & from their very vulgar apprearance and manners am quite at a loss to conceive how Robert could spend so much of time in their company — I said as little to Kemble as I could, as he seemed to be a composition of meaness, deep cunning & artifice & in short every thing that was bad; as *we* left the house the word 'damn'd' (with a theatrical stamp) came from his mouth but we could not make out the rest — We are more greived than ever for poor Robert from this specimen of the family with which he has thus imprudently connected himself; and he will no doubt soon repent of not having followed the advice of you and Mother —

We got a stage beyond Harrowgate last night by taking post horses from Leeds, & shall get back tomorrow night & hope you will let us hear from you very soon how my Mother & Bess are —

your affectionate Son
Richard Arkwright —

We wish to hear soon account of John —

Kemble was at first very much agitated & seemed conscious of having improperly acted & alarmed when I said the marriage was illegal —

But Robert's judgement — the memoirs and letters of Greville, of Harriet, Countess Granville[63] and of Thomas Moore[64] all confirm — was in this instance superior to that of his brothers. For a short time at Lumford Park,[65] near Bakewell, then at Stoke Hall, a stately stone mansion near Curbar, and from 1837 at Sutton Hall,[66] Frances became the engaging centre of the Arkwright circle. And more, a frequent visitor to Stoke Hall was Sarah Siddons,[67] by this time a confirmed friend of Richard Arkwright, who with his wife took up her invitations to call upon her when in London.[68] Frances Arkwright's story from the time of her marriage is best told by her cousin Frances Ann

Kemble in *Record of a Girlhood*:

Mrs. Arkwright went home to Stoke, to the lovely house and gardens in the Peak of Derbyshire, to prosperity and wealth, to ease and luxury, and to the love of husband and children. Later in life, she enjoyed, in her fine mansion of Sutton, the cordial intimacy of the two county magnets, her neighbours, the Dukes of Rutland and Devonshire, the latter of whom was her admiring and devoted friend till her death. In the society of the high-born and gay and gifted with whom she now mixed, and among whom her singular gifts made her remark-able, the enthusiasm she excited never impaired the transparent and childlike simplicity of her nature. There was something very peculair about the single-minded, simple-hearted genuineness of Mrs. Arkwright which gave an unusual charm of unconventionally and fervid earnestness to her manner and conversa-tion. I remember her telling me, with the most absolute conviction, that she thought wives were bound implicity to obey their husbands, for she believed that at the day of judgement husbands would be answerable for their wives' souls.

It was in the midst of a life full of all the most coveted elements of worldly enjoyment, and when she was still beautiful and charming, though no longer young, that I first knew her. Her face and voice were heavenly sweet, and very sad; I do not know why she made so profoundly melancholy an impression upon me, but she was so unlike all that surrounded her, that she constantly suggested to me the one *live* drop of water in the middle of a globe of ice. The loss of her favourite son affected her with irrecoverable sorrow, and she passed a great portion of the last years of her life at a place called Cullercoats, a little fishing village on the north coast, to which when a young girl she used to accompany her father and mother for the rest and refreshment, when the hard life from which her marriage released her allowed them a few days' respite by the rocks and sand and breakers of the Northumberland shore. The Duke of Devonshire, whose infirmity of deafness did not interfere with his enjoyment of music, was an enthusiastic admirer of Mrs. Arkwright, and her constant and affectionate friend. Their proximity of residence in Derbyshire made their opportunities of meeting very frequent, and when the Arkwrights visited London, Devonshire House was, if they chose it, their hotel. His attachment to her induced him, towards the end of his life, to take a residence in the poor little village of Cullercoats, wither she loved to resort, and where she died.[69]

Twenty-five years after Robert's marriage that of his younger brother John, then aged forty-four, to Sarah, twenty-three-year-old daughter of Sir Hungerford Hoskyns, Bart, of Harewood, Herefordshire, was preceded (apparently unn-ecessarily, as it turned out) by doubts and anxieties among John's family and friends. 'I confess he is so great a favourite of mine & I feel so much interested for his happiness, that I cannot fancy Miss H. will be the proper wife for him,' Margaret,[70] wife of the Rev. N. W. Robinson, wrote to his brother Joseph on 17 April 1829.[71] '23 years difference in age, I think *unfortunate*; persons who know her say her manners are artificial & that she has a very high spirit. Lady H. is so deceitful that I cannot fancy a daughter of hers & Sir Hungerford is such a snob & so abominably proud, but love is blind, they say, & Miss H is young & pretty looking.' And on 9 May 1829 Richard confessed to misgivings in a letter to his father:

> I conclude the subject of Johns letter to you is to state that he has thoughts of being married, I am not surprised at it altho when I saw him he did not admit that it was so, but did not deny the probability of such an event. I am very glad to hear it. I hope the young Lady is not too young, but I believe they have had some thoughts of it a good while. I do not exactly know her age, it has been long talked of *for them* among the Ladies.

'I am now on the tiptoe of expectation, respecting the affair I spoke of to you when we last met, and . . . I hope to communicate very shortly to you that the Lady has made up her mind,' John wrote to Joseph on 3 November 1829. A little over five months later he married.

Whatever Arkwright's own thoughts at the time Robert and John married, he did not seek to influence the political or other actions of his family, except perhaps where financial considerations were involved. This is made clear in letters from Richard, whose instinct was to stand firm against the claims for Catholic Emancipation being pressed by Daniel O'Connell. He wrote to his father from 30 Old Bond Street on 10 February 1829 of events in Parliament:

> I do not suppose that you will expect to hear any thing from me upon the subject which so much occupies every one at this time which you will not have learnt from the Papers, in which you will have seen much about Peel, the Duke of Wellington seems to have had less than his share of reproach from the protestant Journals — O'Connell has arrived in town I believe this morning he is at an Hotel in Dover Street where there is a crowd trying to get a sight of him at the Window. Nobody seems to know what he intends to do, as to taking his seat.
>
> It is expected that Peel in moving for leave for his Association Bill to night will state fully the substance of it. It seems that nothing short of a suspension of the Habeaus Corpus act will enable them to put down the Association. I cannot help thinking that those who now talk so triumphantly of the Emancipation Bill, as if passed, will be much disappointed at the intended enactments, and that it is the policy of the Duke in the first instance to get the Association well put down if possible, as a matter of previous necessity; and that his bill of concession will be such as to afford all possible security to the Portestants . . . [and] the catholics will be much disappointed, that it should fall so far from their expectations.

On 6 March 1829 Arkwright voted against Peel's motion that a committee of the whole House be set up to consider the laws imposing civil disabilities on Roman Catholics. He wrote to his father on 9 March:

You probably can form a pretty accurate opinion of what is going on here upon the Catholic question from the two opposing newspapers which you see, and the degree in which it excites the mind of the Public — I should long since have written to ask your opinion upon this question had you not always upon similar occasions declined to give it to me — I have therefore after the most embarrassing consideration, of all I have heard and seen taken upon myself in the exercise of my honest judgment to decide for myself — I think you will not be surprised to see my name in the list of the minority & I trust I have come to this decision with as little undue bias upon my mind as possible. Upon almost any other question, I should have been disposed to give up as much as possible my opinion to that of Ministers, who are so much better able in general to judge of all the bearings of questions, but upon this, I could not have been satisfied without judging for myself upon the Principle of the Measure ——— I have been told that with such feelings, I should do my duty better by abstaining altogether from giving a vote — This I could not consent to, as I think it right, that, having those opinions as I have, I should not shrink from the expression of them as to the Principle — I shall not prolong my letter by giving you any more of my reasons, but only to say that having very much attended to all that has been said & done in & out of Parliament, I should not have been satisfied with myself by any other conduct. I understand that it is the intention of the Minority, of which Bank[e]s is considered ·he leader in the House of Commons, to protract the discussion as much as possible ——— The friends of the Measure have been very much surprised at the largeness of the Minority, when it is recollected that so many parties have united, and that individual members have been induced to join them from various considerations — The majority in the House of Lords is variously estimated ———no doubt it will be considerable, and it is said that the King has decidedly made up his mind as a matter of necessity to go through with the measure — It is really a dreadfull thing to have at the head of the Protestant party one of the Royal Dukes[72] under such imputations as those stated against him and of which there seems too little doubt of the existence of proofs. They will I fear be brought before the public in a very short time — I hope you will excuse so long a letter upon the subject of myself and my opinions, but I could not resist the inclination to communicate them to you —

In the Commons three days later Arkwright spoke in defence of Francis Mundy,[73] whose presentation for a 'petition from Derby against further Concessions to the Catholics', signed by 8,876 people, had been attacked by Lord George Cavendish[74] as having been 'got up by the True Blue Club' and as unrepresentative of 'the sober sentiments of the people'.[75] 'I could not be surprised if Lord George should upon the presentation of the other petitions have recourse to the same means of vilefying them & of venting his violent feelings of opposition to the Independent Party in the County. If so I think I shall be much disposed to say a little more, as M.ʳ Mundy appears to by unwilling to state the case openly,' Richard wrote to his father from London on 17 March 1829, adding, 'I . . . am glad to think from the observations you made respecting the Great Question that you do not think I have come to the wrong decision upon it.'

Although perhaps rather surprisingly Arkwright thus gave approval to his son's vote against Peel's motion (Richard went on to vote against the second and third readings of the Roman Catholic Relief Bill) he viewed with less apprehension than many of his circle the campaign for parliamentary reform.

Richard, who had accepted with reluctance his father's decision that he should not contest the 1831 election, wrote to him from Sutton Scarsdale on 2 May 1831:

> I am very busy here superintending my workmen instead of being at Leicester ready for tomorrow morning. I cannot but regret the decision you came to upon this matter, but probably it was the best which could be come to. I do not feel however quite satisfied in these times of great public excitement upon a subject which if allowed to go too far, is certain to entail dangers upon the country. I know you do not feel strongly upon this subject, & I believe your opinions are not that much is to be apprehended.

The supposed dangers were spelt out by Sir James Wigram, Arkwright's son-in-law, who wrote to him on 23 May 1831:

> I hope you think favorably, or at least without alarm, of the changes that are taking place. For myself I am full of the most fearful forebodings. There will not henceforth be a Member of the House of Commons who will hold his seat *independently* of the people — In other words, the people will henceforth possess the power of commanding majorities, by requiring pledges upon every subject which is in favor with the people. I cannot, with such power absolutely vested in the hands of the people, imagine that annual parliaments are very far distant, for, without annual parliaments, the people will not be all in all; with Annual parliaments, what will become of the Funds? and the tithes? and the Lords & the King? &c. It seems to be very generally thought, from Lord Greys speeches about a year or two back, and Sir James Graham's publications, that a reduction of the national debt by some forced measure may be expected at no remote period.

Five days later Richard told his father of his reactions to the election and of his plans for the future:

> The Elections being now over we have only to await the Determination of Ministers as to the Quantum and the Time of Reform which they shall think fit to give us. It is quite clear that they will have a very great majority in the House of Commons, and I am quite surpris'd to find that I was wrong in my expectations as to the Result of the Elections, and I have to thank you for having prevented my embarking in an Election . . . which would certainly have brought on very great expence and annoyance and probably disappoint-ment . . . . No one I think can guess what will happen within the next three months. I cannot help being glad that I have not a seat in Parliament as perhaps

I might lend my aid to do harm as likely as good. For I cannot but think very ill of the ministers who have led us into this state which appears to me so dangerous.

I have lately had a letter from M.ʳ Wilmot wishing to know if I would in the event of a Dissolution come forward for the County, and if in the Event of their being four members for the County, I would come forward with Sir George Crewe. . . . To this, I return'd for answer, that in the present state of things, I thought it would be better to remain quiet to see what was likely to happen, and that at all events *I* did not feel disposed to put myself forward, however gratified I might be to be placed in that situation of Member for the County. The same proposition has been made to me today by Sir Roger Greisley[76] (to whom I have given the same answer,) that is, to unite with him. I shall be glad to hear that you think I have done right upon this occassion. I think there is considerable alarm & anxiety upon the subject of the State of the public Excitement, not the Bill only, but the Sovereignty of the People, alias Mob.

On 25 June 1831 Richard advised his father, 'I have lately received many letters from Derbyshire urging me very much to declare publickly my intention to offer myself at the next Election, I have not however thought right to depart from the determination to which I came with your approbation and advice.' He had, he went on, received similar requests from Leicestershire: 'to these of course I have paid very little attention as I take for granted, that you would be much better satisfied with the Representation of Derbyshire, to which we all belong'. But Richard was never again to stand for Parliament. He died after a short illness at Normanton Turville on 27 March 1832 and was buried in the family vault at Cromford eight days later.

In matters of finance, as in political affairs, Arkwright was hesitant in giving advice. This is clear from James Wigram's letter to him of 23 May 1831:

I am in great distress about my Trust property to which you refer. This time last year, the property which was settled on my marriage was unimpared in amount, the rise on one part having compensated for the fall on the other. I made arrangements for a mortgage on the principle that security was, in my case, a principal thing to be looked to and had this arrangement been completed I should now be at my ease. My intended mortgage, however, made some arrangements with the Westminster office which disappointed me & prevented my realising at that time. Ever since, the West India & East India Stock have been rapidly wasting and *at this time* all holders of the securities [or rather insecurities] are sellers & no persons buyers. I could not realise my money in either of those stocks without actually forcing a sale, and if I were to do that, I should not lose less than between £6,000 and £7,000 pounds. I cannot tell you the uneasiness this gives me, as my exertions in my profession are quite unequal to the repair of calamities like those I speak of. I have the good fortune ot be very hard worked which keeps my mind from dwelling on the subject. You do not, I know, like giving advice, but I really should feel obliged by your hinting to me whether, if you were in my situation, you would realise now *at any rate* or wait for the chance of things improving. I have a very eligible mortgage at $4\frac{1}{2}$ per cent offered me if I can make up the whole amount of the money wanted which is £50,000 and this I have no doubt might be managed by looking about me.

Arkwright's approachability led to pleas for assistance from, among others, friends and acquaintances who found themselves in financial straits. One such request came from Henry Bache Thornhill, now up at Christ Church, Oxford:

Ch. Ch. April 21ˢᵗ 1799.

Dear Sir

From imprudent expences since I have been here I find my bills amount to £200 & as I [am] going to leave Oxford in June or July they must be paid soon. If I tell my father of them I know he will pay them, but not without much uneasiness, & perhaps that opinion which he has always had of me would be altered. The Dean of Christ Church[77] who is an old friend & schoolfellow of my fathers has assisted me as far as it is in his power, & told me he would have offered to lend me two hundred pound if he could possibly have spared it, as by so doing he might have been the means of preventing much uneasiness to my father & perhaps a quarrel between him & me & advised me if I thought I had any friend or relation who would lend me the money without mentioning it to my father; (as I was the properest person to tell him of it, if he must know it) & when my father, if he should afterwards hear of it would approve of before any other person; to apply to him & entrust him with my imprudence confidenti/ally. I had not the least idea of mentioning it to any body but my Father untill I consulted the Dean whose advice I have followed. If therefore you will lend me two hundred pound you will confer the greatest obligation upon me, & I will repay you with the interest as soon as it is in my power. With compliments & best wishes to all at Willersley I remain

yours sincerely
Henry Thornhill

I must beg of you not to mention the recᵖᵗ of this to *any one*.

And in 1811 Arkwright received an even more urgent request from Old Etonian John Simpson, eldest son of his one-time partner in the Manchester mill:

Dear Uncle

I hardly know how to begin this letter; it is with the most unpleasant feelings that I now write to you but being in a most serious predicament with respect to money matters, I do hope for your advice & assistance, before I mention the circumstance I shou'd wish to say any thing I could in exterpation but feel that

[286]

not much can be said. The fact is that being last week at Chester races it was my unfortunate lot from a previous knowledge of Martin Hawke who happened to be there also, to be introduced to his party. A L.ʳ Col. Chas Morgan not of the best character was one to whom (I confess it with fear) I have lost upwards of two thousand pounds. I imagine there remains nothing for me to do but that it should be paid. Good may arise out of evil I now feel & I hope not too late that it is *absolutely necessary* to pay the strictest attention to business which at the same time that I hope it will be a benefit will from the attention that is requesite lead to less expence than I have hitherto been at. You may suppose from my past conduct that resolutions so suddenly formed my not stand but the shock which I experienced when thought was awakened was such that I do not hesitate in saying my resolutions as to business & as to my future conduct are those that will merit your approbation. I think at the same time necessary to state that from engagements entered into some time ago *my whole time* will be dedicated to business by degrees. I am the more astonished when I reflect upon the sum I have lost & in some measure attribute it to too great a confidence in myself for I was warned in the morning to be on my guard agˢᵗ my companions; to prevent *anything of the kind in future* I have laid down a rule never to play however small the amount. I never before lost one hundred pounds. I was a subscriber to the Manchester & Stockport hounds but have this day declined subscribing any longer. I hope you will not think me tedious in entering into these particulars. If you that I attend properly to business & do the best in my power I shᵈ hope you would not think I did wrong in expecting a proportionate allowance. I have not informed my Mother as I do not see any end it would answer but to make her uneasy. Pray do not judge me too harshly. I am willing to do an thing you point out *that it is in my power to do.*

I shall be very uneasy‘until I hear from you
to mention everything
at once the total sum
I should require wᵈ
be about three thousand
pounds. I cannot say more
but must by my conduct show how sincerely I
respect.

I am your affectionate Nephew
John Simpson

Manchester
may 14ᵗʰ
1811

In the absence of Arkwright's detailed accounts for these years we have no means of knowing whether he rose to these occasions or not. Given the amount of Thornhill's request, it seems unlikely that his plea would have gone unans-wered but, whatever the outcome, Henry was to remain indiscreet in financial affairs. In 1801 he married Helen, daughter of Charles Pole, of Liverpool, and had his residence in Montague Place, London. In 1809 his father gave him the Pleasley estate 'for his further and better advancement in life'; twelve years later Henry, now an officer in the Royal Horse Guards, made his will, leaving, amongst other bequests, 'the standard taken from the French by my brother William at the Battle of Ortheze' to be placed in the family house at Stanton. He went on the explain that on his father's death he would inherit several other large estates in Derbyshire and took the liberty of leaving them in trust for his wife and family. Unfortunately for this arrangement Henry died before his father and, to provide for his heirs, the trustees were obliged to auction the Pleasley estate, which went to William, father of Florence Nightingale, for £38,000.[78]

As to John Simpson, he died at Salthorp, Wiltshire, on 19 March 1867, worth less than £10,000.[79] And this despite bequests of £18,000 from his bachelor uncle Samuel and £2,000 under Arkwright's own will. He had earlier received £10,000 from the £80,000 estate of his father in 1802,[80] another £20,000 from the same source on coming of age and an additional £10,000 on the death of his mother in January 1812. And it could well have been that when on 31 July 1811 — less than three months after John's unfortunate encounter with the grandson of Admiral Lord Hawke and with the MP for Monmouthshire at the Chester races — Elizabeth Simpson drew up her will she felt obliged to state, 'In consequence of my Husbands Will my Eldest Son John Simpson will have ten thousand pounds at my Death, is the reason I have not considered him in this Will.'[81]

Arkwright's affairs afforded a stark contrast to those of his nephew. 'Men of business generally take care to have written documents to refer to,'[82] he had complained to Lord Essex when his agent admitted to having no records of the farm stock on the Hampton Court estate. And, true to his own precepts, he maintained throughout his long life extensive and up-to-date summaries of his many and varied financial involvements.

On sheets of paper — sometimes extended and often patched and repatched when fragile through use — he set out such information as 'A Statement of All Property from 1792 to the Latest Period', a document which included figures of 'Profits at Bakewell & Cromford', the 'Prices of Yarn & Cotton Commenc-ing: 1792' (details of the 'Market Price of Cotton Per annum' — 'List Price' and the 'Difference' — as well as the 'On hand Value of Cotton [&] Yarn'). In the final columns Arkwright gave an annual estimate of his 'Capital' together with details of its 'Yearly average increase'. On other lists he set out the increase (always an increase) in his capital 'each year', its 'Increase in every 5th Year' and 'Therefore in each 10th Year'. Also painstakingly recorded was an annual valuation of each of his estates, details of government funds purchased together with their current market values and all other sources of income.

In Wills's *Complete Clerical Almanak for the Year 1823* (London, Price 2s. 6d. in Marble Paper) and in several small notebooks Arkwright set out less personal financial and business information: the prices of Funds, Consols, bank stock, India bonds and Exchequer bills at various times from 1792 together with their average prices; details of the 'Depreciation in [the] price of bullion from 1800 to 1821'; the qualifications required of the Governor, Deputy Governor and Directors of the Bank of England, as well as those required for a vote at the General Court; a note of 'Deeds deposited at Smith's and another that 'Property tax eased 5 April 1816'. Also recorded in one or other (and sometimes in several) of the notebooks are the names of almost a score of 'Permissions to Angle at Skerne', the numbers of deer at Sutton Scarsdale, as well as those of pheasants, woodcocks, hares and rabbits killed there on two occasions in January 1826 and 1827, details of 'Wine in the Cellar' at Willersley at various times and the purchase between 1807 and 1825 of two phaeton, three post-chaises and one gig.

In small green notebooks (probably of the 1820s) are listed the names of his London suppliers, among them William Ashley, 'Biscuit-baker' of 26 Broad Street, Ratcliffe Highway; James Lynn, who had his 'Barrelled Oyster-ware-house' at 70 Fleet Street; Deane & Roughton, 'wholesale Druggists', of 19 Walbrook; Larken Varnham & Co. of 4 Copthill Court, from whom he bought tea, and Carbonnell & Son, wine merchants, of 182 Regent Street. Also noted were the names of three London solicitors (John Hopton Forbes, of 5 Ely Place; Samuel Amory of Amory & Coles, 25 Throgmorton Street, and E. L. Ogle, of 3 Clement's Lane) and King and Whitaker, attorneys of 5 Gray's Inn Square.

An entry in one of the notebooks reads, 'History of Cott[o]^n Manuf[acture,] Longman Hurst & Co', an apparent reference to J. R. McCulloch's unsigned article in the *Edinburgh Review* of June 1827 reviewing Guest's *A Compendious History of the Cotton-Manufacture: with a Disproval of the Claim of Sir Richard Arkwright to the Invention of its ingenious Machinery*. It is unfortunate that we have no information as to Arkwright's reaction to McCulloch's tribute to Sir Richard and his criticisms of the 'very meagre, prejudiced and superficial work' of Guest in supporting the claims of Thomas Highs to the invention of the water-frame.

Arkwright, like Sir Richard in his later life. displayed an interest in the rudiments of grammar, setting out and repeating in successive notebooks a list of 'Double Negations', some of the examples being taken from Shakespeare. The Old and New Testaments, Pope and Samuel Richardson's *Clarissa* all furnished illustrations of the use of *I* and *me*.

Also recorded are the dates of the deaths of Samuel Oldknow and Samuel Simpson, the latter followed by a detailed breakdown of his estate ('*His own Valuation*'), amounting in all to £122,041. And it was Samuel's brother Richard who set out in one of Arkwright's notebooks moves in chess as well as the following:

[289]

Two Gentlemen cutting
for partners at whist
each cut a King
then each cut fours
then each cut nines
then each cut aces
then each cut knaves.

Aug.ᵗ 8 1836
the writer of this was one of the
parties. Richᵈ Simpson.

Other entries in Simpson's handwriting read:

At a Country Seat nʳ Coimbra in Portugal is a vast kitchen, the most curious circumstance connected with which is, that it is traversed by a River, in wᶜʰ the Cooks can catch the fish according as they have need of them.

Jeremy Taylor says 'Strange that for the Stomach wʷʰ is scarce a span long, there shᵈ be provided so many furnaces, & ovens, huge fires, & an army of Cooks, Cellars swimming with wine, & Grannaries sweating with Corn; & that into one belly shᵈ enter the vintage of many Nations, the spoils of distant Provinces, & the Shell fishes of several Seas.'

In June 1825 Arkwright began to record in his notebook his own weight and, less frequently, that of his wife, of his son Richard, his ailing daughter Frances, Samuel Simpson and a family friend, Miss Judith Robson, probably a sister of the Rev. Richard Swann Robson, of Rawcliffe in Snaith, near Goole, a frequent angler on the Skerne estate. The records were continued until July 1834, and although Mrs Arkwright is listed on only a single occasion (9 August 1825, when she weighed nine stone) it could well have been the decline in her health, which began about this time, that prompted Arkwright to continue his practice.

Two years earlier (14 April 1823)[83] John Arkwright, writing from Hampton Court ('I am but just returned from a short visit into Derbyshire where I saw all Brothers & Sisters Uncles & Aunts Cousins & Connexions Except Peter's family Richard and some of Robert's young ones. Robert and his wife were at Alderwasley'), had told his brother Joseph that he had found his parents 'particularly well' and preparing for their usual spring visit to London.

But by the late summer of 1825 news from Rock House revealed that Mrs Arkwright was far from well, although the precise nature of her complaint is not made clear. 'I think you will not be much surprised to hear that my Mother has had another attack of the same nature as those from which she has lately suffered,' Richard wrote to his brother Joseph on 5 September. 'She is now apparently gradually recovering from it, and Dr Forester and Dr Poyser have confident hopes that she will so far recover from the effects of it as to be as well as she was before the last attack. They are disposed to attribute this attack in great measure to a want of management of herself.' And on 21 October[84] James Wigram filled in some detail in a letter to Joseph: 'I have dined twice at Willersley and, on both occasions, saw you Mother who spends two or three hours in the morning, in the music Room, and nearly the same time in the evening. She is certainly grievously altered in appearance and I fear the case is one in which a perfect recovery cannot with reason be hoped for.'

By June 1826 Arkwright believed his wife to be improving, as, early the following year, did her doctor: 'My Mother saw D[r] Warren whose opinion appears to be very satisfactory,' wrote Anne to Joseph on 3 February 1827[85] 'He considers the hardness in the side as proceeding from the Liver but that the uneasiness she feels will be removed by taking Calomel repeatedly, & using external Menthol applications. We therefore hope there is no more cause for anxiety about her tho' I fear she will be some time before she is in robust health.'

But it was not to be. On 20 February 1827 Mrs Arkwirhgt suffered a 'very sudden & alarming apoplectic seizure' which rendered her 'incapable of speaking & her situation . . . most alarming'. On 22 February her condition 'became quite hopeless' and she died at 1.30 a.m. the next day. Arkwright and his sister, Mrs Hurt, were at her bedside.[86]

As Arkwright's daughter married and his sons left Willersley to manage his estates the large family gatherings almost inevitably became less frequent. Nevertheless each year just before Christmas most of his family still contrived to be in Derbyshire to celebrate his birthday. Thus on 17 December 1823[87] John wrote to Joseph from Hampton Court of his intention to visit Willersley 'where or whereabout I shall be till the Derby ball on the 31st inst.'. And, he went on, 'I conclude from your letter that you are not intending to keep Xmas in Derbyshire. My Father tells me he intends to Decline keeping his Birthday in future as it seems inconvenient to some of you family men.'

Charles Arkwright had written on 6 March 1823[88] to Joseph from Dunstall in much the same vein: 'The next time I go to London I will, if you are at home, give you a call, that I may not forget you and pass without knowing you. I suppose you and your family do not intend ever visiting these part again.' 'We are much disappointed not to see you here, as it is such a rare occurrence,'[89] he told him on another occasion, and on 4 February 1824[90] he wrote, 'I shall be happy to attend your summons at any time. I shall be glad of the opportunity of seeing my Godson with his brothers and sisters, as well as their parents who are becoming quite strangers to us . . . . Now that you are blessed with all these bairns we despair of ever again seeing you in this country.'

But family gatherings around Christmas continued, and John, writing to Joseph from Willersley on 22 December 1827,[91] described one such occasion:

You was the only one of the Boys absent on my Father's Birthday. George & Mr Simpson with Emma & Elizabeth & Mary Anne from the Rock completed our party. My Father was in pretty good spirits, but not quite so much as he usually is. There are now always some of the Alderwasley girls in the house for Mrs Hurt is still with her husband at Strelley and has been so ever since his attack. He is now rapidly improving . . . .

I think my Father wonderfully well, but he fancies himself weak. The fact is, he walks all day long and, when he has tired his companion, he is surprised that he is tired himself. He eats heartily, his faculties are but little, if at all, impaired, but he does not sleep well. I believe people at his age never sleep well, and do not require much. I hope he may live and enjoy life many years. I see no reason why he may not.

At this gathering news was passed round of two shooting accidents. John's 'sincere Friend', thirty-one-year-old Thomas Andrew Knight,[92] of Downton Castle, Herefordshire, had been accidentally killed by one of his two shooting companions, while 'poor Bache Thornhill' was said to be 'now in an hopeless condition'. The vicar of Bodenham was also thought to be failing fast:

I have told you before now of the state of Mr Robinsons health. He appears to be gradually becoming weaker and I have mentioned to my Father my apprehensions on his account. And though I think it may be premature, my Father, wishing to know your sentiments with regard to Bodenham had desired me to write to you as he would himself have written. I wish therefore you would write to me immediately whilst I am at Willersley and say how far you can. and whether you wish to have the next presentation. My Father seems anxious that all arrangements on these matters should be clearly understood, in case anything should happen to him . . . . Poor Mr Robinson is breaking I fear. He has given up his fiddle and can hardly get on horseback and cannot walk without assistance.

But the Arkwrights need not have concerned themselves overmuch about the Rev. Nicholas Waite Robinson, who was to live for another fifteen years. He died at his residence in Queen Square, Bath, on 18 November 1842 at the age of ninety-one and was succeeded as vicar of Bodenham by Richard's grandson, the Rev. Henry Arkwright.

Arkwright survived his friend by five months. He remained active to the end, keeping his accounts and maintaining track of his income until a fortnight before his death. But on 19 April 1843 Arkwright had a stroke. Dr James Heygate, physician to the Derbyshire General Infirmary, was summoned to Willersley, presumably on the recommendation of Thomas Poyser, the Wirksworth surgeon who regularly attended the family. It was of no avail; Arkwright died four days later on Sunday, St George's Day, at the age of eighty-seven.

The funeral took place the following Saturday, soon after ten o'clock. 'It was,' the Derby Mercury[93] reported, 'conducted in the most unostentatious manner, the corpse being borne from Willersley to Cromford Chapel by labourers belonging to the estate, and followed on foot by male relatives and friends, to the number of twenty-four persons.' Eight friends — among them Jedediah Strutt, grandson of Sir Richard's partner — served as pall-bearers, and a number of the clergy and magistrates of the neighbourhood preceded and attended the coffin. 'An immense crowd of orderly and respectably dressed people had assembled previous to the hour named for the melancholy ceremony, amongst whom there seemed but one feeling, namely, that of sincere and unmitigated regret. Although market day at Cromford the shops were wholly closed without an exception, and no business whatever appeared to be transac-ted till after the conclusion of the mournful ceremonial.' The funeral service was performed by the Rev. Robert Morgan Jones, vicar of Cromford, and the body was interred in the family vault between those of Sir Richard and of Mary, his own wife.[94]'Old Arkwright died at the age of eighty-seven,' Greville noted in his memoirs on 7 May 1843. 'The world had long been looking for his death with great curiosity to know what he was worth. It was generally reported that his property exceeded seven millions sterling.'[95] It was an estimate Greville had first heard almost ten years earlier when, on a visit to Stoke Hall, Arkwright's son, Robert, told him that 'it was reported by those who were better informed than himself of his Father's circumstances, that he is worth from seven to eight millions'.[96]

Arkwright had made his will, a remarkable sixteen-page document, on 16 December 1841, just three days before his eighty-sixth birthday. The main beneficiaries were his five sons. Peter, who after Eton had gone not to Cam-bridge but into the mills, now succeeded to the ownership of those at Cromford and Masson as well as to Oldknow's former concerns at Marple and Mellor. With these went the Cromford and Willersley estates, together with those at Marple and Mellor, the Manchester warehouses and various properties (includ-ing the paper mill at Masson) and mineral rights in and about Cromford and Wirksworth.

Arkwright's other sons, Robert, John, Charles and Joseph, each received the estates upon which they were already settled. Charles, however, was given Skerne in addition to Dunstall, and Joseph Normanton Turville as well as Mark Hall. For each there was a legacy: £40,000 for Peter £100,000 for Robert, £50,000 for John, £120,000 for Charles and the same for Joseph. But no son was to be released from any debt owed to his father. The residue of Arkwright's estate was 'equally to be divided' among his five sons, 'share and share alike'. This worked out at exactly £263,745 17s each.

Frances, Arkwright's youngest surviving daughter, had long suffered from indifferent and poor health. The £6,250 she had received under the will of Sir Richard would not, Arkwright believed, be sufficient to maintain her and he therefore left sufficient money for the purchase of £30,000 of $3\frac{1}{2}$ per cent

Reduced Bank Annuities, the income from which was to provide for her needs. To his daughter Anne, the wife of Sir James Wigram, he left £25,000 and also the income from £50,000, which on her death was to go to her children, the eldest of whom, James Richard Wigram, received £20,000 and his eight brothers and sisters £5,000 each. Frances Edward Hurt, the husband of Arkwright's late daughter Elizabeth, was bequeathed land and various properties in the parish of Crich; their son Francis received £35,000 and each of their six daughters £14,000.

To each of his other thirty-nine grandchildren (including the Hurts and the Wigrams there were fifty-five in all) Arkwright left £5,000. In his later years at least, the birth of each grandchild was carefully noted, and Arkwright even went so far as to consult the tables of William Morgan and John Finlaison in an attempt to estimate, as his accounts put it, how many of them 'Will not survive'. Although Arkwright had a lifelong passion for exactitude in financial above all other matters, in this instance at least he was surely carrying things too far.

The five children of Arkwright's late half-sister, Mrs Susanna Hurt, each received £5,000, while the nephews and nieces of his late wife (John, Richard and Francis Simpson and Mrs Mary Gilbert) were left £2,000.

Cromford chapel was endowed with £4,000, which was to be invested 'upon Government or real security or securities at interest'. The income from this was to go towards ' the Salary of the Organist, the Clerk of the Chapel and also in repairing and beautifying the Chapel'.

Lastly there were smaller bequests. 'Tokens of Rememberance' each of £100 went to nineteen persons, among them the Rev. Richard Ward, incumbent of Cromford chapel for upwards of forty years, the Rev. Robert Morgan Jones, its minister since 1839, and Thomas Poyser, the Wirksworth surgeon. To his old butler, Joseph Hunt, and to his wife, Fanny Hunt, his housekeeper, Arkwright left £100 each. All other domestic servants and George Stafford, his gardener, received a year's wages. The Derbyshire General Infirmary, the General Hospital near Nottingham and the Manchester Infirmary were each bequeathed £200.

The announcement of Arkwright's death gave rise to immediate (and renewed) speculation as to how much he was worth. 'He died,' reported the *Morning Herald* on 1 May 1843, ' . . . possessed of not less than seven millions sterling in personal property alone, irrespective of landed estates.' The *Inverness Courier*[97] stated 'on what is considered good authority' that Arkwright 'has left behind him a fortune quite unparalleled in the annals of ancient or modern accumulation'. The *Wiener Zeitung*[98] cited 'a reliable source' in the London *Globe* for the view that 'the recently deceased Mr. Arkwright left an inheritance that is nearly without parallel'. According to the Augsburg *Allgemeine Zeitung*[99] he was 'reputed to have been the richest private person in Europe'. *The New*

York Herald[100] simply announced, 'Richard Arkwright the richest commoner in Europe died on the 23*d* of April.' 'He is supposed,' reported the New Orleans *Times-Picayune*,[101] 'to have held more, in every description of funds, than any other British subject'. So much so that the *Morning Herald* expressed concern that the sale of stocks would have a depressing effect on the market.

There were attempts to compare Arkwright's fortune ('a modern Croesus', the *Globe*[102] called him) with those of other capitalists: with the Peels and with the as yet unmarried heiress Angela Burdett-Coutts in England; with Salomon Heine, the Barings, the Hopes and the Rothschilds in England and in continental Europe; with the late Stephen Girard and with John Jacob Astor in the United States.

But estimates as to the size of Arkwright's fortune and speculations as to how it compared with the accumulations of other very wealthy persons were at best hazardous. When on 24 May 1843 his will was proved in the Canterbury Prerogative Court by his sons Robert, Peter and Charles (John and Joseph, the remaining executors, were not present) the 'Effects [were] sworn to exceed £1,000,000.' This was, however, only a nominal amount, since at the time estates were not sworn to a specific sum.

For a more realistic measure of Arkwright's wealth we must turn to his own meticulously kept accounts and to figures set out in the official documents drawn up in preparing the probate. These reveal a fortune derived from three main sources: government stock, £1,555,298 11*s* 9*d*; landed estates, £1,012,813, and mortgages, £413,738 19*s* 6*d*. A total of £57,742 10*s* 9*d* was held in three banks: £28,682 16*s* 6*d* with Smith Payne & Smith, £28,335 0*s* 6*d* with the Arkwright Bank at Wirksworth, and the remainder — £724 13*s* 9*d* — with Pares & Co. of Leicester. 'Book and other Debts' came to £68,104 16*s* 5*d* and 'Bonds, Bills, Notes, and Interest due at the Death' £30,698 4*s* 3*d*. Four of the smaller items related to Willersley Castle: in the language of the official documents, 'Cash in the House' amounted to £1,260 2*s*; 'Furniture, Plate, Linen, China, Books, Pictures, Wearing Apparel, Jewels, and Ornaments' were valued at £4,031 0*s* 6*d*; 'Wine and other Liquors' at £263 18*s* 6*d* and 'Horses and carriages, Farming Stock, and Implements of husbandry' at £392 4*s* 6*d*.

The Times[103] carried no obituary but printed a near 500 word piece, 'The Founder of the Arkwright Family', about Sir Richard, 'the first member of this new wealthy, distinguished, and remarkable family, who made a noise in the world'. The younger Arkwright is referred to merely as the inheritor of his father's fortune, which he greatly increased, or, as the *Gentleman's Magazine* put it, 'Inheriting the wealth of his father, and the still more valuable endowments of his sagacious and comprehensive mind, Mr. Arkwright commenced life with prospects vouchsafed to few.'

These assessments are, however, misleading in that they fail to give Ark-wright credit for having done much to create his own fortune. On Sir Richard's death in 1792 Arkwright inherited the residue, £193,000, of his father's estate. He had himself been a mill owner since 1783, when he began cotton spinning at Rocester, and on acquiring Bakewell the same year he estimated his own capital at £20,011. He was worth £45,045 in 1785, £101,900 two years later, £145,000 in 1789 and £249,500 in 1792.

Living comfortably but without ostentation at Willersley, one might almost be tempted to suppose, Arkwright was resting on his laurels and, if not actually drawing on his father's fortune then certainly not adding to it. But in many ways Arkwright was no less a remarkable man than Sir Richard. Behind the diffident and modest exterior of an essentially private person reluctant to appear in public life lay an astute businessman, shrewd, sensible and successful in his judgements. He had become a millionaire by 1805, a double millionaire by 1823 (the year his holdings of government stock passed the million mark), a landed estate millionaire by 1828 and a treble millionaire by 1839. He died worth £3¼ million, almost certainly the richest commoner of the first half of the nineteenth century.

Arkwright held the offices of Justice of the Peace and Deputy Lieutenant of Derbyshire and (like Sir Richard fourteen years earlier) became High Sheriff in 1801. Of his six sons, Richard, the eldest, was twice elected Member of Parliament for Rye before his death at the age of fifty in 1832; Robert and Peter both served as Justice of the Peace, High Sheriff and Deputy Lieutenant of Derbyshire, while John and Charles became Justice of the Peace and High Sheriff of their adopted counties, Herefordshire and Staffordshire; the Rev. Joseph, Arkwright's youngest son, was a Justice of the Peace for Essex and Hertfordshire.

Only Peter, who since leaving Eton some forty years earlier had assisted his father in the day-to-day running of the Cromford and Masson mills, remained active in cotton. Arkwright's great wealth had enabled his sons (Peter included) to enter the higher reaches of landed society, and their progeny, usually after Eton or Harrow, followed by Christ Church, Oxford, or Trinity College, Cambridge, made their careers in the Church, Parliament, the law or the army.

The Arkwright estates were the conspicuously-visible sign of affluence in a society which measured social esteem in acres. But of even greater importance were the family's holdings in the Funds, an investment which afforded a higher return than land, in addition to being more marketable. From little or nothing Sir Richard, in just over twenty years, had made a fortune entirely in cotton; his son, no less lacking in business acumen, died a far richer man and set up his own sons simultaneously as landowners and Fund holders extraordinary. And, like the older landed aristocrats, both classes thought of themselves as England.

NOTES

1 Unless otherwise stated material in this chapter is drawn from A.F. MSS; *G.M.*, 1860, p. 310; Stapylton, *Eton Lists*, p. 27B (1796).
2 *G.M.*, 1812, p. 93; Stapylton, *Eton Lists*, p. 25B (1796).
3 *G.M.*, 1809, pp. 185⁄6; Stapylton, *Eton Lists*, p. 27A (1796).
4 *G.M.*, 1841, pp. 90⁄1; Stapylton, *Eton Lists*, p. 38B (1802).
5 C. Hollis, *Eton: History*, London, 1960, pp. 178–9.
6 *Derby Mercury*, 26 January and 2 February 1797; Glover, *Peak Guide*, pp. 128⁄30.
7 A party of French, sent to seize Bristol, were driven north by the wind and landed near Fishguard in 1797. They mistook red⁄cloaked women onlookers for guardsmen and surrendered.
8 Warner, *Northern Counties*, I, p. 146. 'One spring behind the new bath is called, from this circumstance, the petrifying well; hath the property of incrusting in a short time any substance exposed to its action, with calcareous matter.'
9 *G.M.*, 1858, p. 425. Joseph Pilkington Brandreth, MD, of Broad Green, near Liverpool, died 1858 aged seventy⁄six.
10 Stapylton, *Eton Lists*, 1791⁄99: 'Henry Lewis Hexter, brother of late Writing Master at Eton died early'.
11 For *Bell's Weekly Messenger* see Peter Prince, 'John Bell and the *Universal Advertiser*', *Business History*, XI, 1969.
12 George Anderson Pelham (1785⁄1835), MP, brother of Lord Yarborough (*G.M.*, 1835, p. 221), and Charles Anderson⁄Pelham (1781⁄1846), first Earl of Yarborough, MP. He was for many years Commodore of the Royal Yacht Squadron and noted for his princely hospitality to the members. He died on board his yacht *Kestrel* off Vigo. (*G.M.*, 1846, pp. 532⁄3); Burke's *Peerage and Baronetage*.
13 Warner, *Northern Counties*, I, p. 115, 'at Derby, Carr's porcelain manufacturing (likely belonging to Mr. Dewsbury) is carried on'.
14 Presumably the Cromford minister; Arkwright intended to keep them swotting.
15 Glover, *County of Derby*, II, p. 6. Pedigree of Hurt. Mary Hurt (daughter of Frances, died 1783, aged sixty⁄one) married George Moore, of Appleby, in 1780. (Mary's brother was Francis, died 5 January 1801, aged forty⁄one.)
16 Cited by Hollis, *Eton*, p, 185, and see W. Thackeray, *Memoirs of Hawtrey*, for the headship of Dr Goodall.
17 *Derby Mercury*, 8 October 1812.
18 Glover, *Peak Guide*, p. 121.
19 *Annual Register*, 1850. *App. to Chron.*, p. 275.
20 Jones, 'Arkwrights in Herefordshire', pp. 59⁄64.
21 *Ibid.*, p. 60, citing John Biddulph's diary, 2 August 1828, Hereford City Library, local collection.
22 The only date on this letter is 'Cambridge November 9th'.
23 Not all his brothers and sisters got theirs at twenty⁄one.
24 W. Addison, *The English Country Parson*, London, 1947, p. 217; A. L. Drummond, *The Churches in English Fiction*, Leicester, 1950, p. 84 n. 2.
25 20 November 1814.
26 Son of Sir Robert Wigram, Bart, married at Matlock by the Rev. Joseph Arkwright.
27 Arkwright II's daughter, Mrs Elizabeth Hurt (1780⁄1838), who in 1802 married Francis Edward Hurt.
28 Holcombe.
29 *Music and Friends, or Pleasant Recollections of a Dilettante*, (1838), I, p. 233.
30 W. O. Henderson, *Industrial Britain under the Regency*, London, 1968, p. 137.
31 Burke's *Landed Gentry*.

32 *G.M.*, 1841, p. 647; *L.G.*; 1879.

33 Burke's *Peerage and Baronetage*.

34 Married 21 August 1798 (*G.M.*, 1798, p. 809).

35 *Derby Mercury*, 31 January 1805, 26 March 1807.

36 *Derby Mercury*, 22 May 1802.

37 Arkwright and Toplis Accounts.

38 Arkwright Accounts.

39 Glover, *County of Derby*, II, p. 518.

40 *Derby Mercury*, 27 January 1836. Peter Arkwright also gave £100.

41 Also: *Derby Mercury*, 31 October 1838; Glover, *Peak Guide*, 1830, p. 128; Adam, *Gem of the Peak*, p. 88. See also P.P. 1839 (42) XLII, *Educational Provisions*, pp. 50-1, and P.P. 1840 (227) X, *Select Committee on Regulation of Mills and Factories*, p. 54.

42 For Webb see Colvin, *British Architects,* p. 874; Britton and Brayley, *England and Wales*, III, pp. 522-3.

43 *Transactions*, III, 1822, pp. 95-8.

44 For the Chapel Walk see Adam, *Gem of the Peak*, pp. 68-70.

45 5 August 1840.

46 MP for Windsor, 1806-10, and 'for more than 40 years a Liveryman of the Company of Stationers, but better known for his famous Windsor Ale' (*G.M.*, 1813, p. 291).

47 Letter to Arkwright II dated 2 April 1795.

48 John Smith died at the Chapel Lodge, Cromford, on 27 September 1834, aged seventy-three (*Derby Mercury*, 8 October 1834), a few months before Frank Ogden, 'Old Frank', for many years in service with the Arkwrights (*Derby Mercury*, 6 May 1835).

49 Letter, Henry Walshman to Arkwright II, 2 July 1795.

50 Greville, *Memoirs*, II, p. 47.

51 The 14 ft statue, costing £10,500 (inclusive of £1,500 worth of metal donated by the Chancellor of the Exchequer), was completed by Chantrey's successor and erected at the recently Royal Exchange on 18 July 1844, the anniversary of Waterloo. (*G.M.*, 1837, p. 630; 1844, p. 179; 1844, p. 197.)

52 *Derby Mercury*, 6 May 1840.

53 *G.M.*, 1843, p. 656.

54 Arkwright MSS at Essex, 634 D/DAr C10/7.

55 Fitton and Wadsworth pp. 189-190.

56 *Derby Mercury*, 29 May 1794.

57 *Derby Mercury*, 15 May 1794.

58 *Derby Mercury*, 22 March 1798.

59 *Derby Mercury*, 17th May 1798.

60 *Derby Mercury*, 3 May 1798.

61 J. C. Cox, *Three Centuries of Derbyshire Annals*, I, London, 1890, pp. 198-200, 207, 208, 399.

62 F. A. Crisp *Visitation of England and Wales*, VII, London, privately printed, 1907, p. 17. Says married at Newcastle on 27 April 1805 (this corresponds with letter) but *G.M.*, 1805, p. 66, gives 27 June 1805, as does J. A. Venn, *Alumni Cantabrigiensis*, Part II, I, Cambridge, 1940, p. 70.

63 Hon. F. Leveson-Gower, *Letters of Harriet, Countess Granville, 1810–1845*, third edition, London, 1894, I, p. 32; II, pp. 47, 183, 185-6 187, 395.

64 Lord J. Russell (ed.), *Memoirs, Journals and Correspondence of Thomas Moore*, V, London, 1854, pp. 215, 216, 250-1, 252, 253-4.

65 Where in 1807 the Arkwright's first child George, later MP for Leominster, was born (*G.M.*, 1807, p. 886).

66 *Derby Mercury*, 18 January 1837.

67 Thomas Campbell, *Life of Mrs Siddons*, II, London, 1834, p. 371, 371 n., . . . Mrs Arkwright at Stoke in Derbyshire.'
68 *Ibid.*, p. 371.
69 London, 1878, I, pp 37-8.
70 *G.M.*, 1842, p. 338. 23 January 1842, 'At Bristol Margaret wife of the Rev. N. W. Robinson Vicar of Bodenham Herefordshire'.
71 Arkwright MSS at Essex, letter 241.
72 Probably a reference to Ernest Augustus, Duke of Cumberland (1771-1851), then charged in the popular press with incest. He had previously been publicly accused of murder and was to be so again. (See E. Halevy, *The Liberal Awakening, 1815-1830*, New York, 1949, p. 273.) Brothers Clarence and Sussex were in favour of Catholic emancipation (Greville, *Memoirs*, I. pp. 258–9).
73 MP for Derbyshire.
74 MP for Derbyshire.
75 Hansard, pp. 988-9.
76 Roger Gresley (1799–1837), eighth baronet, MP for Durham City 1830-31; New Romney, 1831; Derbyshire South, 1835-37 (Stenton, *British M.P.s*, II).
77 Cyril Jackson (1746-1819), Dean of Christ Church, 1793-1809, an ex-pupil of Manches-ter Grammar School, and tutor to Canning, Sir Robert Peel, Charles Wynn. (See *D.N.B.*)
78 S. Pigott, *Hollins: a Study of Industry, 1784-1949*, Nottingham, 1949, pp. 61-2.
79 Somerset House, Will, John Simpson, 1867.
80 L.C.R.O., Will, John Simpson, 1802.
81 L.C.R.O., Will, Elizabeth Simpson.
82 Jones, 'Arkwrights in Herefordshire', p. 59.
83 Arkwright MSS at Essex, letter 348.
84 Letter 106.
85 Letter 310.
86 Letters 272 and 288.
87 Letter 249.
88 Letter 85.
89 Letter 158.
90 Letter 330.
91 Letter 308.
92 *G.M.*, 1828, pp. 87-9.
93 3 May 1843.
94 Cost of Funeral, £509 0s 5d.
95 Greville, *Memoirs*, V, p. 90.
96 Greville, *Memoirs*, III, p. 5.
97 24 May 1843.
98 20 May 1843.
99 30 April 1843.
100 1 May 1843.
101 23 May 1843 (the statement first appeared in the (London) *Standard*, 2 April 1843).
102 Cited *Manchester Guardian*, 20 May 1843.
103 18 May 1843.

BIBLIOGRAPHY

PRINCIPAL MANUSCRIPT COLLECTIONS CONSULTED

In the possession of the Arkwright family. Miscellaneous papers, uncatalogued, principally to the patent trials and partnerships, and letters, account books etc. concerning business, estate, family and social subjects.

Birmingham Reference Library. Correspondence and papers forming part of the Boulton & Watt collection.

Blair Castle. The Atholl MSS, particularly papers, deeds, etc. relating to Arkwright's activities in Scotland, especially at Stanley.

British Museum. Papers relating to lands in the Cromford area subsequently purchased by Arkwright and originally part of the Wolley MSS.

Chatsworth House. The Arkwright MSS relating to the Bakewell mill and the Chatsworth letters concerning Georgiana, Duchess of Devonshire.

C.I.S. Miscellaneous plans, deeds, etc. relating to the Arkwright mill at Manchester.

Derby Public Library. The Pares MSS; the Strutt MSS; the Hurt MSS.

Derbyshire County Record Office. The Cressbrook Papers, the Gell MSS, Land Tax records, Enclosure Awards, etc.

Essex County Record Office. The Arkwright MSS relating to the Arkwrights at Mark Hall.

Guildhall Library, London. Royal Exchange Registers; Sun Fire Office Registers.

Lancashire County Record Office. The Derby Muniments, Land Tax, deeds, books, etc., relating to the Arkwright family and Preston in the earlier period.

Manchester Central Reference Library. The Owen MSS; Burials Register of St John's Church; microfilm copies of James Whitaker's Minute Book and part of the Samuel Oldknow Papers in the Seligman Collection at Columbia University.

Preston Borough Records. Guild records, Court Leet records, Register of Apprentices, Council Minute Book, Poor Tax records, etc., relating to the Arkwright family and Preston in the earlier period.

P.R.O. Exchequer, Treasury, Board of Trade, and Customs and Excise records.

Scottish Record Office, Edinburgh. Material relating to Arkwright's activities in Scotland.

Sheffield Central Library. The Barker Papers; plan of Cromford Moor Longsough.

Signet Library at Edinburgh. Papers relating to the development of the cotton-spinning industry in Scotland.

U.M.I.S.T. E. G. Holiday documents relating to the early Arkwright partnerships.

OFFICIAL PUBLICATIONS

PARLIAMENTARY PAPERS:

1816 (397) III, *Select Committee on the State of the Children employed in the Manufactories of the United Kingdom.*

1818 (90) XCVI, *House of Lords Committee on the Health and Morals of Apprentices, and others, employed in Cotton and other Mills etc.*

BIBLIOGRAPHY

1819 (66) III, *House of Lords, An Account of the Cotton and Woollen Mills and Factories in the United Kingdom etc.*

1819 (24) CX, *House of Lords Committee on the State and Condition of the Children employed in the Cotton Manufactories of the United Kingdom.*

1829 (32) III, *Select Committee on the Law relative to Patents for Inventions.*

1831–32 (722) VI, *Committee of Secrecy on the Bank of England Charter.*

1833 (690) VI, *Select Committee on Manufactures, Commerce and Shipping.*

1833 (450) XX, *Royal Commission on the Employment of Children in Factories, first Report.*

1834 (167) XIX and XX, *Royal Commission on the Employment of Children in Factories, Supplementary Reports.*

1834 (596) XLIII, *Report of Factory Inspectors.*

1839 (159) XIX, *Report of Factory Inspectors.*

1839 (42) XLII, *Report of Factory Inspectors on the Educational Provisions of the Factory Acts.*

1840 (227) X, *Select Committee on the Regulation of Mills and Factories.*

1841 (311) X, *Special Report of Inspectors of Factories on Accidents to Children and Young Persons.*

OTHER

House of Lords Sessional Papers, 1781–82 to 1786, reprinted by Oceana Publications, New York.

House of Commons Sessional Papers of the Eighteenth Century, LI, ed. S. J. Lambert, Delaware, 1975.

House of Commons Journals.

Hansard.

THESES

D. Evans, 'Mather Brown, 1761–1831: a critical study', PhD, 1972, Courtauld Institute of Art, University of London.

C. D. Saggus, 'Social Identification, Attitudes and Relationships in the 1780s of those Cotton Manufacturers of Manchester listed in the Trades Directories of the Period', PhD, 1974, Emory University; Ann Arbor, Mich., and London, 1977.

NEWSPAPERS AND PERIODICALS

Annual Register, Aris's Birmingham Gazette, Augsburg Allgemeine Zeitung, Bell's Weekly Messenger, Derby Mercury, Derbyshire Courier, Farmer's Magazine, Gentleman's Magazine, Glasgow Mercury, London Globe, Inverness Courier, London Gazette, Macclesfield Courier, Manchester Examiner, Manchester Guardian, Manchester Mercury, Manchester Weekly Advertiser, Mechanics's Magazine, Morning Herald, Nottingham Journal, Preston Guardian, Staffordshire Advertiser, London Standard, Stockport Advertiser, The European Magazine, The Monthly Magazine and British Register, The New York Herald, The Quarterly Review, The Times, Wiener Zeitung.

BOOKS AND ARTICLES

W. A. Abram, *Parish of Blackburn, County of Lancaster: History of Blackburn, Town and Parish*, Blackburn, 1877.

— *Preston Guild Merchant, 1882: Memorials of the Preston Guilds*, Preston, 1882.

W. Adam, *The Gem of the Peak*, London, 1851.

W. Addison, *The English Country Parson*, London, 1947.

Advance, U.M.I.S.T. April 1967, No. 2.

J. Aikin and W. Enfield, *General Biography*, London, 1799.

D. G. C. Allan, 'A proposed national reward for mechanical wool spinning, 1785–9', *Journal of the Royal Society of Arts*, CX, 1962.

BIBLIOGRAPHY

Arkwright Society, *Local History Trail No. 11, Wirksworth*, 1971, revised 1978.
— *Arkwright and the Mills at Cromford*, 1971.
T. S. Ashton, *Economic Fluctuations in England*, Oxford, 1959.
— *The Industrial Revolution, 1760–1830*, Oxford, 1948.
H. O. Aspinall, *The Aspinwall and Aspinall Families of Lancashire*, Exeter, 1923.
J. Aston, *The Manchester Guide*, Manchester, 1804.
— *A Picture of Manchester*, Manchester, 1816.
W. E. A. Axon, *Lancashire Gleanings*, Manchester, 1883.
E. Baines junior, *History of the Cotton Manufacture in Great Britain*, London, 1835.
E. Baines, *History of the County Palatine and Duchy of Lancaster*, IV, London, 1836.
W. W. Rouse Ball and J. A. Venn, *Admissions to Trinity College*, Cambridge, III, London, 1911.
T. C. Barker, *Pilkington Brothers*, London, 1960.
B. T. Barton, *Bolton and District Historical Gleanings*, III, Bolton, 1883.
The Earl of Bessborough (ed.), *Georgiana: Extracts from the Correspondence of Georgiana, Duchess of Devonshire*, London, 1955.
L. Bonaparte, *Memoirs of Lucien Bonaparte by himself*, I, translated from the French, London, 1818.
W. Bray, *Sketch of a Tour into Derbyshire and Yorkshire*, London, editions of 1778 and 1783.
T. Brayshaw and R. M. Robinson, *A History of the Ancient Parish of Giggleswick*, London, 1932.
J. M. Britton and E. W. Brayley, *The Beauties of England and Wales*, III, London, 1802.
B. Bryan, *Matlock Manor and Parish*, London, 1903.
Burk's *Dictionary of the Landed Gentry*, 1849.
— *Dictionary of the Peerage and Baronetage of the British Empire*, 1859.
— *General and Heraldic History of the Landed Gentry*, 1937.
Burdett's Map of Derbyshire, 1762–67.
J. Butt, *Industrial Archaeology of Scotland*, Newton Abbot, 1967.
J. Byng, *The Torrington Diaries, 1781–94*, I–IV, London, 1935.
T. Campbell, *Life of Mrs. Siddons*, II, London, 1834.
T. Carlyle, *Chartism*, London, 1840.
W. H. Chaloner, introduction to MSS letter in *B.J.R.L.*, XLVIII, 1965.
— 'Robert Owen, Peter Drinkwater, and the early factory system in Manchester, 1788–1800', *B.J.R.L.*, XXXVII, 1954.
C. W. Chalklin, *The Provincial Towns of Georgian England: Study of the Building Process*, London, 1974.
J. D. Chambers, 'Population change in a provincial town: Nottingham, 1700–1800', in L. S. Pressnell (ed.), *Studies in the Industrial Revolution*, London, 1960.
R. W. Chapman (ed.), *The Letters of Samuel Johnson*, I, Oxford, 1952.
S. D. Chapman, *The Early Factory Masters*, Newton Abbot, 1967.
— 'The Peels in the early English cotton industry', *Business History*, XI, 1969.
— 'James Longsdon (1745–1821), farmer and fustian manufacturer: the small firm in the early English cotton industry', *Textile History*, 3, 1970.
H. Coleridge, *The Worthies of Yorkshire and Lancashire*, London, 1836.
F. Collier, *The Family Economy of the Working Classes in the Cotton Industry 1784–1833*, Manchester, 1964.
H. M. Colvin, *A Biographical Dictionary of English Architects, 1660–1840*, London, 1954.
A. J. Cooke, 'Richard Arkwright and the Scottish cotton industry', *Textile History*, 10, 1979.
— (ed.) *Stanley - its History and Development*, Dundee, 1977.
B. Cooper, *Transformation of a Valley*, London, 1983.
Rev. J. C. Cox, *Notes on the Churches of Derbyshire*, II, Chesterfield and London, 1877.

— *Three Centuries of Derbyshire Annals*, I, London, 1890.
— 'The Wolley manuscripts', *D.A.J.*, XXXIII, 1911.
B. Cozens-Hardy, *The Diary of Sylas Neville, 1767–1788*, London, 1950.
F. A. Crisp, *Visitation of England and Wales*, privately printed, London, 1917.
G. W. Daniels, *The Early English Cotton Industry*, Manchester, 1920.
E. Darwin, *The Botanic Garden*, II, first combined edition, London, 1791.
D. P. Davies, *A New Historical and Descriptive View of Derbyshire*, Belper, 1811.
D. Defoe, *A Tour through England and Wales*, II, Everyman's edition, London, 1928.
W. Dobson, *History of the Parliamentary Representation of Preston*, Preston, 1868.
A. L. Drummond, *The Churches in English Fiction*, Leicester, 1950.
S. Dumbell, 'The cotton market in 1799', *Economic History*, I, 1926–29,
M. M. Edwards, *The Growth of the British Cotton Trade 1780–1815*, Manchester, 1967.
E. Ekwall, *The Place Names of Lancashire*, Manchester, 1922.
W. Hume Elliot, *The Story of the 'Cheryble' Grants*, Manchester and London, 1906.
F. Elrington Hall, *The Judges in Ireland, 1221–1421*, II, London, 1926.
W. Emerson, *The Principles of Mechanicks*, London, 1773.
Encyclopaedia Britannica:
1810 edition, article 'Cotton'.
1824 edition, article 'Cotton Manufacture'.
W. English, *The Textile Industry*, London, 1969.
F. Espinasse, *Lancashire Worthies*, I and II, London and Manchester, 1874.
W. Fairbairn, *Treatise on Mills and Millwork*, II, London, 1863.
J. Farey, *General View of the Agriculture and Minerals of Derbyshire*, I, London, 1811.
Lady K. E. Farrer (ed.), *Correspondence of Josiah Wedgwood*, London, 1906.
James Finlay and Co. Ltd, privately printed, 1951.
R. S. Fitton and A. P. Wadsworth, *The Strutts and the Arkwrights, 1758–1830: Study of the Early Factory System*, Manchester, 1958.
R. S. Fitton, 'Samuel and William Salte, an eighteenth-century linen house', *Explorations in Entrepreneurial History*, second series, VI, 1969.
Rev. J. M. Fletcher, 'William Newton, "The Minstrel of the Peak"', *D.A.J.*, XXXIV, 1912.
J. Foster, *Alumni Oxonienses, 1715–1886*, III, London and Oxford, 1888.
E. J. Foulkes, 'The cotton-spinning factories of Flintshire, 1776–1866', *Journal of Flintshire Historical Society*, XXI, 1964.
G. J. French, *Life and Times of Samuel Crompton*, London, 1859.
W. Gardiner, *Music and Friends, or, Pleasant Recollections of a Dilettante*, I, London, 1838.
K. Garlick and A. D. Macintyre, *The Diary of Joseph Farington*, V, New Haven, 1979.
P. Gaskell, *Artisans and Machinery: the Moral and Physical Condition of the Manufacturing Population*, London, 1836.
S. Glover, *The History and Gazetteer of the County of Derby*, II, Derby, 1833.
— *The Peak Guide*, Derby, 1830.
Hon. F. Leveson-Gower, *Letters of Harriet, Countess Granville, 1810–1845*, I and II, London, 1894.
C. C. F. Greville, *The Greville Memoirs*, I, II, III, V, London, 1834.
L. H. Grindon, *Manchester Banks and Bankers: Historical, Biographical, and Anecdotal*, Manchester, 1878.
R. Guest, *A Compendious History of the Cotton Manufacture: with a Disproval of the Claim of Sir Richard Arkwright to the Invention of its ingenious Machinery*, Manchester, 1823.
C. Hardwick, *History of the Borough of Preston*, Preston and London, 1857.
Sir J. Hawkins, *The Works of Samuel Johnson, together with his Life, and Notes of his Lives of the Poets*, XI, 1787.
H. Heaton, 'Non-importation, 1806–1812', *Journal of Economic History*, I, 1941.

[303]

BIBLIOGRAPHY

W. O. Henderson, *Britain and Industrial Europe, 1750–1830: Studies in British Influence on the Industrial Revolution in Western Europe*, Liverpool, 1954.
— *Industrial Britain under the Regency*, London, 1968.
W. C. Henry, 'A biographical notice of the late Peter Ewart Esq.', *Memoirs of the Manchester Literary and Philosophical Society*, new series, VII, 1844.
G. Henson, *The Civil, Political and Mechanical History of the Framework Knitters in Europe and America*, I, Nottingham, 1831.
A. Hewitson, *Preston Court Leet Records, Extracts and Notes*, Preston, 1905.
R. L. Hills, *Power in the Industrial Revolution*, Manchester, 1970.
— 'Hargreaves, Arkwright and Crompton: why three inventors?' *Textile History*, 10, 1979.
C. Hollis, *Eton: History*, London, 1960.
J. S. Harford, *Some Account of the Life, Death and Principles of Thomas Paine*, Bristol, 1820.
W. Hutton, *History of Derby from the remote Ages of Antiquity to the Year 1791*, London and Derby, 1791.
J. James, *History of the Worsted Manufacture in England from the Earliest Times*, London and Bradford, 1857.
D. J. Jeremy (ed.), *Henry Wansey and his American Journal*, Philadelphia, 1970.
— *Transatlantic Industrial Revolution*, Oxford, 1981.
E. L. Jones, 'Industrial capital and landed investment: the Arkwrights in Herefordshire, 1809–1843' in E. L. Jones and G. E. Mingay (eds.), *Land, Labour and Population in the Industrial Revolution*, London, 1967.
T. S. Jones, *The Life of . . . Willielma, Viscountess Glenorchy*, Edinburgh, 1822.
F. A. Kemble, *Records of a Girlhood: Autobiography*, I, London, 1878.
J. Kennedy, 'Observations on the Rise and Progress of the Cotton Trade in Great Britain', *Memoirs of the Manchester Literary and Philosophical Society*, second series, III, 1819.
— 'A brief memoir of Samuel Crompton', *Memoirs of the Manchester Literary and philosophical Society*, second series, V, 1831.
— 'My early recollections', written 1825, in *Miscellaneous Papers*, Manchester, 1849.
F. D. Klingender, *Art and the Industrial Revolution*, London, 1972.
E. B. Leach, 'The parish registers of Lancashire', *T.L.C.A.S.*, 1946.
C. H. Lee, *A Cotton Enterprise, 1795–1840: a history of M'Connel and Kennedy, fine cotton spinners*, Manchester, 1972.
Jean Lindsay, 'An early industrial community: the Evans' cotton mill at Darley Abbey', *Business History Review*, XXXIV, 1960.
— 'The Butterley coal and iron works, 1792–1816', *D.A.J.*, 1965.
M. L. Loane, *John Charles Ryle, 1816–1900*, London, 1935.
D. Loch, *Essays on the Trade, Commerce, Manufactories and Fisheries of Scotland*, II, Edinburgh, 1778.
London County Council, *Survey of London*, XVIII, London, 1937.
R. Longrigg, *The History of Foxhunting*, London, 1975.
J. Loudon, *Manchester Memoirs*, London, 1916.
B. Love, *Manchester as it is*, Manchester, 1839.
J. Lunn, *Leigh*, published for the Borough Council, Town Hall, Leigh.
D. S. Lysons, *Magna Britannia*, V, London, 1817.
D. C. M. M'Connel, *Facts and Traditions collected for a Family Record*, privately printed, Edinburgh, 1861.
M. H. Mackenzie, 'The Bakewell cotton mill and the Arkwrights', *D.A.J.*, LXXIX, 1959.
— 'Calver Mill and its owners', *D.A.J.*, LXXXIII, 1963, and LXXXIV, 1964.
— 'Cressbrook and Litton mills', *D.A.J.*, LXXXVIII, 1968.
P. Mantoux, *The Industrial Revolution in the Eighteenth Century*, London, 1948.
E. W. Marrs junior (ed.), *The Letters of Thomas Carlyle to his Brother Alexander, with related Family Papers*, Cambridge, 1968.

J. D. Marshall, 'The cotton mills of the Upper Leen', *Transactions of the Thoroton Society*, LX, 1957.

R. Meeson and W. Newland Welsby, *Reports of Cases in the Courts of Exchequer and Exchequer Chamber, from Hilary Term 6 Will. IV to Easter Term 10 Vict. XVII*, V, London, 1837–49.

G. E. Mercer, 'Mr. Moore of the Adelphi', *Journal of the Royal Society of Arts*, CXXVII, 1979.

E. Meteyard, *A Group of Englishmen (1795–1815), being Records of the Younger Wedgwoods and their Friends*, London, 1871.

J. O. Mitchell, *Old Glasgow Essays*, Glasgow, 1905.

J. Montgomery, *The Theory and Practice of Cotton Spinning*, Glasgow, 1836.

H. Moore, *Picturesque Excursions from Derby to Matlock Bath, and its Vicinity: being a Descriptive Guide*, Derby, 1818.

P. Morgan, *Annals of Woodside and Newhills: Historical and Genealogical Abstracts*, Aberdeen, 1886.

C. P. Moritz, *Travels of Carl Philipp Moritz in England in 1782*, London, 1924.

A. A. Mumford, *The Manchester Grammar School, 1515–1915*, London, 1919.

L. B. Namier, *The Structure of Politics at the Accession of George III*, London, 1929.

The New Statistical Account of Scotland, 1834–45.

J. Nichols, *The History and Antiquities of the County of Leicester*, IV, Part II, London, 1811.

B. Nicolson, *Joseph Wright of Derby*, I and II, London, 1968.

B. Nightingale, *The Story of the Lancashire Congregational Union, 1806–1906*, Manchester, 1906.

J. E. Norton (ed.), *The Letters of Edward Gibbon*, III, 1956.

J. Ogden, *A Description of Manchester, by a Native of the Town*, Manchester, 1783.

The Old Statistical Account of Scotland, 1791–98.

R. Owen, *The Life of Robert Owen, Written by Himself*, Philadelphia and London, 1857.

R. Dale Owen, *Threading my Way*, London, 1874.

Colonel J. Parker, 'A Calendar of the Lancashire Assize Rolls preserved at the Public Record Office', *Record Society of Lancashire and Cheshire*, XLVII, 1904.

J. Paterson, *History of the County of Ayr*, II, Ayr, 1847.

T. Pennant, *The History of the Parishes of Whiteford and Holywell*, London, 1796.

G. Penny, *Traditions of Perth*, Perth, 1836.

Sir R. Phillips, *A Personal Tour through the United Kingdom: describing Living Objects and Contemporaneous Interests*, II, London, 1828.

W. H. Pierson junior, 'Notes on early industrial architecture in England', *Journal of the Society of Architectural Historians*, 8, 1949,

S. Pigott, *Hollins, A Study of Industry, 1784–1949*, privately printed, Nottingham, 1949.

J. Pilkington, *A View of the Present State of Derbyshire*, I, Derby, 1789.

W. Pole, *The Life of Sir William Fairbairn, Bart., Partly Written by Himself. Edited and completed William Pole, F.R.S.*, London, 1877.

Sir U. Price, *An Essay on the Picturesque as compared with the Sublime and the Beautiful*, I, London, 1810.

T. Read, *The English Traveller*, III, London, 1746.

P. H. Reaney, *A Dictionary of British Surnames*, London, 1958.

A. Rees, *The Cyclopaedia, or, Universal Dictionary of Arts, Sciences, and Literature*, London, 1819, for article on 'Manufacture of cotton'.

R. Reid, *Glasgow Past and Present*, Glasgow, 1884.

E. Robinson, 'James Watt and the law of patents', *Technology and Culture*, 13, 1972.

A. G. Rose, 'Early cotton riots in Lancashire, 1769–1779', *T.L.C.A.S.*, 73 and 74, 1963–64.

Lord J. Russell (ed.). *Memoirs, Journal and Correspondence of Thomas Moore*, V, London, 1854.

E. Saunders, 'An eighteenth-century provincial architect: Joseph Pickford of Derby', *Country Life*, November 1972.

R. B. Schofield, 'The promotion of the Cromford Canal in 1789: a study in canal engineering', *B.J.R.L.*, LXIV, 1981–82.

J. C. Scholes, *History of Bolton*, Bolton, 1892.

A. Seward, *Letters of Anna Seward*, IV, Edinburgh, 1811.

A. Seymour-Jones, 'The invention of roller drawing in cotton spinning', *Transactions of the Newcomen Society*, I, 1920–21.

R. Sharpe France, 'A history of the plague in Lancashire', *Historical Society of Lancashire and Cheshire*, XC, 1939.

J. F. D. Shrewsbury, *A History of the Bubonic Plague in the British Isles*, Cambridge, 1970.

Sir J. Sinclair, *The Correspondence of the Right Honourable Sir John Sinclair, Bart.*, I, London, 1831.

S. Smiles, *Self Help*, London, 1859.

—— *The Huguenots: their Settlements, Churches and Industries*, London, 1867.

—— *Lives of the Engineers: Boulton and Watt*, London, 1867.

D. M. Smith, *Industrial Archaeology of the East Midlands*, Dawlish and London, 1965.

Rev. J. F. Smith, *The Admission Register of the Manchester School*, I and II, 1866 and 1868.

L. T. Smith (ed.), *The Itinerary of John Leland*, II, London, 1946.

R. Southey, *Letters from England*, ed. J. Simmons, London, 1951.

H. E. C. Stapylton, *The Eton School Lists from 1791 to 1850*, London, 1864.

M. Stenton, *Who's Who of British Members of Parliament*, Hassocks, Sussex, 1976.

G. Stewart, *Curiosities of Glasgow Citizenship*, Glasgow, 1881.

Lady J. M. Strachey (ed.), *Memoirs of a Highland Lady: the Autobiography of Elizabeth Grant of Rothiemurchis afterwards Mrs. Smith of Baltiboys, 1797–1830*, London, 1898.

D. M. Stuart, *Dearest Bess: the Life and Times of Lady Elizabeth Foster, afterwards Duchess of Devonshire*, London, 1955.

H. A. C. Sturgess (compiler), *Register of Admissions to the Honourable Society of the Middle Temple*, I, London, 1849.

Sir A. J. Sykes, *Concerning the Bleaching Industry*, Manchester, 1925.

H. C. Syrett (ed.), *The Papers of Alexander Hamilton*, VIII, IX, X, XV, New York and London, 1965.

J. Tann, *The Development of the Factory*, London, 1970.

—— 'Arkwright's employment of steam-power: a note of some new evidence', *Business History*, XXI, 1979.

—— 'Richard Arkwright and technology', *History*, 1973.

W. Thomas, *Original Designs in Architecture*, London, 1783.

R. Thornhill, 'The Arkwright cotton mills at Bakewell', *D.A.J.*, LXXIX, 1959.

J. H. Thornton, 'The Northampton cotton industry – an eighteenth century episode', *Northamptonshire Natural History Society and Field Club*, XXXIII, 1959.

G. Unwin *et al.*, *Samuel Oldknow and the Arkwrights*, Manchester, 1924.

A. Ure, *The Cotton Manufacture of Great Britain*, I, London, 1836.

—— *The Philosophy of Manufactures*, London, 1835.

J. and J. A. Venn, *Alumni Cantabrigienses*, Part II, I, Cambridge, 1940, Part II, V, Cambridge, 1953.

C. B. Wadstrom, *An Essay on Colonisation*, London, 1794.

A. P. Wadsworth and J. de Lacy Mann, *The Cotton Trade and Industrial Lancashire, 1600–1780*, Manchester, 1931.

J. W. Walker, *The History of the old Parish Church of All Saints, Wakefield*, Wakefield, 1888.

M. L. Walker, *A History of the Family of Need of Arnold, Nottinghamshire*, London, 1963.

BIBLIOGRAPHY

R. Warner, *A Tour through the Northern Counties of England and the Borders of Scotland*, I, Bath, 1802.

W. Watson, '"Observations in Bakewell": beginning on the 31 May 1774', *D.A.J.*, XI, 1889.

J. Wheeler, *Manchester: its Political, Social and Commercial History, Ancient and Modern*, Manchester, 1836.

G. S. White, *Memoirs of Samuel Slater*, Philadelphia, 1836.

P. A. Whittle, *Bolton-le-Moors, and the Townships in the Parish*, Bolton, 1855.

C. Woodham-Smith, *Florence Nightingale, 1820–1910*, London, 1950.

A. Young, *The Farmer's Tour through the East of England*, I, London, 1771.

Unsigned, *A Letter to the Spinners and Manufacturers of Cotton Wool upon the present situation in the Market*, London, 1792.

— A Short Tour in the Midland Counties of England performed in the Summer of 1772. Together with a similar Excursion undertaken September 1774, *London (note inside book: 'Presumed to be the work of Thomas Quincey of Manchester, father of Thomas De Quincey')*.

— Answers to certain Objections made to Sir Robert Peel's Bill, *Manchester, 1819*.

— Letters on the Utility of Machines, *1780*.

ARKWRIGHT OF WILLERSLEY.
CO. DERBY.

| CHARLES b.1782 | RICHARD=CAROLINE 1808 b.1785 dau. of Robert Shuttleworth | FREDERICK NICHOLAS d.young | JOHN OCTAVIUS d.young | EDWARD=CAROLINE 1823 NICHOLAS dau. of b.1795 Joseph Strutt |

GENEALOGIES

overleaf
The Arkwright family

below
The Hurt family

1780
CHARLES = SUSANNA
1758–1834 | 1761–1835
son of Francis Hurt | dau. of Richard Arkwright
of Alderwasley and | and Margaret Biggens
Mary, dau. of Thomas |
Gell of Wirksworth |

1822	1811	1805		
JOHN FRANCIS=MARY,	SUSANNA=JOHN	MARY =PETER	FRANCES	MARGARET
THOMAS (WOLLEY) dau. of	RYLE	ANNE son of	d.1831	d.1790
Adam Wolley		1786–1872 Richard		
		Arkwright of		
		Willersley		

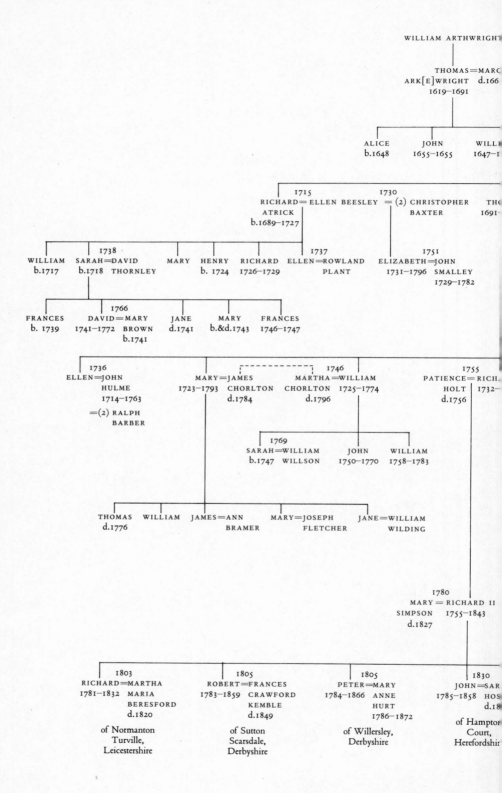

WILLIAM ARTHWRIGHT

THOMAS=MAR(
ARK[E]WRIGHT d.166
1619–1691

ALICE   JOHN   WILL
b.1648   1655–1655   1647–1

1715   1730
RICHARD= ELLEN BEESLEY = (2) CHRISTOPHER   THO
ATRICK   BAXTER   1691–
b.1689–1727

                                   1737   1751
WILLIAM SARAH=DAVID   MARY HENRY RICHARD ELLEN=ROWLAND   ELIZABETH=JOHN
b.1717   b.1718 THORNLEY   b. 1724 1726–1729   PLANT   1731–1796 SMALLEY
                                                              1729–1782

                  1766
FRANCES DAVID=MARY   JANE   MARY   FRANCES
b. 1739 1741–1772 BROWN d.1741 b.&d.1743 1746–1747
                  b.1741

   1736   1746   1755
ELLEN=JOHN   MARY=JAMES   MARTHA=WILLIAM   PATIENCE=RICH.
      HULME   1723–1793 CHORLTON CHORLTON 1725–1774   HOLT 1732–
      1714–1763   d.1784   d.1796   d.1756
      =(2) RALPH
         BARBER

                      1769
                 SARAH=WILLIAM   JOHN   WILLIAM
                 b.1747 WILLSON 1750–1770 1758–1783

   THOMAS WILLIAM JAMES=ANN   MARY=JOSEPH   JANE=WILLIAM
   d.1776   BRAMER   FLETCHER   WILDING

                                                     1780
                                                MARY = RICHARD II
                                                SIMPSON 1755–1843
                                                d.1827

   1803   1805   1805   1830
RICHARD=MARTHA   ROBERT=FRANCES   PETER=MARY   JOHN=SAR
1781–1832 MARIA   1783–1859 CRAWFORD 1784–1866 ANNE   1785–1858 HOS
         BERESFORD   KEMBLE   HURT   d.18
         d.1820   d.1849   1786–1872
                                                              of Hampton
   of Normanton   of Sutton   of Willersley,   Court,
   Turville,   Scarsdale,   Derbyshire   Herefordshir
   Leicestershire   Derbyshire

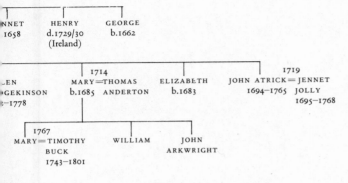

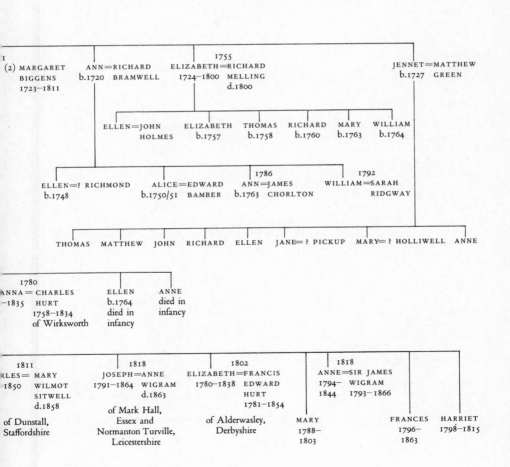

 NNET HENRY GEORGE
1658 d.1729/30 b.1662
  (Ireland)

1714   1719
LEN MARY=THOMAS ELIZABETH JOHN ATRICK=JENNET
GEKINSON b.1685 ANDERTON b.1683 1694–1765 JOLLY
–1778   1695–1768

1767
MARY=TIMOTHY WILLIAM JOHN
  BUCK   ARKWRIGHT
 1743–1801

I
(2) MARGARET ANN=RICHARD ELIZABETH=RICHARD   JENNET=MATTHEW
 BIGGENS b.1720 BRAMWELL 1724–1800 MELLING b.1727 GREEN
 1723–1811   d.1800

 ELLEN=JOHN ELIZABETH THOMAS RICHARD MARY WILLIAM
  HOLMES b.1757 b.1758 b.1760 b.1763 b.1764

      1786   1792
ELLEN=? RICHMOND ALICE=EDWARD ANN=JAMES WILLIAM=SARAH
b.1748 b.1750/51 BAMBER b.1763 CHORLTON RIDGWAY

THOMAS MATTHEW JOHN RICHARD ELLEN JANE=? PICKUP MARY=? HOLLIWELL ANNE

1780
ANNA = CHARLES ELLEN ANNE
–1835 HURT b.1764 died in
 1758–1834 died in infancy
 of Wirksworth infancy

 1811   1818 1802   1818
RLES= MARY JOSEPH=ANNE ELIZABETH=FRANCIS ANNE=SIR JAMES
–1850 WILMOT 1791–1864 WIGRAM 1780–1838 EDWARD 1794– WIGRAM
 SITWELL d.1863 HURT 1844 1793–1866
 d.1858   1781–1854
of Dunstall, of Mark Hall, of Alderwasley, MARY FRANCES HARRIET
Staffordshire Essex and Derbyshire 1788– 1796– 1798–1815
 Normanton Turville, 1803 1863
 Leicestershire

INDEX

Arkwright mill at, 63–5, 86 n. 57 and n. 66,
213, 215–16, 224
opposition to Arkwright's patents, 37, 78, 93,
98, 99, 100, 117
opposition to Arkwright's tax proposals, 211,
213
reaction to Arkwright's death, 218
warehouse at, 65–6, 87 n. 80
see also 4, 5, 10, 14, 53, 101, 128, 138, 139, 210,
225, 226, 239
Manchester Board of Health (1796), 154
Manchester Committee for the Protection and En-
couragement of Trade, 93, 99, 100
Manchester Committee of the Society for Abolition of the
Slave Trade, 215
Manchester cotton mills, 148–51, 213
Manchester Guardian, 227
Manchester Infirmary, 210, 294
Manchester Mercury, 64, 75, 98, 117, 147, 175, 185, 187,
217
Manchester Volunteers, Royal, 210
Mansfield, James, attorney, 101, 136, 137–8
Mansfield, Lord, 137
Mansfield & Pinxton Railway, 245
March, Richard, mechanic, 103, 104, 109
Marriott, Thomas, cotton master, 148
Marsden, Thomas, 56
Marsden, Thomas, spinner, 175
Marshall, Thomas, mill superintendent, 81
Marshall, William, merchant, 78
Marsland, Henry, cotton master, 93, 124, 125
Marsland, John, cotton master, 157
Marsland, Peter, cotton master, 148
Masson
chapel at, 187, 293
mill at, 81–4, 89 n. 156, 146, 155, 169, 187, 196, 224,
229
Master Cotton Spinners, Committee of, 157, 163
Matlock, Derbyshire, 27, 29, 73, 140, 142, 162, 218, 273
Matlock Old Bath Association for the Protection of Fish
and Game, 210
May, Johann Georg, 271
Melling, William, 6, 19, n. 42, 210, 216, 218–19
Mellor, Derbyshire, 154, 226, 235, 237, 238, 239, 293
Mellor, John, factory worker, 159
Merryweather, George, cotton master, 156
Michell, Rev. John, 106
Middleton, Derbyshire, 162, 273
Middleton, Lancashire, 10
Miller, John, 26
Miller's Green, Wirksworth, Derbyshire, 57
Milligan, James, 102, 103, 104
Milne, Alexander, merchant, 75
Mitchell, William, cotton master, 157, 167
Mitchell, William, spinner, 175
Montagu, Frederick, 35
Monteith & Bogle, cotton masters, 146
Moore, George, 263

Moore, Jonathan, victualler, 71
Moore, Mr, attorney, 105, 124
Moore, Thomas (1779–1852), 280
Mordaunt, Charles Lewis, cotton master, 93, 94, 96, 97,
105, 117, 118
Mordaunt trial, 105: *and see* patent trials
More, Samuel, mechanic and secretary of Society of Arts,
103, 104, 108, 109, 123, 153, 196
Morewood, Helen, 242
Moritz, Karl Philipp, 22
Morley, Charles and Benjamin, cotton masters, 100
Morning Herald, 294, 295
Morris, Henry, yarn dealer, 12
Mosley, Sir John Parker, 63
Mundy, Edward Miller, 242, 277
Mundy, Francis Noel Clarke, 242, 283
Murray, Adam and George, cotton masters, 148, 150,
151, 156, 158, 167, 175
Murray, Catherine, 150
Murray, Captain George, 184
Murray, Isabella, 150
Murray, General James, 75, 76
Murray, Wilhelmina, 184
muslins, 77

Nall, Robert, hosier, 28
Nares, Sir George, 100
Need, Elizabeth, 43, 46
Need, John, mill manager, 46
Need, Samuel, hosier, 27, 31, 36, 42–5, 46, 51, 91, 187
Neild, James, 154
Neville, Sylas, 204
'new draperies', 10
New Lanark, Lanarkshire, 64, 73–4, 75, 78, 146, 164,
224
New York Herald, 294–5
Newcastle, Duke of, 242, 244
Newton, William, carpenter and 'Ministrel of the Peak',
61
Nightingale, Peter, landowner and millowner, prose-
cuted by Arkwright, 105, 107–13, 118, 119,
140, 183, 184, 192, 207
Nightingale, William, 288
Normanton Turville, Leicestershire, 231, 266, 267, 270,
285, 293
Northampton, 12, 13, 28
Northwich, Cheshire, 100, 149
Nottingham, 22–3, 26–7, 30, 46, 76, 100, 102, 103, 125,
130, 134, 209, 210, 214, 224, 266
Nottingham Journal, 26, 75, 203
Nuttall, George, agent, 232, 233

O'Connell, Daniel, 282
Ogden, James, 64
Oldham, Lancashire, 147
Oldknow, Samuel, cotton manufacturer
and Arkwright the Younger, 154, 234–9